FOURTH EDITION

COMMUNICATION

FOR TODAY'S STUDENT

KAREN TURNER WARD

Kendall Hunt
publishing company

Cover design and chapter openers created by Mario Lawrence

Kendall Hunt
publishing company

www.kendallhunt.com
Send all inquiries to:
4050 Westmark Drive
Dubuque, IA 52004-1840

Printed in the United States of America

CONTENTS

PREFACE

I recently asked a group of students what they believed will be the technological advances and challenges in the year 2040? I encouraged them to let their imaginations run wild and tell me how technology will evolve and perhaps even improve our way of life? Needless to say, the responses I received and the discussion sparked from my questions were fascinating. From 3D flat-screens to Google Glasses, technology has transformed the way we live from day to day. With all the advancements we have made, it makes you wonder where else will technology take us? What could possibly be next?

When Alexander Bell created the first practical telephone in 1875, it is safe to assume that he had no idea that his invention would revolutionize the way humans communicate for nearly 150 years. While Bell's dream of instantaneous communication was built upon the hope of bringing people together, his invention in many ways proved to be the catalyst for the deterioration of interpersonal communication today. Let's not place the blame on Alexander Bell's shoulders. That would be grossly unfair. Yet, we cannot ignore our current technological landscape. Just think for a moment, as of right now the biggest store in the world has never had a physical storefront. The largest car rental company in the United States doesn't own a single car. How did Amazon, Uber and the invention of the phone influence communication?

Aside from improving our movie nights at home, how have we used technology to impact our lives? Hands down, the greatest impact technology has made in this day and age is how we communicate with one another. In 2014, communication has reached extraordinary boundaries that we could never have imagined. Phones can now facilitate video messaging which allows us to communicate with people, states, and even continents away, and social apps have now made it possible to display our lives to the world connecting those whose paths may never have crossed with ours.

As with anything, technology has its drawbacks when it comes to communication between humans. It's impossible to walk into a restaurant without witnessing at least one person on their mobile device, instead of engaging in a face-to-face conversation with their dinner companion. With the Internet being the major facilitator of communication today, it has now replaced the schoolyard where bullies lurk and torment their victims. Internet bullying is a growing epidemic that does not discriminate and has dire consequences. The very thing that was created to bring us closer has undoubtedly driven us apart.

The great Steve Jobs, the mastermind behind the Apple empire, once said, "Technology is nothing. What's important is that you have a faith in people, that they're basically good and smart, and if you give them tools, they'll do wonderful things with them." Technology has had such a profound impact on the world and the way we communicate that it has drastically changed the landscape of opportunities for today's students. *Communication for Today's Student* is a fresh approach to the communication issues that have become increasingly critical to professional and personal success in contemporary society. This innovative and interactive text incorporates theory and practice to successfully prepare students to become effective communicators, thus giving them the necessary tools to compete in today's job market. You will find this online integrated learning approach provides the guidance students need to identify and implement creative solutions, regardless of the communication context. We live in a world where we share the experience of a moment with millions of other people, a world where it is not just important, but imperative that students are empowered with the knowledge and skills to brave the challenges presented in every type of communication situation. So, let's get started!

ACKNOWLEDGEMENTS

Maya Angelou once said, "If you get, give. If you learn, teach." Those words have become a life motto for my career as an educator. Early on in my life I had several teachers who bestowed upon me the gifts of knowledge and service. Those individuals help shape my life and inspired me to do the same for others. I've never hidden the fact that I didn't have all the answers, but the answers I did have I was willing to give. And the knowledge I did learn, I had no choice but to teach it to others. That's the hope I have for *Communication for Today's Student* as it goes into its fourth edition.

I would have never dreamt of developing a communication textbook if it weren't for the many students that inspired me over the course of my thirty year career in the classroom at Hampton University. While every student was special, there are a few that I must acknowledge. To Torenzo Blair, Tash Hawthorne, Mia Wynn, Sydney Adams, Victoria Rowland, Reverend Christiana Reed, and Stephen Westly I thank you for your thirst of knowledge and for being the constant force driving me to become a better professor. I hope that you take the knowledge you learned and teach it to all those who share your same passion and thirst. It's your responsibility, a responsibility that you were destined to complete.

I would like to thank the faculty in the Department of Fine and Performing Arts at Hampton University. Thank you for all your input and never-ending support. I am so honored to have you as colleagues.

To Mr. Mario Lawrence, thank you for sharing your artistic vision and skill in the creation of the beautiful cover. I extend a special thanks to Mr. Charles Long for serving a photographer for this project.

I would like to extend my sincere gratitude to Dr. Charrita Danley for her contributions to this project. To Patra Johnson and Janice Bennet, I thank you for your unyielding support and your unselfish and giving spirit. You are true friends.

To Ms. Virgelia Jade Banks, thank you for believing in me and for serving as the constant physical reminder of my greatest work.

I would be remiss if I didn't extend my appreciation to the entire team at Kendall Hunt. Amanda Smith and Elizabeth Cray, thank you for your consistent support and encouragement, but most of all, patience. A special thanks to my editor,

Mr. Curtis Ross. I thank you for changing my life and opening doors I never dreamt would be presented to me. I am so blessed to call you a friend.

And lastly to Dr. William R. Harvey, President of Hampton University, I extend my sincere appreciation for your guidance and confidence. You took a chance on a young, enthusiastic academician over thirty years ago and instilled in her through your wisdom, leadership and vision, "that there's no such word as no."

COMMUNICATION FOR TODAY'S STUDENT
AN INTRODUCTION

After reading this chapter, you should be able to:

- ☑ Define communication.
- ☑ Explain the communication process as it relates to a situations in your life.
- ☑ Discuss the different models of communication.
- ☑ Describe the function of each element in the communication process.
- ☑ Explain the importance of ethical communication.

Key Terms

Channel
Communication
Computer-Mediated
  Communication (CMC)
Context
Culture
Decoding
Encoding
Ethical
External noise
Interactive Communication

Intercultural Communication
Intrapersonal Communication
Internal Noise
Lean medium channels
Linear Communication
Message
Noise
Nonverbal feedback
Norms
Public Communication
Public Speaking Anxiety

Physiological noise
Psychological noise
Rich medium channels rules
Semantic noise
Sender-receivers
Small-group Communication
Symbol
Transactional Communication
Verbal feedback

Keynote
Speaker

1 Scenario

"Come on, how long does it take to make a smoothie." Nathalie muttered to herself.

The Student Center was fairly empty, only a few people left over from the 12-2 activity jam. It was the third 12-2 she missed in the past month. Studying for Mr. Fields' calculus class had taken over her social time.

"Machine acting up. Give us a few minutes." The lady yelled from around the counter.

"UGHHH." Nathalie growled loudly causing everyone in the vicinity to stop in their tracks.

Noticing the disapproving stares, she dropped her head and sauntered away. She plopped down in an open booth, pulled out her iPhone and few taps later was on the Instagram app. As soon as the feed refreshed, a familiar face popped up: Chris. Nathalie's eyes softened as she scrolled the multiple picture post he uploaded 30 minutes prior.

Chris Matthews was class president, captain of the basketball team, on the pre-law track and the object of Nathalie's affection. Chris had been Nathalie's crush since the summer they met in Pre-College. They met at the welcome party thrown by the school for the incoming freshmen. Chris and her shared a dance. Nathalie hoped that something would have happened between them in the fall. And while they remained friendly, nothing else transpired between them.

"Don't just stare at me. Give me some double tap love." A voice chuckled from behind her.

Nathalie's eyes grew big. She knew that baritone from anywhere. She watched as Chris walked from around and took a seat across from her. He smiled at her expression.

"Hey you," Chris grinned. "I didn't mean to creep up on you, but since you creeping on my page that makes us even, right?"

Nathalie couldn't help but giggle. "What can I say it's a nice feed you curated."

"Where you been hiding?" Chris eyed her, "You've been ghost."

Natalie eyed him flirtatiously, "You've had to have been looking for me to know I've been ghost. You checking for me, Christopher?"

Chris' eyes widened, clearly taken aback by Nathalie's boldness. Nathalie was taken back by her boldness too. But she was tired of Chris leaving her in awe. It was her turn to return the favor.

"Smoothie ready!" The lady yelled, breaking Nathalie and Chris' stare.

Nathalie stood up, "See you around maybe."

Nathalie walked over to the smoothie stand and grabbed her smoothie, not looking back at Chris. Chris hurried over to her before she could make it out the nearby exit.

"Hey my boys and I are having a party tonight." He held up his phone, displaying his twitter feed. "I've been tweeting about it all day. Just having something to take our minds off midterms. Are you and your friends gonna roll through?"

Nathalie paused to face Chris, staring at him head on. "I have a scholarship and gpa to maintain. If I'm going to skip out on a night of studying, I'll need a personal invitation."

Chris bit his lip. He liked this version of Nathalie. "I want you to come to my party. Will you come?"

"Thanks, maybe I'll show up." Nathalie smirked.

"I'll be watching the door all night." Chris said as he backed up towards the door. "See ya later Nathalie."

Chris walked out, leaving Nathalie looking after him. Nathalie stood there wondering what would happen between her and Chris at the party and whether they had a future.

What are some factors that may impact the interpersonal communication between Nathalie and Chris in the cafeteria?

Respond Here

Let's Communicate

Communication is a part of every human being's daily life. From an infant's cries for milk, to a teenager's request to drive, to a college student's questions in class, to Chris and Nathalie's discussion of the party, to an employer's instructions to employees, communication is taking place. Many people take communication for granted because it happens so often in our daily interactions with one another. However, communication should never be taken for granted; it is the foundation of our human interaction.

Children communicate with their parents and caregivers to ensure that their basic needs are being met. Students communicate with teachers and professors to ensure that they are acquiring the knowledge being taught and meeting the expectations that have been set. As individuals, we communicate with our peers to form relationships and friendships. As family members, we communicate with those who are related to us as we build familial bonds based on shared relationships. As employers and employees, we communicate to meet the goals and objectives set before us and to fulfill the mission of our organizations.

Communication with our parents and caregivers ensures our basic needs are met.

These are but a few examples of the ways in which we communicate. If you were to take a few moments and reflect upon your daily activities as a college student, you would notice that they involve a significant amount of communication with various individuals for unique purposes in different settings and contexts. Take a moment to think about the communication that you have had over the past 3 hours. How many individuals were involved? What was the purpose of the exchange? Was it successful?

Why Study Communication?

Having thought of how often you communicate and knowing that you have been actively engaged in some form of communication since birth, you may wonder why it is important for you to be enrolled in a communication course. Well, it is important for you to be enrolled in this course because it teaches you how to communicate effectively. The fact that you engage in communication daily, does not mean that your communication is effective.

How many times have you felt that the person you were talking to did not understand what you were saying? How often have you wished that people would "get the point"? Have you ever felt that no matter how many times you explained yourself, the listener did not respond appropriately? Have you ever tried to think of other ways to say what you wanted to say? Has a person's facial expressions ever signaled to you that you said the wrong thing? Have your facial expressions ever hurt someone's feelings? Have you ever said something you wished you could take back? Has your tone of voice ever been inappropriate for the situation? Have you ever been in a situation similar to Nathalie and Chris?

More than likely, everyone reading this text answered "yes" to several of the questions. That is why it is important for you to take a communication course. This course will prepare you to communicate effectively in both your personal and professional lives.

Personal Communication

Personal communication is the foundation of building relationships. As a college student, a great deal of your personal communication revolves around your interaction with family members and friends. These are the people who you consider a part of your circle, the people that you trust with your thoughts and feelings. These are the people who influence you.

Communication is a direct reflection of identity. Who you are is largely determined by your personal communication. Consider the children whose parents tell them, "You can be anything you want in life!" These children usually have a positive self-image and believe that the sky is the limit for them. Unfortunately, there are other children who are sometimes told, "You will never amount to anything!" Not having the encourage-

Children whose parents tell them, you can be anything you want in life usually have a positive self-esteem.

ment and the reinforcement necessary for a positive self-image, these children sometimes fall prey to the negative communication spoken into their lives and do not reach their potential.

As you can see, your personal communication with family members and friends can affect who you are as a person. In college, you meet many new people from different places with different backgrounds, cultures, and ways of thinking. Many of these individuals become your life-long friends. It is important to communicate positively with your peers in order to not only learn from them, but to also provide them with the support and encouragement that they need to be successful students. What you say and hear makes a difference in your life and the lives of others. Therefore, it is important to say the right thing, at the right time, inthe right manner. It is important to communicate effectively in your personal communication with family and friends.

Professional Communication

As a college student, you are preparing yourself for the professional world of work. Consequently, you must be prepared to communicate on a professional level. The communication styles and techniques you engage in with your family, friends, and peers are often more informal than the communication expected in the professional world.

The way in which you communicate professionally is a major factor in your success as a professional. You must communicate with your employer, other employees, business partners, clients, and various constituencies related to your profession of choice. No matter what career path you choose, at some point, you must engage in professional communication with other people.

One of the first instances when an employer gets an opportunity to evaluate your communication skills is during the face-to-face interview. At this time, both your verbal and non-verbal communication skills are on display. You should want potential employers to be impressed by your ability to communicate, but they will not be impressed if your communication in the interview is the same as your communication with family and friends.

It is important to know the difference between various modes of communication and when it is appropriate to use each. You will learn this information in your communication class. Becoming an effective communicator in your professional life is just as important as becoming an effective communicator in your personal life. This text will teach you both.

Now that you understand why it is important for you to study communication, you will be introduced to the foundations of effective communication, the different types and methods of communication will be explained to you, and you will be prepared to become an effective communicator in various settings and situations.

In order to become an effective communicator, you must know what communication is and be equipped with the tools necessary to communicate effectively.

Communication: Defined

Communication is a process described as the exchange of ideas using symbols which represent abstract and concrete ideas. Like all processes, the communication process is comprised of elements or components. The critical components work together to fulfill the objectives of the process.

To understand fully how the communication process works, let's use the model to explicate the role each element or component plays in the process.

The Communication Model

In our opening scenario between Nathalie and Chris, we can see the communication model in action.

When Nathalie decides to go with Chris to the party, she was engaging in **intrapersonal** communication. Chris took a seat next to Nathalie and began engaging in conversation. At this point, Nathalie and Chris become sender and receiver within the communication process and engage in **interpersonal** communication.

What does this mean? Once a communicator gets an impulse or has a mental image in mind, it must take the form of a **symbol**, or words in this case. The process of transforming mental images into words and placing these words into logical messages with meaning is called **encoding**. The process continues as the sender sends the message to the intended recipient or receiver, who in turn, **decodes** the message and attaches meaning to it. The message can be verbal or nonverbal, conscious or unconscious.

Photo courtesy of Charles Long

The critical components work together to fulfill the objectives of the process.

Photo courtesy of Charles Long

Communication is a process in action.

The message can travel on various types of channels to include telephone, letter, text, computer mediated and, of course, the most common channel, face-to-face.

Once the message is perceived and understood by the receiver, the decoding process occurs and that process is reversed. The receiver's feelings and thoughts are sent back to the sender for decoding. In the case of Nathalie and Chris, when Chris sat down next to Nathalie and began sharing comments about his Instagram feed, they were operating as sender and receiver. Basically, the couple was sending messages back and forth using a face-to-face channel. Each communicator was engaged in the process and was giving feedback to the messages they received. At some points in their communication, they gave **nonverbal feedback** and at other points their messages took the format of **verbal feedback**. Feedback, whether verbal or nonverbal is essential in gauging how our message is received. We use feedback to adjust our encoding or as a way to self monitor. For example, after telling your best friend in a harsh tone to stop arriving late for dinner every time you decide to meet, you decide to rephrase the criticism once you see your friend begin to tear up.

Sometimes feedback may lead to misunderstanding a message. Therefore, it is important that we use caution when interpreting and before responding.

Most communication in interpersonal situations is two way. Each time the opportunity is given for the receiver to react to the message, the communication is open to feedback and is characterized as two-way. Where the communication process takes place is as critical as these elements are to the process of communication. The place that communication occurs is called the **context or setting**. The context refers not only to the time, place or physical or social environment, but also the personal perceptions, attitudes, beliefs and background each speaker brings to the communication context or setting. This, of course, affects how the sender and receiver will respond to the message being sent and, therefore, affects the feedback of each. Control of the context or environment is important when communicating effectively. Nathalie and Chris have their communication in the Student Center which of course is the physical environment, but an even greater factor in their communication with each other is the fact that they are attracted to each other and have been previously involved. Both parties are affected by the rules and norms of communication. According to Hamilton and Creel, rules are standards of acceptable behavior in a communication context that are explicitly stated while norms are behavioral standards that are implied. As we read the exchange between Nathalie and Chris, do we question the whether the location of the conversation is one that is appropriate? Is this conversation one that should take place between the two parties at all?

Photo courtesy of Charles Long

Communication open to feedback is characterized as two-way.

As Nathalie and Chris discuss and deliberate about going to the party that night, they communicated openly and freely because they had shared knowledge and experiences. They were successful in communicating their mental images because they were able to understand one another. There was no breakdown in the communication context or setting, even though there may have been the presence of what social scientists like to call "noise." When speakers approach communication from different contexts, this can lead to ineffective communication. When noise occurs in the communication context, it also interferes to the success of the process. **Noise**, or interference as some like to call it, is anything within the communication context that prevents the message from being transmitted successfully.

Photo courtesy of Charles Long

Messages can travel on various channels.

There are two types of noise: external and internal.

External noise or interference includes any factors outside of the communicators that make it difficult or prevent the message from being understood. For example, the loud engines of a plane flying overhead when you are speaking to someone on your outdoor deck or a fluorescent light flickering off and on as your history professor is lecturing. While noise in these examples may not prevent the message from being heard or even understood, the noise serves as a road block to the smooth transmission of the message. **Internal noise** refers to interference which occurs within the speaker. A speaker who has a speech impediment, may be difficult to understand. A person with a severe headache may find it difficult to concentrate to decode a message. Thus, in both cases, the successful transmission of the message would be affected. There are three types of internal noise: psychological, physiological and semantic. Oftentimes, internal noise will manifest itself as psychological idiosyncrasies. **Psychological noise** consists of attitudes or beliefs held by a communicator that may interfere with the communicator's ability to express or understand the intent message. For example, speech apprehension or a reaction resulting from a negative interaction with someone previously may impact successful communication. **Physiological noise** occurs when any aspect of the physical apparatus causes the speaker to be ineffective in the transmission of the message. Physiological noise can range from a physical pain to hunger or even fatigue. Just like psychological and physiological noise, semantic noise can be disruptive to the successful transmission of the message. **Semantic noise** involves any interference that deals with language. Examples of semantic noise include the unwanted or inappropriate use of profanity or slang. A speaker's strong dialect could be viewed as semantic noise as well. In these cases, the noise is caused by people's emotional response to the words or use of the language.

Noise is interference in the process. Sometimes noise is external, other times it may be internal or psychological.

As we examine Nathalie's and Chris' interaction in the Student Center, we recognize the role each plays in the communication process and the results of their communication encounter. As we examine the process, we can describe each element. We might make the assumption that communication is **linear**, which asserts that communication is one-way and that the message carried on the channel flows from the sender to the receiver. Often referred to the action model of communication, the linear model has one

Communication is shared knowledge and experiences.

very important omission. In linear communication, there is no feedback. Given that there is no feedback, how would we know the message is understood? As we see in the case of Nathalie and Chris, this is not the way communication flows in an interpersonal communication context.

LINEAR COMMUNICATION

SENDER   ENDCODES → MESSAGE → DECODES   RECEIVER
          CHANNEL(S)   CHANNEL(S)

If we take the linear approach a step further and add feedback from the receiver back to the sender, the communication is interactive. Originally introduced by communication theorist, Wilbur Schramm in 1965, the **interactive model** operates under the assumption that once the message is received and understood by the receiver, the process is complete.

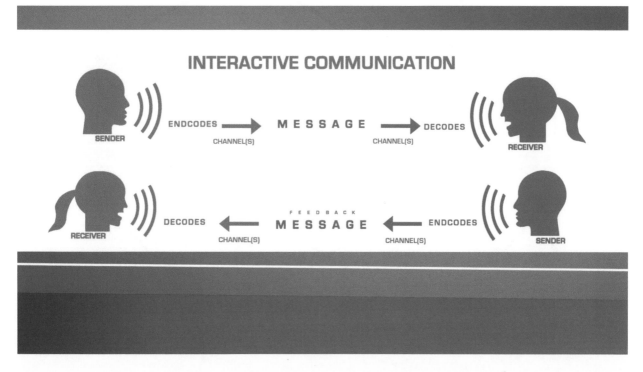

In the interactive model, once Chris suggests that Nathalie has been going "ghost" and she responds you had to have been looking for me to know I've been ghost. We know that this is not true in the case of Nathalie and Chris nor is it true in most communication contexts. The **interactive model** presumes the message of the sender will match the message that is decoded by the receiver. The interactive model does not allow for misunderstanding or, in some cases, totally misunderstood messages. The transactional model does.

Communication Is Transactional

According to Dean Barnlaund, the **transactional** model most adequately describes how the process of communication occurs when it is the most effective. The transactional model has three identifiable characteristics. The first characteristic is that communication is "continuous." Communicators are constantly and simultaneously encoding and decoding messages. For example, in the case of Nathalie and Chris, even when Chris turns and walks to the door as if to terminate the information exchange, he was communicating with Nathalie. What message was he sending? How does Nathalie respond?

The second characteristic of communication as a transactional process is all "communicators play roles." We communicate with our friends differently from the way we communicate with our minister. Our language choice differs significantly in many cases. Our topics or subject matter may differ. Since Nathalie and Chris are involved in a relationship, the language they choose to use with each other facilitates the needs of their interpersonal relationship. For example, Chris refers to his friends as "my boys" when talking with Nathalie. His language choice is specific to the communication with Nathalie. In a different context, for example speaking to his math professor he may choose to refer to his "boys" as his "friends." Their degree of disclosure is significantly, different from the degree of disclosure that each has with their other classmates or even their instructors.

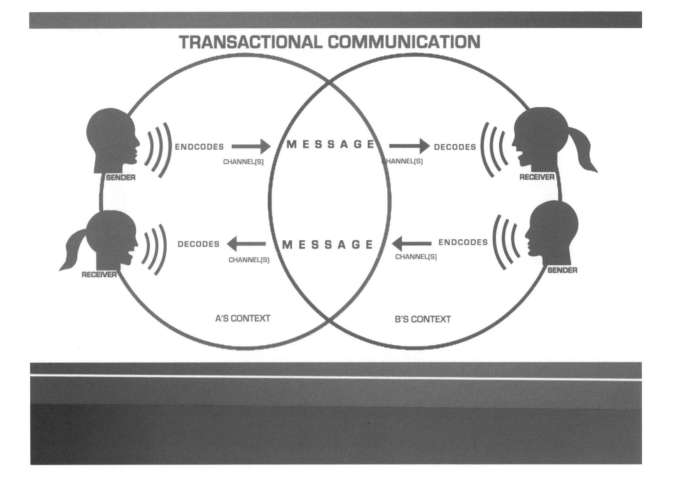

The last characteristic of the transactional theory is that "all communication has a past, present and future." As communicators, we receive and send messages based upon what has occurred in our past. We act upon these messages based upon our experiences. Can you think of an experience that you have had in the past that has affected the manner in which you interacted with someone recently? Those experiences will have an impact upon how we communicate in the future.

Types of Communication

The communication context can occur within several types of communication. While the types share characteristics, they each have their own identity. Let's look at each to gain a clear understanding of the different types that are most often used: intrapersonal, interpersonal, small group, public, intercultural and computer mediated communication.

Intrapersonal Communication

Intrapersonal communication can be best described as communication within oneself. Intrapersonal communication is the ongoing dialogue that you have in your head. The alarm goes off. You sit up in the bed to think, "Man, how I would love to go back to sleep for twenty more minutes." You have just engaged in a conversation in which you are both the sender and receiver. As the sender and receiver, you are actively involved in the encoding and decoding of messages within yourself! As you encode yourself generated messages, you are continuously providing feedback. The stronger our ability as intrapersonal communicators, the greater understanding we have of ourselves. In essence, strong intrapersonal communication yields increased ability to recall and retain information. Strong intrapersonal communication leads to an increased ability to solve problems and make responsible decisions. In our story of Nathalie and Chris, when Nathalie is standing in the Student Center waiting for her smoothie to be made and she thinks, *Come on, how long does it take to make a smoothie?* she is engaging in intrapersonal communication. Most importantly, as we engage in this ongoing internal processing, we increase our ability to communicate effectively with others.

Interpersonal Communication

Interpersonal or dyadic communication is an interaction between two people. Interpersonal communication occurs whenever one person willingly or unwillingly exchanges information with another. Our success in life is greatly affected by our effectiveness in interpersonal communication. From our engagement in social relationships, to our effectiveness on the job, to our successful completion of an employment interview, we are dependent upon our ability to communicate effectively one-on-one as well as to develop and maintain relationships. The majority of the college student's communication takes place within the interpersonal communication context. As a student engages in other contexts, a student will find him/herself communicating in multiple dialogues within larger groups.

Small-Group Communication

Small groups are a critical part of a student's life. If you are on the track team, a member of the editiorial board of the school newspaper, a cast member of the Christmas play at church or a member of a group of students working on a class project, you are a member of a small group. Most students prefer not to work in small groups because they believe that working in a group requires more work than working alone. This perception often factors directly into the effectiveness of the group. The key to a positive small group interaction is to learn strategies that help you function effectively within the group to achieve a positive outcome. These essential strategies, coupled with the type of leader who takes the authoritative role within the group, leads to a successful and positive group experience, minimizing anxiety.

Small groups are a critical part of a students life.

Public Communication

You have been asked to introduce the speaker for Founder's Day at Ogden Hall. While you have made a few group presentations in your biology class, you have never even stepped on the stage of the 1800 seat Ogden Hall auditorium. Suddenly, you feel sick and break out in a sweat, and you cannot stop shaking. You are suffering from stage fright or public speaking anxiety. Research shows that the fear of speaking in public is second to the fear of dying. Yes, dying.

Truth of the matter is, all successful people will at some point engage in public communication. The success of this communication context is greatly dependent upon a speaker's ability to make a connection with the audience regardless of its size.

Public communication can be described as a communication context in which the membership becomes too large for more than one or two people to speak. By its nature, the audience provides nonverbal feedback to the speaker. The audience is unable to provide verbal feedback due to the numbers of the participants. This provides a greater need for the speaker to connect with the audience to convey a message by keeping the audience engaged and involved.

Public communication differs from small group communication but how?

Good public speakers employ skills that accomplish their goals. While some public speakers demonstrate an innate talent for this communication context, most speakers develop such skills by observation and practice.

Intercultural Communication

The tragedy of 911 greatly impacted our view of culture and diversity in the field of communication. The term culture has almost as many definitions as the word communication. For communicators today, a successful relationship greatly depends on one's ability to demonstrate communication competency across cultures. For our exploration and discussion, **culture** will be referred to as shared perceptions and expectations of a group of people. As we further explore these communication patterns and expectations, our engagement with other cultures becomes more socially positive and, in some cases, professionally productive. Based upon the premise that culture is learned, dynamic and pervasive, we can begin to understand the role culture plays in the success of our relationships. Good commu-

When is computer mediated communication preferred over face-to-face communication?

nicators must develop a personal approach to maintain successful diverse interpersonal relationships. *Communication For Today's Student* will assist in reaching your goals with regards to culture and diversity.

Computer Mediated Communication

The major difference between **Computer Mediated Communication** (CMC) and face to face communication is control. CMC can be described as the use of computer networks to exchange information and to facilitate the interactive sharing of information. This exchange differs from other types of communication as it occurs over a single channel, whether it is via emails, discussion groups, chat, IM, web pages or news groups. CMC best facilitates our communication goals and objectives when coupled with digital literacy. This broadens the scope of our communication and affects our ability to process and exchange information in a manner in which social and economic subjectifiers can be eliminated. That being said , today we have numerous ways in which to communicate, and our choices have created an ongoing battle between **lean medium channels** and **rich medium channels**. Simply put, today's student is faced with the challenge of communicating using CMC which is considered a lean medium channel or face to face which is considered a rich medium channel. There is a clear disadvantage when using CMC and we have all experienced it. CMC does not allow us to express nonverbal messages. We attempt to substitute with symbols and emoji but there is a wide margin of misinterpretation. So, why would today's student choose CMC over face-to-face communication? The reasons range from personal preferences to accepted social risks.

Ethics in Communication

When we communicate with individuals, we have an unspoken expectation that the information being shared with us is true. How would you feel if you had a long conversation with a friend and later discovered that everything you had been told was a lie? What would you think if you attended a seminar on increasing your finances, completed all of the steps outlined for you to follow, and discovered that your finances never increased? In each of these situations, you would more than likely be extremely disappointed or possibly hurt and angered. To avoid such situations happening to you or causing them to happen to others, it is pertinent that you practice **ethics** in your personal and professional communication.

When is computer mediated communication preferred over face-to-face communication?

As you communicate with others, you must decide what to say and what not to say. You must decide whether to present factual information or fictitious information. You must decide whether to tell half of the story or the whole story. You must decide whether to tell the truth or tell a lie. You must decide whether or not to practice ethical communication. The decision to be ethical in your communication is a decision that will impact your listener(s) and, ultimately, you. It is a decision that must be made with much thought and careful consideration.

The best decision to make when it comes to ethics in communication is the decision to be ethical. As the communicator, you should want to share information that is accurate and factual with the listener, whether for personal or professional purposes. When you practice ethics in communication, those with whom you communicate will be able to trust you. When you tell your employer that you have completed a task, he or she will trust that it has been done. If you tell your friends that you will meet them, they will trust that you will be there.

From this point forward, it is important for you to take a moment before you speak and consider the ethics of what you are saying. Is the information accurate? How will it affect the listener? Should I share this information or keep it to myself? Once you begin taking ethics into consideration, you will have made one more giant step towards becoming an effective communicator.

Let's Get Started

In Chapter 1, you were introduced to the foundations of communication. We discussed the importance of studying communication and how it can affect our personal and professional lives. The communication process was defined, and we used the Communication Model to explicate the role that each element of communication plays in the process. You learned that communication is transactional. The Nathalie and Chris scenario served as our reference and guide to the explication. You were introduced to the types of communication (intrapersonal, interpersonal, small-group, public, intercultural, computer-mediated) and presented a discussion on the ethics of communication.

This text will provide the opportunity to engage in activities that introduce you to and familiarize you with the theories of effective communication that will be useful to you, both personally and professionally.

The topic of Chapter 2, *Perception and Listening*, examines the manner in which individuals process information. The chapter covers the factors that influence perception as well as the steps to effective listening. Chapter 3, *What is the Power of Verbal and Nonverbal Communication*, will identify the differences between verbal and non-verbal messages and how each is used in the communication process. Chapters 4, 5, and 6 are all related to the role communication plays in relationships. *Understanding Interpersonal Relationships* describes the essential elements that draw people together and explains the role of emotional intelligence in communication. *Building Relationships* discusses the stages of relationships as they are formed and dissolved. The chapter also addresses conflict resolution within relationships. *Intercultural Relationships* defines culture, identifies the characteristics of culture, and evaluates the impact cultural values have on interpersonal communication. Additionally, the chapter provides strategies to enhance effective interpersonal communication in diverse relationships.

The second half of the textbook provides the blueprint for successful oral presentations. In Chapter 7, *Researching Your Topic*, the text offers strategies for accessing, analyzing, and using information in your speech. You are also given guidelines for the using various forms of support. *Organizing Your Ideas and Structuring Your Outline*, Chapter 8, teaches you how to generate the main points of the speech and presents patterns for organizing the points. The chapter also offers guidance in planning the outlines sentence and keyword of the speech. Chapter 9, *Delivering The Speech*, addresses the methods of delivery and the aspects of vocal and physical delivery.

After all of the foundational materials are presented, the next two chapters focus on two unique purposes for speaking. First, Chapter 10 addresses *Speaking to Inform* and expands upon the types of informative speeches and the goals of informative speaking.

Second, Chapter 11 addresses *Speaking to Persuade* by an examination of the elements of persuasion, inductive and deductive reasoning, emotion, and logic. The chapter also discusses the speaker's ethical responsibility when preparing a persuasive speech.

The last two chapters in the text deal with groups. In Chapter 12, *What are the Roles of Leadership and Power in Group Dynamics?*, the differences between leadership and power are identified. The chapter offers the six bases of power that are typical in a small group as well as ways to deal with conflict within small groups. The closing chapter, *Small Group Presentations*, presents the characteristics of small groups and the role and responsibilities of individuals within small groups. The chapter offers suggestions for presenting in small groups and identifies small group formats.

By the time you have completed reading the text and completed the related assignments, both in class and on the website, you will be equipped with all of the tools necessary to be an effective communicator in both your personal and professional lives. These tools will last a lifetime and contribute to your success as an individual. Now, let's get started!

Communication is important to our everyday lives.

Communication for Today's Student

Chapter 1 – Communication for Today's Student: An Introduction

Exercise 1.1 – Communication Journal

I. Good communication skills are guaranteed to make us more successful in life.

Establish a communication journal for one week which chronicles your communication experiences within each context:

Communication Contexts

Intrapersonal
Interpersonal
Intercultural
Small Group
Public

Communication Journal

Day 1 Context:	
Day 2 Context:	
Day 3 Context:	
Day 4 Context:	
Day 5 Context:	
Day 6 Context:	
Day 7 Context:	

Be prepared to share your journal entries with the class.

As you record your experiences consider the following for inclusion, if applicable:
- Are the elements of communication represented in the communication experience?
- What is the channel that the message is being transmitted upon?
- Was there any noise involved, and if so, what type?
- Was there anything that you would like to change about your communication experience?
- Would you consider the experience positive or negative?
- How would you approach changing the outcome of that experience?

II. Choose one context to illustrate, Using photos from your
    photo library to create an illustration.
    Label the elements!

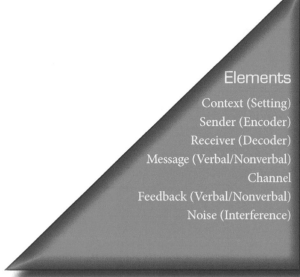

Elements

Context (Setting)
Sender (Encoder)
Receiver (Decoder)
Message (Verbal/Nonverbal)
Channel
Feedback (Verbal/Nonverbal)
Noise (Interference)

III. Describe in one or two paragraphs what occurs in your include the dialogue that may have occurred.

- Identify the sender and receiver?
- In what communication context does the illustration occur?
- Is there any noise in the context? Which type?
- What type of channel does the message travel upon?
- Did your sender or receiver demonstrate any nonverbal behavior?

Communication for Today's Student

Chapter 1 – Communication for Today's Student: An Introduction

Exercise 1.2 – Credo for Communication Ethics

The National Communication Association published a ***Credo for Communication Ethics*** which describes the expectations of ethical behavior. The document condemns such behavior as distortion, intimidation, coercion, intolerance, and hatred; while it advocates truthfulness, accuracy and honesty, freedom of expression and so on.

With a partner, document a media event in which ethical communication practices where in question according to the standards of the ***Credo***. Prepare a 2 to 3 minute speech to explain why the situation was one in which the National Communication Association would condemn or advocate based upon the Credo and why? Be sure to cite the specific principle from the ***Credo***.

For example:

Bill Mahr's use of the NWord on his HBO Television show

Kim Kardashian and Taylor Swift public feud over the song Famous

Kathy Griffin's use of the beheaded image of President Trump

NCA Credo

NCA Credo for Ethical Communication, available at www.natcom.org
Reprinted by permission of the National Communication Association.

NCA Credo for Ethical Communication
(Approved by the NCA Legislative Council in 1999)

Questions of right and wrong arise whenever people communicate. Ethical communication is fundamental to responsible thinking, decision-making, and the development of relationships and communities within and across contexts, cultures, channels, and media. Moreover, ethical communication enhances human worth and dignity by fostering truthfulness, fairness, responsibility, personal integrity, and respect for self and others. We believe that unethical communication threatens the quality of all communication and consequently the well-being of individuals and the society in which we live. Therefore, we, the members of the National Communication Association, endorse and are committed to practicing the following principles of ethical communication:

We advocate truthfulness, accuracy, honesty, and reason as essential to the integrity of communication.

We endorse freedom of expression, diversity of perspective, and tolerance of dissent to achieve the informed and responsible decision-making fundamental to a civil society.

We strive to understand and respect other communicators before evaluating and responding to their messages.

We promote access to communication resources and opportunities as necessary to fulfill human potential and contribute to the well-being of families, communities, and society.

We promote communication climates of caring and mutual understanding that respect the unique needs and characteristics of individual communicators.

We condemn communication that degrades individuals and humanity through distortion, intimidation, coercion, and violence, and through the expression of intolerance and hatred.

We are committed to the courageous expression of personal convictions in pursuit of fairness and justice.

We advocate sharing information, opinions, and feelings when facing significant choices while also respecting privacy and confidentiality.

We accept responsibility for the short- and long-term consequences for our own communication and expect the same of others.

PERCEPTION AND LISTENING

After reading this chapter, you should be able to:

☑ Define perception.
☑ Discuss the three interactive processes of perception.
☑ Describe the three principles of perception.
☑ Identify the errors in perception.
☑ Distinguish between hearing and listening processes.
☑ Identify the seven steps to effective listening.
☑ Recall the four listening styles and identify the focus of each.
☑ Explain the four motivations to listen and recall a potential pitfall of each.
☑ Recognize the six common listening misbehaviors.

Key Terms

Perception	Meaningfulness	People-oriented listening	Pseudo listening
Selection	Listening	Action-oriented listening	Monopolizing
Organization	Hearing	Content-oriented listening	Disconfirming
Interpretation	Paraphrasing	Time-oriented listening	Defensive listening
Subjectivity	Positive feedback	Appreciative listening	Selective listening
Physiology	Negative feedback	Comprehensive listening	Ambushing
Culture	Dual perspective	Evaluative listening	
Stability	Discriminate listening	Empathetic listening	

2 Scenario

"Chris, how could you forget the cake?"

Chris bit his lip as he sped down the road, towards the bakery.

Dr. Vera was celebrating her thirtieth year working at the university, and her students in the history department were planning a big bash for her. Jillian was in charge. She was the perfect person for the job. She organized everything. She had workers from Buildings and Grounds decorate the banquet room in the student center with Dr. Vera's favorite colors. She had the campus food service department cook all of Dr. Vera's favorite dishes. She then made sure all her favorite students who had graduated would be there to celebrate. Everything worked out, except trusting Chris to pick up the ice cream and cake. Chris returned with the ice cream, but no cake. The bakery had just closed, and Chris and Jillian were racing down street, hoping someone was still there.

"I swear you said Mark picked up the cake," Chris said, defending himself.

"Mark picked up the ice cream!" Jillian yelled.

Chris was known for making colossal mistakes like this, which is why Jillian was reluctant about giving Chris such a big responsibility.

"You never listen, Chris!"

"I do, too, listen. I just misunderstood."

"No, you never take the time to just stop and listen!"

Chris pulled up to the bakery, and Jillian jumped out of the car and raced up to the door. The main lobby was pitch-black, but she could see a little light from the back. She banged on the door, hoping someone was there so that Dr. Vera's bash wouldn't be ruined.

Are you a good listener?
What can you do to improve your listening skills?

Respond Here

What Role Does Perception Play in Critical Thinking?

To engage in critical thinking, we have to begin with the most fundamental of our skill abilities: our perceptions. The concept of **perception** can be defined in many ways, but simply put, it is our set of beliefs concerning what is out there. For more detail, let us consider two views. John Chaffee, a professor of humanities specializing in critical thinking, says that perceiving involves actively selecting, organizing, and interpreting what is experienced by your senses.[8] Thus, perception involves what you can see, hear, feel, smell, and taste; you use these sensations to experience and to make sense of the world. Communication Professor Julia T. Wood says that perception is an active process of selecting, organizing, and interpreting people, objects, events, situations, and activities.[9] It is how we attach significance to the world around us.

If you're on a sports team, you may identify more closely with other athletes.

Process of Perception

If we combine the previous definitions, perception involves our senses, employs a process of interaction, and results in an understanding of some experience in order to make sense of the world. Returning to Wood's definition, perception involves three interactive processes: selection, organization, and interpretation:

Selection. First is **selection**. Because your senses are bombarded by sights, sounds, and smells (at the minimum), you have developed a method of focusing that narrows your attention to selected stimuli. Stop reading right now and focus on the sounds around you. Did you notice them as you were holding this book? Can you close your eyes and picture what page you were on? Are there any pleasant or unpleasant smells around you? Reflect on the stimuli you were actively conscious of and those you eliminated from awareness.

We all try to structure perception in order to make sense of them.

This selection of stimuli is necessary and typical of perceptions; you cannot make all stimuli relevant, so you focus on the ones that you have defined as important to whatever task you are currently engaged in.

Perhaps you remember a time when a pot boiled over. Even though dinner was important, your attention had been drawn away by a phone call. One perception (the phone's ring) shifted your perception away from the boiling pot. This perceptual process is important for a communicator, because you can use it to your advantage. We know that some stimuli will draw attention because they are particularly relevant, immediate, or intense. If you talk about something that your listener relates to, it is likely that issue will draw greater interest. If you attempt to catch initial attention by a soft voice, it is unlikely that will work, simply because it is not very intense. If your audience cannot see what you are showing them, their visual limits will likely result in their tuning out.

Organization. The second perceptual process is **organization**. We all try to structure perceptions in order to make sense of them. You will learn later that there are many strategies for structuring public speeches, group meetings, and interviews to accomplish desired goals. For now, we will simply say that each of us applies certain cognitive patterns, or perceptions. Those patterns are developed through experience. If you have never smelled certain spices, then you cannot sort them into the correct meaning of what kind of food is cooking; if you have developed stereotypical patterns that suggest all members of a certain ethnic group have a certain intellectual level, then you might assume that a new colleague from that group has that intellect.

Interpretation. **Interpretation** happens when you assign meaning to your perceptions. Once your brain has selected and organized the stimuli, it has to create meaning. For instance, if you are given a set of numbers, how do you know what they mean?

231 7620

904 38 7231

5468 9960 0075 1234

The first set appears to be a phone number, without the area code. The second set might be structured like a social security number. The third set appears to be similar to a credit card number. How do you know this? Part of your interpretation comes from the way the numbers are structured (organized), but part has to come from your experience. If you have never seen a social security number, you cannot interpret the second set in that way; it might not have any meaning. Similarly, if someone you know suddenly stops talking to you, you recognize the change in a pattern, but you interpret what has "caused" this silence to occur based on your own experiences, beliefs, values, and attitudes. Did Joan stop talking to you because you hurt her feelings? Is she sick and hoarse? Each of those interpretations is different, but they are based on the same initial perception of silence. Depending on your interpretation, your next communication encounter with Joan will be markedly different.

Other strategic perceptual techniques will be developed later in this text, but you need to remember that an audience's perceptions will greatly influence your ability to communicate successfully with them. The process of perception, involving selection, organization, and interpretation, describes the active steps we engage in to develop meaning.

Perception Principles

Three basic principles of perception might offer a deeper understanding of the complexity of the perception process. **Subjectivity**, **stability**, and **meaningfulness** describe the various filters that each of us employs when we attempt to create meaning from stimuli.

Subjectivity. **Subjectivity** refers to perceptions that are unique to your personal experience, views, or mental state. The most obvious source of subjectivity is your **physiology**; you differ from another in your physical sensory ability. Next time you are at the grocery store, look at what people are wearing on their feet. Some will be in sandals, others in boots, some in shoes, and some may try to shop barefoot! Each person's footwear choice indicates a degree of sensitivity to temperature and texture. Similarly, what might be hot chili to you might be mild to another. Music that is "too loud" for some may be "too quiet" for others. Ten million American men—7 percent of the male population— either cannot distinguish red from green, or see red and green differently from most people. This is the most common form of color blindness, but it affects only 0.4 percent

Photo courtesy of Charles Long

The most obvious source of subjectivity is your physiology; you differ from another in your physical sensory ability.

Perception Principles

Subjectivity—Perceptions that are unique to your personal experience, views, or mental state. Sources include:

Physiology: physical sensory ability

Culture and experiences: beliefs, values, norms and ways of interpreting experiences

Psychological: affected by the perceptual choices you make

Selective exposure: you choose consistent information

Selective attention: you choose to pay attention to known stimuli

Selective interpretation: you interpret ambiguous stimuli to be consistent with what you know

Selective retention: you remember more accurately those things that are consistent with what you know

Stability—The predictability that we need in life; managed in two ways:

Assimilation: you interpret the stimuli you receive to fit what you already know or expect

Accommodation: you change what you know to fit the incoming perceptual data

Meaningfulness—Refers to the ways that we project comprehension or understanding onto perceptions; achieved in several ways:

Contrast: you say something is like (or unlike) something you know

Familiar versus the novel: you understand what you've experienced, but something new is much more difficult to understand

Closure: you fill in details of an incomplete picture

Repetition: if it happened before, you expect it to happen again

of women.[10] That knowledge might impact your strategic choice of color on a graph. In the same way, about 10 percent of the population is left-handed; this means that some of us experience an anti-lefty bias that assaults us; scissors are useless, power tools (such as circular saws) are dangerous, and pens smear and make writing illegible. In giving instructions, it might be important to consider handedness. Consider how awkward it might be for a leftie to learn to use a tool meant for the right-handed worker. Many physiological states can influence perception. When you are tired or ill, you may be less able to react to a friend's humor and may take offense at a comment that normally would not make you blink.

A second subjectivity source involves psychological aspects created by our culture and experiences. **Culture** refers to the community of meaning to which we belong (beliefs, values, norms, and ways of interpreting experience that are shared by those around us). As Americans, we tend to subjectively view the world through basic assumptions of various rights: to freedom of speech, to pursue religious beliefs, to be all that we can be. Other cultures do not have those assumptions, yet we do not become aware of that until we are questioned. For instance, in the United States, many adoptive families openly celebrate how their families were created, and they consider the birth parents as part of their extended family. In other countries, adoption is still a shameful state, and if one is forced to make a decision to place the child for adoption, it is shrouded in secrecy and mystery.

To envision this aspect of subjectivity, consider your reactions to the following examples. Past Olympic media coverage highlighted the adoption stories of 2006 American bronze medalist (men's mogul) Toby Dawson, adopted at age three from South Korea, and 1984 gold medalist Scott Hamilton, adopted at six weeks from the United States. Run-D.M.C. group member, Darryl "D.M.C." McDaniels, revealed on a 2006 VH1 documentary that he was adopted as an infant but only learned that at age thirty-five.[11] Wendy's

Many physiological states can influence perception.

founder Dave Thomas started a foundation to celebrate adoption, because he had been adopted from foster care. Your beliefs and experience with adoption, whether you have a member of your family who is adopted or if you are adopted, will impact the way that you view these stories, and, in turn, whether you donate to adoption causes, watch programs about adoption, or even consider adoption yourself.

In the same way, modern Western culture integrates technology and speed into nearly everything about living: we expect things to happen quickly (instant messages, instant photos, instant oatmeal). How does our speed expectation impact our perceptions of other cultures where patience and leisure are the norm, such as Mexico and Nepal?

Psychological subjectivity is affected by the perceptual choices that you make, either intentionally or not.[12] *Selective exposure* suggests that you choose to seek consistent information or to expose yourself to certain contexts where you will feel comfortable with the stim-

Are we twins? Are we the same? Are we sisters?

uli. For example, you may attend only one style of play (let's say musicals) rather than going to Greek tragedies, comedies, farces, or melodramas, because psychologically, a musical is pleasant to your eyes and ears. You know what to expect and feel at ease with the context, story line, characters, and addition of music to the overall experience.

Selective attention suggests that people choose to expose themselves or pay attention to certain stimuli already present, to key in on certain phenomenon, because these are more similar to their experiences or beliefs. Perhaps you listen only to one kind of music because that is what you know; the thought of going to a country concert when you are an opera fan may just be too much to ask! If you engage in *selective interpretation*, you interpret ambiguous stimuli so that it becomes consistent with what you know. Imagine that you are given some new food to taste, and it looks pretty much like chicken. You may interpret what you taste as a unique flavor of barbeque chicken, only later to find out that it was alligator! *Selective retention* suggests that you will remember more accurately messages that are consistent with interests, views and beliefs than those that are in contrast with your values and beliefs. Because of the vast amounts of information you are bombarded with, you decide what to keep in the memory, narrowing the informational flow once again. When parents ask children to do household chores, those children seem to have an uncanny ability to remember only the chores that are the easiest or the ones they want to do. Perhaps you are more likely to remember the parts of your professor's lecture that you agree with and to forget the parts that do not correspond to your beliefs.

Stability. A second perception principle, **stability**, refers to the predictability that we need in life. The concept of organization suggests that we pattern what we perceive in order to get stimuli to "fit" into our preconceived ways of thinking. Stability can be managed in two basic ways. *Assimilation* is when you interpret the stimuli you receive to fit what you already know or expect. In simple terms, you "bend" the incoming information so that it fits what you know. If you know that your family always orders sausage pizza, that first bite you take of that pizza will taste like sausage, because you are certain that's what they order. Until you are informed that the topping is really tofu, you expect that the pizza guy has brought you sausage. *Accommodation* occurs when you change what you know to fit the incoming perceptual data. For instance, if you believe that your friend is honest but you see her looking on someone else's test, you might change your perception of what constitutes cheating.

If you engage in selective interpretation, you interpret ambigious stimuli so that it becomes consistent with what you know.

Meaningfulness. Finally, **meaningfulness**, the third perception principle, refers to the ways that we project comprehension or understanding onto perceptions. This is achieved in several ways. You might employ *contrast*, where you say that something is like (or unlike) something that you know. Is the latest reality show anything like *Survivor*, which you cannot stand? You might compare a political candidate to an earlier politician you admired, giving him your vote. Someone you are interviewing with might think that you are too similar to the person she just fired, so she cannot take a chance on you.

A second technique is through the *familiar versus the novel:* You can understand something that you have experienced, but something new is much more difficult to understand. Until you have had your house burn down around you, it is hard to really understand the range of emotions of those who have lived through this. You might never have heard of being a CASA volunteer, so you cannot imagine volunteering for this valuable child advocacy service when you hear a speech about it.

With *closure*, you fill in the details of an incomplete picture. You are given an assignment, but once you try to complete the task, you realize that you do not know exactly what is expected. When you cannot reach your instructor, you make some decisions about what you think she means for you to do. Even *repetition* is a means for creating meaningfulness; if something has happened

You are given an assignment, but once you try to complete the task, you realize that you do not know exactly what is expected.

before, then you expect it to happen again. If you have been snubbed by a colleague several times, you will not be able to attribute friendship meaning when that person suddenly treats you as his best buddy in a meeting; you might assume his behavior is a political move.

Errors in Perception. Perceptions are fundamental to critical thinking, and they are confounded by multiple opportunities to be imperfect. There are many reasons for these perceptual errors, and understanding their source may make for a more perceptive communication event. One reason is that we are influenced by the immediately obvious. You observe two children fighting on a playground, and you immediately assume that the one who is hitting the other must have started the fight. When you intercede, you concentrate your message on the "guilty" one. We also cling to those first impressions, because again, our interpretations are rarely questioned. If a church is the place you first meet someone, you might think that she is a devout member of that church, even though it might be her first time

Perceptions are fundamental to critical thinking, and they are confounded by multiple opportunities to be imperfect.

there. Third, we assume that others think like we do, so we do not question our perceptions. Maybe you like junk mail, cyberjokes, and the like, so you pass them on. Others may despise getting bombarded with this same material. Maybe your mother appreciates "constructive criticism," but you do not. As previously noted, we have different sensory abilities, so our facility to see or hear something is likely different from someone else's; where a road sign may be perfectly clear to you, the passenger, your friend the driver may miss it because he cannot see that far.

We also have different experiences through our culture, education, character, and activities, so our perceptions are impacted. If you are a football fan, you may watch the game from a technician's point of view, noticing how the linebackers play defense and the variety of coaching plays. A non–football-loving friend who attends the game with you may focus on the cheer squad and the band. In another example, a builder sees the new house construction differently than the first-time homeowner. Finally, different perceptual expectations may be part of the context: Where you are may determine what you expect to see or to hear. A car accident is perceived quite differently by the drivers, witnesses, and attending officer. What each party communicates about that experience will likely be significantly different. If you are at a concert, you probably expect to hear music and not a political pitch, so your perception of the politician who uses the concert as a fundraiser will probably be negative.

What can you gain from this brief foray into perception? The knowledge you gain from your perceptions is vivid, personal, and often accepted uncritically. Your perceptions are experiential, selective, perhaps inaccurate, and likely evaluative. Every dimension of what you know is directly impacted by your perceptions. You cannot engage in critical thinking without considering your perceptions. The same is true of your listener: you cannot communicate with another until you have considered his or her perceptions.

We have different experiences through our culture, education, characters, and activities, so our perceptions are impacted.

How Does Listening Fit into Critical Thinking?

When you need to check your spelling, do you write the word down to see if it feels right? Do you need to see the word to check it? Or do you sound out the word? What about your behavior when you meet someone for a second or third time. Do you remember that person by what you did together, or do you remember where you met? Is it easier for you to remember a name or what you talked about? One last scenario: When reading, do you prefer action stories, descriptive scenes, or narratives where the characters talk? Each one of these situations reveals something about your learning style, or the different approaches that people take to acquire knowledge. In each case, the first example suggests a tactile learner (learn by feeling or touching); the second is a visual learner (learn by seeing); and the third is an auditory learner (learn by listening). Your preferred styles guide the way you learn. They also change the way you internally represent experiences, the way you recall information, and even the words you choose. Everybody has a mix of learning styles; you may have one dominant style, or you may even use different styles in different circumstances. But why is this important to know in a chapter about audience?

When you create and then present a message, you want to adapt it to your audience in order to create shared meaning. You'll consider how you can organize thoughts through vivid words; you'll try to keep your ideas moving by effective structure and transitions. Your ideas may be supported by presentational aids that supplement your words, ones that give your audience something else to look to for understanding. These strategies will help the visual learners who think in pictures and the tactile persons who need action or hands-on information. But you'll also need to consider how your audience perceives ideas through listening, auditory processing. Just as writing clarifies and documents the spoken message, verbally clarifying the spoken message before, during, and after a presentation enhances listening comprehension. You could create a well organized and supported speech about the needs for reducing truck emissions, but if you don't present it in a way designed to enhance our listening, it's likely that your message won't have an impact. Listening is an essential dimension of our critical thinking skills.

Listening

Multiple definitions of listening exist, but we'll use the one from the International Listening Association, which defines **listening** as the active process of receiving, constructing meaning from, and responding to spoken and/or nonverbal messages.[13] It involves the ability to retain information as well as to react empathetically and/or appreciatively to spoken and/or nonverbal messages.[14] This complex definition offers several important considerations.

Listening is *active*. Ralph Nichols, one of the earliest scholars to study listening, said listening is "not involuntary," and that it is a skill that is the "oldest, most used, and the most important element to interpersonal communication."[15] **Hearing** is a passive physiological process where the ear receives sound. Brownell says that the accurate reception of sounds requires you to focus attention on the speaker, discriminate among sounds, and concentrate.[16] That means that the listener has to be physically able to hear; the physiological receptors must be working. But it also puts a burden on the speaker: you have to make sure that your audience is in a position to hear the sounds you're about to make; you have to consider your volume, rate, and pitch, along with the acoustics. Hearing becomes listening when you engage in the active, psychological activity that requires effort and motivation.

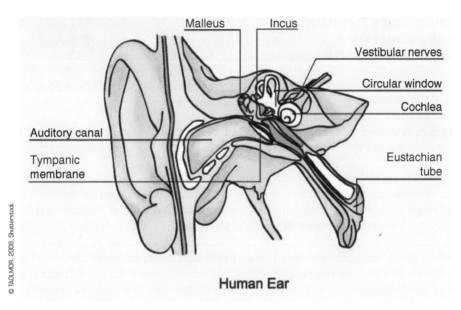

Human Ear

Listening is an active process; hearing is the passive physiological process where the ear receives sound.

Listening is a *process* with implications for speaker and listener. The term *process* implies an activity that is continuous and ongoing. We usually take this process for granted, but there is a major difference between hearing and the complex task of listening. In fact, you could have excellent hearing and still be a terrible listener. This process is also transactional; listening can't occur unless both a sender and a receiver are involved. Have you ever left a lecture feeling cheated because you didn't get much out of the message? Did you then blame the teacher? Don't be lulled into thinking that effective interaction is the sole responsibility of the sender; successful communication is a shared enterprise, a process involving the sending and receiving of messages.

Receiving is a physiological activity in which verbal and nonverbal messages stimulate our senses. If a sound is made, your eardrums vibrate. You can see the nonverbal behavior of people all around you. In addition when receiving, you focus on specific stimuli and reject others.

Constructing meaning occurs as you interpret the stimuli, creating understanding for yourself that you later use as future referents. At the same time you are placing meaning on the stimuli that meets your prior perceptions, you are inferring what the message means to the speaker. You try to fit the message into ideas you already recognize, into what you know about the speaker, into your immediate context, and into your culture. That means that you also have to place that meaning into previously created categories; there simply are too many stimuli for us to keep them all, so we sort and interpret. At the same time, you judge the message for its usefulness and accuracy. That leads to the need for retaining, remembering, or storing the message for later recall.

Reacting is when you respond to the message, providing feedback to the sender. Some examples of responding behaviors are focusing your eye contact on the person you are listening to, using facial expressions to encourage the person to continue, adjusting your posture to lean toward the speaker, or asking questions.

Listening involves our *interpretation of nonverbal cues* that add to meaning. You listen with more than just your physical ability to receive sounds. Listening cues can include perceptions of the speaker's vocal pitch and volume, rate of speaking, use of verbal fillers (such as "uh," "um," "OK," "you know," and "like"), facial expression, eye contact, gestures, and posture. Think of it this way: you listen with more than just your ears! Research tells us that spoken words only account for 30 to 35 percent of the meaning. The rest is transmitted through nonverbal communication that only can be detected through visual and auditory listening.[17]

Photo courtesy of Charles Long

Listening involves our interpretation of nonverbal cues that add to meaning.

As you can see by this definition, listening involves those perception skills of selection, organization, and interpretation. You have to be able to perceive sounds, select which ones to keep, and then organize them into meaning that you can reflect back to the sender. Now, armed with a sense of what constitutes listening, let's look at some of the research findings on effective listening.

There are many reasons to put effort into effective listening. Listening has been identified as one of the top skills employers seek in entry-level employees as well as those being promoted.[18] Listening accounts for approximately one-third of the characteristics perceivers use to evaluate communication competence in co-workers.[19] Listening is an important component in how people judge communicative competence in the workplace.[20] Further, individual performance in an organization is found to be directly related to listening ability or perceived listening effectiveness. Consider your life right now as a student. Research tells us that college students spend nearly half of their communication time listening, about one-third of it speaking, and less than one-third of it reading and writing.[21] Effective listening is associated with school success, but not with any major personality dimensions.[22] A number of research studies show that there is a correlation between listening and academic success. A student with high grades also usually has the strongest listening skills; students with the lowest grades usually demonstrate the weakest listening skills.[23] Listening also impacts us in intrapersonal and interpersonal ways. Confident individuals listen to message content better than individuals who lack confidence.[24] Listening is tied to effective leadership.[25] Those with a high peopleorientation have a low apprehension for receiving information.[26] In health care contexts, the largest indicators of patient satisfaction with physician's communication skills include empathy and listening. Effective listening has been called a significant predictor for patient satisfaction.[27] As you can tell, the research on listening is broad, but one significant conclusion can be made: Successful listening improves communication.

Key Strategies for Effective Listening

To help you remember some of the key strategies involved in effective listening, remember the following acronym: **BIG EARS**. Each of these strategies is discussed in the paragraphs that follow.

Be Open to the Message. Listening is difficult enough to begin with, but when we fail to prepare ourselves to receive messages, it becomes even more so. Effective listening requires you to employ effective nonverbal listening behaviors, control message overload, and manage your preoccupations and other distractions.

First, we need to be aware of our nonverbal listening behaviors. The next time you are sitting in class listening to a lecture, take a moment and consider the role your nonverbal behaviors play in the listening process. Do you look like you are open to receiving messages? Maintaining an open body position, engaging in eye contact, and responding to the lecture by nodding your head are all examples of nonverbal behaviors that communicate a willingness to listen.

Next, focus on ways to manage the multiple sources of information that are competing for your attention. Remember our discussion of perception and the role of selective attention and exposure? Effective listening behaviors require you to dedicate your attention to a particular message. The next time you are tempted to watch *Grey's Anatomy* while carrying on a phone conversation with your mother, think twice. One of the sources will ultimately win out over the other—will it be the television show or your mother?

Table 2.1 Key Strategies for Effective Listening (BIG EARS)

B	Be open and receptive to the message
I	Interpret the message
G	Give feedback
E	Engage in dual perspective
A	Adapt your listening style
R	Reduce noise
S	Store the message

Finally, identify ways to manage the multiple preoccupations and distractions that can impair your ability to listen. Look beyond superficial factors that may be hindering your ability to focus on the message. While a professor's distracting delivery style or prehistoric clothing choices may cause your attention to focus away from the lecture being delivered, these are not excuses to disregard the source's message. Remain focused on the content of the message. On average, Americans speak at a rate of 125 words per minute. However, the human brain can process more than 450 words per minute (Hilliard and Palmer 2003) and we can think at a rate of 1000–3000 words per minute (Hilliard and Palmer 2003). So what happens with all that extra time? Often we daydream or we become bored because our brain can work faster than the speaker can talk. Therefore, it is important to dedicate

Manage multiple preoccupations and distractions that can impair your ability to listen.

yourself to relating the information to existing information that you already know. While this can be challenging at times, chances are that it will prove to be extremely useful. Ask yourself questions during a conversation or lecture such as, "How will this information benefit me?" or "How will this information benefit my relationship with the source?" Being open to receiving messages is the first step to ensuring an effective listening experience.

Interpreting the Message. Interpretation refers to the cognitive processes involved in listening. Recall our discussion of the role of interpretation in perception. We pointed out that associations are often made between stimuli and things with which we are already familiar. Interpretation is also a key element in listening, and in verifying that the meaning we assigned to the message is close to that which was intended by the source. Some strategies to assist in interpretation of messages include asking questions, soliciting feedback, and requesting clarification. These strategies will help you interpret the source's message more accurately. Consider the following interaction between Maya and Raj:

Maya: I hate biology.
Raj: Why?
Maya: Well, I guess I don't hate it, but I am upset I did poorly on the first exam.
Raj: Why did you do poorly?
Maya: Because I studied the wrong chapters.
Raj: So, do you dislike the material?

Maya: Well, no, I actually enjoy the teacher and the book.

Raj: So, you like biology but you are upset you studied the wrong material?

Maya: Yes, I actually like the course; I am just mad because I know I could have received an A if I had studied the right material.

Because Raj asked Maya to provide additional information to help clarify why she hated biology he was able to interpret Maya's situation more clearly. In fact, it changed the meaning of the message entirely. Maya's initial message was that she hated biology and it turns out that she actually enjoys biology. Raj was able to accurately interpret the message because he asked questions and solicited feedback. But soliciting feedback is not the only element involved in listening. **Paraphrasing** is another useful strategy for clarifying meaning and ensuring that you have accurately interpreted a message. Paraphrasing involves restating a message in your own words to see if the meaning you assigned was similar to that which was intended. But this is still not enough. Effective listening also requires you to provide the source with feedback to communicate that you have both received and understood the message.

Give feedback. Feedback serves many purposes in the listening process. By providing feedback to the source, we are confirming that we received the message and were able to interpret and assign meaning to what was being communicated. Feedback can be either positive or negative and communicate its own message. **Positive feedback** includes verbal and non-verbal behaviors that encourage the speaker to continue communicating. Examples of positive feedback include eye contact, nods, and comments such as, "I see," and "Please continue." **Negative feedback** is often discouraging to a source. Examples of negative feedback would be disconfirming verbal comments such as "You are over-reacting" or "I don't know why you get so upset," or negative nonverbal responses such as avoidance of eye contact, maintaining a closed body position (e.g., crossed arms), or meaningless vocaliza-

What kinds of positive feedback show that you are interested and listening?

tions such as "Um-hmm." Positive feedback communicates interest and empathy for the speaker, whereas negative feedback often results in feelings of defensiveness.

Engage in dual-perspective taking. **Dual-perspective taking**, or empathy, refers to the attempt to see things from the other person's point of view. The concept of empathy has been a primary focus of the listening process required of social workers and counselors. Norton (1978) explains this by theorizing that all people are part of two systems—a larger societal system and a more immediate personal system. While it is often possible to gain insight into an individual's societal system, truly understanding someone's personal system is often a more difficult task. Consider the phrase, "Put yourself in another person's shoes." Do you think it is possible to truly put yourself in another person's shoes? This would require us to be able to tap into their unique background and experiences in order to perceive things exactly as they do. But is this ever really possible? Our position is that it is not. This may help explain why we find it difficult to respond to a friend who is going through a difficult break-up. Our initial response may be to respond with a statement like, "I know exactly how you feel. I've been through dozens of broken relationships." But this is not necessarily the best response. There is a unique history to your friend's relationship that you

Empathetic listening requires an attempt to see things from your friend's point to view.

can never truly understand. While you cannot fully put yourself in her shoes, you can communicate empathy by attempting to see things from her point of view. Dual-perspective taking requires a receiver to adapt his listening style to accommodate a variety of situations.

Adapt your listening style. Effective communicators are flexible in their communication style and find it easy to adjust both their speaking and listening styles, based on the unique demands of the receiver, the material, or the situation. Duran (1983) defines communicative adaptability as a cognitive and behavioral "ability to perceive socio-interpersonal relationships and adapt one's interaction goals and behaviors accordingly" (320). Duran and Kelly (1988) developed the Communicative Adaptability Scale. Their scale suggests we can adapt our communication in six different ways which include: social composure (feeling relaxed in social situations), social experience (enjoying and participating socially), social confirmation (maintaining the other's social image), appropriate disclosures (adapting one's disclosures appropriately to the intimacy level of the exchange), articulation (using appropriate syntax and grammar), and wit (using humor to diffuse social tension). You can determine the extent to which you are adaptable on these six dimensions by completing the Communication Adaptability Scale on page 49.

Adapt your listening style.

Reduce noise. Noise refers to anything that interferes with the reception of a message. Our job as listeners is to focus on ways to reduce the noise that interferes with the reception of messages.

Oftentimes, this is easier said than done. While we are able to control some forms of physical noise that interfere with listening (e.g., cell phones or radios), other types of physical noise may be more difficult to manage (e.g., a neighbor mowing her yard). Obviously, the less noise there is, the better our chances of effectively receiving the message. Reducing psychological and physiological noise may be more difficult. Sometimes it is difficult to listen to a professor's lecture knowing that you have a big midterm exam in the class that follows, and gnawing hunger pains that begin during your 11:00 A.M. class can impair listening as well. Consider ways to manage these potential distractions and maximize listening potential—be prepared for that exam, be sure to eat something before leaving for class. Planning ahead for potential distractions to listening can ultimately assist you in receiving a message that you can store in memory for future reference.

Store the message. A final strategy in the listening process involves storing what we have received for later reference. This process involves three stages: remembering, retention, and recall. Have you ever been impressed with a doctor or a professor because they remembered, retained, and recalled your name? This is not an easy task. Nichols (1961) demonstrated that immediately after listening to a ten-minute lecture, students were only able to remember about fifty percent of what they heard. As time passes, so does our ability to remember. Nichols' study suggested that after two weeks, most listeners were only able to remember about twenty-five percent of what they had heard. The following are strategies that can be used to enhance message retention.

1. Form associations between the message and something you already know.
2. Create a visual image of the information you want to remember.
3. Create a story about what you want to remember to create links between ideas. *Suppose your mother asks you to go to the store to pick up soda, laundry detergent and paper cups. You can enhance your ability to remember the information by creating a story which links the ideas such as, "Sam dropped a paper cup full of soda on her jeans and now they need to be put in the laundry machine."*
4. Create acronyms by using the beginning letters of a list of words to assist your recall. BIG EARS is an example of this tool.
5. Rhyme or create a rhythm to organize information. Creating a song or rhyme that is unusual or humorous typically helps trigger recall.

Listening Styles

Reflecting on your own interpersonal relationships, did you ever notice that individuals have different listening styles? Or perhaps you have noticed that an individual's listening style changed when the topic changed. Have you considered your own listening style and how it may change with the person or topic? For example, with our friends we might pay more attention to their feelings and when we listen to co-workers we may be more focused on the content of the message. Research has identified four predominant listening styles (Watson, Barker, and Weaver 1995). Listening style is defined as a set of "attitudes, beliefs, and predispositions about the how, where, when, who, and what of the information reception and encoding process" (Watson, Barker, and Weaver 1995, 2). This suggests that we tend to focus our listening. We may pay more attention to a person's feelings, the structure or content, or particular delivery elements, such as time. The four listening styles are people-oriented, action-oriented, content-oriented, and time-oriented. There is no optimal listening style. Different situations call for different styles. However, it is important to understand your predominate listening style. Let us take a closer look at each of these listening styles.

People-Oriented. First, people-oriented listeners seek common interests with the speaker and are highly responsive. They are interested in the speaker's feelings and emotions. Research shows a positive relationship between the people-oriented listening style and conversational sensitivity (Cheseboro 1999). This makes sense since people-oriented listeners try to understand the speakers' perspective and therefore are more sensitive to their emotional needs. They are quick to notice slight fluctuations in tone and mood. For example, they may comment, "You really look upset," or "You smile every time you say her name." Although you must consider the individual and the situation, this style may work best when we are communicating with our friends or family about sensitive issues.

Action-Oriented. An action-oriented listener prefers error-free and concise messages. They get easily frustrated with speakers who do not clearly articulate their message in a straightforward manner. They tend to steer speakers to be organized and timely in their message delivery. They grow impatient with disorganized speakers that use ambiguous descriptions or provide unrelated details. For example, an action-oriented listener may use the phrase "Get to the point," when the speaker is telling a lengthy story or may interrupt a speaker and say, "So. . . . what did you do?" The action-oriented listening style may work best when there is little time for extra details and decisions need to be made quickly.

Content-Oriented. Unlike the people-oriented listener, the content-oriented listener focuses on the details of the message. They pick up on the facts of the story and analyze it from a critical perspective. They decipher between credible and noncredible information and ask direct questions. They try to understand the message from several perspectives. For example, they may say, "Did you ever think they did that because . . ." or "Another way to think about the situation is . . ." Because they analyze the speaker's content with a critical eye, the speaker may feel reluctant to share information because they do not want to hear alternative perspectives. Additionally, they may feel intimidated by the criticalness of content-oriented listeners since they are engaged by challenging and intellectual discussion. The content-oriented listening style works best in serious situations that call for vital decision-making.

The people-oriented listener focuses on feelings and emotions.

Time-Oriented. Finally, time-oriented listeners are particularly interested in brief interactions with others. They direct the length of the conversation by suggesting, "I only have a minute," or they send leave taking cues (such as walking away or looking at the clock) when they believe the speaker is taking up too much of their time. This type of listening is essential when time is a limited commodity. Usually, time is precious in the workplace. A day can be eaten up by clients, co-workers, supervisors, and other individuals needing our attention. Time-oriented individuals protect their time by expressing to others how much effort they will devote to their cause.

Gender and Cultural Differences in Listening Styles

Some researchers suggest there are gender differences when it comes to listening styles. In the mid-1980s, Booth-Butterfield reported that "males tend to hear the facts while females are more aware of the mood of the communication" (1984, 39). Just about twenty years later, researchers' findings were consistent in indicating that men score themselves higher on the content-oriented listening style and women score themselves higher on the people-oriented listening style (Sargent and Weaver 2003). In addition, Kiewitz and Weaver III (1997) found that when comparing young adults from three different countries, Germans preferred the action style, Israelis preferred the content style, and Americans preferred the people and time styles.

Although no listening style is best, it is imperative to understand your own listening style and to recognize the listening styles of others. Depending on the situation and the goals in communicating, you may need to adjust your listening style. In addition, recognizing the listening style in others will help direct your responding messages. For example, if you notice your boss is engaging in action-oriented listening style, you may want to produce a clearly articulated message. He may become irritated if you include miscellaneous information or use confusing vocabulary.

Motivation to Listen and Potential Pitfalls

When we do anything, we have some kind of motivation, or purpose. Sometimes this motivation is driven by our goals, dreams, and interests. Other times motivation may be a result of guilt, responsibility, or shame. Consider your motive for attending school. Perhaps you are a student because you have set a goal to graduate or maybe you are motivated out of a sense of responsibility to your parents. Either way, motivation drives behavior. Have you ever considered your motivation for listening? Researchers have identified five listening motivations (Wolvin and Coakley 1988). Certain motivations for listening lend themselves to particular listening barriers. Therefore, let us examine each of these motivations independently and offer potential pitfalls for each. Table 2.2 presents some guidelines for effective listening.

Table 2.2 Guidelines for Effective Listening

Effective listeners do their best to avoid these behaviors:
1. Calling the subject uninteresting
2. Criticizing the speaker and/or delivery
3. Getting overstimulated
4. Listening only for facts (bottom line)
5. Not taking notes or outlining everything
6. Faking attention
7. Tolerating or creating distractions
8. Tuning out difficult material
9. Letting emotional words block the message
10. Wasting the time difference between speed of speech and speed of thought

Source: Nichols, R. G., and L. A. Stevens. 1957. *Are you listening?* New York: McGraw-Hill.

From *Are You Listening?* by R.G. Nichols and L.A. Stevens

Discriminate listening. First, we may listen for the purpose of discriminating. The purpose of **discriminate listening** is to help us understand the meaning of the message. In certain situations we want to discriminate between what is fact and what is an opinion. Or perhaps we try to discriminate between what is an emotionally-based argument and what is a logically-based argument. One example of a situation in which we might engage in discriminate listening is in the workplace when we attentively listen to how a co-worker responds to our new recommendation. Here we are trying to determine if they agree or disagree with us. Another example is engaging in listening in the classroom when the teacher suggests that portions of the lecture will be on the exam. In this example, we are discriminating between what the teacher believes is important material for the exam and what

In certain situations we want to discriminate between what is fact and what is an opinion.

is not going to be on the exam. Furthermore, we tend to use discriminate listening when we are trying to determine whether someone is lying to us.

Potential pitfall. Often when we are trying to discriminate between messages, we selectively listen to certain stimuli while ignoring others. For example, if someone does not maintain eye contact with us, we may jump to conclusions regarding her trustworthiness. If discrimination is your motivation, it is important to *keep an open mind and attend to the entire message.*

Appreciative listening. Another motivation we have for listening is appreciative listening. The purpose of appreciative listening is for the pure enjoyment of listening to the stimuli. This may be listening to your favorite tunes on your iPod, attending the opera, a musical or the movies, or listening to the sounds of the waves crashing on the shore.

Potential pitfall. With appreciative listening it is important to be proactive. In order to be successful in appreciate listening you must *decrease noise.* You can do this by controlling distractions. For example, turn off your cell phone. Sometime you can even choose your physical environment. If you are going to the movies, you can choose a particular seat away from potentially "loud" patrons. Or you may choose to go to the movies with a partner that will not inhibit your pleasure-seeking experience by talking or asking questions throughout.

Appreciative listening is for the pure enjoyment of listening to the stimuli.

Comprehensive listening. We also may be motivated to listen in order to grasp new information. Comprehensive listening involves mindfully receiving and remembering new information. When our boss is informing us of our new job duties or a friend is telling you when they need to be picked up at the airport we are engaging in comprehensive listening. Our goal is to accurately understand the new information and be able to retain it.

Potential pitfall. Often there are several messages that the speaker is sending and it is the job of the listener to determine which messages are the most important. With comprehensive listening it is critical to *recognize the main ideas and identify supportive details.* If you are unsure, *seek feedback or paraphrase the message.* For example, you may ask, "So you are flying Southwest and you need me to pick you up at baggage claim at 10:00 P.M., correct?"

Evaluative listening. When our motivation goes beyond comprehending messages to judging messages we are engaging in evaluative listening. **Evaluative listening** involves critically assessing messages. This occurs when a salesperson is trying to persuade us to buy a product or when we listen to political speeches. We are evaluating the credibility and competency of the speaker and the message. Our goal here is to create opinions and sound judgments regarding people and information.

Potential pitfall. Prejudices and biases may interfere with our listening ability when we are motivated to listen for evaluative purposes. For example, individuals who identify with a particular political party are quick to judge the messages of an individual representing an alternative party. It is important to be **aware of your own preconceived notions** and not let that impede on your ability to effectively interpret the speaker's message.

Empathetic listening. The last motivation to listen is for empathetic reasons. The purpose of empathetic (or therapeutic) listening is to help others. For example, we may meet up with our friends to discuss their most recent romantic episodes or we may help our family members make tough financial decisions. Our goal is to provide a supportive ear and assist in uncovering alternative perspectives. Often, just by listening our friends will identify their own issues or our family members will uncover their own solutions to their problems. Other times, they may ask for suggestions or recommendations.

Potential pitfall. It is critical to distinguish if the speaker indeed wants you to be an active participant in offering solutions or if he wants you "just to listen." Sometimes we assume that solutions are being sought, but what is really wanted is someone to act as a "sounding board."

Common Listening Misbehaviors

There can be severe consequences when we choose not to listen effectively. One study found that the second most frequently occurring mistake made by education leaders deals with poor interpersonal communication skills and that the most frequent example given for this type of mistake was failure to listen (Bulach, Pickett, and Booth 1998). The perception that we are not listening may be because we lack appropriate eye contact with the speaker, we appear preoccupied or distracted with other issues, or because we do not provide the appropriate feedback. When we send these signals, the speaker interprets our behavior as not caring. This can damage internal and external business relationships. These behaviors can have severe consequences. Another study examined the top five reasons why principals lost their jobs (Davis 1997). The results of this study found that the most frequently cited response by superintendents focused on failure to communicate in ways that build positive relationships. The results of this study can be applied to situations outside of the educational setting. So, how do people communicate in ways that do not build positive relationships? This section will identify the six common listening misbehaviors.

Pseudo-listening. Pseudo-listening is when we are pretending to listen. We look like we are listening by nodding our head or providing eye contact, but we are faking our attention. This is a self-centered approach to listening. Let us be honest, when we are pseudo-listening we are not "fooling" anyone. We are not able to ask appropriate questions and we are not able to provide proper feedback.

Monopolizing. Listeners that engage in monopolizing take the focus off the speaker and redirect the conversation and attention to themselves. Often, monopolizers interrupt the speaker to try to "one up" the speaker. They may try to top his story by saying "That reminds me . . ." or "You think that is bad–let me tell you what happened to me. . . ."

Disconfirming. Listeners that deny the feelings of the speaker are sending disconfirming messages. Examples of disconfirming messages include: "You shouldn't feel bad . . ." or "Don't cry . . . there is no need to cry." This misbehavior discourages the source to continue speaking and decreases perceptions of empathy.

Defensive listening. An individual who engages in defensive listening perceives a threatening environment. Defensive communication has been defined as "that behavior which occurs when an individual perceives threat or anticipates threat in the group" (Gibb 1961, 141). Defensiveness includes "how he appears to others, how he may seem favorable, how he may win, dominate, impress, or escape punishment, and/or how he may avoid or mitigate a perceived or anticipated threat" (141). In other words, defensiveness is a process of saving "face." The issue of face is associated with people's desire to display a positive public image (Goffman 1967). An example of defensive listening is, "Don't look at me, I did not tell you to do that. . . ."

Selective listening. Selective listening happens when a listener focuses only on parts of the message. She takes parts of the message that she agrees with (or does not agree with) and responds to those particular parts. We reduce cognitive dissonance or psychological discomfort, screening out messages that we do not agree with, to remain cognitively "stable." For example, if we recently bought a new SUV, we may choose not to pay attention to messages suggesting that SUV's are not environmentally sound. We would, however, choose to pay attention to messages that suggest SUV vehicles rated higher on safety tests.

Photo courtesy of Charles Long

Defensive listening occurs when one perceives a threatening environment.

Ambushing. Ambushers will listen for information that they can use to attack the speaker. They are selectively and strategically listening for messages that they can use against the speaker. Often ambushers interrupt the speaker. They do not allow the speaker to complete his thought and jump to conclusions. Ambushers make assumptions and get ahead of the speaker by finishing his sentences. They are self-motivated and lack dual perspective.

What are some examples of common listing misbehaviors that you have experienced lately?

Respond Here

Communication for Today's Student

Chapter 2 – Perception and Listening

Exercise 2.1

In this chapter we learn that perception, according to communication professor, Julia T. Wood, is an active process of selecting, organizing and interpreting people, objects, events, situations, and activities. Simply put, it is how we attach significance to the world around us.

The following is a dyad exercise. Your professor will place five topics on the board. After the topic is placed on the board, you and your partner will each record the word in the first column below, indicated by the numbers 1-5. In the second column you are to record the first word (or words) that come to mind. Do not reveal your responses to your partner. If you believe your reaction is positive, place it in the blue shaded box. If you believe your reaction is negative, place it the red shaded box. For example, your professor may place the topic 'basketball' on the board. You may place the word, 'boring' in the red box because you really have an interest in the arts and think that the game of basketball is mundane. On the other hand, your partner may respond with word, 'playoffs' and place it in the blue box because she is on the girls basketball team and is hopeful that her team will win the playoffs this season.

How many of your responses landed in a blue box?

How many landed in a red box?

Did any of your color responses overlap with your partners?

Share with your classmates how the process of perception determined your responses.

Topic 1		
Topic 2		
Topic 3		
Topic 4		
Topic 5		

Communication for Today's Student

Chapter 2 – Perception and Listening

Exercise 2.2

Have you ever considered your motivation for listening? Researchers have identified five listening motivations. After listening to the Larry and Palmer story, answer the following questions? Once you have been given the correct answers, give yourself 2 points for each correct answer.

1. What is Larry's last name? What is Palmer's last name?

2. In what town do they live?

3. How long have both young men been participating in the performing arts?

4. Larry won the All District, State and Regional voice competitions for how many consecutive years?

5. Palmer served as an intern for what Company?

6. Palmer will have an opportunity to audition for what dance company in May?

7. What University have both students applied to attend in the fall?

8. Who has the higher GPA, Larry or Palmer?

9. What score did Palmer receive on his SAT? What score did Larry receive?

10. Both students applied for the _____ scholarship for the amount of _____.

11. Which of the following is not a show in the upcoming season, **Grease, Anything Goes, Blues for an Alabama Sky** or **Rent**?

What's your score? Are a good listener? Why or why not? Listen as your instructor tells you how you might become a better listener. Try this exercise with a friend not in your class.

Of the five motives for listening, which did you just participate in?
What were some of the most obvious pitfalls?
Review the answers that you got correct. Discuss why you believe you remembered each answer.

The instructor reads this aloud to the class at a rapid rate.

Larry Lattimore and Palmer Patterson attend the gifted high school in a small town named Vienna, Virginia. Both students have been participating in the performing arts since elementary school. In addition to their extracurricular arts credits, Larry and Palmer have served in some capacity in each production since freshmen year. Larry won the All District, State and Regional voice competitions for three consecutive years. Palmer has had extensive dance training. In addition, he has interned each summer with the Alvin Alley Dance Company. Palmer was selected to participate in the Dance Theatre of Harlem spring concert when his dance coach submitted his name and recital tape to the Company. In addition, he has been invited to audition in May to become a full time member of the Chuck Davis African Dance Company. Both Larry and Palmer have applied to attend United Union University's School of the Arts in the fall. Larry has a 3.56 GPA and received a 26 on the ACT. Palmer has a 2.8 GPA and received 2000 on his SAT. Both students have excellent recommendations. The School has under taken an ambitious season next year that includes: ***Anything Goes, The Wiz, Blues for an Alabama Sky, Rent***, and ***Othello***. Both Larry and Palmer have applied for the University' Denzel Washington for $35,000 scholarship. Neither Larry nor Palmer will be able to attend the University if they do not receive this substantial financial opportunity. The department's recruitment team recognized immediately what wonderful assets these two perspectives students would be to the department. They also recognized the department could use two male actors with Larry's and Palmer's training to work on the upcoming season. At the completion of the tour of the theatre facility, the audition and interview, the committee decided to announce the recipient of the scholarship. Unfortunately, only one student can receive the scholarship.

WHAT IS THE POWER OF VERBAL AND NONVERBAL COMMUNICATION?

After reading this chapter, you should be able to:

- ☑ Define language.
- ☑ Discuss the basic principles of language.
- ☑ Discuss the three models that help explain how meaning is created including the semantic triangle, Sapir-Whorf hypothesis, and the muted group theory.
- ☑ Identify the strategies for using language effectively.
- ☑ Describe the characteristics of nonverbal communication.
- ☑ Discuss the six functions of nonverbal messages to include complementing, substituting, repeating, contradicting, regulating, and deceiving.
- ☑ Discuss the types of nonverbal communication including body movement, use of space, dress and appearance and eye contact.

Key Terms

Language	Regulative rules	Trite words	Adaptors	Chronemics
Symbols	Constitutive rules	Loaded words	Personal space	Haptics
Grammar	Semantic triangle	Empty words	Primary territory	Paralanguage
Intersubjective	Referent	Derogatory language	Secondary territory	Olfactics
Meaning	Reference	Equivocal words	Public territory	Oculesics
Denotative meanings	Dual perspective	Kinesics	Intrusion of territory	Clothing and artifacts
Connotative meanings	Regionalisms	Emblem	Eye contact	
Phonological rules	Jargon	Illustrator	Expectancy violations	
Syntactical rules	Slang	Regulator	theory	
Semantic rules	Clichés	Affect display	Proxemics	

3 Scenario

Chris smiled he looked down at his iPhone 7. He scrolled through Samantha Washington's Instagram page, admiring all her photos.

"Are you on her Instagram . . . again?" Chris's best friend and roommate Darien asked, as he walked into their room.

"I know, man," Chris stated, shaking his head as he clicked on a photo of Samantha tying her sneakers while dressed in her cheerleading uniform. She looked up at the camera through her bangs, smiling. "I'm officially pathetic," he sighed.

"I'm glad you realize it," Darien said, shaking his head. "Why don't you just talk to her?"

"Talk to Samantha!" Chris exclaimed, popping up from his bed.

"Yes, talk to her," Darien frowned. "She ain't Beyoncé, dude."

Samantha was one of the head cheerleaders at school, and Chris developed a crush on her the day she walked into his oral communication class. In his world, she was Beyoncé.

"Man, I can't think straight when she's around," Chris admitted.

"You just need an approach," Darien responded. He looked up at the ceiling searching for an idea, when he found one his eyes bulged. "Oh, man, I got it!" he exclaimed.

"What?" Chris asked slowly. Darien was known for his crazy ideas.

"Make her your WCW!" he smirked.

"What?"

"That's how everyone hooks up nowadays." Darien stated, grabbing his laptop. "See, all you have to do is pick out your favorite picture of her – I know your stalker self has one – and post it on your page." "Do that and I'm sure you'll get her attention."

"Man, I don't know," Chris replied wearily.

"Look, if you don't risk your pride a little, you reap no benefits when it comes to love," Darien mused. "Just do it. She's used to dudes being too intimidated to approach her. You'll stand out."

Darien had a point. Chris scrolled through her pictures and took a screenshot of his favorites. After he was done and everything was ready to submit, he had Darien look at it for his approval.

"This is cool," he surmised. "Kudos for you for not using any of her suggestive pictures. She'll think you really like her for her and not for her body, blah, blah, blah."

Chris chuckled. "So you think it's fine. No typos, right?" he asked.

"Uh . . . My #WCW is our campus's own Samantha Washington. She's got beauty and brains . . . you're good man."

Chris inhaled deeply and hit submit. He watched as it popped up on his screen.

"I guess all I have to do is wait," Chris sighed.

In your opinion, did Darien give Chris good advice? Why do you think Chris was so careful in selecting the photos and the language he intended to use on the post?

Respond Here

Introduction

Using words to describe magic is like using a screwdriver to cut roast beef.
—*Tom Robbins, twentieth century American author*

Better wise language than well-combed hair.
—*Icelandic Proverb*

All credibility, all good conscience, all evidence of truth come only from the senses.
—*Friedrich Wilhelm Nietzsche, nineteenth century German philosopher*

Eloquence is the power to translate a truth into language perfectly intelligible to the person to
whom you speak.
—*Ralph Waldo Emerson, nineteenth century U.S. poet, essayist*

Get in touch with the way the other person feels. Feelings are 55 percent body language,
38 percent tone and 7 percent words.
—*author unknown*

The limits of my language means the limits of my world.
—*Ludwig Wittgenstein, twentieth century philosopher*

The eyes are the windows to the soul.
—*Yousuf Karsh, twentieth century Canadian photographer*

The difference between the right word and the almost right word is the difference
between lightning and a lightning bug.
—*Mark Twain, nineteenth century American author*

Dialogue should simply be a sound among other sounds, just something that comes out of the
mouths of people whose eyes tell the story in visual terms.
—*Alfred Hitchcock, twentieth century film director*

Through these quotations, you've just been exposed to the *power of verbal and nonverbal communication* to define our beliefs, expose our values, and share our experiences. The words that you use and the nonverbal behaviors that accompany them are critically important as you communicate, because they have the ability to clarify your ideas to others or to confuse them. In this chapter, you'll learn about verbal language and nonverbal communication, to discover how they are used to create shared meaning.

What Is Language?

So what do we know about language? Linguists estimate that there are about 5,000 to 6,000 different languages spoken in the world today; about 200 languages have a million or more native speakers. Mandarin Chinese is the most common, followed by Hindi, English, Spanish, and Bengali. However, as technology continues to shrink the communication world, English is becoming more dominant in mediated communication. According to Internet World Stats, which charts usage and population statistics, the top ten languages used in the Web are English (31% of all Internet users), Chinese (15.7%), Spanish (8.7%), Japanese (7.4%), and French and German (5% each). English is one of the official languages of the United Nation, the International Olympic Committee, in academics and in the sciences. English is also the language spoken by air traffic controllers worldwide. Yet the English that we speak in the United States is really a hybrid, using vocabulary taken from many sources, influenced by media, technology, and globalization. Let's consider what all of this means for you as you try to share meaning with others.

Language is a shared system of symbols structured in organized patterns to express thoughts and feelings. **Symbols** are arbitrary labels that we give to some idea or phenomenon. For example, the word *run* represents an action that we do, while *bottle* signifies a container for a liquid. Words are symbols, but not all symbols are words. Music, photographs, and logos are also symbols that stand for something else, as do nonverbal actions such as "OK," and "I don't know." However, in this section, we're going to focus on words as symbols. Note that the definition of language says that it's structured and shared. Languages have a *grammar* (syntax, a patterned set of rules that aid in meaning). You've learned grammar as you've been taught how to write, and it's become an unconscious part of your daily communication. Take, for example, this sentence:

Verbal language and nonverbal communication are used to create shared meaning.

The glokkish Vriks mounged oupily on the brangest Ildas.

Now, we can answer these questions:

Who did something? The Vriks mounged.
What kind of Vriks are they? Glokkish
How did they mounge? Oupily
On what did they mounge? The Ildas
What kind of Ildas are they? Brangest

You might have difficulty identifying noun, verb, adverb, and adjective, but because you know the grammar of the English language, you're still able to decipher what this sentence is telling you because of the pattern, even if the symbols themselves lack meaning for now. That leads to the next part of the definition: *symbols must be shared in order to be understood.* George Herbert Mead's Symbolic Interaction Theory asserts that meaning is **intersubjective;** that means that **meaning** *can exist only when people share common interpretations of the symbols they exchange.* So if you were given a picture of Vriks and were told that these were ancient hill people of a particular region of the country, you'd have a start at meaning!

English is the language spoken by airline pilots and air traffic controllers all over the world.

In order to get a grasp on language, this section will uncover basic principles about language, introduce to you a few theoretical perspectives, and then will suggest language strategies to enhance your communication.

What Are the Basic Principles of Language?

There are some basic principles of language. It is arbitrary, it changes over time, it consists of denotative and connotative meanings, and it is structured by rules. Let's look at these more closely.

Arbitrary

"Language is arbitrary" means that *symbols do not have a one-to-one connection with what they represent.* What is the computer form that you use if you take a test? Is it a bubble sheet? A scantron? An opscan? Each of these names has no natural connection to that piece of paper, and it's likely that at different universities, it's called different names. Because language is arbitrary, people in groups agree on labels to use, creating private codes. That's why your organization might have specialized terms, why the military uses codes, and why your family uses nicknames that only they understand. The language that you create within that group creates group meaning and culture. The arbitrary element of language also adds to its ambiguity; meanings just aren't stable. To me, a test is the same as an exam; to you, a test might be less than an exam. If you say to me, "I'll call you later," how do I define the term later? We often fall into the trap of thinking that everyone understands us, but the reality is, it's an amazing thing that we share meaning at all!

Symbols often do not have a one-to-one connection with what they represent.

Changes over Time

Language *changes* over time in vocabulary, as well as syntax. New vocabulary is required for the latest inventions, for entertainment and leisure pursuits, for political use. In 2007, the top television buzzwords included surge and *D'oh,* while in 2006, they were *truthiness* and *wikiality.* How many of those words play a role in your culture today? Words like *cell phones* and *Internet* didn't exist fifty years ago, for example. In addition, no two people use a language in exactly the same way. Teens and young adults often use different words and phrases than their parents. The vocabulary and phrases people use may depend on where they live, their age, education level, social status, and other factors. Through our interactions, we pick up new words and phases, and then we integrate them into our communication.

How is your language different from your parents' and grandparents'?

Consists of Denotative and Connotative Meanings

Denotative meanings, the literal, dictionary definitions, are precise and objective. **Connotative meanings** reflect your personal, subjective definitions. They add layers of experience and emotions to meaning. Elizabeth J. Natalle examined this dichotomy in a case study of urban music, examining how our language has evolved over the years to include more negative connotation regarding talk about women as compared to talk about men. Think about *chick, sweetie, sugar pie* and *old maid,* versus stud, *hunk, playboy,* and *bachelor.* Do you get a different image? Using a study of rap music, she attempted to clarify how urban music names a particular world, creates male community, and has implications for power and gendered relationships.

A simpler way to consider denotative and connotative meanings is to examine the terms President Bush used to describe the terrorists who crashed the planes on Sept. 11, 2001. Bush's labels

on that day in various locations began with "those folks who committed this act" (remarks by the president when he first heard that two planes crashed into World Trade Center) to "those responsible for these cowardly acts" (remarks by the president upon arrival at Barksdale Air Force Base) to "those who are behind these evil acts" and "the terrorists who committed these acts" (statement by the president in his address to the nation). Consider how the connotative meaning shaped the image of the perpetrators.

David K. Berlo provided several assumptions about meaning:

- Meanings are in people.
- Communication does not consist of the transmission of meanings, but of the transmission of messages.
- Meanings are not in the message; they are in the message users.
- Words do not mean at all; only people mean.
- People can have similar meanings only to the extent that they have had, or can anticipate having, similar experiences.
- Meanings are never fixed; as experience changes, so meanings change.
- No two people can have exactly the same meaning for anything.

What does this sign's language mean to you?

These ideas echo the idea that when you use words, you need to be aware of the extent to which meaning is shared. For example, when an adoptive parent sees those "adopt a highway" locator signs, it's probable that that person sees something different than others might. "Adopt a" programs might be seen as confusing and misleading others about the term *adoption*. An adoptive parent might say that you don't adopt a road, a zoo animal, or a Cabbage Patch doll. Adoption is a means of family building, and it has a very subjective, emotional meaning. To the town official who erected the sign, it's a representation of the good work being done by some group to keep the highway clean.

Structured by Rules

As we understand and use the rules of language, we begin to share meaning. Think of rules as a shared understanding of what language means, as well as an understanding of what kind of language is appropriate in various contexts. Many of the rules you use weren't consciously learned; you gathered them from interactions with other people. Some, however, were learned aspects of your culture.

Phonological rules *regulate how words sound when you pronounce them.* They help us organize language. For instance, the word lead could be used to suggest a behavior that you do (you *lead* the group to show them the way) or a kind of toxic metallic element (*lead* paint in windows is harmful to children). Do you enjoy getting a *present*, or did you *present* one to someone else? Another example of phonological rules is demonstrated by your understanding of how letters sound when they're grouped in a particular way. Take for instance the letters omb. Now put a t in front of them, and you have *tomb*. Put a c in front, and it becomes *comb*. Put a b in front, and you have *bomb*. See how the sounds shift?

The way we make singular nouns plural is also phonological. It's not as simple as adding the letter s to the end of a word. The sound changes too: dog/dogs (sounds like a z at the end); cook/cooks (sounds like an *ess*); bus/buses (sounds like *ess-ez*). English has many inconsistent phonological rules like these, which makes making errors quite typical, especially for nonnative English speakers.

Syntactical rules *present the arrangement of a language, how the symbols are organized.* You saw that earlier in the "glok-kish Vriks" example; you're usually unaware of the syntactical rules until they're violated. In English, we put adjectives prior to most nouns: I live in a red house. In French, you live in a house red (the adjective follows the noun).

Semantic rules *govern the meaning of specific symbols.* Because words are abstractions, we need rules to tell us what they mean in particular situations. Take, for example, the headline, "School Needs to Be Aired." What does that mean? Is the school so smelly that it needs to be refreshed? Or are the needs of the school going to be broadcast or spoken in a public forum? Words can be interpreted in more than one way, and we need semantic rules to lead us to shared meaning. Although these three kinds of rules help us to pattern language, there are also rules that help us guide the entire communication event.

You can count on a close friend for comfort when you have a problem.

Regulative rules *tell us when, how, where, and with whom we can talk about certain things.* You know when it's OK to interrupt someone; you know when turn-taking is expected. You may be enrolled in classes where you are expected to express your opinion; in other classes, you know to hold your tongue. How do you feel about public displays of affection? When is it OK to correct your boss? These regulative rules help us to maintain respect, reveal information about ourselves, and interact with others.

Constitutive rules *tell us how to "count" different kinds of communication.* These rules reveal what you feel is appropriate. You know that when someone waves or blows kisses, that person is showing affection or friendliness. You know what topics you can discuss with your parents, friends, teachers, co-workers, and strangers. You have rules that reveal your expectations for communication with different people; you expect your doctor to be informative and firm with advice, and you anticipate that your friend will compliment you and empathize. As we interact with others, we begin to grasp and use the rules. For instance, when you start a new job, you take in the rules on whom to talk with, how to talk with supervisors and co-workers, and what topics are appropriate, along with the mechanics of how to talk and the meaning of job-specific words. Interestingly enough, you might not even be aware of the rules until they're broken!

How Do Theorists Describe Language and Meaning?

Can you picture a book, a pen, a laptop, and a horse? Your ability to conjure up these images means that you've been exposed to the symbols that represent them in the English language. How about the picture shown on the right? What do you see? If you said "keys," then that shows how you have acquired language; you've been taught that these things are associated with the symbol "keys." How are you able to do those connections? There are a great number of perspectives related to language, meaning, and symbols. In this section, you'll be exposed to three models that present varying perspectives on the way that meaning is created.

Semantic Triangle

One of the models that demonstrate how words come to have meaning is the **semantic triangle.** Ogden and Richards suggest that a major problem with communication is that we tend to treat *words* as if they were the *thing.* As a result, we confuse the symbol for the thing or object.

At the bottom right hand of the triangle is the **referent,** the thing that we want to communicate about that exists in reality. As we travel up the right side, we find the **reference(s),** which consist of thoughts, experiences, and feelings about the referent. This is a causal connection; seeing the object results in those thoughts. Another causal connection exists as you travel down the left side of the triangle, to the *symbol,* or *word.* That's the label we apply to that referent.

The problem is that there is not a direct connection between a symbol and referent; it's an indirect connection, shown by the dotted line. According to this model, it's that indirect link between *referent* and *symbol* that creates the greatest potential for communication misunderstandings. We assume that others share our references, and we think that they must use the same label or symbol because of that shared state of being. A simple example should help.

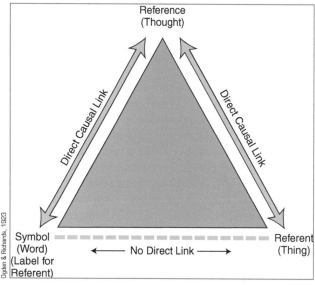

The Semantic Triangle—Ogden & Richards, 1923.

A mom is teaching her son words by reading simple children's books—books about tools, farms, trucks, zoos, and dinosaurs. Usually, this reading activity happens on the front porch. One day, the mom sees the neighbor's cat sneaking up on her birdfeeders, and under her breath, she mutters something about the "stupid cat." The next day, the toddler goes off to day care, and when mom comes to pick him up, she's met by the teacher. She laughingly tells how she was reading a book about animals that day, and when she got to the page with cute kittens on it, the little boy yelled out, "Stupid cat." The embarrassed mother just learned a lesson about the semantic triangle. For her, the referent (cat) evokes images of bird-murdering, allergy-causing felines (references). She creates the label "stupid cat." (symbol). When the boy sees a picture of one, he naturally thinks that is what those things are called. Unfortunately, that's not the universal name!

You can experience the same thing: If you tell others that you own a dog, what referent do you think they apply the label to? The semantic triangle is a practical tool that helps us to understand the relationship of referent, references, and symbol, or thing, thoughts, and word. It reminds us that one word doesn't necessarily evoke the same meaning in any two people.

Sapir–Whorf Hypothesis

Another theoretical approach to language is the *Sapir–Whorf hypothesis* (also known as the theory of linguistic relativity). According to this approach, your perception of reality is determined by your thought processes, and your thought processes are limited by your language. Therefore, language shapes reality. Your culture determines your language, which, in turn, determines the way that you categorize thoughts about the world and your experiences in it. If you don't have the words to describe or explain something, then you can't really know it or talk about it.

For example, researchers Linda Perry and Deborah Ballard-Reisch suggest that existing language does not represent the reality that biological sex comes in more forms than female and male, gender identities are not neatly ascribed to one's biological sex, and sexual orientation does not fit snugly into, "I like men, I like women, I like both, I like neither," choices. They also assert that evolving new language such as the word *gendex* (representing the dynamic interplay of a person's sexual identity, sex preference, sexual orientation, and gender identity) can work against biases and discrimination. Another example is the concept of *bipolar disorder.* It used to be called manic depressive, and it refers to a mood disorder characterized by unusual shifts in a person's mood, energy, and ability to function. But if you don't know what that illness is, you might just agree with a family member who says, "You're just going through a phase." The lack of language restricts our ability to perceive the world. Reality is embedded in your language.

Muted Group Theory

As these perspectives suggest, the *words* that you use are powerful. They have the ability to express attitudes and to represent values. Communication scholar Cheris Kramarae developed *the muted group theory* to suggest that power and status are connected, and because muted groups lack the power of appropriate language, they have no voice and receive little attention. Kramarae noted, "The language of a particular culture does not serve all its speakers, for not all speakers contribute in an equal fashion to its formulation. Women (and members of other subordinate groups) are not as free or as able as men are to say what they wish, when and where they wish, because the words and the norms for their use have been formulated by the dominant group, men." She asserts that language serves men better than women (and perhaps European Americans better than African Americans or other groups) because the European American men's experiences are named clearly in language, and the experiences of other groups (women, people with disabilities, and ethnic minorities) are not. Due to this problem with language, muted groups appear less articulate than men in public settings.

The muted group theory suggests that language serves men better than women.

The task of muted groups is to conceptualize a thought and then scan the vocabulary that is suited to men's thinking for the best way to encode the idea. The term sexual harassment is an example. Although the act of harassment has existed for centuries, it wasn't until sex discrimination was prohibited by Title VII of the 1964 Civil Rights Act. It also took the Clarence Hill–Anita Thomas hearing in 1991 to make the term *gender discrimination* part of the popular dialogue, as the media focused attention on the workplace issue.

Because they are rendered inarticulate, muted groups are silenced in a variety of ways. Ridicule happens when the group's language is trivialized (men talk, women gab). Ritual creates dominance (the woman changes her name at the wedding ceremony but the man doesn't). Control happens as the media present some points of view and ignore others (we don't hear from the elderly or homeless). Harassment results from the control that men exert over public spaces (women get verbal threats couched as compliments when they walk down the streets). This theory affirms that as muted groups create more language to express their experiences and as all people come to have similar experiences, inequalities of language (and the power that comes with it) should change.

Each of these perspectives demonstrates how language impacts meaning. They show how we believe meaning comes into being, how we are limited by the language we possess, and how language wields power. By now, you should be sensitive to the many ways that you can miscommunicate, or at least communicate ineffectively through language choices. How can you become more sensitive to strategic language choices?

How Can I Use Language Effectively?

Communication scholar Julia T. Wood says that the single most important guideline is to engage in a dual **perspective**, recognizing another person's point of view and taking that into account as you communicate. Wood suggests that you should understand both your own and another's point of view and acknowledge each when you communicate. You'll see that concept played out throughout this text; you need to consider your audience's beliefs, attitudes, and values as you create your message. Here are some strategic tips for effective language use to maintain that dual perspective.

Use Accurate Language

Make sure you are using the term correctly, and if you're unsure if the audience will understand your meaning, define it. You'll learn about defining in the chapter on informative speaking. Remember, what makes perfect sense to you may be gobbledygook to me. When the doctor tells you that you have a rather large contusion, do you know what that is?

Use Appropriate Language

Appropriate means that the language you use is suitable for the context, for the audience, for the topic, and for you. Some occasions call for more formal language (proposals to a client), while others will let slang pass (texting a friend). Some audiences expect technical language, while others need simple terms. Off-color humor might work in certain instances and with specific groups, but you probably shouldn't choose to use it at a church gathering. You need to

It's important to use appropriate language for the occasion.

consider if your audience utilizes regionalisms (words or phrases that are specific to one part of the country) or jargon (specialized professional language) as you speak with them.

Your topic also can determine suitable language. Some topics call for lots of vivid language and imagery, while others are better suited to simplicity. If you are honoring your boss upon his retirement, then the topic probably calls for words that evoke appreciation and emotion. But if you're telling someone how to put together a computer table, then simple explanatory words are expected. Finally, you need to use words that are appropriate to you. You have developed your own style of language over the years; do you use the same words as your parents? Don't try to use words that just don't flow easily from your mind; it's not going to sound like you.

Use Unbiased Language

Biased language includes any language that defames a subgroup (women; people from specific ethnic, religious, or racial groups; people with disabilities) or eliminates them from consideration. Even if you would never think about using language that defames anyone else, you can fall into using language that more subtly discriminates. Sexist language is replete with this: We use the masculine pronoun (he, him) when we don't have a referent. So if you personify "the judge," "the executive," "the director," as male by using the pronoun *he*, you eliminate one whole subgroup from consideration.

The same holds true when you use the word *man* in occupational terms, when the job holders could be either male or female. Examples are fireman, policeman, garbage man, chairman; they're easily made nonsexist by saying firefighter, police officer, garbage collector, and chair or presiding officer. Finally, while the generic use of *man* (like in mankind) originally was used to denote both men and women, its meaning has become more specific to adult males. It's simple to change the word to be more inclusive: mankind becomes people or human beings; man-made becomes manufactured; the common man becomes the average person.

The Associated Press *Stylebook* has a lengthy entry on "disabled, handicapped, impaired" terminology, including when to use (and not to use) terms such *as blind, deaf, mute, wheelchair-user,* and so on. A separate entry on *retarded* says "mentally retarded" is the preferred term. The World Bank advises using *persons with disabilities and disabled people,* not handicapped.

Use appropriate labels when referring to sexual orientation. The terms *lesbians, gay men,* and *bisexuals or bisexual women and men* are preferred to the term *homosexuals* (because the emphasis on the latter is on sex, while the former all refer to the whole person, not just the sex partner he or she chooses). In general, try to find out what the people's preferences are, and be specific when applicable. For instance, if all the subjects are either Navajo or Cree, stating this is more accurate than calling them Native Americans.

Avoid Verbal Distractions

If you divert the audience from your intended meaning by using confusing words, your credibility will be lowered and your audience may become lost. The following are distractions:

- **Slang** *consists of words that are short-lived, arbitrarily changed, and often vulgar ideas.* Slang excludes people from a group. Internet slang was usually created to save keystrokes and consists of "u" for you, "r" for *are,* and "4" for for. Poker slang includes *dead man's hand* (two pair, aces, and eights); to act (make a play); and *going all* in (betting all of your chips on the hand). *Daggy* means out of fashion or uncool; *fives* means to reserve a seat.
- **Cliches** or **trite words** *have been overused and lose power or impact.* The Unicorn Hunters of Lake Superior University keeps a list of banished words that is regularly updated. In 2007, it listed words such as combined celebrity names (*Brangelina* and *Tomcat*), *awesome* (because it no longer means majestic), and *undocumented alien* (just use the word illegal).
- **Loaded words** *sound like they're describing, but they're actually revealing your attitude.* When speaking of abortion, consider the different image created by the terms *unborn child* or *fetus.* Are you *thrifty* but your friend is *cheap*? How about your brother; is he one of those *health-nuts* who is dedicated to the cult of marathoning? Colorful language is entertaining, but if it distorts the meaning or distracts the audience, then don't use it.
- **Empty words** *are overworked exaggerations.* They lose their strength because their meaning is exaggerated. How many products are advertised as *new and improved or supersized*? What exactly does that mean?
- **Derogatory language** *consists of words that are degrading or tasteless.* If you use degrading terms to refer to ethnic groups (*Polack* for a person of Polish descent; *Chink* for someone from China; *Spic* for an Italian) then you are guilty of verbal bigotry.
- **Equivocal words** *have more than one correct denotative meaning.* A famous example is of a nurse telling a patient that he "wouldn't be needing" the books he asked to be brought from home. Although she meant that he was going home that day and could read there, the patient took that to mean that he was near death and wouldn't have time to read. One time while evaluating a debate, an instructor encountered students arguing the issue of the legalization of marijuana. The side arguing for the legalization used the Bible, citing chapter and verse and asserting that God created the grass and said, "The grass is good." This sent the other side into a tailspin as they tried to refute the biblical passage. This simple equivocal use of the term grass lost the debate for the opposition!

What Should You Take from This Section on Language?

Because our language is arbitrary and evolving, it's easy to be misunderstood. You can attempt to enhance shared meaning by remembering that language is a shared system of symbols; through language, you share ideas, articulate values, transmit information, reveal experiences, and maintain relationships. Language is essential to your ability to think and to operate within the many cultures (community of meaning) that you travel through. You should be sensitive to the words you choose as you attempt to connect with others. Now let's turn our attention to the other means by which you create meaning: your nonverbal communication behaviors.

What Is Nonverbal Communication?

Pretend you are hoarse and the doctor has told you not to speak at all for the next three days. Nor can you IM or text or do any other computer-related communication. How would you do the following?

- Let your friend know that you can't hear her. Or tell her that she's talking too loudly.
- Tell your lab partner that you want him to come where you are.
- Show the teacher that you don't know the answer to the question she just asked you.
- Let a child know that he needs to settle down; his play is getting too rough.

- Tell your significant other that you're not angry, and everything is OK.
- Express disappointment over a loss by your team, which always seems to lose the lead in the last two minutes.
- Signify that you're running late and have to leave.

How hard would it be to make yourself understood? What you've just attempted to do without verbal language is present a message nonverbally. We all constantly send nonverbal messages, giving our receivers all types of cues about ourselves. An awareness of nonverbal communication is important: your nonverbal behaviors present an image of yourself to those around you. They tell others how you want to relate to them, and they may reveal emotions or feelings that you either are trying to hide or simply can't express.

In the remainder of this chapter, you will be introduced to some of the elements of the study of nonverbal communication in the hopes of creating a greater awareness of these elements of the message. You will examine *definitions* of nonverbal communication, its *functions,* and *types* of nonverbal communication. Along the way, we will provide examples and illustrations to help you understand the applications of various nonverbal behaviors and how they can be used to help you interpret the messages of other people. You should also gain some insight into how to use nonverbal behaviors to enhance your own communication.

What Is the Nature of Nonverbal Communication?

Although nonverbal communication is a complex system of behaviors and meanings, its basic definition *can be* fairly straightforward. Here are four definitions for comparison:

1. All types of communication that do not rely on words or other linguistic systems
2. Any message other than written or spoken words that conveys meaning
3. Anything in a message besides the words themselves
4. Messages expressed by nonlinguistic means

Taking these definitions and the body of related research into consideration, we propose a very simple definition: nonverbal communication is *all nonlinguistic aspects of communication.* That definition covers quite a lot of territory. Except for the actual words that we speak, *everything* else is classified as nonverbal communication. The way you move, the tone of your voice, the way you use your eyes, the way you occupy and use space, the way you dress, the shape of your body, your facial expressions, the way you smell, your hand gestures, and the way you pronounce (or mispronounce) words are all considered nonverbal communication. Some of these behaviors have meaning independent of language or other behaviors; others have meaning only when considered with what is said, the context and culture in which a communication event takes place, and the relationship between the communicators.

Maybe you're getting a hint of the richness of nonverbal expression. Without any formal training, you already are able to interpret messages that others send nonverbally. Your skill level, however, may not be as strong as you think, so keep in mind the goal of increasing strategic communication as you continue. Researchers have also been fascinated with the extent to which nonverbal communication impacts meaning, and their findings provide glimpses into the impact of nonverbals on shared meanings and culture. If nothing else, by the end of this section, you will discover that the study of nonverbal communication has come a long way since it was referred to only as *body language!*

What can you say about his nonverbal communication?

What Are the Characteristics of Nonverbal Communication?

Ambiguous

Most nonverbal behaviors have no generally accepted meaning. Instead, the connection between the behavior and its meaning is vague or *ambiguous,* leaving understanding open to various interpretations. The meaning we apply to words is fairly specific, but the meaning we give to nonverbal communication is nonspecific. The meanings you attribute to nonverbal behaviors are heavily dependent on the relationship between you and the others you're interacting with, the nature of the communication event, the content of the words that accompanies it, and the culture in which the event takes place. For example, consider the ubiquitous "thumbs up" hand gesture. In the United States it means, "OK" or "very good." In some eastern cultures, however, it is considered an insult and an obscene hand gesture. In Great Britain, Australia, and New Zealand, it could be a signal used by hitchhikers who are thumbing a lift; it could

In the United States, a thumbs-up is appropriate for celebrating.

be an OK signal; it also could be an insult signal meaning "up yours" or "sit on this" when the thumb is jerked sharply upward. In Indonesia, the thumb gesture means "good job" in response to someone who has completed an excellent job, or "delicious" when great food is tasted. In another context, if you smile at a joke, that's understood in an entirely different way than if you do it after someone misses a chair and falls to the ground. A smile could also show affection, embarrassment, or even be used to hide pain or anger. As you can see, it is possible to find several meanings for the same nonverbal behavior, and it is possible to find several nonverbal behaviors that mean the same thing.

Continuous

With verbal communication, if you stop speaking, listeners can't attribute any more meaning to your words. Nonverbal communication, by contrast, is so pervasive and complex that others can continue to gather meaning, even if you are doing absolutely nothing! The mere act of doing nothing can send a message; you might blush, stutter, wring your hands, or sweat unintentionally, causing others to react to you. You might not mean to send a message, but your lack of intention to communicate doesn't prevent other people from assigning meaning to your behavior. In addition, your appearance, the expression on your face, your posture, where (or if) you are seated, and how you use the space around you all provide information that is subject to interpretation by others.

Sometimes Unplanned and Unconscious

Nonverbal communication can be either unconscious or intentional, but most of our nonverbal behaviors are exhibited without much or any conscious thought. You rarely plan or think carefully about your nonverbal behaviors. When you

What can you tell by this boy's expression?

are angry, it is naturally expressed on your face as well as elsewhere in your body. The same is true for how your voice changes when you're nervous, how your arms cross when you're feeling defensive, or how you scratch your head when you're unsure of something. These expressions and behaviors are rarely planned or structured; they just happen suddenly and without conscious thought.

Sometimes Learned and Intentional

Saying that some nonverbal behaviors are natural or occur without conscious thought doesn't mean that people are born with a complete inventory of instinctive nonverbal behaviors. Much of your nonverbal behavior is learned rather than instinctive or innate. You learn the "proper" way to sit or approach, how close to stand next to someone, how to look at others, how to use touch, all from your experiences and your culture. You have been taught their meaning through your experience in interactions with other people. As a result, you can structure some nonverbal behaviors to send intentional messages, such as disapproval when you shake your head from side to side or give a "high five" to show excitement. However, unlike the formal training you received in reading, writing, and speaking, you learned (and continue to learn) nonverbal communication in a much less formal and unceremonious way, and you use it in a much less precise way than spoken language. But *because* many of these behaviors are learned, you can actively work to improve your nonverbal skills. There is a debate as to whether unintentional nonverbal behaviors really count as communication. Since others incorporate their understanding of our nonverbals as part of shared meaning, we're going to say that intentional and unintentional nonverbals both are worth recognizing here. Our position is that it's nearly impossible not to communicate nonverbally.

More Believable than Verbal

Communication textbooks have been saying for years that, when verbal and nonverbal messages contradict each other, people typically believe the nonverbal message. Because nonverbal is more spontaneous and less conscious, we don't or can't manipulate it as easily as we can control verbal communication. When you were younger and your parents thought that you might be lying to them, they would say, "Look me in the eye and say that again." Your face was more believable to them than what you were saying verbally. Your nonverbal messages would tell them the truth. How could this be so?

Research suggests that between 65 percent and 93 percent of the meaning people attribute to messages comes from the nonverbal channel. There is a small fudge factor in those percentages, however, because the Mehrabian and Ferris study assumed up to 93 percent of meaning came from nonverbal messages in situations *where no other background information* was available. The reality is that many factors affect the meaning given to messages, including how familiar the communicators are with the language being spoken, cultural knowledge, and even individual differences in personality characteristics.

Regardless of the exact percentage of meaning that comes from the verbal or nonverbal channels, we still appear to get more meaning from the nonverbal channel. Unless you are very good at controlling all your nonverbal behaviors, your parents can probably still know when you are not telling the truth.

What Are the Functions of Nonverbal Communication?

Types of nonverbal communication will be described a little later in the chapter, but you first need to understand what part nonverbals play in the communication process. Nonverbal communication performs six general functions that add information and insight to nonverbal messages to help us create meaning. Those functions are complementing, substituting, repeating, contradicting, regulating, and deceiving.

Complementing Verbal Messages

If someone shakes your hand while saying "Congratulations" at your college graduation, the handshake gives added meaning to the verbal message. Gestures, tone of voice, facial expressions, and other nonverbal behaviors can clarify, reinforce, accent, or add to the meaning of verbal messages. For instance, if you are angry with a friend and are telling him off, pounding your hand into your fist would add depth to your meaning. These nonverbal behaviors are usually not consciously planned, but they are spontaneous reactions to the context and the verbal message.

Substituting for Verbal Messages

You can use a nonverbal message *in the place* of a verbal message. A substituting behavior can be a clear "stop" hand gesture; it can be nodding the head up and down to say yes; or it can be a shoulder shrug to indicate "I don't know." When you use this kind of gesture, you don't have to supply any verbal message for the meaning to be clear to others. However, keep in mind that your nonverbals may be interpreted differently, given what you have learned from your context and culture. As an example, someone in Japan might act in a controlled fashion, while someone from the Mideast might seem more emotional, even when both are feeling the same intensity of emotion. Your interpretation of those postures, without accompanying verbals, might lead you to the wrong conclusions.

Repeating Verbal Messages

If a stranger on your college campus asks you for directions to the administration building, you might reply, "Carty Hall is two blocks south of here." While you are delivering the verbal message, you also *repeat* the message by pointing to the south. The gesture reinforces the meaning of the verbal message and provides a clear orientation to listeners who are unfamiliar with the campus.

Nonverbal messages can substitute for verbal messages. What specific messages are being sent by the young girl in these photos?

Contradicting Verbal Messages

Nonverbal messages sometimes *contradict* the verbal message. It can be done by accident, such as when you say "turn right" but you point to the left. Or it could be done without thinking (unconsciously), such as when you have a sour expression on your face as you tell your former girlfriend how much you "really like" her new boyfriend. Finally, you could use planned nonverbal behaviors, such as a wink of the eye and a sarcastic tone of voice, to contradict the verbal message, "Nice hat!" A famous example of this contradiction happened in September 1960, when 70 million U.S. viewers tuned in to watch Senator John Kennedy of Massachusetts and Vice President Richard Nixon in the first-ever televised presidential debate. The so-called Great Debates were television's first attempt to offer voters a chance to see the presidential candidates "in person" and head to head. Nixon was more well known, since he had been on the political scene as senator and two-term vice president. He had made a career out of fighting communism right in the midst of the Cold War. Kennedy was a relative newcomer, having served only a brief and undistinguished time as senator; he had no foreign affairs experience. Expectations were low for Kennedy; there seemed to be a huge reputation disparity between them.

During the debate, their points were fairly even. But it was the visual contrast between the two men that was astounding. Nixon had seriously injured his knee, had lost weight, and had recently suffered from the flu. When the first debate came, he was underweight and pasty looking, with a murky 5:00 shadow darkening his lower face. He wore a white, poorly fitting shirt and a gray suit that nearly blended into the background set, and he refused to wear make-up, even though he was advised to do so. Kennedy supplemented his tan with make-up, wore a dark suit, and had been coached on how to sit and where to look when he wasn't speaking. Kennedy's smooth delivery made him credible, because he came off as confident, vibrant, and poised. Nixon looked tired, pasty, and uncomfortable (he sweated heavily).

Polls taken after the first debate showed that most people who listened to it on the radio felt that Nixon had won, while most who watched it on television declared Kennedy the victor. Those television viewers focused on what they saw, not what they heard.

Contradictory messages can be difficult for others to interpret, so it's important to monitor your nonverbal behaviors. People have a tendency to prefer the meaning of the nonverbal message when it conflicts with the verbal, so when you say turn right, you should try to point to the right. Or if you don't want your former girlfriend to know how jealous you are of her new boyfriend, try to guard against making that sour face. Most adults, however, will interpret the "Nice hat" comment as sarcasm and clearly understand the message.

Gestures are very important in establishing speaker credibility in debates.

Regulating the Flow of Communication

Nonverbal behaviors help us to control the verbal messages we're presenting. To prevent chaos when two are more people are engaged in conversation, we use a system of signals to indicate whose turn it is speak. Think about that. How do you know when it is appropriate for you to begin speaking in a group or in a classroom? When you're talking, no one is there saying, "Now, it's your turn." You might use tone of voice to indicate that you want to speak and silence to show that you're ready to yield the floor. If you don't want to be interrupted, you might not make eye contact with the potential interruptor. If you expect an answer, you might directly look at the other person. You probably also use nonverbals to let others know that you're trying to control their talk. Have you ever started to put your computer or lecture materials away before the professor is done speaking? You use nonverbal behavior to indicate that you want to speak, that you are finished speaking, that you want to continue speaking, or that you do not want to speak at all. The nonverbal signals include tone of voice, posture, gestures, eye contact, and other behaviors.

Deceiving Listeners

Sometimes, your nonverbal behaviors are attempts to mislead somebody or hide the truth. This deception doesn't have to be malicious or mean. If you're a poker player, you might wear sunglasses in order to shield your eyes; pupils dilate when you're excited, and you want to keep that excitement close to your vest. Sometimes, you deceive to protect yourself or the other person, like when you pat someone on the back and say, "Everything will be all right," even when you know it won't.

There are many movies based on the premise that you can learn to nonverbally behave like someone you're not in order to deceive others. In *Tootsie* (1982), Dustin Hoffman becomes the female star of a television soap opera. Robin Williams stars as *Mrs. Doubtfire* (1993), dressing as a woman so he can see his children. In *The Birdcage* (1996), Robin Williams attempts to teach Nathan Lane how to do an exaggerated John Wayne walk to disguise his effeminate stroll. *Mulan*

(1998) is a young woman wanting to fight the Huns in the place of her father, so she poses as a male to join the army. Big *Momma's House* (2000) stars Martin Lawrence, who plays an FBI agent who goes undercover and dresses as a heavy-set woman. In *White Chicks* (2004) Shawn Wayans and Marlon Wayans are sibling FBI agents who must protect two cruise line heiresses from a kidnapping plot. Finally, in *The Lord of the Rings: The Return of the King* (2004), Éowyn dresses as a soldier to be allowed to fight with the men.

A great deal of research on deception has practical implications. For instance, some occupations, such as lawyers and actors, require you to act differently than you might feel. Research has found that they are more successful at deception than the rest of the general population. People who monitor themselves have been found to be more effective in hiding deception cues than are people who are not as self-aware. Just think about the last time you told someone a "white lie." Were you a little nervous? How did you show that? Did the words come easily? Did you stammer or have to search for words? When you fib, you have to weigh the consequences of being caught versus the need to fib (telling a child that Santa or the Easter Bunny exists). You have to look and act sincere and believable, even though you're churning inside. If you can look composed and natural, then you are more likely to be a successful liar. In fact, research tells us that people with a greater social skills repertoire and more communication competence will generally be more proficient, alert, confident, and expressive, and less fidgety, nervous and rigid, making them more skilled at deception than others.

Now that you see the many roles that nonverbals can play in communication, let's turn from the functions to the categories of nonverbal communication.

What Are the Types of Nonverbal Communication?

Although many types of behaviors can communicate, available space and the focus of this book limit our discussion of nonverbal communication to body movement (kinesics), the use of space (proxemics), dress and appearance, and eye contact (occulesics). Vocalics, or paralanguage (the use of the voice), is covered in the chapter on delivery.

Body Movement/Kinesics

(Birdwhistell first identified kinesics, or the study of our use of the body to communicate. It includes gestures, posture, facial expressions, and other body movements. Five research themes have emerged in kinesics: the use of emblems, illustrators, regulators, affect displays, and adaptors. A brief look at all five themes will provide a good orientation to the complex ways that we can use our bodies to send messages.

Emblems. An emblem is a nonverbal behavior that has a distinct verbal referent or even a denotative definition, and it is often used to send a specific message to others. The verbal referent is typically one or two words of a short phrase. For example, the "thumbs-up" hand gesture is listed in many dictionaries and is defined as a *gesture of approval*. There is a high level of agreement about the meaning of an emblem within cultures, but not usually across cultures.

Most emblems are created with the hands, but we can create them in other ways. For example, a shoulder shrug suggests "I don't know," or a wrinkled nose indicates that "something stinks." But the emblems we are most familiar with are usually hand gestures. Try to make the gesture that goes with each of the following meanings:

- "Sit down beside me."
- "Follow me."
- "I can't hear you."
- "Be quiet!"
- "Shame on you!"
- "OK."
- "I promise."
- "What time is it?"
- "Good bye!"

In addition to everyday conversation, emblems are used by divers while under water, by police officers directing traffic, by construction workers, and by catchers, pitchers, and managers during baseball games. Don't forget the very familiar and more or less universal signal some people use to indicate displeasure with other drivers! Keep in mind, though, that the emblems you know are not always shared. The hand gesture we use for "come here," with the hand palm up with the index finger extending in and out three or four times, has a very different meaning in Latin America. It means that you are romantically interested in the person, and is considered a solicitation. Emblems can replace the verbal or reinforce it.

Bikers use emblems when manuvering in traffic.

Illustrators. An illustrator is a gesture that is used with language to emphasize, stress, or repeat what is being said. It can be used to give directions, show the size or shape of something, and give clarification. Can you imagine trying to explain to a new parent how to "burp" a baby without using illustrators? Can you give directions to the campus library with your hands in your pockets? Sure you could, but the illustrators add much meaning and clarification to your directions or instructions; they help with that function of clarifying. In a study done several years ago, speakers were found to be more persuasive when they used illustrators than when they did not. More recent research has even extended the importance of illustrators. Robert Krauss found that gestures do more than amplify or accent verbal communication. They also help people retrieve ideas and words, such as when you try to define a term with a spatial meaning such as underneath, next to, and above, which Krauss calls *lexical retrieval*. If not done to excess, "talking with your hands" can be a very good thing!

Regulators. A regulator is a turn-taking signal that helps control the flow, the pace, and turn-taking in conversations, and you learned about their coordinating role earlier. If a group of people are talking and trying to share meaning, they must take turns speaking, and taking turns requires cooperation among the communicators. To accomplish this cooperation, along with the content of the conversation, participants must also communicate about who will speak next and when that turn will begin. Regulators help us with this task.

Can you make judgements about the nature of the emotions in these photos?

Weimann and Knapp and Argyle identified four categories of turn related signals in a typical conversation:

1. *Turn requesting* signals: These are used by a nonspeaker to take the floor. Nonverbal regulators used to request a turn include rapid head nods, forward leaning posture, and increased eye contact with the speaker.
2. *Turn yielding* signals: The speaker uses these to give up the floor. Nonverbal regulators used to yield a turn include increased eye contact with a nonspeaker, leaning back from a forward posture, or a sudden end to gesturing used while speaking.

3. *Turn maintenance* signals: These are used by the speaker to keep the floor (i.e., continue speaking). Nonverbal signals used to keep the turn include speaking louder or faster (increasing volume or rate of speech), continuing to gesture, or avoiding eye contact with the person requesting the turn.

4. *Back channel* signals: Nonspeaker refuses a turn that has been offered by the speaker. Nonverbal signals used to refuse a turn include nodding the head and avoiding eye contact with the person exhibiting a turn-yielding signal.

Affect displays. An **affect display** is a form of nonverbal behavior that expresses emotions. Although this behavior is most often associated with facial expressions, affect can also be expressed through posture and gestures. These behaviors cannot only express the type of emotion being experienced, but can also express the intensity of the emotion. A smile suggests that you are happy. A slumped-over posture and a scowl on your face can suggest that you are unhappy, while your clinched fists and tense muscles can communicate just *how* unhappy you might be.

Affect displays express emotion.

The emotions communicated by your face and body can affect the way you are perceived by other people. People who smile spontaneously are often considered by others to be more likable and more approachable than people who do not smile or people who just pretend to smile.

What do these adaptors tell you about the internal feelings of the people in the photos?

Adaptors. Adaptors are behaviors that can indicate our internal conditions or feelings to other people. We tend to use these behaviors when we become excited or anxious. Think about the kind of things that you do in communication situations when you feel nervous or excited. Do you scratch your head? Bite your nails? Play with your glasses? Rub your nose? You might not know, because most people are not aware of displaying these behaviors.

Adaptors are generally considered the least desirable type of nonverbal communication. Self-touching in this way could be a distraction to the audience, and it is often perceived as a sign of anxiety. One study found that deceivers bob their heads more often than people who tell the truth. Cultural guidelines may prohibit these behaviors, too. Wriggling your nose or having a disgusted facial look to show that you're repulsed seems to have a universal meaning.

However, in some cultures, people are socialized to mask emotional cues, and in others they're taught to emphasize them. Latin Americans will usually greet friends and relatives more personally than do Americans. Everyone hugs, including the men. Men usually also greet woman with *besitos,* meaning they touch cheeks while making a kissing noise with their lips. Women also greet other women with *besitos.* These little kisses are purely friendly and have no romantic meaning. Maslow and colleagues suggested that the anxiety displayed by adaptors can be interpreted by other communicators as a sign of deception; you are anxious because you are not being honest with the others and you fear being discovered!

Personal Distances

Hall recognized characteristic distances maintained between people in the U.S. culture, depending on their perceived relationships. The distance categories are *intimate, personal, social,* and public.

Type	Distance	Who Is Permitted/Context
Intimate Distance 	touching to 18 inches	**Who:** Spouses and family members, boyfriends and girlfriends, and very close friends. Context: A date with your spouse.
Personal Distance 	18 inches to 4 feet	**Who:** Good friends and people you know well. Context: Having lunch with a good friend or co-worker.
Social Distance 	4 feet to 12 feet	**Who:** Business associates, teachers, and people you know but with whom you have a professional but less social relationship. Context: A business meeting, small group discussion, or an employment interview.
Public Distance 	12 feet and beyond	**Who:** A person you don't know; a stranger on the street. **Context:** Giving a presentation to a large group; walking downtown on a public sidewalk.

Photo courtesy of Charles Long

Use of Space/Proxemics

The study of proxemics is typically divided into two applications: The use of personal space and how people claim and mark territory as their own. Most of us don't even think about the impact of space on our relationships, but research has shown that your use of space can influence shared meaning and impact your relationship. Knapp and Hall found that our use of space can seriously affect our ability to achieve desired goals. Both applications can be used and managed by people to communicate fairly specific messages, and they can provide evidence to help us make judgments about person using the space.

Relationships affect the way we use space. Based on the use of space, describe the relationships in these photos. Be specific about the nonverbal clues that indicate the relationship.

Personal space. When you consider the idea of **personal space,** think of a small amount of portable space that you carry around with you all the time. You control who is and who is not permitted inside of that space. Permission to enter that space is granted based on the relationship you have with that person, the context of the encounter, the culture in which you live, and your own personal preferences and tolerances. For example, you would be likely to allow business and professional colleagues to be reasonably close to you; you would allow good friends to be very close to you; and you would allow romantic partners to be closer still, even to the point of touching. In addition, you might allow people that you don't know to be very close to you in the appropriate context, like a crowded elevator or a busy airport.

Sometimes we allow our personal space to be violated.

When someone enters your space without permission, you can interpret it as a lack of courtesy, or even as a threat. You will feel uncomfortable, so you can either wait for the trespasser to move out of your space, or you can move away until you feel comfortable again.

The range of personal space varies across cultures. The box describes spaces typical to the culture in the United States. If you visit the United Kingdom, you will notice that these spaces are slightly expanded; that is, the British prefer just a bit more distance between people. By contrast, many Eastern cultures, including Asia and the Middle

People mark their territory in many ways.

East, prefer a smaller distance. When these cultures meet, people from the United States often feel "crowded" by people from Asian cultures, while people from Japan might think that Americans are "cold" or "stand-offish" because of the increased interpersonal distances. As you can see, there is no shortage of opportunities for misunderstanding! Burgoon suggests that we want to stay near others, but we also want to maintain some distance—think about the dilemma this causes! Try to be sensitive to cultural norms when you assign meaning to the use of personal space.

Territoriality. We also have a tendency to claim space as our own. We have just looked at personal space, which is portable space that you carry around with you. Territory, by contrast, is not mobile; it stays in one place. You can think of territory as a kind of extension of you that is projected on to space or objects. Space that you occupy or control, and objects that belong to you or that you use regularly, are all important to you. If any person not authorized by you occupies that space or touches those objects, you feel violated and threatened. To help describe this kind of attachment to places and things, we turn to Altman, who classified territory into three categories: primary, secondary, and public.

Primary territory is space or those items that you personally control. This includes personal items that only you would use, like your clothes and your toothbrush. It also includes the private spaces in your house like your bathroom and bedroom. Many people treat still other places as primary territory such as their car, their office at work, and even their refrigerator!

Secondary territory is not your private property. That is, it is not owned by you, but it is typically associated with you. Examples of secondary territory include the desk you always use in class, the seat you always sit in at the office conference table, your favorite fishing spot at the lake, or your usual table at the library.

Public territory is available to anyone, so any space that you try to claim is only temporary. You might define your space on the beach by using markers such as blankets, beach chairs, or umbrellas. Or you might spread out your books and notes at the library to claim space on a work table. Our use of the territory lasts as long as we are using it, or as long as other people respect our markers.

Most of us pay little attention to these claims of space, and we probably don't even realize that we do it. However, these claims come clearly to our attention when they are violated. It seems like there is almost nothing worse than walking into the classroom on the day of the big exam to find someone else in your seat! Sure, any seat will work just as well, but that is *your* seat where you feel most comfortable and confident. We tend to feel violated whenever any unauthorized person uses our space or touches our stuff!

Lyman and Scott identified three levels of **intrusion of territory:** violation, invasion, and contamination. A *violation* happens when your space or your stuff is used without your permission, like when a neighbor borrows one of your tools without asking first. An *invasion* occurs when an unauthorized person enters the territory that you have claimed with markers. They might move your books and notes at the library (while you were looking for a book) and take over your space at the table, or they could cut in front of you in a check-out line at the grocery store. Finally, a *contamination* occurs when space that you claim is used without your authorization, but your evidence of the use is not the presence of the user but objects left behind. For example, you arrive at your office in the morning to find cups and fast food wrappers on your desk. There is nobody in your office, but you know somebody *was* there, and he or she was eating at your desk. Territory that you claim as your own should not be used by anyone without your permission. How you respond to territory depends very much on who invaded the territory and why it was invaded, which you'll see explained in expectancy violations theory, which follows later in this chapter.

Clothing and Artifacts

Your appearance, along with the way you dress, influences the way other people respond to you. In some situations, your appearance can be the primary factor that determines the response of others. *Physical attractiveness,* as well as personal grooming and hygiene, weigh heavily on judgments that are made about you every day. If that's not enough pressure, along with protecting you from the environment and fulfilling cultural requirements for modesty, *clothing* is also a potent source of nonverbal information about you. Morris tells us that clothing sends continuous signals about us and who we think we are. For example, watch the scene in the 1990 movie *Pretty Woman* when the character played by Julia Roberts first enters a "high-class" clothing store and is treated poorly by the staff. What about her appearance led to that treatment?

Among other qualities, clothing can suggest social and economic status, education, level of success, or trustworthiness and character. Morris suggests that clothing can be a cultural display and one that communicates something special about the wearer. People have a tendency to express certain values central to their belief systems that indicate the kind of people they perceive themselves to be. Katz tells us that we hold and express particular attitudes to satisfy this need and that those attitudes reflect a positive view of ourselves. Clothing and appearance are consistent with this concept. For example, if you consider yourself to be the "artistic" type, or a successful business person, or a talented athlete, your clothing choices will likely reflect that self image.

Clothing is a potent source of nonverbal information about you.

Gordon et al., suggests that clothing fulfills a number of symbolic functions:

- Traditional and religious ceremonies often involve specific clothing.
- Self-beautification (real or imagined) is often reflected in clothing.
- Clothing expresses cultural values regarding sexual identity and practice.
- Clothes differentiate roles and levels of authority.
- Clothing is used in the acquisition and display of status.

Think about the way you dress and why you make those clothing choices. What are you trying to say? Are you trying to fit in? Are you trying to identify yourself with a particular group? Are you trying to show respect for an occasion or person?

Clothing is not the only aspect of appearance to consider. Think of the other personal choices people make with tattoos, body art, and personal grooming. What are the impacts of blue hair, black nail colors, Mohawks or dreadlocks, multiple piercing and colorful tattoos? You have the right to communicate about yourself in any way you want, but remember that if you go against cultural norms, you may be creating perceptual barriers that impede communication. Your appearance is a prime source of information that others use to make judgments about you. Try to use some care when making choices about how you should look in particular situations. You can always maintain your individuality, but you should also dress to show respect for the occasion and the people that you will be coming into contact with. If you have to give a presentation for a business group, for example, you can show your respect for the group by dressing in more formal attire. Wearing jeans with ripped out knees may say a lot about who you think you are, but wearing the suit for the business group also communicates who you think you are. You are someone who combines your own needs with a respect for the needs of other people!

How could her tattoos impact others' perceptions?

Eye Movement/oculesics

In many Western cultures, including the United States, making **eye contact** with another person is considered a sign of sincerity, caring, honesty, and sometimes power or status. Pearson found that men sometimes use eye contact to challenge others and to assert themselves. Women tend to hold eye contact more than men, regardless of the sex of the person that they're interacting with. Some Eastern cultures view eye contact with others as an impolite invasion of privacy and they especially disapprove of eye contact with a person of higher status. In another study, it was found that inner-city African-American persuaders look continually at the listener, and African American listeners tend to look away from the persuader most of the time. The opposite is true of middle-class Whites; as persuaders, they look only occasionally at the listener, and White listeners look continuously at the persuader. This could explain why the two groups could have incorrect inferences about the amount of interest the other has when they communicate.

By making eye contact with others, you can find clues about their level of understanding and interest.

We consider the use of eye contact to be an essential tool for achieving communication goals. In U.S. culture, how does it make you feel when someone will not make eye contact with you? Do you trust this person? Do you suspect his or her motives?

Eye contact helps us communicate in at least four ways: It can open a channel of communication, demonstrate concern, gather feedback, and moderate anxiety.

Open a communication channel. You can let others know that you would like to communicate with them by simply looking at them. A brief moment of eye contact can open a channel of communication and make other messages possible.

Demonstrate concern. Engaging other people in eye contact during conversations shows a concern for them, as well as your commitment that they understand your message. In addition, eye contact can be used to communicate liking and attraction.

Gather feedback. If you would like information about what other people are thinking, take a look at their eyes. You won't be able to read thoughts, but you can certainly find clues to indicate that they are listening, that they understand the message, and perhaps that they care about what you are saying. The old adage that speakers should look at the back wall of the room when giving a public speech is pretty bad advice; you will miss out on critical information about the frame of mind of audience members, as well as other feedback essential to achieving your goals.

Moderate anxiety. When speakers get nervous or anxious during a public presentation, they have a tendency to avoid eye contact with the listeners by either looking at the floor, the back wall of the room, or at their notes. As they continue to stare at the floor, anxiety (fear of unknown outcomes) continues to build. Occasionally, but rarely, anxiety can build to the point at which it completely takes over, and the speaker freezes. You can avoid this scenario through *careful preparation* for the event, and by allowing the listeners to provide you with support. By *establishing eye contact* with members of your audience, you will see listeners smiling at you or expressing support with their posture, head nods, or other behaviors. Not looking at the audience or conversational partners removes your opportunity to get or give supportive feedback. When others notice your anxiety, they usually want to help you. Look at the audience, feel the support and try to relax, and then refocus on your communication goals.

How Does Theory Describe Nonverbal Behavior's Impact on Relationships?

Have you ever played elevator games with strangers? You know, you enter an empty elevator and take the "power position" by the buttons. At the next floor, someone enters and either asks you to push the button for a floor or reaches in front of you to select a floor and then retreats to the opposite corner away from you. There's no further talk or eye contact. The next person who enters does the same thing, finding a corner. Everyone faces the doors, anticipates its opening, watching the numbers change as if by magic. If others enter, their volume drops to a hush, or they stop talking until they leave. Now, have you ever tried *this?* Get on an elevator and keep walking until you face the back wall. After all, that's how you entered, right? Go stand right next to the power person, real close. Keep talking real loud. Sit down on your backpack or luggage. What do you think will happen? How will others react to you?

One theory that attempts to explain the influence of nonverbal communication on meaning and relationships is **expectancy violations theory.** Judee Burgoon said that "nonverbal cues are an inherent and essential part of message creation (production) and interpretation (processing)." Expectancy violations theory (EVT) suggests that we hold expectations about the nonverbal behavior of others. It asserts that when communicative norms are violated, the violation may be perceived either favorably or unfavorably, depending on the perception that the receiver has of the violator. Burgoon's early writing on EVT integrated Hall's ideas on personal space (which you read about earlier) as a core aspect of the theory. EVT says that our *expectancies* are the thoughts and behaviors anticipated when we interact with another.

We have expectations of how others ought to think and behave. Levine says that these expectancies are a result of social norms, stereotypes, and your own personal idiosyncrasies, and these expectancies cause us to interact with others. We have both preinteractional and interactional expectations. *Preinteractional expectations* are made up of the skills and knowledge you bring to an interaction; *interactional expectations* are your skills and knowledge that let you carry out the interaction.

Another basic idea of EVT is that we learn our expectations from our cultures: You've learned what kind of touching is appropriate with whom, how to greet a stranger, and where to stand in relationship with another, for example.

Finally, EVT says that we make predictions about others based on their nonverbal behavior. So how does this work? Let's say you're standing in line at the grocery store, and the person in front of you looks at what you're about to buy and then makes eye contact with you. At first, you might be uncomfortable, thinking that the person is judging you by the way she is eyeing your groceries. If she then gives you a warm smile and points to her big pile containing the same things, you might feel a bit more comfortable. You've made predictions based on nonverbal behavior: The person is not threatening or judging you negatively.

But EVT is about *violations* of our expectations. Burgoon says that when people deviate from expectations, that deviation is judged based on the other's ability to reward us. A reward could be something as simple as a smile, friendliness, or acknowledgment of competence. This potential to reward is called *communicator reward valence,* which is the interactants' ability to reward or punish and the positive and negative characteristics they have. Someone in power, like your professor for instance, may have more communicator reward valence than a stranger, because the professor has the power of grades and probably has more credibility for you. If someone violates our expectations, these deviations cause *arousal,* an increased attention to the deviation. Cognitive arousal is mental awareness of the deviation; physical arousal involves physiological heightening. For instance, if a person stares at you, you might wonder why he's doing that (cognitive arousal) or you might start to sweat (physical arousal). Once arousal happens, threats occur. Your *threat threshold* is the tolerance you have for deviations; how threatened do you feel? Maybe you don't mind if another person stands too close; maybe you can't put up with someone staring at you. The size of your threat threshold is based on how you view the person who is deviating from your expectations; what is that other's communicator reward valence? Then you add in the *violation valence,* which consists of your positive or negative value placed towards the deviations from your expectations.

When someone violates one of your expectations (for instance, he touches you when you didn't expect it), you interpret the meaning of that violation and decide if you like it or not. If you don't like it, then the violation valence is negative; if the surprise was pleasant (even though you didn't expect it), then the violation valence is positive. The theory predicts that if a violation is ambiguous, then the communicator reward valence will influence how you interpret and evaluate the violation. If the person is someone you like, then you'll positively evaluate his violation; if you don't like him, then you'll negatively evaluate his violation. Take a simple example of how someone is dressed. On an interview, there are certain expectations of how you should look. If you go in wearing jeans and a t-shirt and the company wants its workers to wear suits, then you've violated expectancies. It's pretty likely that you don't have any power here, or any way to reward the company for hiring you. Thus, the interviewer will evaluate you negatively, feeling aroused that you

Do You Know All the Types of Nonverbal Communication?

Kinesics	Proxemics	Chronemics	Haptics	Paralanguage
The use of body language to send messages; includes gestures, facial expressions, posture, and body movements	Communicative behavior through the use of space and distance; best explicated by using zones and territories	Communication through the way we conceptualize and adhere to time	The way humans communicate by using or not using touch; closely linked to culture	Nonverbal behavior that focuses on how something is said and not what is said; includes vocal characteristics such as rate, pitch, volume, vocal quality, dialect, articulation and diction, fillers, dialect, etc.
Olfactics The communicative attributes of smell and scents; can be responsible for strong reactions both positive and negative	**Oculesics** The communication that takes place through eye behavior: the least controllable area of the face	**Clothing and Artifacts** The manner in which we communicate through our clothing choices and preferences as well as the adornment of our bodies with accessories; serves the purpose of beautification or identification		

didn't understand such a basic concept like appropriate attire. However, what if you are a highly sought-after, uniquely imaginative individual that the company has been pursuing? Your violation of the dress code might be seen positively; you're bold and creative, just like they thought. EVT is an interesting theory that focuses on what we expect nonverbally in conversations, as well as suggesting what happens when our expectations aren't met. It's very practical in applications across many contexts.

What Are the Key Points to Remember about Nonverbal Communication?

Nonverbal communication is a complex combination of behaviors that form a source of information used by other people to make sense of messages that you send. Even though much of your nonverbal behavior is spontaneous and unconscious, you should realize that it contributes a significant percentage of the meaning that people attribute to your messages. As such, you should try as hard as you can to be a good self-monitor and pay close attention to your nonverbal behaviors. However, nonverbal behavior is also a source of information for you. It can help you to more accurately interpret the communication of others, so pay attention!

Be careful to not overgeneralize the meanings of particular nonverbal cues. The specific meaning of any nonverbal behavior is typically dependent on multiple factors, including (but not limited to) culture, the relationship between the people communicating, the specific communication context, and individual characteristics of the participants. You wouldn't want others to make stereotypical assumptions about your behavior, so make sure that you don't make those same assumptions about the behavior of others. Gather as much information as possible before reaching conclusions. Sometimes a touch is just a touch!

Summary

Verbal and nonverbal communication are powerful, critically important elements in the creation of shared meaning, because they have the ability to clarify your ideas to others or to confuse them. It's not always easy to use language or nonverbal behavior correctly, because both are arbitrary and ambiguous. The relationship that words or movements have with ideas is not based on a concrete characteristic; instead, you are relying on the ability of the audience to associate your symbols with their cognitions (beliefs, attitudes, and values). You've been exposed to some theoretical explanations of how these attempts to create meaning work in our lives. We interpret language and nonverbal communication because of our particular culture, which provides a frame of reference on how to assign meaning. In order to be a competent communicator, you need to remain aware that your words aren't always understood as you mean them to be and that your nonverbal behavior can supplement or contradict those words.

Communication for Today's Student

Chapter 3 – What Is the Power of Verbal and Nonverbal Communication?

This is a two part exercise.

Exercise 3.1 – Principles of Language

Part One

There is power in verbal language. Language is a shared system of symbols and structures in organized patterns to express thoughts and feelings. Let's explore further the basic principles of language by identifying the following terms as they relate to how we use language.

VERBAL LANGUAGE TERMS	DEFINITION	EXAMPLE FROM SCENARIO
Appropriate language		
Unbiased language		
Accurate language		
Syntactical rules		
Constitutive rules		
Phonological rules		
Regulative rules		
Semantic rules		

VERBAL LANGUAGE TERMS	DEFINITION	EXAMPLE FROM SCENARIO
Slang		
Cliché		
Loaded words		
Empty words		
Equivocal words		
Derogatory words		

Part Two

Write a creative and engaging scenario about Nathalie and Jerrome using the terms you have just defined. Indicate when you use each term by placing the term in parenthesis behind the example.

The story begins . . .

> Nathalie and Jerrome were Precollege students at Harmony University. They met at a pool party at Harmony gym when Jerrome walked over to Nathalie and said "Hello, my name is Jerrome. What's up?" (semantic rules)

Be prepared to share your journal entries with the class.

Communication for Today's Student

Chapter 3 – What Is the Power of Verbal and Nonverbal Communication?

Exercise 3.2 – Observations

Nonverbal Communication includes all nonlinguistic aspects of communication. The types of nonverbal communication include: Kinesics, oculesics, and proxemics, dress and appearance. You are also encouraged to refer to any of the categories included on the chart on page _____. Give a brief definition of each. Then, visit one of the sites listed below and record examples of each as you observed the nonverbal "types" in action. Record your time and place on the record chart and be very specific when you describe your observations.

Choose one site: Student Center
                        Cafeteria
                        Local fast food restaurant
                        Library
                        A dorm lobby

Name: _____

Place: _____

TYPE OF NONVERBAL BEHAVIOR	DEFINITION	OBSERVATION
Kinesics		
Oculesics		
Proxemics		
Clothing and Artifacts		
Choose one additional to describe behavior:		

Be sure to . . .

Describe who you observed in each type.
Tell us what was unique about the behavior.

Be prepared to share your journal entries with the class.

UNDERSTANDING INTERPERSONAL RELATIONSHIPS

After reading this chapter, you should be able to:

- ✅ Discuss the theory of emotional intelligence and its relevance to interpersonal communication.
- ✅ Describe the foundation and types of attraction.
- ✅ Describe the essential characteristics of the types of relationships.
- ✅ Discuss the manner in which conversations establish and facilitate interpersonal relationships.
- ✅ Explain self disclosure, why it's important, and how the Johari Window and Social Penetration Theory clarify the self disclosure process.
- ✅ Explain the strategies that are utilized for establishing and maintaining good relationships.
- ✅ Discuss the impact of electronically mediated communication on relationships.

Key Terms

Attraction
Bid
Biographic stage
Blind pane
Close relationship
Common ground stage
Conversation
Cyber bullying
Cyber stalking

Electronically mediated
   communication
Emotional intelligence
Empathy
Hidden pane
"I" messages
Interpersonal communication
Intrapersonal
   communication

Johari window
Localized attraction
Magnetic attraction
Open pane
Personal stage
Physical attraction
Receivables attraction
Reflective attraction
Rules theory

Scripted conversation
Self disclosure
Small talk
Social penetration model
Stereotypic conversation
Unknown pane
Virtual attraction
"You" messages

Facing image Photo courtesy of Charles Long

4 Scenario

"Carla! SLOW DOWN!" Ariel yelled as she tried to keep up with Carla on her bicycle.

"Come on, slow poke!" Carla yelled back as she increased speed down the rocky trail.

Carla loved to go biking on the weekends. After several months of convincing and begging, she finally got Ariel to agree to go with her. However, she was beginning to think that leaving Ariel back on campus was the best thing to do.

Ariel complained the whole time about the heat, the bugs, the dirt, and how tired she was during biking. Carla didn't know what Ariel thought she was going to experience. She had seen her come in exhausted and dirty from the weekend excursions, so she had to have known this was going to happen.

"I'm turning back," Ariel declared, abruptly stopping.

"What?" Carla huffed, obviously frustrated. "You can't be serious."

"Oh, I am," Ariel said matter-of-factly. "This girl is done."

Carla rolled her eyes as she slowed down. She turned her bike around. "Wait a second." Before Carla knew it, her wheel hit a rock and sent her flying over the edge into a prickly bush.

"Ouch!" Carla yelped.

"I got you," a voice called out to her from beyond the bush.

The sun was shining bright in her eyes, shielding the face of the stranger who reached out to help her. As she stood to her feet, the glare disappeared and she laid her eyes on the young man who picked her up from the bush.

"Hey, you alright?" he asked as he held up four fingers. "How many fingers am I holding up?"

Carla mumbled, "Four."

"Oh my gosh! Carla, are you ok?" Ariel screamed. She was already in drama mode, and Carla knew she was in for an earful.

"She's alright," the guy said, smiling down at Carla. "What's your name, beautiful?"

"Her name is—" Ariel started.

"No no no," the guy chuckled. "I need to hear her say it. What's your name?"

"Carla Renolds," Carla answered, thankful that the man had silenced Ariel.

"What year is it?" he asked next.

"2014."

"She's fine." The guy ushered Carla over to a nearby tree stump.

"Thank you . . ." Carla drifted off.

"Brian, my name is Brian."

"Thank you, Brian. I should be fine now." Carla tried to stand up, but a sharp pain in her knee stopped her. She looked down to see blood flowing down her knee.

"Oh gosh, she's bleeding," Ariel screamed.

"It's ok," Brian reassured her. "I have a first aid kit in my pack."

For the next 20 minutes, Ariel questioned Brian as he tended to Carla's knee. They found out that Brian was a medical student with hopes of becoming a pediatrician. Carla just sat there quietly watching his skillful handiwork. He worked quickly, and before they knew it, he was already heading back to his bike.

"Thank you again," Carla said, mounting her bike.

"Hey, Carla," Brian called, jogging back over to her. He passed her his card. "Call me sometime."

"Oh, it's ok," Carla waved him off. "I have a doctor."

"Well, that's good," Brian chuckled, "but I wasn't looking for a new patient. I was hoping to take you out for dinner."

Carla's eyes grew wide. "Oh, ok. I'll call you."

"Great," Brian smiled. "You ladies have a great day and be careful."

Brian got back on his bike and disappeared down the trail with Carla looking after him. Ariel peddled over to Carla and looked after him as well.

"That was something," Ariel giggled. "If there are fine doctors like that on this trail, I'm coming back every weekend."

Why do you think Ariel is attracted to Brian?
Do Ariel and Brian show any personality traits that are indicators
that they may be able to enjoy a good relationship?

Respond
Here

When Brian stops to provide first aid to Carla after her tumble from her bike, he initiates communication with Carla that may lead to a close personal relationship with various possible outcomes. In the collaborative work, Close Relationships, Harold Kelley, a pioneer in social psychology, describes a close relationship as "one that is strong, frequent and that lasts over a considerable period of time"(Kelley, Berscheid, Christensen, Harvey, Hurston, Levinger, McClintock, Peplau, and Peterson 1983). The degree of closeness ranges from intimacy found between family members to that of close friends to that of romantic partners. Some common characteristics of close relationships include emotional reciprocity, trust, breadth and depth of disclosure, enjoyment, and respect. Another important factor to remember about close interpersonal relationships is that not only do they vary in degree, but as humans, we need them. In fact, we seek companionship and without it we naturally possess a feeling of incompleteness or emptiness. No matter how much we try to deny the need by rationalizing it with statements like, "I'm a loner" or "I can do bad all by myself," these are simply excuses for failed attempts at closeness and bad choices in previous relationships.

Interpersonal communication is defined as one person interacting with another, often in an informal unstructured setting. Most theorists agree that interpersonal communication is the most critical aspect of successful personal relationships. In one of his early works, entitled *Personal Relationships*, Kelley asserts that there are critical components of an interpersonal relationship: 1. Interdependence in the consequences of specific behaviors, 2. Interaction that is responsive to one another's outcomes, and 3. Attribution of interaction events to dispositions. In this theory, Kelley merged three of his major areas of study including interdependence, attributions and personal relationships (Kelley 1970). In the interdependence theory, also referred to as the Social Exchange Theory, Kelley along with his partner, John Thibaut asserted that by using patterns of interdependence in interactions, they could identify the extent to which one partner in an interpersonal relationship can affect and or control the other's outcome (Thibaut and Kelley 1959). In the attribution theory, Kelley proposed that people attribute behavior to whatever it covaries with, which generally includes three major questions. These three questions center around the concepts of *consistency*, *distinctiveness* and *consensus*. Is the behavior consistent with people in this situation? Does the behavior vary across different situations? Do *most* people engage in this behavior in this situation? (Kelley 1973)

Men without close social ties are two or three times more likely to die earlier than men who have them.

As relationships develop, it becomes more and more apparent that each relationship can only be as strong as the individuals involved in the relationships. Therefore, before we make an attempt to engage in a relationship, it is important to first make a concerted effort to understand ourselves. In a previous chapter, we looked at the manner in which a person communicates within themselves. **Intrapersonal communication** is described as the understanding of self. Intrapersonal communication involves your thoughts, feelings and the way you look and feel about yourself. In many ways, intrapersonal and interpersonal communication are interdependent because it is unlikely that you will have a strong interpersonal relationship if you suffer from inner turmoil.

Managing your emotions does not mean that you never feel angry, worried, or anxious. It's important that you control these emotions rather than letting them control you.

Emotional Intelligence

In our scenario earlier involving Brian and Carla, we are led to believe that they may engage in an interpersonal relationship in the future. We gather from their brief interaction that there is at least a possibility that they may become involved. Perhaps their relationship may begin as friends and later develop into a relationship with much greater breadth and depth. But, let's not get ahead of ourselves. Brian and Carla should first determine if they are ready to pursue a close relationship. Brian and Carla can determine this by assessing their emotional maturity or emotional intelligence. *Emotional intelligence* is described as the ability to understand and get along with others. According to theorist Daniel Goleman, emotional intelligence can be determined by assessing attributes and behaviors within five categories: *Being Self-Aware*, *Managing Emotions*, *Motivating Yourself*, *Recognizing Emotions in Others*, and *Handling Relationships* (*Goleman* 1995).

Being Self-Aware

Do you know how you would react in an emergency? Do you know what you would say if you were falsely accused of a crime? What would say if you a stranger asked you for a ride? How would you respond to a malicious rumor? If you believe you know what you would do or how you would behave in these or similar situations, you may have a good understanding of self. It is important to recognize your emotional triggers so that you can put distance between the action and reaction. Being able to do so is an indication that you have reached a level of emotional maturity as well as a confirmation that you have the ability to engage in a relationship with another person. A clear example of self-awareness occurs when Carla, from the earlier scenario, decides to take Brian up on his offer and decides to call him. After calling and texting Brian several times with no response, Carla becomes angry and frustrated. She discloses to Ariel that she is so disappointed in herself for trusting that Brian was sincere when he asked her to call him. In her frustration, she declares to her friend, "If I never see Brian again, it will be too soon. And, if I do see him again, I plan to give him a piece of mind that he will never forget." In a later discussion with Carla, Ariel discovers that after allowing herself some distance from her emotions and the way she was feeling, Carla decided to call Brian once again. When she does, Brian disclosed that his phone had been stolen and he was without a phone for five days. Had Carla not given herself some time to take an objective perspective of the situation, she may have forfeited the possibility of close interpersonal relationship. When she finally had a opportunity to speak to Brian, she was composed and could rationally articulate her feelings. She did not deny her disappointment but she did alienate Brian by acting irrationally.

Managing Emotions

What would you do if someone physically threatened you? How would you react if you discovered a friend has betrayed a confidence? How do respond to bad news? How do you respond to good news? Anger, joy, anxiety, worry are all emotions that humans experience during various situations in life. It is normal to feel these emotions, but abnormal if we do not recognize when and to what degree we express these emotions. For example, it is normal for us to be upset when a close friend betrays a trust either by disclosing information you have discussed in confidence or by revealing information that has been obtained because of the closeness you share. It is not normal to fly into a violent rage when you discover the betrayal. When we are able to manage our

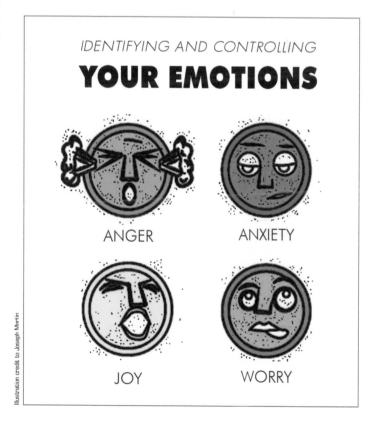

IDENTIFYING AND CONTROLLING

YOUR EMOTIONS

ANGER

ANXIETY

JOY

WORRY

Illustration credit to Joseph Martin

emotions, we reach a level of maturity at which we can express our feelings in an appropriate manner. When Carla calls Brian and does not receive a response for days, she manages her anxiety when he is non responsive. Her behavior is an indication that she has control over her emotions and is a good sign that she has a high emotional intelligence.

Motivating Yourself

Think back to your junior year in high school. Did you take the initiative to complete your college application or did you do so only after numerous reminders from parents and guidance counselors? Do you wait until the day before or the day of the exam to study or the week of a due date of a paper to begin researching and writing? Do you allow laundry to pile up and run over the bin before you decide to take care of it? Setting goals and demonstrating the discipline to achieve them is an essential ingredient in a successful life. Self control and the ability to resist impulses are key to motivation. As we develop our emotional intelligence, we are able to overcome temptations that interfere with our ability to accomplish what we set out to do. It takes a great deal of self-motivation for Ariel to finally decide to go biking with Carla. In fact, Ariel at one point on the ride decides to turn back. Had it not been for Carla's accident, Ariel probably would have returned home. Ariel complains the entire time she is on the trail about everything, including the heat, bugs, dirt, and, most of all, about being exhausted. Ariel will discover that there are numerous influences on self-motivation. According to Goleman, two of the most powerful influences are the ability to remain positive and optimistic.

Recognizing Emotions in Others

When you witness fellow students emotionally distraught, do you console them? A classmate freezes on a presentation in front of the class, do you applaud and assist the student with removing the visual aid as you talk about how interesting the topic was? Our ability to identify with another person's feelings and circumstances is an essential part of the human experience. When we demonstrate a high emotional intelligence, we do not simply show pity nor express sympathy. We empathize with them. Empathy is a distinguishable emotion that humans experience because of our ability to recognize as well as share someone's feelings. It is a human trait we express when we say we feel sorry for Carla when she fell from the bike. This is an indication that we can feel and express pity in appropriate situations. When we lean over and whisper to a friend how we sympathize with Carla because we know how we would feel if we had taken that fall in front of a group of people, we are showing sympathy. To feel pity and sympathy for Carla is only part of recognizing the emotions of others. Recognizing the emotions of others is our ability to momentarily feel as another person does. It is not only our ability to see the path of others but to walk the path of others as well. **Empathy** is defined by Ronald Adler and George Rodman as the ability to recreate another person's perspective; to experience the world from the other's point of view (Adler and Rodman 1991). The ability to empathize with others is a strong indicator of high emotional intelligence.

Courtesy of D'Marcus Butler

The ability to empathize with others is a strong indicator of high emotional intelligence.

© 2012 Courtesy of JaxonPhotoGroup

Who is most popular in this picture? Is popularity their main goal?

Handling Relationships

Have you ever wondered why some students are more popular than others? Do you sometimes ask yourself how is it that some students can garner favor with professors and administrators while others do not?

Have you questioned why some of your friends are selected for opportunities while others with equal ability are never selected? Upon close examination, we are more than likely to find that the students selected are described as the students who possess positive attitudes, a strong worth ethic and exude synergy. Additionally, these students consistently demonstrate an astute ability to achieve both personal and academic objectives. Students who can achieve this balance project a positive energy and tend to connect with others because of their ability to achieve balance. Carla and Ariel find Brian attractive and enjoy the attention they receive from him. They assume Brian is popular because he's attractive, intelligent, and outgoing. Why do you think Brian is popular? Theorists would argue that Brian's popularity can be attributed to his ability to achieve balance in his relationship and in his life.

What's Your Score?

It is not surprising to learn that Goleman's theory of emotional intelligence has met some opposition. Many believe that the theory of emotional intelligence is much too broad to be fully explained using these five simple categories. An individual's emotional maturity is as complex as the individual. Some assert much more complexity than is claimed by Goleman's theory. Most theorists can and do agree, however, that if individuals exemplify behavior which is indicative of the attributes within the categories, they are more likely to be successful in their relationships with others.

Let's see how high your emotional intelligence is. In order to obtain a useful assessment, it important that you respond honestly and accurately.

Before you begin completing the chart, review the five categories once again. Next, rank yours behavior in each category using the numbers 1(Low) through 5(High). Lastly, total your scores to determine your rank.

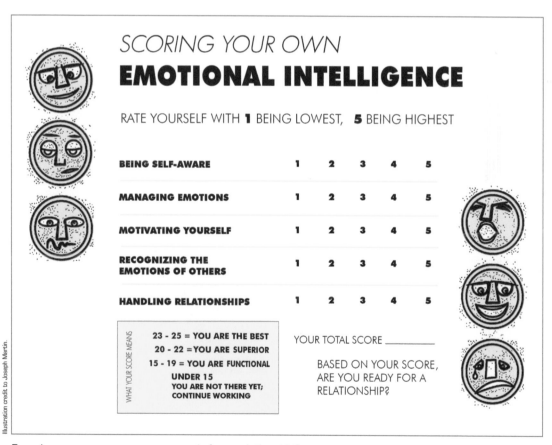

Based upon your score, are you ready for a relationship?

Strategic Flexibility

Self-concept is a combination of the way you view yourself and the value you place on yourself. Your self-concept is influenced by several factors: 1. the way others view you; 2. the way you compare yourself to others; 3. the values, beliefs, and attitudes taught within your culture; and 4. the way you evaluate yourself. All of the factors that determine your self-concept also influence your perception and emotional intelligence (DeVito 2005). As your perception level increases, your emotional intelligence is likely to increase and you will probably develop a high self-concept.

Your ability to engage in strategic flexibility is directly impacted by how you view yourself, how you perceive others, and your level of emotional intelligence. Strategic flexibility allows you to determine which emotions you should use in which situations. All of the emotions that you experience are not necessarily meant to be expressed every time they present themselves. As you mature, you are better able to identify your emotions as well as the situations that trigger them.

The more you engage in strategic flexibility, the better you become at controlling your emotions and associated behaviors. For instance, if you find yourself in a situation which you have already experienced, you instinctively know how to respond to that situation by using appropriate behaviors. Responding in such a manner increases your ability to communicate effectively and to achieve desired results.

Using strategic flexibility enables you to gain more control of your emotions and behaviors. When you have the ability to discipline and control your own behaviors, you become more secure within yourself. As a secure individual, you will become a better communicator in that you will be more willing and able to listen to and understand those who attempt to communicate with you. Ultimately, this will cause you to form more substantive and long-lasting relationships.

Attraction Driven Interaction

Individuals are driven to interact with others based on their attraction to them. The foundation of this is usually based one of the types of attractions described in this section.

Physical Attraction

Physical attraction is determined by one person's appeal to another person's physical qualities. You may find yourself physically attracted to a person based on various physical attributes. The various attributes which individuals usually find attractive are height, body build, facial features, style of dress, voice, etc. Many times people are also sexually attracted to a person for the same reasons. However, physical attraction alone does not function well as the basis of a long-term relationship (Beebe, Beebe and Ivy 2010).

Receivables Attraction

When individuals seek to interact with someone, they desire to receive something from that interaction. However, what they desire to receive may be different for each person. Some individuals desire interaction to gain a friend, while many others desire to a romantic

Photo courtesy of Charles Long

There are many factors that make up attraction to others. Physical attraction, perceived gain, similarities, differences, and proximity are some of them. What are the likely factors at play here?

partner. What individuals desire to receive is primarily based upon what their personal needs may be at the time. For instance, people who feel unsupported may desire to interact with someone who will provide them with support. Similarly, people who feel unloved will desire interaction with someone who might offer to love them.

Reflective Attraction

People usually interact with individuals who are reflections of themselves. The reflection is usually based on similarities. The areas of similarity that generally attract people to one another are beliefs, values, interests, and attitudes (Beebe, Beebe and Ivy 2010). For this reason, people often desire to interact with those individuals who "look like" them.

Magnetic Attraction

Relationships which are built on differences are usually exciting, but not stable. This is based on the fact that differences often cause conflict over a period of time, as related to beliefs, values, interests, and attitudes. Though magnets connect powerfully initially, they often lose strength over time and fall apart.

Localized Attraction

The concept of localized attraction suggests that people are more likely to interact with those who are near them physically and geographically. For instance, when developing relationships with peers, college students are more likely to develop relationships with individuals who live in their dormitories or take the same classes as they do because they share physical spaces and experiences. However, when these same individuals graduate from college and relocate to other regions, their level of contact usually decreases because of the physical distance between them (Beebe, Beebe and Ivy 2010).

In today's age computers, cell phones, and the internet, the concept of localized attraction is not as powerful as it was at one time. Now, individuals who are not physically near each other have many opportunities to communicate through emails, text messages, video chats, etc. Because of the existence of the above-mentioned communication options, localized attraction no longer has such a major impact on interpersonal interaction (Beebe, Beebe and Ivy 2010).

Specific interests may be so similar that they outweigh any differences.

Virtual Attraction

Since technology has become one of the norms in today's society, many individuals have interpersonal interactions in the virtual world. When communicating virtually, individuals do not have the advantage of viewing individuals' body language or hearing their voices. Instead, they must rely on the language used in emails, text messages, etc. The disadvantage is that people have the ability to hide their true selves behind the computer screen. The person presented virtually may be totally different from the person that exists in the flesh. As an example, many people become attracted to a person they have met on line, only to be disappointed when they actually meet them.

All relationships begin, and in some cases end, because of attraction. In relationships, it is sometimes not evident, until the relationship is in trouble, what attracts you to your partner. Now that you have an understanding of the six foundations for attractions, read the following story about Brain and Thomas. After reading the story, take a moment to discuss the questions that follow.

"Stop fidgeting," Thomas said.

Brian snapped out of his thoughts, realizing that he was fidgeting. He tried to sit still, but his nerves were getting the best of him. This was not how he envisioned his Saturday going.

"Maybe we should turn back," Brian thought out loud.

Thomas shook his head. "Not happening. We drove three hours on a Saturday to get here."

"Look, this is stupid," Brian said. "We're driving to someone's house unannounced."

"Why wouldn't we be welcomed?" Thomas asked sarcastically. "This is your girlfriend's house after all, right?"

"Enough man . . ."

"It's not like you haven't met her before or anything," Thomas continued. It's not like you've never seen her ever in your life!"

"Are you done?" Brian yelled.

Brian knew that this whole situation was crazy. He knew it from the beginning. From the first day Brittany befriended him on Facebook, he knew this whole situation was too good to be true.

In the beginning, they just talked. Brian had just lost his father to colon cancer and felt more alone than ever. Brittany listened to him. She slowly brought him back to life, in a way. As the relationship grew deeper and more intimate, he expressed his need to see her. He tried to get her to Skype and FaceTime, but she refused or stood him up.

Last spring break, they made a pact to meet each other down in Florida. Brian showed up, but Brittany did not. She didn't even return his calls, texts, or messages until after he was already home. Her excuse was sketchy, but he forgave her and continued on with the relationship.

It wasn't until Thomas decided to investigate, that things began to unravel. Thomas took one of Brittany's pictures from Facebook and dropped it in Google image. The image came on Brittany's page, as well as another page. He befriended the "other Brittany" and saw that she had several of the same pictures as Brian's Brittany.

Brittany also claimed that she was a member of her university's cheerleading team. After pulling up the roster from the university's sports page, Thomas found that there wasn't a Brittany on the team. Even after Thomas presented Brian with the information, Brian didn't believe it.

Thomas tracked down Brittany's address and finally convinced Brian to go to her house and prove him wrong.

"Look, I'm sorry, but what this girl is doing is unhealthy and not fair to you," Thomas sighed. "You need to confront this. This whole thing cannot go on anymore."

Brian nodded. "You're right. She owes me an explanation."

Thomas pulled into a driveway. The house looked decent. "Well, go get it," he said to Brian.

Brian exhaled deeply and stepped out of the car. He slowly walked up to the porch. Three pink-painted rocks sat next to the door with the names "Lisa," "Candice," and "Brianna" drawn on them. He rang the doorbell and waited for the door to open. He could hear voices, and one was familiar. He could hear Brittany yelling that she would answer the door.

Brian smiled as the door opened, but it quickly disappeared. This wasn't Brittany. He didn't know who this young woman was, but she knew him. He saw the flash of familiarity and horror cross her face.

"Brittany?" Brian questioned.

"No," she said softly. "I'm Brianna."

Dishonesty on the Internet is not uncommon today. In 2010, an independent documentary called Catfish was released, detailing dishonesty on the Internet. The film revolved around Nev Schulman, a young photographer who begins an online friendship with a young kid and later a romantic relationship with her older sister. As he grows closer to the family, he suspects that they are not who they say they are. After a thorough investigation with the help of his brother, Nev uncovers the truth and discovers that the young woman he had engaged with online was actually an older woman using the photos of a family friend's daughter.

The film garnered a lot of the attention and shed light on a growing epidemic. Since then, MTV has produced a successful television show centered on the two brothers in the film helping other people who may be engaging with dishonest people online. The term 'Catfishing' is a verb widely used in our culture.

At what point in the relationship should Brian have become suspicious?
What do you think is the true source of Brian's attraction to Brittany?
What type of attraction is needed for a relationship to be successful?
Can you be attracted to someone in more than one way?
What do you think Brian discovers after Brianna introduces herself to him?

Interaction Motivated Connectedness

Once people's attractions to others have driven them to interaction, they may be motivated to connect even further through communication. The desire for such a communication connection is based on the needs of individuals which are presented below.

Fun

People often find communication to be a fun activity. When you pick up the phone and call a friend, you usually expect the conversation to be an exciting exchange. The conversation may include a little dorm gossip or a discussion of current events, pop culture, or sports. No matter the topic, the motivation for the conversation is usually to have a little fun.

Socialization

Socialization is the desire to interact with others. Because it creates a sense of belonging, socialization is often the motivation individuals have for joining sororities and fraternities, attending parties, and hanging out with friends. Socializing with others can improve a person's health. Therefore, the desire to create and maintain a healthy lifestyle is a motivating factor for socializing with friends, family, and co-workers.

Avoidance

When people have no desire to complete a task or participate in an activity at particular time, they often avoid it through communication. Instead of writing the paper for class, they pick up the phone and call a friend. As opposed to going to the library to study, they go to the student center to hang out with friends. People also use the internet for avoidance by surfing the web or emailing when their focus should be a different computer-based activity, such as posting to the discussion board for an on-line course.

Affection is important to human happiness.

Release

Communicating with family and friends often motivates individuals to release. It gives them the opportunity to clear their minds of issues of concern (whether personal, educational or professional) and talk about things that are less stressful. After a long day of school or work, most people rely on communication to change their focus to something more relaxing.

Relationship Roles

A good friend once told me that when you are lying on your death bed, "How many of us would say, wish I had spent more time at work?" We are more likely to say, "I wish I had spent more time with my family and friends." When we consider what makes us happy in life, it usually involves being with people we enjoy. As we explore the fundamental aspects of interpersonal communication, we must begin with a discussion on the roles that people play in our lives. Relationships are defined as sets of expectations two people have for their behavior based on the pattern of interaction between them (Littlejohn 2002). When we attempt to classify relationships, we must start by recognizing the rules that apply to each type of relationship. In Shimanoff's relationship *rules theory*, he purports that relationships are held together by adhering to certain rules. Successful relationships are based upon our ability to master the social skills from their development to their maintenance (Shimanoff 1980).

In this section, we will investigate the types of relationships, including acquaintances, friends, co-workers, and intimates. Let's also look at the rules that apply to each.

Acquaintances

Acquaintances are defined as people we know by name and talk with as the opportunity arises, but our interaction is largely impersonal. Typically, our interaction with an acquaintance is because of a relationship that is defined by three factors: location, membership, and circumstances. Often times as one of the previous factors change so does the relationship. Carla and Natalie are members of the Student Government Association. They consider themselves acquaintances because they interact in that organization and rarely do they communicate outside of that context.

Friendship

If you sat down and made a list of all of your friends, how many names would end up on your list? For some of us the list would be quite long, and for others there would be very few names. Friendship is defined as a relationship between two people that is mutually productive, established and maintained through perceived mutual free choice, and characterized by mutual positive regard (Devito 2005). There are different types of friendships. According to John Reisman, there are three types of friendship including reciprocity, receptivity, and association (Reisman 1979). The most rewarding type of relationships are those that are based on reciprocity because they are based upon equality. There is a mutual giving, mutual sacrifice, and mutual generosity. The second type of friendship, receptivity is characterized where one person is the major giver and the other, the major receiver. The relationship is unequivocal, but the persons involved feel a degree of satisfaction. Lastly, a friendship of association is characterized by casual involvement and interaction. Even though term "friend" is used, it is more accurately defined as "friendly" (Resiman 1981).

Co-Workers

Most adults spend the majority of their time in the work environment. This environment involves a great deal of interaction between co-workers and their supervisors. Employers rarely equate productivity to a positive work environment and job satisfaction. However, an employee's job satisfaction greatly depends upon the environment and the successful interaction with coworkers. Co-workers must remember that to be successful in the work environment, they must have the ability to actively listen and respectfully respond to each other. In addition, they must be able to trust their co-workers. Co-workers should never reveal too much information about themselves. In fact, some topics should never be discussed among co-workers.

Intimates

In an intimate relationship, partners reach the highest level of disclosure. They share commitment and in most cases become romantically involved. We consider intimate relationships as those with whom we share our deepest feelings. It is not wise nor recommended to have multiple intimate relationships because of the costs and rewards that are experienced as a result of such relationships. Leslie Baxter suggests eight rules that couples should follow when involved in a romantic relationship (Baxter 1986):

1. Recognize that each has a life beyond the relationship.
2. Have and express similar attitudes and interests.
3. Reinforce each other's self esteem.
4. Be real, open and genuine.
5. Be faithful to each other.
6. Spend substantial time together.
7. Obtain rewards commensurate with your investment compared to the other party.
8. Experience inexplicable "magic" when together.

No Small Matter: Effective Conversations and Small Talk

The Conversation Formula

Successful interpersonal relationships are facilitated by effective communication. The effectiveness of interpersonal communication depends upon the quality and quantity of the information shared. Interpersonal communication or conversations establish and facilitate interpersonal relationships whether they are with family members, friends, colleagues or acquaintances. According to Roy Berko, Andrew Wolvin and Darlyn Wolvin, a *conversation* is an interaction with at least one other person (Berko, Wolvin, and Wolvin 2001). When we first encounter another person and a bid is accepted, the next interpersonal exchange takes the format of what is referred to as *scripted conversations*. Scripted conversations consist of a pattern of questions and answers with very little variation. Scripted conversations are often frequently referred to as *stereotypic* because they" follow clear, even rigid, rules in well-defined situations

When most people begin conversations, they engage in small talk.

(DeFleur, Kearney, and Plax 1993)." Scripted conversations can appear relaxed. The exchange can take on the appearance of spontaneity. Sometimes if the parties in the exchange make a strong connection, there will be a sense of comfort. If the two parties are on an equal level of power, the scripted conversation is typically less socially awkward and less rigid. The potentiality of the relationship progressing beyond the initial contact depends greatly upon the parties' ability to follow a scripted conversation which authors Melvin DeFleur, Patricia Kearney, and Timothy Plax state is analogous to a "play script" (DeFleur, Kearney, and Plax 1993). Once our interest moves beyond the obvious, typically the physical attraction and sometimes awkward scripted conversations, the parties will enter into the most important communication in which we can engage, *small talk*.

The Small Talk Formula

Small talk is defined as "discussions that focus on topics of general interest and have little emotional or personal significance (DeFleur, Kearney, and Plax 1993)." Without question, small talk is a skill. It is a skill upon which every successful dyadic social relationship depends. Small talk usually lasts no longer than fifteen minutes and is most likely to occur in what we would consider informal communication contexts such as sports events, wedding receptions, bars, parties and meetings or conferences. A typical progression of small talk may begin with information that is biographic and moves to that which that is considered more of a personal nature. During the ***biographic stage*** of small talk, the information that is exchanged usually consists of items such as your name and residency. You may also discuss your profession or occupation. When the conversation progresses to the **personal** *stage*, the discourse tends to include items of a more personal nature such as your interests and hobbies. You may possibly even discuss mutual friends and acquaintances. The final stage in small talk, the ***common ground stage*** occurs when both parties have exchanged enough information so that there is a presumption of minimal risks. During this time, the parties may adjust their nonverbal orientation. If they were standing, they may decide to find a comfortable place to sit down. If they were sitting, they would perhaps move to a quiet area in the room, separating themselves from others and intentionally excluding them from their discussion. In observing the nonverbal of the two parties, people in the room will assume that the two parties are having a private conversation. In this stage, the discussion includes not just factual information but stage the parties discover that there are common factors between them which not only link them together but allow them to feel safe. Because there is a presumption of trust during the common ground stage, the parties feel comfortable progressing to more indepth sharing.

The success of small talk is formulaic. If the two parties follow the socially acceptable pattern of small talk progression, the chance that the relationship will continue is greater. As we follow the scenario below, identify the places in the conversation that Carla and Brian break the socially acceptable pattern of small talk.

Carla: Hello Brian. How are you?

Brian: I'm good. You?

Carla: I'm fine. On my way to the library.

Brian: Oh yea, I'm walking that way too.

Carla: It's such a sunny day. I wish the library had a courtyard.

Brian: They had one at my old high school library. But they had to close it when the principal was caught selling drugs there.

Carla: My, my, my. That is simply awful. Do you use drugs, Brain?

Brian: Really? Are you serious?

Brian and Carla get off to a great start making small talk. Both parties stay within the accepted pattern of small talk until Brian takes the conversation in a serious direction by introducing the principal's behavior as the cause of the demise of his former school. The conversation moves beyond small talk when the parties discuss matters which involve feelings, beliefs, attitudes. Another sign that the time for small talk has exceeded is when the parties arrange to meet or talk in the future. They may exchange numbers so they can keep in touch or so they can arrange to have lunch or dinner.

You may ask yourself why small talk, a direct and simplistic communication exchange is stressed as critical to the success of relationships? Theorist Mark Knapp proposes that small talk is so important that it should be labeled, big talk (Knapp 1978). Small talk is viewed as a critical skill in communication because without it, relationships cannot and will not progress to the next stage in which more in depth information is shared. During the small talk period of interpersonal communication, each party can, without risks or commitment, assess if they are interested in furthering the interaction. Mark Knapp calls this process, 'an audition for friendship." Thespians understand and accept that some auditions will be successful while others will not. When we encounter someone for the first time, we remember that all small talk does not lead to the establishment of a closer relationship. Let's examine the factors that help us become more effective communicators when engaging in small talk.

Illustration credit to Joseph Martin.

Tips for Small Talk

1. **Stick to the script.** There is an accepted conversational pattern that should always be adhered to when engaging in small talk. Adhering to the structure ensures the parties will be comfortable with the information being exchanged and that the information will be interpreted correctly. Always keep the conversation positive and light.

2. **Read the nonverbal cues.** When engaging in small talk, it's important to pay close attention to what is being said, but it is just as important to pay attention to nonverbal cues. Often times, the word choice does not coincide with what is being expressed nonverbally. Therefore, always be observant of facial expressions, body movement and gestures, and eye movement. While participating in small talk, eye contact, nodding affirmatively and smiling are signs of interest. When nonverbal cues such as these are displayed, the receiver will perceive the interest goes beyond preliminary physical attraction.

3. **Ask questions.** One way to establish and stimulate small talk is by asking questions. In many ways, questions serve to pull the speaker into the conversation and maintain the movement of the dialogue. Keep in mind, most people's favorite subject is themselves.

4. **Minimize distractions.** It is considered rude and disrespectful to take phone calls, text or engage in extensive conversation with others while participating in small talk. Conversational focus involves paying attention to the speaker and giving feedback throughout the interaction. Conversational focus also helps us remember important information such as names, places and affiliations.

5. **Listen.** When participating in small talk, listening is critical. While listening to the speaker, the listening style may need to change from one type to another depending on the individual and the information being shared. In chapter two, we looked at the four listening styles and established which style you, as a communicator, use most often. During small talk, you may be a people–oriented listener at one point as you discover how the other party is feeling about the gathering you are currently attending. Later, as they begin to tell a story about their difficulty finding the location of the party, you may switch to an action-oriented listening style because you want them to get to the point they are trying to make, and so on. Most importantly, you never want to be accused of being a pseudo-listener, someone who is pretending to listen; nor a monopolizing listener, someone who is intent on redirecting the conversation back to themselves; nor a selective listener, someone who focuses on certain parts of the message and ignores other parts. Once listening misbehaviors such as these are detected, termination of small talk is inevitable.

Small talk should never be viewed as trivial or meaningless. In fact, quite the opposite is true. Small talk serves as the bridge between first impressions based primarily upon physical attractiveness and close relationships. You should never take small talk for granted and never minimize its importance. Research supports that small talk may be the most critical communication skill you can develop.

Relationship Call and Response: Bids and the Bidding Process

In any relationship, the individuals involved must engage in a call and response process in order to communicate successfully with each other. This is commonly called the bidding process. In relationship call and response, a call or bid is a request to feel emotionally connected. This "call" may take the form of a verbal question or statement or it may be a non-verbal gesture, look, or touch. The "response" to the call is the other person's answer to the request, which may be either positive or negative.

Some people are likely to be better at bids and responses than others.

Learning the Process

In order for the call and response process to work effectively, the individuals learn the unique ways in which their partners communicate a call and respond to a call. Both the call and response should be communicated in a positive manner. Partners should always respond to a request for emotional connection. A lack of response to a call will likely have a negative impact on the relationship.

Engaging in the Process

In order to engage in the call and response process, each individual must be willing to share with the other their method of sending out a call, their desired response to the call, as well as their method for response to calls. In this way, each partner will be able to identify the calls their partners send out and respond to them in an appropriate manner. Their willingness to receive and respond to each others' calls for emotional connectedness will have a positive impact on their relationship.

"I" Messages and "You" Messages

Thomas Gordon, communication theorist, suggests one way to prevent defensive and self-serving behaviors is by using what he termed "I" messages or owned messages (Gamble and Gamble 2009).

"You always talk when I'm trying to listen to the news." "You need to spend more time with me and get off of that computer." "You should stop acting like a slob and clean up this house." According to Thomas, communicators have the choice of sending either evaluative or nonevaluative feedback when engaging in discourse. The previous statements are considered "You" Messages because they all contain the word, "You." These statements cast blame and pass judgment on the receiver. When communicators replace "You" statements with "I" statements, they are more likely to elicit the type of behavior desired. In many instances, we choose words that place blame on the other party without taking into consideration the affect these words may have once they are spoken. While using "I" messages cannot guarantee the desired response will be obtained, one can be assured that using "You" messages will hinder the growth of a relationship.

Models of Self Disclosure: Social Penetration and The Johari Window

Today, many people use Twitter, Facebook, YouTube, Instagram, and various other forms of social media to manage the release of information about themselves. This trend is an indication that information that was typically mutually shared to achieve intimacy, including the intellectual, emotional and physical aspects of oneself, is no longer considered private. In fact, more often than not, such intimate details are placed on social media pages for everyone to see. People are more open to disclosing unedited intimate facts about themselves without realizing the consequences of their actions on future relationships. *Self disclosure* is the process of deliberately revealing information about oneself that is significant and that would not normally be known to others (Adler and Rodman 2012). Prior to the penetration of social media into our lives, self disclosure was dependent upon the nature of the relationship. Ask yourself, if the same can be said for today?

Telling a secret might be one form of self-disclosure.

The Social Penetration Model

For decades, social scientists have studied behavior in an attempt to understand the dynamics of self disclosure. What has evolved from their work are models which explicate how self disclosure factors into the development of interpersonal relationships. One model is *The Social Penetration Model*. Developed by social psychologists Irwin Altman and Dalmas Taylor, The Social Penetration theory model examines disclosure by measuring the breadth and depth of the information disclosed as relationships develop (Altman and Taylor 1973). The model consists of the layers, with varying widths and depths, through which the self-disclosure passes in developing relationships. Breadth refers to the range of information shared, whereas depth is the level of personal information shared. According to the theorists, as a relationship develops, the breadth and the depth increase. In intimate relationships, the breadth is great but the depth is even greater. The typical progression of a casual relationship to an intimate one occurs when it moves from the periphery to the center of the model. This development occurs slowly over a long period of time. Upon close examination of the Social Penetration Model, we might say it resembles peeling an onion. The outer layer is analogous to the breadth of a relationship. Information shared between romantic couples on this layer can be described as "superficial." As the outside ring or second layer is peeled away, the depth of disclosure increases. Here, the couple may exchange information about their beliefs and attitudes. The third layer reveals more intimate information. The couple focuses on their attitudes, values and most importantly feelings. At this layer, there is a significant investment made in the relationship in that an agreement of exclusivity is established. According to theorists, Stephen Littlejohn and Karen Foss, the couple begins to make future plans as it becomes clear that the rewards of the relationship outweigh the costs (Littlejohn and Foss 2008). Once the next layer is reached in the relationship, it is apparent that you have reached the core. When the core of the relationship is reached, the level of intimacy is at its greatest. Information shared at this level

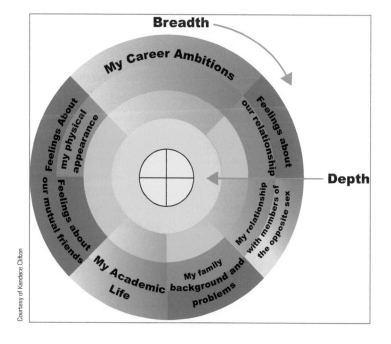

THE JOHARI WINDOW

	KNOWN TO SELF	UNKNOWN TO SELF
KNOWN TO OTHERS (DISCLOSURE AREAS)	**OPEN PANE** XXX	**BLIND PANE** BLIND TO SELF / SEEN BY OTHERS
UNKNOWN TO OTHERS (NON-DISCLOSURE AREAS)	**HIDDEN PANE** OPEN TO SELF / HIDDEN TO OTHERS	**UNKNOWN PANE** UNKNOWN TO SELF AND OTHERS

includes secrets that maybe be perceived as embarrassing or painful. When couples reach the core, they are willing to be vulnerable because a long term commitment such as marriage has been made.

The Johari Window Model

Another model that is used to explain the disclosure process is the Johari Window. The **Johari Window**, developed by Joseph Luft and Harry Ingram describes the relationship between self-disclosure and self-awareness. The Johari Window describes human interaction by depicting the four different levels of knowledge that exist in our relationships with others (Luft 1969). The four window panes are labeled as **open**, **blind**, **hidden**, and **unknown** (Luft 1970). Let's take a closer look at how each pane's designation is determined and the type of information that may be found within each pane.

PANE I—Open

The open pane consists of information that is *known to others* and *known to self.* The open pane includes information that you would willingly disclose to your partner or observations that your partner has shared with you. During your initial meeting, you may observe a person's sex, skin tone, weight, and height. The information freely disclosed by the partners may be names, hometowns, dormitory, courses in which they are enrolled and perhaps career aspirations. After the first few meetings, you may begin to disclose additional facts about yourself like your family composition and your personal likes and dislikes. When Carla meets Brian in the opening scenario, what information would be viewed in the open pane?

PANE 2—Hidden

The hidden pane is sometimes referred to as the secret pane as it contains information that is *known to you* and *not known to others.* This pane may contain information ranging from incidents that happened in your past that you rather not disclose due to fear of embarrassment or the impact that knowledge of this information may have on your future.

Regardless, the information in the hidden pane is considered personal and private and we should be very selective of who and when we disclose it. We can expect, however, to share more information in the hidden window as the relationship grows. As the hidden pane shrinks, the open pane naturally gets expands. Let's imagine Brian and Carla have been dating for two years, what personal and private facts about them may shift from the hidden pane to the open pane?

Pane 3—Blind

The information included within the blind pane includes behavior and idiosyncrasies that are *known to others* and *not known to you*. Has anyone ever accused you of committing an etiquette faux pas that you had no idea that you were guilty of doing? The idiosyncrasies of smacking when you eat or popping gum may be recognized by others. Some may even find these habits offensive. Let's hope that no one would intentionally commit an action that is annoying or offensive, but it happens all the time. These are examples of behaviors that are indicative of the blind pane. One evening when Brian and Carla were having dinner, Brian disclosed to Carla that he has a half brother that was the product of his father's extra marital affair. When Brian chose to disclose this information to Carla, he moved this information from the blind pane into the open pane. Whenever Carla is asked a question about her previous relationships, she begins blinking frantically. Brian asked her one day if the subject made her uneasy because whenever he mentions it, he notices that she reacts with nervous blinking. Prior to receiving Brian's feedback, Carla was unaware that she reacted in that manner. Whenever information moves from the blind pane to the open pane it is due to disclosure and feedback. As the blind pane becomes smaller, the open pane will become larger.

Pane 4—Unknown

While Brian and Carla have been dating for several years, neither of them can be certain that they will one day make a long term commitment, such as marriage. Do you know what you plan to do when you graduate from college? Are you planning to enter the workforce or attend graduate or professional school? Do you plan to move back home with your nuclear family or are you going to establish a residency in another location? The answers to these questions may not be known to you nor to anyone else. Information that is *unknown to you* and *unknown to others* falls within the unknown area or fourth pane. Often times, information that is repressed remains so until we are capable of dealing with it. Sometimes information in this unknown pane remains there until it is accidently discovered. In both cases, time is the key to information moving from the unknown pane to the open pane.

In summary, the Johari Window is an excellent model to use as we examine disclosure and feedback in relationships. Research supports the assertion that men and women disclose information with their partners at different levels and at different stages in relationships. Women are more likely to disclose personal information than their male counterparts. Men are more likely to disclose personal information in casual acquaintances than women (Stokes, Fueherer and Childs 1980). Overall, the more willing you are to communicate your feelings, attitudes, and beliefs and the more apt you are in encouraging feedback from others, the larger your open pane will be.

Improving Self Disclosure: Risks and Rewards

Now that we have a better understanding of interpersonal communication and have examined closely the ways in which we reveal personal information about ourselves to others, let's look at the ways we can improve self disclosure by minimizing the risks and maximizing the rewards. Most people would agree that self disclosure is essential in developing and maintaining a healthy and satisfying relationship. If we desire more than a superficial relationship, there must be self disclosure. As important as self disclosure is, it is equally as risky. In *Motivations Underlying Topic Avoidance in Close Relationships*, Walid Affifi and Laura Guerrero state, "Individuals often choose to avoid disclosure rather than risk the perceived personal or relational consequences" (179). In order to minimize risks and enjoy the rewards of self disclosure, let's look at some essential guidelines.

Guidelines for Self Disclosure

1. Self Disclosure must occur gradually. As we disclose personal information about ourselves, we also make ourselves vulnerable. In doing so, we are susceptible to disappointment. By releasing information gradually, we minimize the likelihood that the person to whom we confide in will use it in an inappropriate or harmful manner. In essence, by managing the release of personal information, we manage damage and increase intimacy.

2. Self Disclosure must be reciprocated. Just as self disclosure must occur gradually, it must also be a two-way process. Unequal self disclosure leads to an unequal relationship which will ultimately come apart. Think for a moment if you would, what would happen if Carla discloses to Brian personal information about her previous sexual activities, but Brian evades any discussion about his previous sexual encounters? This would eventually create an imbalanced relationship. Inevitably, Brian will begin to formulate an opinion of Carla that she will feel compelled to defend. Whenever disclosure is not reciprocated in a relationship, trust issues will ensue. Researchers Valerian Derlega, Sandra Metts, Sandra Petronio, and Stephen Margulis state that people expect a kind of equity in disclosure (Derlega, Metts, Petronio and Margulis 1993).

3. Self Disclosure must be appropriate. The inability to discern when and to whom to disclose personal information will lead to problems in the future. One should reserve disclosure of personal information for relationships that have reached a desired level of intimacy. One way to ensure embarrassment early in a relationship is by revealing personal information in a professional setting to acquaintances or business associates. For example, it would not be wise to reveal intimate personal information at the holiday office party.

Strategies for Good Relationships

Carla and Brian have been involved in a committed relationship for four years now. As their relationship grew to a level of intimacy, they incorporated certain skills and strategies which have helped them develop and maintain what can be characterized as a strong and satisfying relationship. How did they accomplish such a milestone?

The skills and strategies required to maintain long lasting relationships can be learned and enhanced as a relationship develops. Relationships are challenging. Our response to these challenges can be codified with the following specific skills and strategies:

1. Express emotions. In healthy relationships, it is important to understand the differences between expressing your emotions and being "emotional." Once a relationship reaches intimacy, the partners should

Photo courtesy of Charles Long

Once a relationship reaches intimacy, the partners should feel comfortable sharing their feelings and expressions.

feel comfortable sharing their feelings and expressing emotional reactions in appropriate situations. Often times it is viewed as negative when we express emotions. However, in a strong relationship, the expression of emotions will not be perceived as weak or vulnerable but be viewed as a healthy expression in a secure and comfortable relationship.

2. Engage in discourse. When involved in an interpersonal relationship, it is essential that each partner is willing to communicate and engage in constructive discourse. It is not unusual if one partner does more initiating and maintaining of the conversation. In fact, in most relationships this is the norm. This becomes problematic when the least talkative partner refuses to engage. In cases such as these, it becomes difficult, if not impossible to achieve a discourse level known as "relationship talk." **Relationship talk** is discourse about the nature, quality, direction, or definition of a relationship. An interpersonal relationship cannot exist at the intimate state without relationship talk. In such cases, the relationship is more than likely to fail (Beebe, Beebe, and Redmond 2005).

3. Be aware of nonverbal cues. Nonverbal analysis can make a critical difference in the effective communication in an interpersonal relationship. When partners engage in conversation, often times the verbal expression and the nonverbal clues are not in sync. Therefore, it is important to be able to discern and interpret what nonverbal messages are being transmitted. We use sayings such as "you're wearing your heart sleeves" and "it's written all over your face" without giving them much weight. In relationships it is important to keep in mind that the truth may be not be in the words but in the actions. Your ability to interpret can mean the difference between a satisfying relationship and an unfulfilling one.

4. Encourage compromise. A wise man once told me that compromise is not healthy. I adamantly refuted this claim and his assumption. Compromise by its very nature means that the results of a negotiation yields a "win, win" outcome. It is important to remember that when negotiating in a relationship, fairness is tantamount to its success.

5. Express care and affection. Care and affection are simple words. However, they are interpreted differently by different people. Through the process of self disclosure, partners can learn how to best foster and nurture their partner's needs. Once these needs are identified, partners cannot be hesitant to express their desire to meet those needs. This does not in any way require grand gestures, however, frequent and appropriate expressions are appropriate and necessary. For example, Friday flowers may be an expression of affection and appreciation for Carla, whereas Ariel may appreciate an evening of baking cookies with her significant other.

Courtesy of D'Marcus Butler

6. Commit, Commit or Quit. Relationships are in a constant state of change. When you are involved in a relationship, it is important to communicate when your needs are being met as well as when the costs are greater than the rewards. In order for relationships to overcome difficulty there has to be a commitment and a strong desire by both parties to address problems and agree to work collaboratively to reach a solution. If the commitment is not mutual, the relationship will eventually dissolve.

Electronically Mediated Communication and Relationships

If you were born mid-to-late 1990s you have never known a world where computer technology wasn't a part of our daily lives. As a child you probably mimicked your parents talking on a cell phone with your plastic toy phone. Being allowed to have a Facebook page served as a rite of passage in your childhood, and more than likely you had class in a school where computers served as the main tool in the class. Unlike your parents and grandparents, you grew up in world where you can use computer based technology to communicate with anyone from any corner of the world. Communication that involves the use of electronic equipment is known as electronically mediated communication (EMC) (Contributors of Linguistics 2003).

Cell Phones

Cell phones have now become a chief tool used for interpersonal communication. Cell phones not only allow us to talk to one another, but they also serve as an all-in-one and have several features including video cameras, recorders, notepads, task managers, portable libraries, wireless e-mail carriers, address books, and MP3 players.

People now use cell phones to replace the need for face-to-face communication. No matter how significant or insignificant, people can relay messages with cell phones and text messaging to communicate. Cell phones have allowed us to stay connected with one another every second, minute, and hour of the day.

Although the cell phone has been a wonderful tool, it still has its drawbacks. How many times has your cell phone gone off in the middle of a class or another important moment? Cell phones are constantly interrupting us. Their interruptions are so common that reminders to turn off cell phone ringers display on our screens before movies and are printed on the bottom of pages in playbills at theatres. Cell phones are distracting. Cell phones prevent us from communicating face-to-face. Aside from hindering us from participating in the main purpose of their existence, communication, cell phones prevent us from being aware of our surroundings. According to a study performed by the National Highway Traffic Safety Administration, text messaging is by far the worst offense when it comes to distracted drivers. Because text messaging requires visual, manual, and cognitive attention from the driver, it reigns over all other distractions. NHTSA also concluded "texting drivers" are 23X more likely to crash their vehicle (NHTSA 2012).

Internet

According to The Social Skinny, in one year, we will share 415 pieces of content on Facebook; we'll spend an average of about 23 minutes a day on Twitter, upload 196 hours of video on YouTube, and send countless emails (Pring 2012). The internet is a superhighway that extends farther than the eye can see and contains more information than probably all of the libraries in the world. Aside from knowledge, the internet is probably the most universal form of communication.

Positive Aspects of Internet Use

The internet has allowed for business and other work-related tasks to be performed quicker and easier. With the strokes of few keys and clicks of a mouse, e-mails can be sent and documents can be transported from one computer to the next. Conferences and business meetings with people in different states and even countries can be conducted with use of the internet and a camera.

Within the academic arena, the internet can allow students to access information that would have required them hours or even days to search to find. Students use the internet to share notes, interact with one another, and even communicate with their advisors and teachers. The internet has also allowed for older adults to return to school and obtain degrees with the creation of virtual classrooms. Schools like the University of Phoenix, Devry University, and even Ivy League colleges and universities, such as Harvard, Yale, and Columbia are now offering courses that are taught through virtual classrooms. (Cochran 2012)

The internet has broken through our psychological and emotional barriers. With the help of the internet, people who would have never talked face-to-face or at all because of race, religion, creed, or lifestyle differences are now able to connect on a fair playing ground. The internet has created a place where people can connect with others who are that experiencing similar things and share similarities. For example, the *It Gets Better Project* was a movement geared toward empowering and dissuading young gay youth from committing suicide due to bullying. The movement was primarily fueled by positive message videos placed on YouTube by celebrities, parents of gays, and other supporters. The videos received record breaking views, connected several people together and gained national media coverage (Savage 2010).

Negative Aspects of Internet Use

As with everything, too much of a good thing can be bad. The internet has risks. These risks can be intensified with constant, continued use. The internet has served as gateway to cyber addiction, cyber bullying, and cyber stalking.

Cyber Addiction

Cyber addiction is defined excessive computer use that interferes with daily life (Conner 2004). With Facebook, Twitter, Tumblr, and even YouTube on the rise, people are finding easier ways to disconnect with and abandon the people and world surrounding them. Cyber addicts can have different activities on the web that can persuade them into engaging in this type of behavior. Some of these activities can be gambling, compulsive shopping, cyber-sex, and social media. The potential consequences for new Internet users are significant and may be growing. Nearly 20% of the people going on-line will encounter one or more of the following problems.

• Personal neglect
• Compulsive checking and "clicking"
• Isolation and avoidance from people
• Lost productivity
• Depression
• Marital problems
• Sexual addiction
• Gambling away savings.
• Internet abuse in the workplace
• Academic failure.

(Conner 2004)

Cyber Bullying

"Jumping off the gw bridge now. sorry." That was last Facebook status update 18-year-old Tyler Clementi would ever post. On September 22, 2010, Clementi committed suicide by jumping off the George Washington Bridge after his roommate recorded Clementi having intimate encounters with another man (CBS 2010). The Clementi tragedy is a prime example of cyber bullying.

Cyber Bullying involves the use of information and communication technologies to support deliberate, repeated, and hostile behavior by an individual or group, that is intended to harm others (Presley 2010). Online harassment, or cyber bullying, ranges from insignificant annoyances to genuine threats. This type of bulling transcends other forms of bullying because comments and posts on the internet can never be deleted entirely and last forever. The effects of bullying can include the following:

• Depression
• Problems at school
• False sense of security

- Anger and behavioral issues
- Stress and other health related problems
- Substance abuse
- Suicidal thoughts, attempts, and or suicide (Teacher Today 2011)

There are only fourteen states that include cyber bullying under their bullying laws (Hinduja and Patchin 2012).

Cyber Stalking

Have your friends ever called you a "Facebook stalker" because you patrol your crush's Facebook page, looking out for competition that may steal his or her affection? While your intentions may be innocent, others may participate in what is known as cyber stalking. Cyber stalking is threatening behavior or unwanted advances directed at another using the Internet and other forms of online and computer communications. Cyber stalkers target their victims through chat rooms, message boards, discussion forums, and e-mail. Cyber stalking takes many forms such as: threatening or obscene e-mail; spamming, live chat harassment or flaming (online verbal abuse), leaving improper messages on social media profiles, tracing another person's computer and Internet activity, and electronic identity theft.

Similar to stalking off-line, online stalking can be a terrifying experience for victims, placing them at risk of psychological trauma, and possible physical harm. Many cyber stalking situations do evolve into off-line stalking, and a victim may experience abusive and excessive phone calls, vandalism, threatening or obscene mail, trespassing, and physical assault (National Center of Victims Crime 2003).

Social Media and Blogs

Most people can't go days or even a certain number of hours without checking either their Facebook, Twitter, or Instagram accounts. It's also the fasting growing activity on the net. On average, about 11 new twitter accounts are created every second. Also, on a busy day Twitter can see over 175 million tweets (Pring 2012). Around 75 million users post and view pictures and videos on Instagram daily. Needless to say, social media is probably the most preferred form of communication among teens and young adults.

FaceBook and Twitter

Facebook generally sees over a billion posts a day from its 845 million active viewers (Pring 2012). The website serves as a place where friendships can be formed, continued, and even strengthened. Most news and events that happen on college campuses can be circulated through the use of Facebook. Once deemed as a website only visited by young people, the Facebook user has significantly grown older. According to a recent study, 45% of active Facebook users are 65 years old or older. While Facebook has grown older, other social media platforms have emerged and are being utilized by upcoming generations. Facebook and Twitter now go hand in hand with this generation. Twitter allows users to share thoughts with the user's audience of followers. The creation of a relationships or communication with people that was once impossible is now possible. Twitter and Instagram are even used as a tool by celebrities to connect and share their lives with fans. Instagram took sharing your life to another level. With the ability to capture life's biggest moments with the camera on your phone, Instagram provided a platform to share your photos with not only your audience of followers, but (with the help of a hashtag) the whole world. Instagram is so integral to how we perceive one another that one may think they have a sense of who a person is based on their pictures on Instagram.

Blogs

What type of blogs do you frequent on a daily basis? Do you like to visit fashion blogs or Tumblrs to inspire future outfits? Do you like visit movie review blogs so you know what movie you should go out and see or simply wait for it to hit your nearest REDBOX? Blogs have become one of the easiest and fastest publishing tools available. In a blink of an eye, you can set up a domain using a free host and you can write on any topic and generate a following and (with a little business sense) create another source of income.

Summary

In this chapter we have explored the theories that explain the motives for interpersonal interaction, types of relationships, models for relationship development, key strategies for good relationships, and the impact and role of media on relationships. These ideas establish a foundation for understanding how relationships develop and more importantly how to maintain them. As we move to the next chapter, we will gain insight as to how these concepts are interdependent. But first, let's recap:

Most communication theorists agree that interpersonal communication is the most critical aspect of successful personal relationships. Interpersonal communication is defined as, "one person interacting with another often in an informal, unstructured setting."

In the collaborative work, Close Relationships, Harold Kelley, a pioneer in social psychology describes a close relationship as "one that is strong, frequent and that lasts over a considerable period of time." Additionally, Personal Relationships by Kelley states that there are critical components of an interpersonal relationship: 1. Interdependence in the consequences of specific behaviors, 2. Interaction that is responsive to one another's outcomes, and 3. Attribution of interaction events to dispositions.

Before we make an attempt to engage in a relationship, it is important to first make a concerted effort to understand ourselves. Intrapersonal communication is described as the understanding of self. One measure of understanding oneself is emotional intelligence which is described as the ability to understand and get along with others. According to theorist Daniel Goleman, emotional intelligence can be determined by assessing attributes and behaviors within five categories: Being Self-Aware, Managing Emotions, Motivating Yourself, Recognizing Emotions in Others, and Handling Relationships. Successful relationships are based up our ability to master these social skills from their development to their maintenance. In Shimanoff's relationship rules theory, he purports that relationships are held together by adhering to certain rules. In this chapter we investigated the four types of relationships, including acquaintances, friends, co-workers, and intimates.

The effectiveness of interpersonal communication depends upon the quality and quantity of the information shared. A conversation is an interaction with at least one other person. Scripted conversations consist of a pattern of questions and answers with very little variation. Small talk is viewed as a critical skill in communication because without it, relationships cannot and will not progress to the next stage in which more in depth information is shared. We also learned that "You" messages will hinder the growth of a relationship, according to Thomas Gordon.

Self disclosure is the process of deliberately revealing information about oneself that is significant and that would not normally be known to others. Social Penetration and The Johari Window are two models which explain self disclosure.

What's your poison? Is it cell phones, E-mail, instant messaging, blogs, social networking, or even teleconferencing? Or maybe all of the above? No matter what method, EMC is an integral component of interpersonal relationships. The advancements of the internet, cell phones, and social networking have allowed communication to reach new heights. However these tools do contain their risks, and we as users must use them responsibly.

Communication for Today's Student

Chapter 4 – Interpersonal Relationships

Exercise 4.1 – Virtual Johari Window

THE VIRTUAL JOHARI WINDOW

The Johari Window was developed by Joseph Luft and Harry Ingham as way of explaining and understanding the process of disclosure. For this assignment, you will _CONSTRUCT_ the Johari Window. This visual exercise will allow you to understand the process of self-disclosure and self-perception.

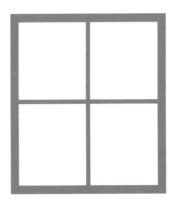

This assignment will either be constructed manually or digitally. In order to construct the Johari Window digitally, Microsoft Office or Adobe Office Suite programs can be used to design this project. Manually: Using a piece of poster board or cardboard, plywood etc., construct the background for the Johari Window. Use four sheets of 8 ½ × 11 paper to make the (four) panes for the background. Label all <u>parts</u>. Use a 2 or 3 dimensional object that illustrates each pane and adhere the object to the pane in additional to labeling the pane. The object should personify the criteria for the pane. Make sure you label the horizontal (x) and vertical axis (y) on the window. Please write your <u>name</u> on the back of the board. In addition, make sure your images are good color representatives for each panel. If you choose to illustrate your window virtually, you can paste/cut items that represent your personal items in each window. Do not forget to label. You will be evaluated on your use of creativity.

Supplies Required:

Foam board, Poster board, or Cardboard

Arts and Crafts supplies

Personal items that represent each panel

BUILDING RELATIONSHIPS

After reading this chapter, you should be able to:

- ☒ Identify the stages in the development and deterioration relationships.
- ☒ Explain the major advantages and disadvantages of engaging in relationships.
- ☒ Discuss the costs and rewards of relationships.
- ☒ Explain how conflict impacts relationships.
- ☒ List and explain the steps in conflict resolution.
- ☒ Discuss the advantages and disadvantages of online relationships.

Key Terms

Aggression	Conflict	Intensifying
Avoidance	Differentiating	Negative criticism
Avoiding	Experimenting	Owned messages
Bonding	"I" messages	Social exchange theory
Circumscribing	Immediate rewards and costs	Stagnating
Coming apart	Initiating	Terminating
Coming together	Integrating	"You" messages

5 Scenario

"Carla waved her hand, signaling the waiter to come over to her table.

"May I have the check, please?" Carla asked rudely.

As the waiter hurried off, Carla shook her head in disbelief. She couldn't believe Brian had stood her up again. This was the fourth time and Carla was fed up. A dramatic change had occurred between them and Carla feared the worst. They were growing apart, becoming more and more distance. At first Carla simply thought that the distance was because of Brian's increased hours at the hospital. Not wanting to appear too clingy, or worse unsupportive about his ambition to become a doctor, she tried to understand. But as time went on they began having fights and then that progressed to them not speaking every day and making no effort to see each other. Not wanting to lose Brian, Carla began trying harder to fight for the relationship. The only thing she received in return was four dinners alone.

The waiter approached the table and passed Carla the bill. She simply placed her money inside and thanked the waiter. As she took the last gulp of her wine she looked across the restaurant. It was the first restaurant where she and Brian had dinner. She remembered how they closed down the place, just laughing and talking. Now she was leaving, alone. She grabbed her coat and walked out of the restaurant. As she slowly walked to the car, she heard someone running down the side of the street.

"Carla!"

Carla recognized the timbre of his voice. She ignored it and continued to walk to her car. It wasn't until Brian darted in front of her, blocking her path that she stopped. There Brian was, all out of breath, two hours late, and in Carla's mind, out of time.

Carla folded her arms across her chest, waiting for Brian to move. He stood upright, his breathing slowly going back to normal, and his gaze focusing on her face. She knew he was assessing her mood. By the look in her eye, Brian knew to tread softly if he wanted to make it out of this unscathed.

"Carla," he began, "I'm so sorry."

"You sure are sorry, Brian," Carla said flatly. "Only a sorry individual would stand up his girlfriend not once, but four times."

"Carla, I was stuck at work."

"Before you tell me a lie, know that I stopped by the hospital today. They said you were off." Carla watched all the blood drain from Brian's face. He wasn't expecting that. Every emotion was etched on his face and Carla smirked. "Now, do you want to run that by me again?"

"You went to my job?" he frowned.

"You can't be serious!" Carla threw her arms up in the air. "Are you serious? That's what you say to me after trying to play me for a fool?"

"Carla, I don't mean to lie to you," Brian said. "I hate doing it."

"Then tell me the truth," Carla said. "Tell me the truth about everything. Tell me the truth about us and where are we going."

"I don't want to hurt you," Brian said softly.

The fear Carla felt earlier resurfaced. It was beginning to form a lump in her throat.

"Too late for that Brian," Carla said. Brian didn't say anything. He just continued to stare at her, afraid to speak. Carla shook her head and exploded. "Brian, just say it! You give people bad news every day. It's your job. So just say it!"

"I cheated on you," he said simply.

The words effortlessly left his lips, but punched her with such a force. The lump in her throat grew bigger and her eyes burned with a familiar feeling that she hated. Brian's hands reached for her, but Carla moved away.

"I'm sorry I shouldn't have . . ."

"No, you did as I asked," Carla finally said. "You ripped the bandage off."

Silence fell over them again. Brian rubbed the back of his neck, while looking up in the night sky. Carla was familiar with the action. He did that whenever he was frustrated. She shook her head. She knew this man like the back of her hand, right down to his mannerisms. She wanted to scream, but couldn't. She wanted to look away from him, but she couldn't.

Brian's eyes refocused on her. He moved towards her again. "We can fix this."

Once again Carla moved from his grasp. "No."

"Carla, don't say that," Brian said. "She didn't mean a . . ."

"She meant a lot if she took you away from me," Carla said.

"Carla!"

"It's over Brian."

Silence overcame them once again for the final time.

Now that he has confessed, what, if anything, could Brian say to prevent Carla from terminating the relationship?

Respond Here

Have you ever been in a committed relationship? How long did the relationship last? What were some of the factors that led to the termination of the relationship? Were there identifiable shortcomings on the part of both parties? In what ways were you and your partner compatible? Was there a sense of romance present throughout the relationship? Was affection reciprocal? If not, when did you first observe that there was less verbal and nonverbal interaction? Did you ever visit an online dating site while you were involved in that relationship? If answering any of these questions truthfully made you feel a sense of anxiety, you are not alone.

In his Relational Development Model, communication theorist Mark L. Knapp describes ten stages of the development and deterioration of relationships. In this model, he identifies five stages of relationship development known as *coming together*. The stages in the coming together process include initiating, experimenting, intensifying, integrating, and bonding. The process of relationship deterioration, labeled *coming apart*, is comprised of differentiating, circumscribing, stagnating, avoiding, and lastly terminating (Knapp 1978).

Knapp further explains that relationships are in a constant state of change. He characterizes the relationship development process as a series of feelings, beliefs, attitudes, behaviors, and actions. While other theorists have proposed concepts on relationship development and decline, Knapp's theory is endorsed by most communication experts for its completeness in capsulating this human phenomena.

Coming Together
Initiating

When Brian and Carla first met, they engage in superficial conversation and small talk. Generally, there is an assessment with regards to physical attractiveness, verbal and nonverbal responses. In the initiating stage, couples formulate their first impressions and decide whether they are interested in pursuing future contact. This stage is particularly challenging to people with shy tendencies. Even though this stage is usually brief, this initial encounter is typically filled with mutual feelings of nervousness, uneasiness and anxiety.

The joys of entering the initiating stage are enormous.

Experimenting

In the experimenting stage, partners seek to go beyond superficial dialogue. They engage in self disclosure with greater breadth. Since self disclosure should occur gradually over a period of time and should never be rushed, it is important that only low risk facts and opinions are discussed during this stage. During the experimenting stage, Brian and Carla may meet for coffee at the local coffee shop and casually discuss topics such as their favorite musicians, athletic teams, or vacations they have taken. This stage is one in which partners make a conscious effort to seek out common interests and experiences.

Intensifying

Brian and Carla have been spending a great deal of time together because they truly enjoy each other's company. In the intensifying stage, couples share information on a variety of topics, in addition to discussing private things. At this stage, trust becomes a major factor. Partners feel comfortable that their secrets

In the intensifying stage, closeness is wanted and needed.

will be kept in confidence and risk taking is done without hesitation. When a relationship enters the intensifying stage the couple may display affection including flirting and touching. With the intensifying stage comes plans for the future and statements of commitment are expressed.

Integrating

The integrating stage is characterized as one in which individual personalities begin to merge. During this stage Ariel, Carla's best friend, began to feel alienated because Carla and Brian were spending so much time together. Couples in the integrating stage may begin to acquire common property, frequent the same social circles, and visit each other's families during holidays. They may, for example, share a favorite song that commemorates their relationship and no longer feel they are obligated to practice courtship inducements. Theodore Avtgis, Daniel West, and Raci Anderson state that in the integrating stage, people expect to see them together, and they are seldom seen apart (Avtgis, West and Anderson 1998).

Bonding

Brian has planned a special evening which will begin with dinner at Carla's favorite restaurant and culminate with a quiet walk on the moonlit waterfront. After the romantic walk, he plans to ask Carla if she would consider becoming his wife after graduation. Brian and Carla have entered into the bonding stage of their relationship. This stage is one in which the couple makes a formal commitment and makes their commitment known to others. Most often, couples discuss future plans, financial interdependence, and possible common employment opportunities. It's important to remember that the bonding stage typically occurs in romantic relationships, however bonding experiences can take place in other types of dyads as well. For example, bonding can occur within military troops, between college roommates, or among fraternity or sorority members. Once a couple has bonded, dissolving the relationship becomes problematic due to legal issues, social stigmas or religious beliefs.

In the bonding stage, the couple makes a formal commitment.

Coming Apart

In the introduction of this chapter, you were asked to reflect on issues regarding previous relationships. As you reflected and began to identify some of the early signs of relationship deterioration, you may have asked yourself, "How could I have not seen the impending outcome of that relationship?" In an ideal world, once a relationship has reached the stage of bonding, the couple would live "happily ever after." However, based upon the percentage of marriages which end in divorce each year, we know that this is not always the case. In 2011, 49% of marriages resulted in divorce (Worldwide Divorce Statistics 2012). The deterioration of a relationship depends upon several factors. Interpersonal theorists assert that the number one reason for relationship failure is lack of communication. Also, the manner in which the relationship is terminated greatly depends upon the stage at which the relationship begins to deteriorate. For example, if the relationship begins to deteriorate in the intensifying stage, there is likely to be greater expression of remorse and regret. If the relationship reaches the intensifying stage, termination may require numerous exchanges both verbal or written. Termination attempted during the experimental stage, may be accomplished by simple avoidance.

According to Mark Knapp, the deterioration of the relationship typically begins with a major conflict or disagreement. Let's examine what happens in a relationship when a couple does not make a concerted commitment to maintain the relationship once it is challenged. The deterioration of the relationship will progress through the following stages: differentiating, circumscribing, stagnating, avoiding, and ultimately, lead to termination.

Differentiating

Communication in the differentiating stage takes on a tone of negativity. Verbal messages in this stage are used to criticize and accentuate perceptions of differences. They often include what Thomas Gordon describes as "You" messages rather than "I" messages which ultimately leads to playing the "blame game". In the differentiating stage there is a focus on individual identities and discourse includes the desire and need for autonomy. There is no band-aid for a relationship once it has reached the differentiating stage, however if the partners in the relationship are willing to make a commitment to negotiate their differences, the relationship may survive. In some cases the relationship may end up even stronger than before. This requires interpersonal communication and conflict management skills. If the couple's relationship survival kit does not include these two tools the relationship is more than likely to continue down the path to termination.

There is no band-aid for a relationship once it has reached the differentiating stage.

Circumscribing

In the circumscribing stage, the communication, interests, and commitment level decreases. Discourse on certain topics is discontinued in an attempt to avoid overt or direct conflict. The relationship often times suffers due to the decrease in intimacy. While the relationship is in turmoil in private, public interaction is disguised to give the appearance to others that the relationship is stable. Since many topics are considered off limits, restoring the relationship becomes increasingly difficult. Once the relationship reaches the circumscribing stage, third party consultation is recommended. If the lines of communication are re-established, the couple may eventually be able to overcome conflict and rekindle the excitement they experienced during the intensifying stage. If this does not occur, the relationship will continue to decline to the stagnating stage.

In the circumscribing stage, the relationship is in turmoil.

Stagnating

The stagnation stage in the decline of a relationship occurs when communication focuses primarily on superficial topics. The relationship shows no signs of growth and it becomes obvious that the couple's need for inclusion,

In the stagnating stage, the relationship shows no signs of growth.

openness, and control are not being met. In the stagnating stage, one or both partners will seek intimacy outside the relationship in order to fulfill the need of socialization. Carla and Brian constantly argue about his relationship with his previous girlfriend. Even though Brian reassures Carla that his previous girlfriend is not a threat to their relationship, Carla refuses to accept it because Brian spends several evenings each week playing "golf" with her. Carla's need for inclusion is not being met while it appears Brian's need of socialization is. The relationship will decline to the avoiding stage if an alternative, which may include confiding in friends, immersing themselves in work, and other social and benevolent activities, is pursued.

Avoiding

Couples can remain in the stagnating stage for what is considered long periods of time if they do not seek help or simply give up. In either case, as the channel of face-to-face communication decreases, the relationship will move to the avoiding stage. In lieu of face-to-face communication, couples will resort to texting, leaving notes, and using other people as the primary means of communicating. Ultimately, nothing short of an intervention can salvage a relationship once it has reached this point. Brian and Carla have breakfast each morning at the kitchen table before going to work. During breakfast Brian reads the daily paper and Carla responds to her messages on her phone. Even

When the channel of face-to-face communication decreases, the relationship will move to the avoiding stage.

though they are sitting at the table together, neither party feels obligated or compelled to talk to the other. It is apparent that the couple has reached the avoiding stage.

Terminating

There have been more popular songs written about the termination stage than any other stage in relationships. In this stage, there is a severing action as a result of the inability to manage conflict and resume communication. The termination stage is rarely met without expressions of grief and sadness either publicly or privately. Termination can be quick or drawn out, hostile or cordial, direct or indirect, but it is important to remember that the termination of one relationship offers an opportunity to begin again, and at such time utilize the lessons learned.

The termination stage is rarely met without expressions of grief and sadness.

Courtesy of Kandace Clifton

Relationships: The Good, the Bad, and the Ugly

There have been numerous studies to determine why people have difficulty committing to a relationship of a serious and romantic nature, yet we still have so many unanswered questions. If we knew that engaging in a relationship would increase our happiness and satisfaction in life, would we hesitate? When we weigh the advantages against the disadvantages of being involved a relationship, what do we expect to find? Do the costs outweigh the rewards? Are we asking the right questions of ourselves and our potential partners? Before we draw any conclusions, let's take a close look at these issues and see if we can find some answers.

The Good: The Advantages

When we consider the advantages of developing strong, long lasting relationships, we can draw some rather basic conclusions. One definite advantage of a relationship is physical and emotional stability. Some studies suggest that elderly people live longer if they own a pet. The British Market Research Bureau in their 2002 research found multiple reasons why pet owners felt their pets were good for them. Seventy–five percent said their pets made them laugh and thereby contributed to better mental health. Sixty–seven percent said that pets offered unconditional love. Sixty-six percent stated that their pets provided companionship and alleviated loneliness. Sixty-four percent said their pets reduced stress and made them feel more relaxed (Palika 2008). The companionship of the pet and its ability to render unconditional love contributes to an individual's emotional health. Emotional health

© Kendall Hunt Publishing

Some of us begin a relationship with no intention of its becoming serious and then discover it has evolved to that level without a decision ever being made.

directly corresponds to physical health. Goleman states that loneliness is one of the major factors leading to premature mortality (Goleman 1995). Another advantage of relationships is increased self esteem. As humans we have a need to be needed. A healthy relationship creates a backdrop for reciprocity. Participating in a relationship when it is a healthy one makes you feel desirable and gives you a sense of worth. Some of the obvious advantages of a relationship include increased social economic status and intellectual stimulation.

The Bad: The Disadvantages

It is unfortunate that relationships, which initially offer so many advantages, often result in so much pain. Once the emotional bond has been established in a relationship, there is a natural progression to increased obligations. Frequently, these increased obligations stretch us beyond our ability to fulfill them. Therefore, it is critical that bonding does not take place until we understand fully the demand of time, money, and emotional expenses that the relationship will entail (Buchholz 1998). Additionally, when one becomes engaged in an interpersonal relationship, it may lead to the exclusion of other valued relationships. Lastly, when a relationship proves too costly to your well being, it can be difficult, if not impossible, to sever. The inability to sever or terminate a relationship can lead to great vulnerability and have the potential to impact the rest of your life.

The Ugly: A Relationship, But At What Cost?

The **Social Exchange theory** claims people make relationship decisions by assessing and comparing the costs and rewards (Thibaut and Kelley 1959). The Social Exchange theory addresses the costs and rewards that affect our decisions to initiate, develop and maintain relationships. In essence, interpersonal relationships can be described similarly to the law of supply and demand. If you possess a resource or provide a commodity that is equal to the desire for that commodity, the result is a balanced relationship. Another way to look at the same principle is from the standpoint of rewards and costs. For example, Thibaut and Kelley assert that there are costs affiliated with any item which is valued. The same can be said with relationships. A relationship may require a party to extend time, money, freedom, loss of status, and the loss of other relationship (Thibaut and Kelley 1959).

Altman and Taylor suggest that relationships can be evaluated in the following three ways: **immediate**, **forecasted**, and **cumulative rewards and costs** (Altman and Taylor 1973). **Immediate rewards and costs** are based upon the present assessment of a relationship. When we first meet someone, we immediately assess whether or not further interaction with that individual would be rewarding. When Brian and Carla first met there was an immediate assessment which led to a long-term relationship. Their assessment when weighing the immediate costs and rewards consisted of physical attributes, scripted conversations, and general small talk.

Forecasted rewards and costs are an assessment of our projected and predicted outcomes. Often times, students will become involved in relationships during their college years because of immediate rewards and costs. They may use forecasting to decide whether they want to remain in that relationship after they complete their education. Carla's parents have enjoyed a long term relationship. While Carla went to college her parent's relationship showed signs of coming apart. Each partner had to weigh the costs and rewards of their relationship. In essence, low immediate rewards/high immediate costs may not cause a relationship to deteriorate if the partners believe that eventually the relationship will improve or result in high forecasted rewards/low forecasted costs.

Lastly, **cumulative rewards and costs** represent the total rewards and costs accrued over a period of time. When couples are asked, "Why do you stay in a relationship that is not satisfying or meeting their needs?" Various reasons are given. Some say, "I've invested a lot in the relationship." Others respond, "What's the alternative?" Regardless of the reasons people may give for staying in a relationship that gives low immediate rewards, it is basically a result of cumulative rewards and costs. Altman and Taylor describe this behavior by comparing it to placing money in a saving account. When your expenses are greater than your income, you may choose to withdraw funds from your savings account. Similarly, when the relationship has greater costs and lower rewards, partners may draw upon prior rewards from their investment in the relationship. It is important to remember, however, just as a savings account can run out of money, so can the stockpile of cumulative rewards be depleted or lose value (Altman and Taylor 1973).

In summary, most of us do not make a conscious assessment of the advantages and disadvantages when we engage in an interpersonal relationship. We do not normally make a list of the costs and rewards of a relationship once we find ourselves involved in one. In fact, most of us become involved in relationships without considering the most critical issues that will lead to the success of a relationship. It is not until we find ourselves in a troubled relationship that we consider why we became involved initially. We must always remember to ask the right questions of ourselves, and more importantly ask the right questions of our potential partner. Frequently, we forget that successful, long lasting relationships must be built on a solid foundation.

Making the Most of Relationships

Whether they involve family members, friends, or a romantic interest, relationships can be challenging. You have more than likely heard that the best strategy to developing and maintaining healthy, long-term relationships is communication. This is true. In order to make the most of your relationships, you must have open and honest communication. This is not to suggest, however, that open communication will totally eliminate relationship conflict.

Relationship conflict occurs when the individuals in relationship have a disagreement. Such conflict is usually viewed negatively, but it can be positive in nature. Conflict is negative when one of the persons involved views the other person negatively after the interaction. However, when conflict results in individuals acknowledging a problem and seeking a solution, it is positive (DeVito 2005).

© 2010. Courtesy of JaxonPhotoGroup

Culture, gender, and power play roles in conflict.

Though conflict is a part of all relationships, they way you handle conflict when it arises is critical to relationship success. In this section, you will learn strategies for avoiding conflict in relationships as well as strategies for resolving conflicts when they occur. Applying these strategies will likely minimize the amount of conflict you experience in relationships and improve your relationship conflict resolution skills.

Avoiding Relationship Conflict

Much of the conflict that occurs in relationships is a result of communication issues. There are several forms of communication that tend to cause conflict in relationships. These include aggression, negative criticism, and avoidance.

Courtesy of DeMarcus Butler

Aggression in communication occurs when one person voices concerns and frustration about a conflict without considering the other person's thoughts or feelings. Aggressive communication is usually very demanding and self-focused (Beebe, Beebe and Ivy 2010). Individuals who practice aggressive communication typically do not respect others' thoughts and opinions (DeVito 2005). Such communication usually results in the recipient of the aggression either responding with aggression or experiencing emotional pain. Continued aggression in a relationship usually causes those involved to distance themselves from each other emotionally.

Negative criticism occurs when one person in the relationship evaluates the other person in the relationship in a negative manner. The criticism may focus on something the person has said or done as well as a particular physical or emotional characteristic of the person. For example, a husband may criticize his wife for not being organized. Though this may be true, the manner and tone in which the husband gives the criticism and his willingness to help the wife improve her organizational skills determine how the criticism is received. When the husband's tone is negative and there is no desire or effort on his part to assist the wife in becoming more organized, his criticism is viewed as negative. When people receive more negative than positive criticism, their confidence in themselves is lowered and they tend not to feel supported by the individual criticizing them.

Avoidance occurs when one or both individuals in a relationship do not address issues of conflict. When conflict is not addressed, it cannot be resolved. Behaving as if a conflict does not exist does not eliminate it. It is, therefore, advisable not to practice avoidance but to deal directly with conflict when it arises.

Resolving Relationship Conflict

Even if you are aware of the forms communication that tend to cause conflict in relationships and make an effort not to engage in such communication, conflict will still occur in your relationships, though probably not as often. When conflict does occur, you can use the steps below to help resolve the conflict. The steps are based on John Dewey's problem solving methods (Dewey 1910).

Identify the Conflict

In order to solve a conflict, you must first know exactly what the conflict is. Often times, there are many problems involved in one particular conflict. Each problem may need its own solution. Therefore, it is necessary to determine specifically what the problem is before attempting to solve it. The more specific you can be, the better your chances of addressing the real issue. Instead of saying that your partner is inattentive to your emotional needs, it is better to say that your partner does not listen or respond when you communicate that you feel lonely. Instead, he continues engaging other activities. By defining the problem in such specific terms, your partner will have an opportunity to understand your feelings about the conflict.

Consider Several Resolutions

There are usually several possible resolutions to a particular conflict. It is important to determine what the possible resolutions are and consider each of them. Some resolutions may work better for one person than the other. However, it is best to select those resolutions that will work better for both parties. As in the situation with the husband and wife above, a resolution that involves the husband turning off the television to listen to his wife when his favorite sports team is playing would not work well for the husband. Setting aside a mutually agreed upon time for the husband and wife to connect emotionally would be a resolution that addresses both of their needs.

Attempt the Resolution

Once you have selected a resolution that will address the needs of everyone involved, attempt the resolution to determine if it is, in fact, viable. In this step, the husband and wife above should identify a time to connect with each other emotionally. During that time, the wife should discuss with her husband her feelings of loneliness and the husband should respond accordingly.

Reflect on the Resolution

After the resolution has been attempted, both parties will have an opportunity to communicate their views of the impact of the resolution on the conflict. Together, they can determine if the conflict was actually resolved or if they should attempt one of the other resolutions that was considered. The wife can tell the husband whether she felt heard, and the husband can tell the wife how he felt about responding to her during the resolution attempt.

Embrace or Release the Resolution

Once the resolution has been reflected upon, the individuals are in a position to either embrace or release the resolution. If they select to embrace the resolution, they should make it a permanent part of their relationship so that the conflict it addresses does not continue to occur. If they release the resolution because they do not find it useful, then they should consider another resolution, attempt it, reflect on it, and either embrace or release it until a viable resolution is determined.

The Internet and Relationships

Relationships are hard enough when you deal with another person face-to-face on a daily basis. The relationship is expected to be filled with its hardships and ups and downs. Try to imagine experiencing these hardships with a person behind a computer screen.

Relationships that are formed online are growing at a rapid rate. According to a study conducted by the Pew Research Center, 66% of online daters have gone on a date with someone they met through a dating site or app. It was also found that 23% of online daters say they have met a spouse or long term relationship through these sites. These sites promote dating online as a fun and easier way to find a perfect relationship. Although this may be true, do people really get to know each other in online relationships? When developing a relationship face-to-face, there is a lesser chance of ignoring or missing warning signs of lies, hidden agendas or misrepresentation. You are equipped with five senses that aid in helping you decide if the person you're embarking on this relationship with is a worthy suitor. Are you able to use them to aid you when dealing with online relationships? What should you look out for when dealing with potentially toxic online relationships? See if any of these scenarios look familiar.

- You receive a random request from an attractive suitor on Facebook Instagram and start a chat session with them. After a minute or two of pleasantries, they start engaging in overly sexual conversation and even feel comfortable enough to ask for racy photos.
- The person you have been in an online relationship bliss for the past month is now out of a job and falling behind in his financial obligations. Because of this, most conversations between the two or you involve his attempts to persuade you to "loan" him money.
- From their Facebook profile, your new online friend looks like one of the most attractive persons you have ever met. You can't wait to meet her, and show her off to your friends. However, when you ask to formally meet, she evades you. When you ask for current pictures of her, she says she's not looking her best at the moment. When you ask if she is willing to have a Skype date, she declines.

If any of these scenarios appear familiar, you are more than likely embarking on a toxic online relationship. The person on the other end of that computer screen may not be honest. The key to any successful relationship is honesty. Relationships are like houses. They cannot be built on a bad foundation. If this happens, the house is sure to crumble and so will a relationship.

There have been successful relationships that have originated online. Internet relationships are becoming increasingly common, but as an educated person you have to make smart decisions and be aware of the warning signs. The transition from the virtual world to the real world is possible. Consider the following tips:

- Be honest from the start.
- Don't exchange personal information too quickly. Move slowly.
- Always be respectful of others and require respect in return.
- Don't ignore red flags or discrepancies.
- Ask for current photos and teleconferencing to make sure you are talking to the person you believe you're talking to.
- Never agree to meet for the first time at a private location. Meet in public when you are ready.

Summary

In this chapter, we focused on the development and deterioration of relationships described by communication theorist Mark Knapp as the "coming together" and "coming apart" process. We identified each as consisting of five stages. The coming together process includes initiating, experimenting, intensifying, integrating, and bonding. The coming apart process is comprised of differentiating, circumscribing, stagnating, avoiding, and lastly terminating. Relationships must grow and matriculate in a balanced manner. If couples progress too quickly to the bonding stage, the relationship will soon terminate. Or in other words, a couple will "fall out of love" before they have "fallen in love." With 49% of marriages in 2011 ending in divorce we found that weighing the advantages and the disadvantages as well as the costs and rewards of relationships to be integral in interpersonal studies.

Thibaut and Kelley's theory of Social Exchange claims that relationships operate similarly to the law of supply and demand. While Altman and Taylor conclude that relationships are evaluated by immediate, forecasted, and cumulative rewards and costs. As certain as we are that at some point in our lives, we will be engaged in an interpersonal relationship, we are just as certain that the relationship will experience conflict.

Conflict in relationships is inevitable, and is the result of communication issues. Behaviors which cause conflict in relationships may tend to stem from one of the following: aggression, negative criticism, and avoidance. John Dewey's five step problem solving method is one approach to solving conflict in relationships. As we look at relationships and how they are developed and maintained, we cannot ignore the trend that cyber dating has increased at a rapid rate.

Lastly, while there are many advantages to online relationships, we would be remiss not to recognize the dangers. The key to all relationships is honesty, and online relationships allow partners to create their virtual reality.

Communication for Today's Student

Chapter 5 – Evaluating and Improving Relationships

Exercise 5.1 – Stages of Relationships

Stages of a Relationship

According to Marc L. Knapp, writer and researcher, relationships are in a constant state of change. Relationships are either coming together or coming apart. Relationships require attention and maintenance. They require servicing. In order to have a long lasting and healthy relationship, it is important to recognize and identify each stage.

You and a partner will identify the stages of a relationship, both coming apart and coming together. Then, identify a popular song that you have heard and that you have on your MP3 player in which the lyrics reflect each stage. Bring your players to class and be certain you can explain and support your selections.

Names

_____

_____

Identify and Cite the Song/Artist(s)

Coming together	Definition	Song Title
Initiating		
Experimenting		
Intensifying		
Integrating		
Bonding		

Coming Apart	Definition	Song Title
Differentiating		
Circumscribing		
Stagnating		
Avoiding		
Terminating		

INTERCULTURAL RELATIONSHIPS

After reading this chapter, you should be able to:

- ☑ Understand three reasons for studying the impact of diversity on interpersonal relationships.
- ☑ Increase awareness of four basic core concepts: knowledge, understanding, acceptance, and skills.
- ☑ Define culture.
- ☑ Differentiate the co-cultural categories of ethnicity, race, region, and social class.
- ☑ Identify three characteristics of culture.
- ☑ Discuss factors which affect our perceptions of others: needs, beliefs, values, and attitudes.
- ☑ Identify three steps in the process of forming stereotypes.
- ☑ Recognize how stereotypes and prejudice influence interpersonal relationships.
- ☑ Describe three forms of prejudice.
- ☑ Explain the three functions that prejudices fulfill in our interpersonal relationships.
- ☑ Evaluate the impact of Hofstede's four dimensions of cultural values on interpersonal communication.
- ☑ Recognize five strategies to enhance effective interpersonal communication in diverse relationships.

Key Terms

Knowledge	Ethnocentrism	Homophily	Attitudes	Discrimination
Uncertainty reduction theory (URT)	Skills	Explicit learning	Stereotyping	Violence
	Culture	Implicit learning	Racial profiling	Acceptance
Passive strategies	Diversity	Perception	Prejudice	High/low context cultures
Active strategies	Socialization	Personal orientation system	Racism	Individualism/collectivism
Interactive strategies	Ethnicity		Race	Power distance
Self-disclosure	Race	Needs	Ageism	Masculine/feminine cultures
Understanding	Regional differences	Beliefs	Sexism	
Acceptance	Social class	Values	Verbal abuse	Uncertainty avoidance

6 Scenario

Chris passed Lee a candle as he rejoined the line of supporters for the candlelight vigil.

Lee looked down at the candle. "So what is the point of a candlelight vigil?" he asked.

Lee was a foreign exchange student from Hong Kong who was assigned to Chris through the student exchange program. It was Chris's job to help familiarize Lee with American culture and the culture of the campus. Because of this, Chris thought that inviting Lee to the vigil for Trayvon Martin was a perfect way to expose him to a particular aspect of American culture.

"A candlelight vigil is an event where we can pay respect to someone who has passed," said Chris.

"Was this Trayvon Martin a friend of yours?" Lee asked as the line began to move.

"No," Chris said. "But I could have known him."

"Why was he murdered?" Lee asked.

Chris went on to tell Lee all about Trayvon Martin as they walked around campus with the other supporters.

"So he was shot because someone felt intimidated by his appearance?" Lee asked in disbelief.

Chris nodded. "Sadly, yes. In America, sometimes people are intimidated by what makes us different."

"In Hong Kong, we see America as this great place that celebrates differences," Lee said. "But, situations like this show me that our perception is not all true."

"I believe we celebrate differences, Lee," Chris said sadly. "But, we have a long way to go."

"We sure do," Lee agreed as he blew out his candle.

Are there any traditions from other cultures that you admire or celebrate?
Are there any traditions from other cultures that intimidate or frighten you?

Respond Here

On July 28, 2006, actor Mel Gibson was pulled over while speeding on Pacific Coast Highway in Malibu, California. As officers were questioning Gibson, he began yelling at them, making anti-Semitic and sexist comments toward the arresting officers.

In October 2006, *Grey's Anatomy* actor Isaiah Washington got into a fight with fellow actor Patrick Dempsey over an alleged gay slur that Washington made about their colleague, T. R. Knight. Even though the incident eventually faded from the spotlight, Washington publicly made an anti-gay comment at the 2007 Golden Globe awards a few months later as he attempted to defend his earlier actions to members of the press.

In November 2006, *Seinfeld* actor Michael Richards erupted into a series of racial epithets targeted toward two African American men attending his performance at the Laugh Factory in Los Angeles. Richards claimed that he was angry at the men for heckling him and allegedly disturbing his comedy routine.

What causes individuals to engage in such negative behavior? Why do people exchange such hurtful words and actions? One reason may be the inability to engage in effective interpersonal communication with those who are different. We make decisions on how to communicate with others based on our beliefs, our values, and our attitudes. As a result, if our beliefs or attitudes toward another individual or group are negative, our communication with them may be negative as well. Why is it that some people fear and apprehend communication with diverse others instead of embracing differences as the added "spice" of interpersonal relationships? In this chapter we will explore a variety of concepts that help explain how our attitudes, beliefs, and values both shape and are shaped by our interactions with others.

Overview

Throughout this text, we have discussed various aspects of interpersonal communication and the roles they play in initiating and sustaining relationships. As we approach the end of the journey of exploring the specifics of interpersonal communication, we would be remiss if we failed to discuss the one variable that *all* interpersonal relationships have in common—they are comprised of diverse individuals. Typically, discussions of diversity focus on things that we can see: race, ethnicity, and gender being the most commonly identified elements when defining diversity. Focusing attention on the obvious differences *may cause us to fail to recognize that cultural attitudes, values, and norms also play a role in our interpersonal relationships.* These are only a few of the less apparent factors that create challenges for relational partners when trying to achieve shared meaning. Consider friends who get upset with one another simply because they differ in their beliefs of how to spend their first weekend out of school. One might want to hang out with family members who were visiting from out of town instead of going out to the exclusive "Summer Kickoff Party" at the hot new nightclub that the other friend had received an exclusive invitation to attend. Differing values for family relationships and friendships contribute to the diversity encountered in this relationship. Maybe you have had a difficult time getting a teacher to understand that your questions are not intended to "challenge his authority," but are attempts to better understand the information being presented in class.

Diversity comes in many shapes and forms. While knowledge of the traditional views of cultural diversity can help you to understand the challenges you may encounter in your own relationships, it is important to focus on the source of many of our communication behaviors and to understand how cultural perceptions impact our view of relationships and communication. We can use the analogy of a coach and a team to understand the influence of diversity on interpersonal relationships and the role communication plays in the process. A good coach would not send a team out on the playing field without preparing them for the game. Plays are taught and rehearsed; team members know what to expect from one another. Practice sessions are conducted so that these preferred ways of acting and reacting can be learned and refined.

© 2012 Courtesy of JaxonPhotoGroup.

Relationships are comprised of individuals who are diverse in many ways.

Sure, there are times when the game plan does not work as planned. The coach and team may become frustrated. They regroup, communicate, and develop an alternate plan. However, if the team continues to run exactly the same play every single game, the chances for success will be slim. Becoming a competent communicator across cultures requires you to develop a similar game plan. You need to be aware of the characteristics that can lead to misunderstandings when communicating with people from diverse backgrounds. Knowing that each person's communication is guided by his unique set of values, beliefs, and attitudes will prepare you for differences in your approaches to conversations. Just as a team needs to study plays, people need to study and understand the various elements that create confusion and miscommunication in cross-cultural encounters. This chapter will help you to develop a personal game plan for becoming a competent communicator in diverse interpersonal relationships. Four core concepts which are essential to enhancing competence include: knowledge, understanding, skills, and acceptance. Let us examine each of these concepts more closely.

The Impact of Cultural Diversity on Interpersonal Relationships

As buzz words such as "diversity" and "cultural sensitivity" continue to permeate discussions regarding relationships in the workplace, the classroom, and our personal lives, there is a need to increase the understanding of both diversity and communication, and their influence on personal relationships. This is an extremely exciting time in our history. Changes in political and social policy, evolving demographics, and technological advances have provided us with vast opportunities for forming relationships with diverse others. Three specific reasons for exploring the impact of cultural diversity on communication in interpersonal relationships are (1) increased awareness of self, (2) appreciation for technological transformations, and (3) understanding of demographic transitions.

Now more than ever, we have opportunities to form relationships with many different people.

Understanding the Self

Perhaps the simplest and most overlooked reason for studying the impact of diversity on our relationships is the opportunity it provides for exploring and understanding our own cultural background and identity. By delving into the cultural factors which influence communication patterns, we begin to gain an awareness of our own reasons for thinking and behaving as we do.

A woman had lived in a small town with a population of 350 all of her life. The population was entirely Caucasian, and the overwhelming majority was Methodist and middle-class. Upon moving to a large metropolitan area, she found the challenges of understanding the cultural differences to be phenomenal. Her knowledge of initiating relationships was limited to experiences in a small, cohesive community. Shortly after moving into her new apartment, she encountered her next door neighbor struggling to bring several bags of groceries from the parking lot to the building. While introducing herself, she attempted to take a couple of bags from her neighbor's car. She was quickly told that her assistance was not needed. She discussed the incident with a roommate. The roommate pointed out, "You have to understand that people in large cities don't just walk up and help one another. Don't be offended. City folks just don't trust people as easily as people you're accustomed to." As she found the first few weeks in the city to be frustrating, her focus was on how "strange" other people were, not on understanding how her own cultural background influenced her perceptions and expectations of others' behavior.

When considering the impact they have on our identity formation, our first instinct may be to focus on interactions with family members and peers. Communication with significant others plays a large role in shaping our sense of self. However, it is essential that we examine the role that culture has played in the process as well. After all, it is likely that the rules and expectations that our family and friends have for our communication behaviors are derived from cultural expectations. Many unspoken guidelines are within different cultural influences.

Technological Transformations

In the 1960s, Marshall McLuhan introduced the notion of a "global village" (McLuhan and Powers 1989). He predicted that mass media and technology would bring the world closer together, a notion considered to be farfetched at that time. But a quick inventory of today's technologies, which provide opportunities for forming diverse relationships, reveals that McLuhan's vision was quite accurate. Airline travel, television, cell phones, and the Internet are just a few of the technologies that have changed the way we communicate. Humans now have the capability to travel around the world in a matter of hours, simultaneously view events as they occur in other cities and countries, and concurrently interact with persons from around the globe.

© Ted Denson, 2012, Shutterstock.

How have cell phones impacted the way we communicate?

Opportunities provided by technology for forming relationships with diverse persons have increased exponentially over the past twenty years. A 2005 survey revealed that nearly 1 billion people worldwide have access to the Internet (http://www.internetworldstats.com/america.htm). In the United States alone, nearly 250 million people use the World Wide Web to find information and to form relationships with others. Teenagers are forming and maintaining relationships via the computer at increasing rates due to social networking sites such as MySpace and Facebook. Some schools encourage students to communicate with intercultural email partners in a variety of subject areas. Internet chat rooms and discussion boards enable individuals to form friendships with others from almost anywhere. An examination of one teen chat site revealed that there were students communicating with one another from seven different states as well as from Canada, Great Britain, and Puerto Rico. As corporate America expands its boundaries to include many overseas partners, work teams will be comprised of members from diverse cultures. People come to the workplace with diverse beliefs, experiences, and expectations about the role of communication in relationships at work. Gergen (1991) emphasizes the fact that new technology has eliminated the barriers of space and time which previously inhibited relationships from forming with diverse individuals. Technology provides opportunities to communicate with persons who come from backgrounds entirely different than our own. Understanding the factors that influence communication will enhance our appreciation of these opportunities.

Influence of Demographic Transitions

Over the past twenty years, the demographic composition of the United States has changed dramatically. And predictions for the twenty-first century indicate that the life expectancy of the population will be longer and that the racial and ethnic composition will be more diverse than ever. Medical advancements have extended the life expectancy of Americans. Immigration patterns have changed dramatically since the 1960s, before then most immigrants came primarily from European countries. Today, nearly ninety percent of immigrants arrive from Latin American and Asian nations. By the middle of the twenty-first century, the majority of the U.S. population will be comprised of today's racial and ethnic minorities. Over the past decade, the number of interracial and interdenominational marriages has increased, and the U.S. workplace has seen a shift from the predominance of white male employees to a more diverse workforce that is also comprised of women and racial and ethnic groups. Opportunities to expand our linguistic, political, and social knowledge abound.

However, not all intercultural encounters are viewed as opportunities. While these demographic shifts create opportunities for diverse relationships, it is important to recognize that they present communication challenges as well. Some intercultural encounters are approached with fear and apprehension. Uncertainty about other individuals creates tension. In July 2005,

The demographic composition of the United States will continue to change and become more diverse.

a series of bombs exploded on subways and a bus in London. Since that time, reporters have pointed to the mistrust, misunderstanding, and fear that have caused members of this city (which once prided itself on its racial, ethnic, and religious diversity), to be more cautious in their interactions with others.

Consequences of changing demographics are being felt in many social institutions. Schools are faced with issues such as bilingualism, differences in learning styles, and challenges of conflict among diverse groups. The Los Angeles school system reported that more than 100 different languages were spoken in classrooms across the county. Yet language is only one piece of a cultural code to be deciphered; other factors include understanding the perceptions and motivations that influence relationships in the home culture. Administrators at Taylor County High School in Georgia were faced with the challenge of how to address a group of students who wanted to host a "white-only" prom:

> Even after schools were integrated in the South, many rural areas still held separate proms for blacks and whites, and Taylor County High School was no exception. The first integrated prom in 31 years was organized by the school's Junior class because they collectively decided they all wanted to be together as a complete group. Every year before that, students and their parents planned separate dances. The proms weren't organized by the school itself, as school officials were concerned about potential interracial dating issues. The year after the first integrated prom, a small group of white students announced that they also wanted a separate dance. One of the students who had initiated the integrated dance said she was bitterly disappointed to hear that some students wanted to go back to the old ways after they had succeeded in bringing about such a change in the school.

Now more than ever, relationship success depends on the ability to demonstrate communication competence across cultures. Achieving communication competence is the ultimate goal in our interpersonal relationships. When the source and receiver are from diverse backgrounds and have unique expectations of communication, this goal may be perceived as difficult to achieve.

Communication Competence: Four Core Concepts

Knowledge

Knowledge refers to the theoretical principles and concepts that explain behaviors occurring within a specific communication context. In other words, increasing your knowledge of communication theories and the concepts used to explain the challenges faced in intercultural relationships will enhance your ability to understand and accept those differences. In addition, knowledge will enhance your interpersonal skills when communicating with diverse others. You have already increased your knowledge base as a result of reading this textbook up to this point. Each of the concepts and theories that have been introduced has enhanced your understanding of the factors that impact communication in interpersonal relationships. Throughout this chapter we will take a second look at some of the theories introduced earlier in the text that have direct implications for intercultural encounters.

Uncertainty reduction theory. Berger and Calabrese's **uncertainty reduction theory (URT)** helps us understand how knowledge can assist us in forming effective interpersonal relationships by predicting the attitudes, behaviors, and emotions of others. As we initiate new relationships, our goal is to reduce our level of uncertainty about the other person (Berger and Calabrese 1975). When crossing cultural lines, alleviating this ambiguity becomes a bit trickier. For example, the notion of what constitutes acceptable disclosures in interpersonal relationships in the U.S. might differ from what is considered proper in other cultures. Is it acceptable to ask about another person's occupation? About her family? How does the other person view status differentials and what rules does he or she adopt for communicating with someone of different status? Berger (1979) identified three primary communication strategies used to reduce uncertainty in relationships. These are: **passive strategies, active strategies,** and **interactive strategies.**

Passive strategies typically involve observation and social comparison. We observe members of other cultures and make assessments as to the differences that exist. When one of your authors arrived in Hong Kong to teach summer classes, she did not speak Chinese. She spent many hours during her first weekend there sitting at the busy harbor, browsing through shopping areas, and walking around campus to observe how people interacted with one another. Through her observations, she learned the cultural rules for personal space, noticed styles of dress and forms of nonverbal greetings, and became familiar with the protocol for communication between students and teachers on campus.

Active strategies require us to engage in interactions with others to learn additional information about the other person. Suppose your professor assigns you to have weekly conversations with an international partner during the semester. Prior to your first meeting, you may decide to ask other international students what they know about your conversation partner's culture, or you may go online and participate in chat rooms that have members from the conversation partner's culture.

Interactive strategies typically involve a face-to-face encounter between two individuals to reduce uncertainty. Typically, partners engage in **self-disclosure** as a means of sharing information about themselves with others. When examining cultural differences in disclosure, it was found that American college students disclose about a much wider range of topics, and to more people outside the family, whereas college students in Korea self-disclose mostly to immediate family members (Ishii, Thomas and Klopf 1993). Consider the following example:

> Alicia was excited to learn that she had been selected to live with an international student in the dorm during her freshmen year. She had been fortunate enough to travel with her parents on business trips to various countries for the past several years and found learning about other cultures to be fascinating. Her new roommate, Kyon, was from Korea. As they were unpacking their things, Alicia told Kyon about her hometown, her summer vacation to Hilton Head Island, and about all of her friends from high school who were attending their college. She shared how frightened she was about the first day of classes, and she laughed as she told Kyon how she had taken her schedule and walked around campus to locate her classrooms for the first day of class. Eventually, Alicia noticed that she had been doing all the talking, so she began asking Kyon questions. While Kyon was willing to discuss the classes she would be taking and the plane trip from Korea, she seemed reluctant to talk about her family, friends, or even her fears about starting college.

Without knowledge of cultural differences in communication styles, Alicia may have become easily frustrated by Kyon's lack of disclosure. After all, in the United States it is common to engage in question-asking and self-disclosure to reduce our uncertainty about others. But understanding that expectations for self-disclosure in Korea are different from those held by Americans will help alleviate the potential frustration and hurt feelings that could occur otherwise.

Knowledge of one's own culture is learned. Cultures teach their members preferred perceptual and communication patterns just as a coach teaches a team the plays. Beginning at a very young age, this learning process instills knowledge about the culture's accepted behaviors. As children enter kindergarten in the U.S., they learn that they need to raise their hand to ask a question in class and to listen quietly while the teacher is speaking. Communication is the channel for teaching these lessons. Members of a culture practice the preferred behaviors and, if they deviate from the endorsed mannerisms they will probably find that they are unsuccessful in their communication. Consider the following example:

A student from Ethiopia shared this story about his experiences in American classrooms. During his high school years, he lost class participation points because of his unwillingness to speak out in class. While he was confused about his low grade, he did not approach the teacher and ask for clarification. Rather, he accepted the teacher's evaluation of his performance. However, what the teacher did not know was that in his culture students are not active participants in class. The teacher is viewed as the authority and the students are expected to listen and learn. Further, to question a teacher's authority would be viewed as extremely disrespectful.

Young children learn quickly that listening quietly to the teacher is the accepted behavior for school.

As we engage in relationships with diverse persons, the knowledge of what constitutes competent communication behaviors is learned. Recent articles have focused on the need for cultural and social knowledge among U.S. armed service workers (McFate 2005; McFate and Jackson 2005). As U.S. military personnel travel overseas for service, it is important that they have a solid understanding of the cultural beliefs and norms that are expected. While the mission of the troops may be to restore order, respect for cultural expectations must still be demonstrated. Even the simple act of eating and drinking could be perceived as being offensive without proper knowledge of cultural norms. Soldiers training for duty in Iraq need to understand that members of Muslim cultures do not eat or drink during the day during the month of Ramadan. By refraining from eating or drinking in front of members of the Muslim culture during this period, U.S. soldiers can display respect for the Muslim culture. Studying the role of values, beliefs, attitudes, and needs in shaping and sustaining relationships can be invaluable. New knowledge can remove some of the barriers that can create communication challenges in relationships with diverse people. But knowledge in and of itself is insufficient for achieving competence. We also need to gain an understanding of why others communicate the way they do.

Understanding

Understanding involves applying knowledge to specific situations in an attempt to explain the behaviors that are occurring. While you may know how uncertainty reduction theory (URT) is defined, it is important to gain an understanding of how it impacts a particular interaction. Understanding involves exploring the roots, or sources of communication, rather than simply explaining the behavior. Imagine this scenario. You attend the funeral of the mother of your close friend who is Jewish. At the end of the ceremony, Jewish tradition calls for friends and family members to shovel dirt onto the coffin, but you are not aware of this tradition. This act makes you extremely uncomfortable, and you decide not to participate in the tradition; you end up offending your friend. Knowledge of the Jewish cultural customs would have assisted you in understanding the negative reaction that resulted from your refusal to participate in the ceremony.

As the twenty-first century opens, the cultural composition of the United States is becoming increasingly diverse. A recent Associated Press news article suggests that the term "minority" may no longer be an accurate descriptor for various U.S. co-cultures (http://www.diversityinc.com/public/16722 print.cfm). Non-Latino whites currently encompass less than fifty percent of the population of Texas, and it is predicted that more than one-third of all Americans will soon live in a state where groups formerly considered minority groups will outnumber Caucasians. Changes in demographics provide more opportunities for individuals to interact with individuals who are from diverse cultural backgrounds. Consider the various relationship contexts we have discussed in this text. The chances are greater than ever before that you will form relationships with teachers, physicians, and co-workers who are from diverse backgrounds.

Broadening our understanding of diversity to understand the influence of a variety of elements such as race, ethnicity, language differences, and religious beliefs is essential for relationship success. In many classrooms across the U.S., Caucasians are no longer the majority. On the surface, twenty-five students may appear to be similar, based on their racial or ethnic status, but it is quite possible that there are twenty-five different cultural backgrounds represented. One aspect of their diverse backgrounds may be seen in the language that is spoken in each of their homes. Nearly seventeen percent of elementary and secondary school students speak a language other than English in their homes (http://www.census.gov/prod/2004pubs/04statab/educ.pdf). Even where racial and ethnic diversity may be minimal, students come from different geographical locations and religious backgrounds and are impacted by their unique family backgrounds. Understanding how each of these elements impacts individual decisions to communicate in relationships is essential. For example, Jack was confused when he saw his friend Adam place a rock on the grave of a close friend who had recently passed away after a car accident. He did notunderstand that Adam's

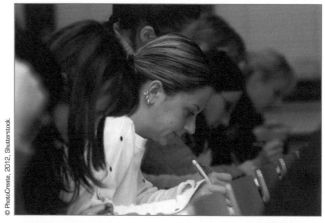

A room full of students appearing to be similar on the surface could have many different cultural backgrounds.

behavior was guided by an old Jewish custom of placing a rock on a loved one's grave as a sign of respect. According to tradition, the rocks were originally used as a way to mark gravesites. As more people visited the site, they added rocks to demonstrate how many people loved and respected the person.

It is important to understand that what works in one relationship may not work in all. Consider our earlier example of the coach and his team. Just as it would be ineffective to run the same play over and over again in a game, communicating with diverse persons in the same manner would not result in satisfying relationships. While this chapter will assist you in building knowledge and understanding of communication differences, acceptance of differences is also key to interpersonal success.

Acceptance

Acceptance refers to our awareness of the feelings and emotions involved in diverse approaches to relationships and communication. It encompasses our willingness to understand the behavior of others. Accepting differences in behavior enables us to be less judgmental and to reject ethnocentric thinking. **Ethnocentrism** refers to the tendency to perceive our own ways of behaving and thinking as being correct, or acceptable, and judging the behaviors of others as being "strange," incorrect, or inferior. Challenges in our interactions are often attributed to external, rather than cultural factors. Consider two co-workers who attempt to influence one another on a project on which they are collaborating. Joe tries to persuade Maynae by directly disagreeing with her proposal and engaging in assertive communication. Maynae's cultural background is one that values saving face. Thus, she avoids directly disagreeing with Joe—rather, she nods her head and proceeds with the project as she planned. Both of them end up frustrated. Joe cannot understand why Maynae did not follow their game plan. Had she not nodded her head and agreed with him? Joe attributes Maynae's actions to her shyness. Maynae is frustrated by Joe's confusion. Did he not understand that she did not want to embarrass him in front of their colleagues? She deduces that he must be in a bad mood and was not paying attention. As they continue to disagree about how to proceed with the project, they attribute the communication difficulty to the other person's mood or to shyness, both reasons being external to cultural factors. In reality, they may have diverse cultural expectations for how to influence others.

Skills

We have discussed many of the specific skills that are central to interpersonal communication throughout this text. **Skills** are the specific communication behaviors which contribute to competent and effective interpersonal communication. Effective listening, assertiveness, responsiveness, nonverbal sensitivity, language comprehension, and conflict management are only a few of the many skills required when interacting in diverse relationships. It is important to note that there is a difference between knowing how to communicate effectively across cultures, and actually being able to engage in the appropriate behaviors. You might understand that the Chinese culture values silence, but because you are an extremely talkative person and are ineffective in practicing silence you may be perceived as being rude when interacting with members of the Chinese culture. While language is an important skill to enhance communication competence, practicing nonverbal skills can also assist in producing effective interpersonal encounters. For example, when dining with friends from Japan, it is appropriate to make loud slurping sounds while eating a meal. The act of slurping is a behavior that is considered to be a compliment to the cook in Japan as it communicates that the food is delicious. But what if you feel very uncomfortable and do not know how to demonstrate the proper slurping behavior because you have never been encouraged to do so? Remaining silent while eating is perceived as an insult in these cultures, but your lack of slurping skills inhibit your ability to communicate your appreciation for the meal.

Culture and Diversity Defined

Culture has been defined by scholars in a number of different ways. In fact, one book identified more than 200 different definitions of culture (Kroeber and Kluckhohn 1952). In the fifty years since these definitions were compiled, attention to the increasing diversity of our world has prompted scholars to create even more. Anthropologists have broadly defined culture as being comprised of perceptions, behaviors, and evaluations. This definition was expanded to include shared ideas of a group which incorporates ethical standards as well as other intellectual components. Other researchers have adopted a descriptive approach to explaining culture. Their definitions include characteristics such as knowledge, morals, beliefs, customs, art, music, law, and values. In this text, we define culture as shared perceptions which shape the communication patterns and expectations of a group of people.

Diversity refers to the unique qualities or characteristics that distinguish individuals and groups from one another. The following is a list of characteristics that contribute to diversity in our interpersonal relationships.

- Age
- Educational background
- Ethnicity
- Family status
- Gender
- Income
- Military experience
- National, regional, or other geographical areas of origin
- Ownership of property and assets
- Physical and mental ability
- Race
- Sexual orientation
- Social class
- Spiritual practice
- Work experience

Diversity takes into consideration specific elements that have tremendous potential for our relationships. Consider the characteristics that you share with your closest friend. Chances are that you formed a relationship based on similarities in some of the areas listed above. Perhaps you are close in age and have similar educational backgrounds. Stop for a moment and consider the relationship implications when there are differences across these characteristics. A couple with different spiritual backgrounds may need to negotiate whose religious beliefs will be followed in raising their children. A daughter who is a lesbian may find it

What characteristics do close friends share?

difficult communicating her feelings about her relationship with her heterosexual parents. Or a soldier may be challenged to convey his beliefs about war and his value of freedom with his friends back home who have not served in the military. When considering the many characteristics of diversity, it is easy to see why many relationships encounter stumbling blocks as individuals attempt to navigate differences in knowledge, experiences, beliefs, and values.

Americans typically learn to value democracy at a young age.

One of the first steps in becoming competent in our relationships involves recognizing the unique characteristics that each relationship partner possesses. Our culture shapes our perception and society teaches us the preferred ways of behaving. The American value for democracy is shared by many members of this country. Beginning in elementary school, we are taught the meaning of democracy. As we grow up, we see people defending their rights to free speech. Thus, our culture begins shaping our perceptions at a very young age. Perception influences and forms our values, beliefs, and attitudes. These shared perceptions are both consciously taught and unconsciously learned. **Socialization** refers to the process of learning about one's cultural norms and expectations. This is critical for an individual to become a functioning member of society. Sources of socialization include parents, peers, teachers, celebrities, political leaders, workplace colleagues, educational materials, and mass media. Perceptions are highly individualized, so much so that we may not realize that others see things differently. It may be easy to overlook the impact that diversity has on our communication patterns. Communication behaviors are often unique to a culture, allowing us to easily identify members of various cultural groups. For example, an employee from Georgia assigned to work on a project with a team from Ohio is likely to be identified by her accent. Forms of address, such as when a child refers to an adult as "Miss Sarah," may also indicate a southern background. Culture is not only reflected in our behavior, it also influences our expectations. We form assumptions about how individuals should behave and what we should expect in our relationships with them. Japan is considered to be a collectivistic culture which values and encourages the accomplishments of groups over individual achievement. A student from Japan may experience difficulty in the U.S. where individualism is valued. He may be uncomfortable in situations where he is "singled out" for his individual academic achievements, preferring to be acknowledged with his class.

While we each have diverse characteristics that make us unique, we also share some aspects in common with other members of our larger culture. These shared characteristics allow us to identify with various groups and help shape our identity.

Co-cultures within the United States

Within the larger cultural context, numerous co-cultures exist, each distinguishable by unique characteristics. It is important to note that individuals are members of more than one co-culture. Consider this. An employee may claim membership as a member of the organization, in addition to being an adult, male, African-American Texan with Republican views, and of the Methodist faith. A total of seven co-cultures are claimed. Multiple memberships may contribute to confusion and miscommunication that occurs in relationships. Suppose you assume that because a teammate on your soccer team likes sports, she would not be interested in classical music or the theatre. As you pass a poster announcing the upcoming cultural arts series on your campus, you make some negative comments about people who attend musical and theatrical events. What you do not know is that your teammate has been a student of classical music since a young age, and that her mother is a trained opera singer. While this scenario is an extremely simplified example, assuming that membership in one group precludes an individual from having interests in other groups can lead to embarrassing situations that can impact relationships. Some examples of co-cultural classifications follow.

Ethnicity

While the terms "race" and "ethnicity" have often been used synonymously, these two categories are unique. **Ethnicity** refers to the common heritage, or background, shared by a group of people. Categories may be established to identify the culture from which one's ancestors came. These include Irish-American, Polish-American, or Mexican-American. While there has been some debate over the connotations associated with the labeling of some of these groups, the intention of naming is simply for identification purposes.

Race

Race is the term used to refer to genetically inherited biological characteristics such as hair texture and color, eye shape, skin color, and facial structure. Terms used to describe different racial categories include Caucasian, African American, and Asian. One situation which impacts our classification of groups results from the increasing number of intercultural marriages and relationships. Previously there were no categories on the U.S. census form to allow individuals to indicate their identification with more than one racial classification. This changed on the 2000 census with the addition of the category "other" to allow citizens to report their racial identification. As a result, individuals can now identify themselves as members of multiple racial groups rather than being restricted to only one racial identity.

Regional Differences

Within a given culture, speech patterns, attitudes, and values may differ significantly depending on the geographic location that an individual calls home. Northern Germans express values which are quite different from those of southern Germans. Those who reside in northern Brazil communicate using nonverbal gestures which are unrecognizable to those from southern Brazil. Accents within a culture also vary depending on the geographic region. Japanese spoken in Okinawa takes on different tones when spoken in Tokyo. English spoken by those who live in the Amish region of Pennsylvania is used differently by Texans. Dodd (1998) observed a variety of **regional differences** in communication styles within the boundaries of the United States. These include variety in the amount of animation, perceived openness, informal rapport, and rate of speech delivery. Even when examining the values of urban versus rural cultures, differences in values are obvious. Rural cultures appear to approach decisions more cautiously and simplistically. Members of urban cultures are more willing to take risks and reach decisions more quickly.

Social Class

Cultures often find that members stratify themselves on the basis of educational, occupational, or financial backgrounds, resulting in classifications and status differentials. Those whose careers produce high financial gain are usually awarded greater power and status in the American culture. Other cultures are more concerned with the amount of education that a person has completed. Stratification often occurs on the basis of homophily, the idea that we choose to be with people who are similar to us. Thus, when initiating relationships, we seek out those in similar careers, with similar educational experiences, and of similar financial status.

In some cultures, it is possible to move from one social class category to another. For example, a person in the U.S. can easily move from one category to another as a result of their economic or educational status. Graduating from college may enable a person to gain a more

When we initiate relationships, we choose to be with people who share our common interests.

Photo courtesy of Charles Long

prestigious job, and thereby allow him to achieve a higher social standing. Other cultures adhere to a philosophy of ascribed roles in society; an individual is born into a particular social class and there is nothing that can be done to warrant movement to a higher level. The caste system in India is one that restricts members from gaining social status. Relationships in these cultures are restricted to those who are in the same social class.

Characterisics of Culture

In the next sections we explain the three primary characteristics of culture: 1) it is learned, 2) it is dynamic, and 3) it is pervasive.

Culture Is Learned

The preferred ways of behaving as a member of a society are learned at a young age. Consider the learning experiences of children. Adults teach them how to say words, which foods can be eaten with the fingers and which should be eaten with utensils, and songs and rituals that are part of the culture. They may be taught that profanity is not acceptable and they are rewarded for saying the Pledge of Allegiance. Children are even taught biases and prejudices. Expectations about the nature of relationships and communication are also learned at a young age. For example, in the United States it is viewed as unacceptable for male friends to hold hands. In some Arab cultures it is not uncommon to see two men engage in this behavior. Society teaches us the behaviors that are accepted by most members of the culture, and, at the same time, instills within us a response mechanism for reacting to violations of cultural norms.

What is acceptable behavior in a culture is learned both explicitly and implicitly. Explicit learning involves actual instructions regarding the preferred way of behaving. A school may print a brochure that specifies the dress code that is required of all students, or a teacher may instruct students to raise their hand before speaking in class. In our families, we learn expectations for communication in relationships. For example, a young girl whose mother has experienced negative relationships with former spouses might be taught to "never trust men" and may find it difficult to engage in disclosure and to form relationships with males. Implicit learning occurs via observation. We are not directly told what behaviors are preferred; rather they are learned by observing others. Our choices of what to wear for a first date or the first day of work are

Children are taught biases and prejudices.

influenced by observing what others wear or by what we have learned from the media. We learn the preferred ways of dressing so as to be accepted by our peers.

Culture Is Dynamic

Over time, events occur that cause change; cultures do not remain static. Consider changes in relationships that occurred after the events of September 11th. In the days and months following the tragedy, people reported that they engaged in more frequent communication with friends and family members. People were more willing to engage in open expressions of affection. Cultures and their members also change as a result of "borrowing" aspects from other cultures. It is quite common to open a fashion magazine and see examples of trends being borrowed from other cultures. For example, many stores and catalogues showcase Asian-inspired t-shirts and jewelry that include Chinese or Japanese writing. It is also quite common to see clothing adopting cultural styles such as the recent style of women in the U.S. wearing kimono style dresses.

Depending on a culture's approach to uncertainty, the encouragement and acceptance of change may occur at different rates. Within the last decade, change has occurred at a rapid rate within the United States. Technological advances make some computers obsolete a year or two after purchase. Food and exercise trends also appear to go through changes as new diet fads are constantly introduced to the culture. In 2003, the Atkins diet gained popularity in the United States and carbohydrates were declared to be taboo. Not only did people begin to alter their dietary habits, restaurants altered their menus by designing and promoting dishes that were "Atkins-friendly." Eventually, doctors began questioning the health issues associated with the Atkins diet, and in 2005, the U.S. Department of Agriculture revised the traditional food pyramid to include

Not all cultures embrace change.

six dimensions recommended for a healthy diet. Not only do cultures change with regard to food and clothing styles, but popular culture also undergoes transitions. The popularity of television shows change as new shows are introduced. What is "hot" one season may be "out" the next.

While you may initially question what impact these changes in various cultural aspects has on our interpersonal relationships, consider the amount of time we spend discussing aspects of culture with others. Friends gather around the water cooler and in dorm rooms to discuss the previous night's episode of Survivor or Desperate Housewives. They analyze the reasons for changes in the cafeteria menu to accommodate society's low carb trend. Changes in our culture provide many topics for discussion and debate in our personal relationships. However, not all cultures embrace change. In fact, some cultures are reluctant to implement change. For example, Germany scores high on uncertainty avoidance. This high score is reflective of the culture's reluctance to change as well as the desire to have strict rules and guidelines in place to maintain order. Some countries, such as Argentina, may find that their members adopt similar religious beliefs. When the majority of a culture's members practice the same religion, there is very little uncertainty about the beliefs held by individuals.

Culture Is Pervasive

Culture is everywhere. Take a moment and look around you. Chances are that you see numerous examples of your culture's influence with one simple glance. Is there a computer on your desk? Perhaps there are posters, photos, or artwork on the walls. Is there a television turned on or music playing? Maybe you are on campus and there are other students nearby. Take a look at the style of their clothes and listen to the words that they are saying to one another. Each of these things demonstrates

the pervasive nature of culture. It surrounds us—in fact, we cannot escape the influence of our culture. If one were to adopt a descriptive definition of culture, this prevalence could be seen as influencing everything: our expectations for relationships, the clothing we wear, the language we speak, the food we choose, and even our daily schedules. Culture is represented not only in our material possessions, but also in the values, beliefs, and attitudes that comprise our personal orientation system. It shapes virtually every aspect of our lives and influences our thoughts and actions. Culture also affects how we initiate and maintain our interpersonal relationships. In many European cultures, it is common for teenagers to go out on large "group" dates, while females in Australia may ask out males and offer to split the cost of a date. In China and Japan, dating is typi-

Culture surrounds our lives and its influence is everywhere.

cally reserved for those who are older, typically in their twenties. Dating was discouraged in India until recently. Families were expected to introduce couples and help them get to know one another socially in preparation for marriage. While online dating has grown in popularity in the U.S. and many European countries, this method of initiating romantic relationships would be frowned upon in cultures that view dating as a time for getting to know one's potential future in-laws.

By taking a moment to consider the impact that culture has on our lives, it becomes clear that culture and communication are inseparable. Our verbal and nonverbal messages are shaped by our culture's influence, and we learn about our culture through the messages we receive from others. Given the level of influence that culture and communication have on one another, it should come as no surprise that the diversity that exists among members of a culture impacts the relationships that they form with one another.

How Diversity Impacts Interpersonal Relationships

Think about the first day in a new school or at a new job. Consider some of the thoughts that may go through your mind. Probably many expectations are formed about the people you see as you walk through the door. Some of the differences may be visible simply by looking at the other person, such as their gender, race, or age. In addition, many "hidden" differences also exist, such as their beliefs, values, and attitudes. Once the realization sets in that we are expected to communicate with someone whose cultural makeup is likely different from our own, we quickly search for any information, or cues, to help us make sense of how to interact in the particular situation. The process which helps us to organize the stimuli that bombards us in a potential communication encounter is known as perception.

In Chapter Two, we defined perception as the process of selecting, organizing, and interpreting stimuli into something that makes sense or is meaningful. Our perception causes us to view relationships and communicate in ways that are potentially different from the ways of others. The perception process may be explained in this way. Think about all the possible things that you could identify by using all five of your senses. Consider all the possible things that you could see, touch, feel, taste, and smell. Literally hundreds of stimuli compete for your attention at a given time! It would be virtually impossible to perceive all of the stimuli at the same time, so we pick and choose which things to pay attention to and ignore the others. Because individuals are selective in what they pay attention to and how they interpret it, each person forms their own perception of behaviors and events. As a result, we each have our own unique view of the world.

The role of selective interpretation was also discussed in Chapter Two. Because of our cultural influences, we may assign different meanings to behaviors. If we do not take the time or make the effort to see what is truly behind our interpretation, serious barriers to effective communication may occur. Imagine the reaction of a teacher who traveled to Hong Kong and, at a celebration dinner, was presented with an appetizer of chicken feet! She perceived the consumption of chicken feet to be disgusting, and her nonverbal behavior of wrinkling her nose and her refusal of the appetizer offended her hosts. The teacher regretted her reaction of obvious disgust, especially after she considered the fact that individuals of other cultures might view her favorite food (a cheeseburger), as disgusting due to their perception of the cow being sacred.

Personal Orientation System

Each individual has a set of predispositions which serves as a guide for thoughts, actions, and behaviors. These predispositions are comprised of one's needs, beliefs, values, and attitudes and are commonly referred to as one's personal orientation system. Communication plans and relationship expectations are developed and organized based on these characteristics. Many of the components of the personal orientation system are learned within the cultural context. Messages are transmitted from parents, teachers, and friends who teach the younger members of society to perceive certain actions as good or bad, fair or unfair. For example, Chinese children are taught to value history and tradition, and stories of the past are viewed as lessons to guide their behavior. Children in the U.S. tend to view stories of the past as entertaining, but instead of following tradition, they are encouraged to find new and innovative ways of doing things. When faced with decisions regarding the proper way to respond in situations, our needs, beliefs, values, and attitudes assist us in guiding our perception of a situation.

Needs

All individuals have needs, strong feelings of discomfort or desire which motivate them to achieve satisfaction or comfort. A strong relationship exists between needs and interpersonal communication, with communication serving as the primary mechanism through which we satisfy needs. If a student needs to have an assignment explained more clearly, he or she must communicate that need to the instructor. If an employee needs assistance in obtaining a copy of a company report, communication with the human resources director or with a supervisor can satisfy the need.

Maslow's hierarchy of needs (1954) organizes the needs which humans must fulfill. A hierarchical structure helps us to understand the importance and priority of having some needs achieved before others. At the most basic level are the physiological needs of humans. These include the need for food, clothing, and shelter. While most cultures are able to devote adequate attention to meeting these needs, others cannot. The next level includes safety needs. Individuals possess a motivation to feel safe and secure in their surroundings. However, cultures differ in their methods for satisfying this need. At the middle of the hierarchy are affection needs. Schutz (1958) identified three basic needs across cultures: affection, control, and inclusion. We have a need to love and to be loved. Esteem needs are

Everyone has a need to love and be loved.

located at the next level of Maslow's hierarchy. Humans have a need to feel good about themselves. Interpersonal communication with others is one mechanism for meeting this need. Things that cultural members say and do impact the fulfillment of these needs. At the highest level of Maslow's hierarchy is self-actualization. This level is achieved when an individual feels that he or she has accomplished all that can be achieved in a lifetime. As the U.S. Army's motto implies, self-actualization is fulfilled when an individual feels that the goal "be all that you can be" has been met.

When applying Maslow's hierarchy to our interpersonal relationships, it becomes apparent that communication is the mechanism through which we meet some of our most basic needs, as well as fulfilling higher levels of need. Communication is the key to understanding individuals' needs and in comprehending the value placed on need fulfillment. Understanding what needs individuals have and their importance enables us to interact more effectively and to avoid misunderstandings. While one person may have a need for power and status, another may possess a strong need for friendship and affection. The intensity with which each of these needs is experienced may cause these two people to interact in very different ways.

Beliefs

A second component of culture which guides our thoughts and behaviors is our belief system. Beliefs are an important part of understanding our interactions with diverse others because they not only influence our conscious reactions to situations, but dominate our subconscious thoughts as well. We are constantly influenced by our beliefs. They are our personal convictions regarding the truth or existence of things. Through our interpersonal communication, we form beliefs about ourselves and our relationships. Based on positive interactions with your family members and teachers, you may believe that you are destined to succeed in college. Less supportive interactions might result in the belief that you will accomplish very little in life. Ultimately, these beliefs impact our communication with others. The formation of the central substance of our belief system begins at a very early age and continues to evolve as we grow and form relationships with others.

When crossing cultural borders, an examination of the beliefs possessed by a culture's members yields some fascinating differences. People from Malaysia believe that it is bad luck to touch someone on the top of the head as it is believed to be the location of the center for spiritual energy. Hawaiians possess a number of beliefs about the messages indicated by the appearance of a rainbow. Consider the superstitious beliefs held by members of the American culture. Walking under a ladder, having a black cat cross your path, and the groom seeing the bride on the wedding day prior to the ceremony are all believed to be signs of bad luck. Our beliefs impact our interpersonal communication.

Because most people do not question social institutions, many of the beliefs of a culture are perpetuated from generation to generation without any thought being given to the reasons for the existence of the beliefs. Some individuals have reported that reactions to their questioning of beliefs have been so negative that they feared rejection in their relationships and simply adopted the accepted beliefs into their own personal orientation system.

Values

Values serve as the guide for an individual's behavior. They dictate what we should and should not do. Kluckhohn (1951) describes values as a personal philosophy, either explicitly or implicitly expressed, that influences the choice of alternative actions which may be available to an individual. This definition highlights the relationship between values and communication in that values are communicated both explicitly and implicitly through our behaviors. The majority of our actions are reflective of the values which are firmly established in our personal orientation system.

Values are often communicated explicitly through verbal communication. Some cultural values are evident in the proverbs shared among people. "A stitch in time saves nine" communicates the value placed on addressing issues or problems when they are small

Friendships are often the most valued things in peoples' lives.

rather than waiting until they grow bigger. Practicality and being satisfied with what you have is expressed in the proverb, "A bird in the hand is worth two in the bush." The Swedish proverb, "Friendship doubles our joy and divides our grief" describes the value placed on friendships. In his book, *A Pirate Looks at Fifty*, Jimmy Buffett communicates his value for family relationships and friendships when he states, "I have always looked at life as a voyage, mostly wonderful, sometimes frightening. In my family and friends I have discovered treasure more valuable than gold."

Nonverbal communication may be a more subtle means for communicating values. Many Asian cultures practice the custom of giving a gift to demonstrate the value for reciprocity and friendship. It is not unusual for students to offer their teachers gifts in exchange for the lessons that are learned. In the American culture, many teachers would be extremely uncomfortable accepting these gifts, resulting in confusion in the student-teacher relationship, possibly making subsequent interactions uncomfortable. It is important to gain an understanding not only of the values held by a culture's members, but also the ways in which individuals communicate these values. By doing so, misunderstandings may be avoided.

Attitudes: Stereotyping and Prejudice

Throughout our lives, each of us develops learned predispositions to respond in favorable or unfavorable ways toward people or objects. These tendencies are known as **attitudes**. A primary goal of this chapter is to assist you in identifying your responses to differences as well as to help you to understand your internal orientations guiding these reactions. If ever we interpret another's cultural customs or actions as being wrong or offensive, it is important to understand our own attitudes and how our culture has influenced their formation. Failure to understand these tendencies can result in irrational attitude formation, producing negative results in interpersonal relationships with diverse others. Two attitude formations to avoid are stereotypes and prejudices.

Stereotyping. Stereotyping results from the inability to see and appreciate the uniqueness of individuals. When generalizations about a group are made and are then attributed to any individuals who either associate with, or are members of, the group, the process of **stereotyping** is evolving. Three steps have been identified in the process of stereotyping.

The first step involves categorizing a group of people based on observable characteristics that they have in common. An international student from Scotland commented that she thought that all Americans would be like the people she saw on Beverly Hills 90210—tan, attractive, and extremely materialistic. As a result, she reported that she was initially apprehensive about forming relationships with many of her American classmates and socialized mainly with other international students.

The second step involves assigning characteristics to a group of people. An example of this step would be a popular magazine characterizing mothers who are employed outside the home as being less dedicated to their children.

Finally, we apply those characteristics to any individual that is a member of that group. An example would be the teacher who assumes that a student-athlete is not serious about academic studies. Following the events of 9/11, some members of Arab cultures have reported that they have been subjected to racial profiling. **Racial profiling** occurs when law enforcement or other officials use race as a basis for investigating a person of criminal involvement. This is a result of applying the single characteristic of race in determining whether a person should be viewed as threatening.

While stereotyping can be irrational, it is actually quite normal. Because humans are uncomfortable with uncertainty, stereotyping enables us to make predictions about our potential interactions with others. In order to become more competent in our interactions with diverse others, it is important to realize that stereotypes *can* and *do* impact our perceptions and our communication.

Prejudice. Another form of attitude which involves negative reactions toward a group of people based on inflexible and inaccurate assumptions is commonly known as **prejudice.** In essence, prejudice involves "pre-judging" individuals. Some of the most common forms of prejudice in the U.S. include racism, sexism, and ageism.

Racism. **Racism** refers to prejudice against an individual or group based on their racial composition. **Race** is a term used to refer to inherited biological characteristics such as skin color, eye color, hair texture, and facial structure.

In her 1995 film entitled *Blue Eyed*, Jane Elliott shares with viewers a diversity training session conducted with adults of various racial and ethnic backgrounds in Kansas City. Blue-eyed members of the group are told that they are inferior to the rest of the group simply based on their eye color. As the film unfolds, it is amazing to watch the confusion, mistrust, lack of confidence, and fear of communication that emerges among members of the group. Elliott explains that while some may consider her decision to discriminate simply on the basis of eye color to be irrational, it is not much different than choosing to treat someone differently on the basis of skin color. She points out that the chemical which produces eye color is the same one that produces skin color.

Ageism. Negative communication toward persons based on their age is referred to as **ageism**. In our culture, some people assume that senior citizens are incapable of making contributions to society and can be considered helpless. In 1967, Congress passed the ADEA (Age Discrimination in Employment Act) to protect older workers against age discrimination. According to

In our culture, some people assume that senior citizens are incapable of making contributions to society and can be considered helpless.

the law, an employer cannot replace an employee over the age of forty with a younger person if the current employee is able to satisfactorily perform her or his job. Sue Sewell, age fifty-one, expresses her frustration of ageism in the workplace:

"Society is missing out on the talent and a wealth of experience of the older worker. I have recently returned to the workplace after a spell at home and have noticed that some younger workers and management are not tolerant of the older worker. I think the older worker is stereotyped as being slow and less likely to be able to pick up new ideas and be able to use new technology. I, like many others in my age bracket, cannot give up work as we have mortgages, bills to pay, and dependents to support. I actually also enjoy being out in the world of work; it makes me feel more a part of society. If the retirement age is to be 70 and beyond as is being mooted at present, then we must have more opportunities for people to be employed whatever their age." (http://www.maturityworks.co.uk/uploads/files/matwrksreport.qxd1.pdf)

Ageism is also communicated when negative prejudices are harbored by adults against teenagers based on the attitude that teens are rude and unruly. While some equate college students on Spring Break with partying and drinking, recent programs have been developed on college campuses to provide students with opportunities to complete community service projects during their break from studies. In 2006, thousands of college students traveled to post-Hurricane Katrina Mississippi and New Orleans and spent their Spring Break vacations assisting in the clean-up process.

Sexism. **Sexism** refers to negative communication directed toward persons of a particular sex. In the United States, sexist attitudes have traditionally been directed toward females. As a result, females have experienced discrimination in the workplace and in other walks of life. While stories of sexism frequently focus on the prejudices against females, men also are subject to sexist behaviors. Consider the father who stays at home and raises the children. As he shops for groceries with the children in the cart or plays with them at the park on a sunny weekday afternoon, he may hear a comment such as, "It's so nice that he's babysitting the children!" Not surprisingly, he may become offended because it is assumed that he is not capable of being the primary caregiver for his children.

Communicating Prejudice

There are three primary means for communicating prejudice. Verbal abuse refers to the process of engaging in comments or jokes that are insulting or demeaning to a targeted group. Consider the impressions that we form of people as a result of their negative verbal behaviors toward others. The racist comments made by *Seinfeld's* Michael Richards may have caused some Kramer fans to question their positive attitudes toward the actor. **Discrimination** involves denying an individual or group of people their rights. While prejudice involves negative cognitions, or thoughts, discrimination is displayed when behaviors are used to express one's negative cognitions. Typically, discrimination is expressed through negative verbal comments made toward a group or an individual, with physical avoidance being the ultimate goal. The most severe form of prejudice is violence. On April 29, 1992, the verdict in the trial involving the 1991 beating of Rodney King by four Los Angeles police officers was read. Only one of the four officers was found guilty of using excessive force; the others were cleared of all charges against them.

As word of the verdict was spread, riots erupted throughout Los Angeles. During the next three days, television viewers witnessed physical attacks, arson, and looting throughout the city. In the end, more than 4,000 people were injured, more than fifty were killed, and the city suffered over $1 billion in damages. This violence demonstrates the potentially extreme outcome of prejudice.

Fortunately, a 2004 study of 2,000 teens conducted by Teenage Research Unlimited (TRU) in Illinois points to changing trends among young Americans. Nearly sixty percent of teenagers reported that they have close friends of different races. Friendships of diverse religious or political beliefs and economic backgrounds are also prominent among today's teens. TRU President Michael Wood summarized the changing views of this

© 2012. Courtesy of JaxonPhotoGroup.

Teens prefer to have friends who share their interests, regardless of their backgrounds.

generation as, "Teens still prefer to hang out with peers who share common ground with them. But that no longer means that their friends have to necessarily *look* the part. It's all about attitudes and actions—about who you are and what you do, not what you are" (http://www.teenresearch.com/PRview .cfm?edit_id=278.) Additional research points to the benefits of multicultural interactions that occur among college students. A 1997 study found that college students who have frequent interactions with students of different racial backgrounds and engage in positive discussions about race and ethnicity tend to have a higher self-concept and report that they are more satisfied with college (Smith and Associates, 1997).

Functions of Prejudice

While prejudice is often based on false, irrational, and inflexible generalizations, it is often considered "normal." Why do individuals form prejudice? Three primary reasons for forming prejudice have been identified.

Acceptance. Acceptance is when a person communicates negative feelings toward a particular group in order to fit in within a desired group. An example of this is when a fraternity member expresses hatred for another fraternity's members. When asked why he has these strong feelings, the only reason offered is "because all Alpha Betas dislike them."

Defend the ego. Another reason for communicating prejudice is to defend the ego. By expressing negative feelings and attitudes toward a group of people, individuals create a scapegoat for their own misfortunes. An employee was overheard expressing his prejudice against women being selected for administrative positions. Upon further questioning, he admitted that he did not actually harbor any ill feelings toward women supervisors. Rather, he was frustrated by the fact that a woman had been offered the position rather than him.

Provide information. A final reason for prejudice is to provide information. As was stated earlier, humans have a need to reduce uncertainty. Unfortunately, many individuals form prejudice as a means for forming knowledge about a group of people with whom little or no contact has been made. Recall our earlier example of the student from Scotland who was reluctant to interact with American students because of the stereotypes formed as a result of watching *Beverly Hills 90210*. Because limited information was available, the student experienced high levels of uncertainty about how to interact with American college students. Prejudices were formed as a means to reduce the level of uncertainty and to provide a framework for building expectations. By forming these negative predispositions, an information base was constructed on which to form expectations about potential interactions.

Cultural Value Orientations

To understand the values shared by a culture's members, a number of scholars have developed models for studying value orientations. These models pose questions designed to measure the intensity with which a culture's members value specific characteristics.

Kluckhohn and Strodbeck (1961) developed one of the first models of cultural value orientation, and it is still being used in research today. Questions are designed to gain insight into such perceptions regarding relationships between humans and humans and nature. Sample questions include:

- What is the basic nature of human beings? Are they inherently evil and incapable of being trusted, or do most humans have a good heart?
- How are social relationships organized? Are relationships viewed as being hierarchical with divisions of power? Or should equal rights be present in all social relationships?

Hall's model of cultural values (1976) represents a continuum of characteristics associated with high-context and low-context cultures. These differences are characterized by distinct differences in communication styles. Cultures which fall at the low-context end of the continuum exhibit high verbal tendencies. This style is associated with a direct approach and verbal expressiveness. A philosophy of "say what you mean" is embraced. High-context cultures, on the other hand, prefer a more indirect style; cues about the intended message are interpreted through nonverbal channels. Whereas persons from a low-context culture expect messages to be direct, those from a high-context culture search the environment for cues. Rather than asking a person whether he or she is happy, high-context cultures would infer these feelings from other cues such as posture, facial expressions, and disposition. Consider the difficulties experienced by a couple who have different cultural backgrounds:

> Alec was confused. He and Miki had been living together for the past year and were engaged to be married in a few months. One evening, Miki was silent as they ate dinner. He knew something was upsetting her, but she kept insisting that things were fine. Miki was extremely frustrated as well. Why did Alec always insist that she tell him what was wrong? Did she always have to put her feelings into words? Why couldn't Alec be more in tune with her nonverbal behaviors and understand that things were not quite right?

This example illustrates the difference between the influence of the low-context approach of the U.S. on Alec's behavior and the high-context approach of Miki's Japanese upbringing. Miki expects Alec to be more aware of the messages that are being communicated via nonverbal channels, while Alec expects Miki to say what is bothering her.

A final model of cultural values is presented by Hofstede (1980). Four dimensions of values were identified by examining the attitudes of employees in more than forty cultures. These dimensions include individualism/collectivism, power distance, masculinity/femininity, and uncertainty avoidance.

Individualism/collectivism. Individualism/collectivism describes the relationship between the individual and the groups to which he or she belongs. Individualistic cultures, such as in the United States, focus on individual accomplishments and achievements. **Collectivism,** or value and concern for the group, is the primary value of many Asian cultures. Consider the cultural differences portrayed in the automobile manufacturing plant in the film *Gung Ho.* Asian managers took great pride in their work as their per-

Individualism/collectivism describes the relationship between the individual and the groups to which he or she belongs.

formance ultimately reflected on their group. They did not dream of taking time off for personal reasons. The American workers, on the other hand, whose behaviors reflected individualism, placed their individual needs over those of the company. Employees would take time off to be at the birth of a child or to keep a medical appointment. These differences in the values of the group versus the self had disastrous outcomes, with the company facing the risk of closing as a result of conflicting cultural values.

Power distance. **Power distance** refers to the distribution of power in personal relationships as well as within organizations. Low power distance cultures have a flat structure with most individuals being viewed as equals. The tendency to show favoritism to individuals based on their age, status, or gender is minimized. High power cultures are depicted by a tall hierarchical structure with distinct status differences. Imagine the frustration experienced by a young intercultural couple who had been married for only a few months. The husband, who was Hispanic, was raised in a culture that places the man as the head of the household (high power distance). His wife, who was raised by a single working mother in New York City, valued her independence. The power differential in her family of origin was low, thus she anticipated that her husband would view her as an equal partner in their relationship. As a result of their differing values for status and power based on their roles as husband and wife, the couple experienced many arguments.

Masculine/feminine. Prevalence of masculine and feminine traits in a culture characterizes Hofstede's (1980) dimensions of masculinity and femininity. Masculine cultures demonstrate a preference for assertiveness, ambition, and achievement. Characteristics of responsiveness, nurturance, and cooperation are associated with cultures at the feminine end of this dimension. Gender roles in these cultures are perceived to be more equal. Cultures such as those found in Japan and Mexico exhibit more masculine tendencies, while those found in Brazil, Sweden, and Taiwan are more feminine.

Uncertainty avoidance. **Uncertainty avoidance** refers to the willingness of a culture to approach or to avoid change. Cultures high in uncertainty avoidance demonstrate a preference for avoiding change. They embrace tradition and order. China and Germany are examples of countries with cultures that avoid uncertainty and embrace tradition. Cultures low in uncertainty avoidance welcome the possibility of change and are more willing to take risks. The United States and Finland are more open to change and are more tolerant of taking risks and adopting new and innovative approaches.

Understanding these dimensions can provide cues as to which values are promoted among members of a culture. This information is useful for determining the appropriate methods to approach interpersonal communication and for providing valuable information that assists in checking the accuracy of one's perceptions.

Cultures low in uncertainty avoidance welcome the possibility of change and are more willing to take risks.

Suggestions for Successful Interpersonal Relationships with Diverse Others

As shown throughout this chapter, perceptions can be faulty. But there are strategies which can enhance accuracy in perception. Each of the suggestions below involves understanding and practicing better interpersonal communication.

- Engage in careful listening and clear communication. Focus on listening for what is really being said, not what you want to hear. Be clear and explicit in your communication. Refrain from using slang or idioms.
- Refrain from judging people based on observable differences such as race, ethnicity, or gender.
- Do not misjudge people based on verbal (e.g., accent or grammar) or nonverbal differences.
- Be patient with yourself. Remember that becoming an effective cross-cultural communicator requires skills and knowledge. It takes time to practice those skills. You may make mistakes, but there are lessons to be learned from those faux pas.
- Practice patience with others. Cultural influences are powerful, and making the transition from one culture's way of thinking and behaving to another's takes time.
- Check for understanding. Do not be afraid to ask for clarification or to ensure that you understood what was being communicated. One simple question now can save offending someone later.

Summary

Throughout this chapter we have discussed the prevalence of diversity in all of our interpersonal relationships. While diversity is most frequently identified based on observable characteristics such as race, ethnicity, or sex, it is important to consider additional variables that influence our communication choices as we interact with others. Individual beliefs, attitudes, and values have a significant impact on the messages we send as well as on our reactions to the messages that we receive. At this point we would like to reiterate the importance of studying and understanding the impact of cultural diversity on our interpersonal interactions—by taking a moment to enhance your own knowledge and skills, you are better equipped to understand the reasons underlying your own communication preferences as well as the communication choices of others.

Communication for Today's Student

Chapter 6 – Intercultural Relationships

Exercise 6.1 – Barriers

Let's begin this exercise on culture by brainstorming the titles of movies that have issues of cultures as their subject matter. We learned that we study culture and diversity and their impact on interpersonal relations for three reasons: 1) to increase awareness of self, 2) application for technological transformations and 3) understanding of demographics transitions. To gain a better understanding of culture and the benefits of diversity, let's prepare the following exercise with a partner.

Part One – Write a brief synopsis of the movie, *Get Out* or any familiar movie whose primary subject matter involves the issue of culture.

A. Identify two (2) examples of cultures.

B. Identify the co-cultures.

Part Two – Define the Barriers and give an example from the movie that illustrates each.

Barriers	Definition	Illustration from Movie
Ethnocentricism		
Stereotyping		
Prejudice		
Racism		
Discrimination		

Part Three – We deal with issues of culture based upon our needs here values, attitudes, and beliefs. Define each. Describe how each has an impact upon the intercultural communication in the movie that you chose.

	Definition	Description
Needs		
Values		
Attitudes		
Beliefs		

RESEARCHING YOUR TOPIC

After reading this chapter, you should be able to:

- ☑ Develop a research strategy.
- ☑ Explain the factors in establishing speaker and message credibility.
- ☑ Analyze the audience.
- ☑ Locate print and online resources.
- ☑ Cite sources within a speech.
- ☑ Identify forms of support.
- ☑ Demonstrate an understanding of the guidelines for citing sources.
- ☑ Establish legitimacy of sources located on the web.
- ☑ Explain the five functions of support.

Key Terms

Analogies	Literal analogies	Research
Biographical sources	Magazines	Secondary sources
Examples	Message credibility	Speaker credibility
Facts	Newspapers	Specialize encyclopedias
Figurative analogies	Opinions	Statistical sources
General encyclopedias	Paraphrase	Statistics
Government documents	Primary sources	Support material
Journals	Quotations	Testimony

7 Scenario

"The library is closing in one hour," the automated voice sang throughout the library, alerting everyone that they had merely an hour to wrap up their activities.

Michelle's eyes grew more and more tired as she stared at the holographic computer screen in front of her. She waved her hand and her Facebook and Twitter timeline rolled away, revealing her research on the Nigerian girls who were kidnapped by a Muslim terrorist group called Boko Haram. She had accomplished a lot today, but she didn't have as much information as she needed. It was so easy getting distracted. Michelle grew frustrated again and waved her hand, bringing her Facebook back up on the main screen. Her FaceTime program popped up and revealed her older sister Melody's call. Melody put on her headset and adjusted her mouthpiece.

"Answer!"

Melody's sweet face popped up on the screen. "Hey, sis."

"Hey, Melody," Michelle smiled. "How's it going?"

"Good, can't complain," Melody frowned. "Where are you? You're not in your room."

"I'm in the library trying to do research," Michelle said, moving her index finger up and down in the air as she scrolled through her Twitter timeline.

"Looks like you're tweeting," Melody scolded.

"Mel, don't chastise me. I'm so tired of researching. I don't know how to present this topic, other than by using what the news outlets are reporting. How can I write a speech and present it from another angle when all I'm getting is one side?"

"Well, before you began, did you develop a research strategy?" Melody asked.

"Uhh . . ."

"That's your problem already," Melody said as she shook her head. "You need to develop one so you can see every avenue you want to explore when it comes to this topic."

"That's true." Michelle nodded. "I can't believe I forgot this important step."

What approach do you use when writing a paper or speech?

Each speaker faces multiple decisions during the speech development process. Sometimes beginning speakers find selecting a topic to be the most difficult aspect of the process. You may feel relief when your instructor approves the topic you have chosen, but your work has just begun. After choosing a topic and developing the general and specific purposes of your speech, it is time for research and to develop appropriate supporting material. Credibility is crucial. To a large extent, your listeners will evaluate your speech on the amount and relevance of research conducted and the types of supporting material used. The extent to which a speaker is perceived as a competent spokesperson is considered **speaker credibility.** A person's background, set of ethics, and delivery are all part of speaker credibility. **Message credibility,** on the other hand, is the extent to which the speech is considered to be factual and well supported through documentation (Fleshler, Ilardo, and Demoretcky 1974). It is this second type of credibility that is the focus of this chapter. Through research, one can find sufficient, relevant, and timely supporting material which will enhance a speaker's message credibility.

We live in an information society that produces far more information than we can use. Books are added to library collections on a regular basis, new information is found quarterly in journals, weekly in magazines, and daily in newspapers. Computers give us access to innumerable websites and ever larger databases. As a result of this galaxy of available information, one of your most important jobs will be to decide what is relevant and what is not, what you should incorporate into your speech and what you should discard. Setting limits on your own research requires that you stay focused on your specific purpose. Do what is required to give an effective presentation; do not allow yourself to be led down an interesting, but unrelated, path.

With all the information available on the computer, it's a big job to decide what material to use and what to discard.

Research is the raw material that forms the foundation of your speech. It gives you the tools you need to expand your specific purpose into a full-length presentation. The raw material may include interviewing experts on your topic and locating print and web-based information. The result of this process is your knowledge of the topic.

Often, research can lead you to deliver a slightly different type of speech than you expected. As facts emerge, you may expand your speech in one place, streamline it in another, and take it apart to accommodate new information. Ultimately, you will piece it together in its final form.

The research process alone is not sufficient. You must determine how to use it most effectively. **Supporting material** is the information used in a particular way to make your case. For example, if you were preparing a speech to inform your class on services available in your community for individuals who are categorized as low income, your *research process* may lead you to an organization that specializes in debt consolidation, another that offers free or low-cost medical care, an agency that gives out food for low-income individuals, and a organization that supplies children with free school supplies. As you develop your speech, one of your points might be that "a variety of services are available in our community." For *supporting material*, these agencies provide *examples* of available services. As the types of supporting material can be quite varied, you must determine what is most suited to the topic and to your listeners.

Develop a Research Strategy

Instructors rarely say, "Go! Prepare an informative speech." Instead, they establish parameters regarding topics, length of speech, minimum number of sources, and types of sources. What is the minimum number of sources required? How many different sources do you need? If you use three different issues of *Newsweek*, do they count as one source or as three? Can you use information from 1980 or 1990, or did your instructor say all material needs to be no more than five years old?

Do you need both print and online sources? Does online access to a magazine count as a print source? Can you use all types of print sources? Does your instructor allow you to count an interview as a source? Can you use your family or yourself as a source? Before you begin to research your topic, make sure you know the constraints of the assignment as specified by your instructor.

The outline at the beginning of this chapter identifies aspects of the research strategy. Supporting material will be discussed later in the chapter. Specifically, in developing your research strategy, you need to address the following aspects.

Before you begin your topic research, make sure you know the parameters of the speech assignment.

1. Analyze the audience
   (What are the needs, interests, and knowledge level of my audience?)
2. Assess your knowledge/skill
   (What knowledge or skill do I have in relation to this topic?)
3. Search print and online resources
   (Based on available resources, where and what will I find the most useful?)
4. Interview, if appropriate
   (Will this speech be helped by interviewing someone with personal knowledge or expertise about this topic?)

Each of these aspects can be viewed as stages. The following section provides a look at each of these stages in greater detail.

1. Start (and End) with an Audience Analysis

Throughout this book we stress the importance of connecting with your audience. Before you determine the general or specific purpose for your speech, consider your audience's needs. As explained in the previous chapter, a careful audience analysis gives you information about who they are and what they value. Understanding your audience helps you develop specific questions that can be answered as you follow your search strategy. For example, suppose you were planning an informative speech explaining prenuptial agreements. You may have some general questions about the topic, such as the following:

When do most people get married?
What are the statistics on the number of marriages and divorces each year?
Who benefits financially and who suffers as a result of a divorce?
What happens to property in divorce?
How expensive is an agreement?
Can people draw up the agreement without legal counsel?

To construct an effective speech that achieves its specific purpose, whether it is informative or persuasive, think about your specifixc audience. So, if you are working on a speech about prenuptial agreements, consider additional questions such as:

Considering the age of my audience, how much do they know about prenuptial agreements?
What do most people think about prenuptial agreements?
What might be this audience's greatest areas of concern or interest regarding the topic?

Answering the more specific questions related to your audience helps you to determine the depth and breadth of information needed to answer your more general questions. By developing questions based on your understanding of the needs of your audience, you can increase the likelihood of establishing an effective speaker-audience connection. Reflect again on your audience *after* you have gathered information to determine whether or not you have collected enough material and if it is the right type of material to meet your audience's needs and interests.

2. Assess Your Own Knowledge and Skills

Some students find topic selection difficult because they think they have nothing to offer or the class will not be interested. Upon reflection, however, you may find you have unique experiences or you have knowledge that others do not. Perhaps you were an exchange student, so you have had firsthand experience of another culture. Maybe you were raised by parents who spoke a different language, and you know what it is like to be bilingual. Maybe you live with an unusual disease.

Do you have unique knowledge that would make an interesting speech topic?

Start your research process by assessing your own knowledge and skills. Most likely, you have direct knowledge or experience related to several topics. Your family may own a monument shop or a restaurant, and you grew up exposed to issues related to these professions. Maybe by the time you started college, you held one or more jobs, joined a political club, pursued hobbies like video games, or played sports such as soccer or rugby. You may know more about Jackie Chan movies than anyone on campus, or you may play disk golf. Examining your unique experiences or varied interests is a logical starting point for developing a speech.

Having personal knowledge or experience can make an impact on your audience. A student with Type I diabetes can speak credibly on what it is like to take daily injections and deal with the consequences of both low and high blood sugar. A student who works as a barista at the local coffee shop can demonstrate how to make a good shot of espresso. CAUTION: Remember the phrase, "Too much knowledge may be dangerous." Sometimes students want to share every detail with the audience, and that information can become tedious or overwhelming.

3. Search Print and Online Resources

Once you have assessed your own knowledge or skills, it is time to search print and online resources for other supporting material. The computer provides a rich playing field that also complicates our lives. We have more choices, but we have to work harder to sift through them.

Your search may result in more questions, including the following: What information is most essential to this topic? What will have the greatest impact? How much background do I need to give? Utilizing a variety of sources is advantageous for a variety of reasons; different sources focus on research, philosophy, or current events. They may be part of a daily publication, or are contained within a one-time publication. Sources target different audiences. We suggest you examine and evaluate materials from various sources to select materials that will help you most.

Avoid wasting valuable time floating aimlessly in cyberspace or walking around the library. Instead, if you need direction, *ask a librarian*. Librarians are experts in finding both print and online information efficiently, and they can show you how to use the library's newest search engines and databases. With new online and print resources being added daily, using the expertise of a librarian can make your job as a researcher much easier.

If you are new to campus, and your instructor has not arranged a library tour for your class, consider taking a workshop on using the library. Your library's home page is helpful. Most college libraries belong to a "live chat" consortium on the web, where students may contact a librarian twenty-four hours a day. Also, you can try the Library of Congress online Ask-a-Librarian Service at www.loc.gov and click on "Ask a librarian."

Narrow your focus It is natural to start with a broad topic. But as you search, the information you find will help you move to a more focused topic, enabling you to define—and refine—the approach you take to your speech. Say you are interested in giving an informative speech about the use of performance enhancement drugs in sports. You need to narrow your topic, but you are not quite sure what aspects to consider. Choose a search engine, such as Google, Yahoo!, AltaVista, or Excite.

Try conducting a **key-word search** on Google for "drugs in sports." This is very general. The key-word search leads you to a list of records which are weighted in order of amount of user access. You may have more than a million records or "hits" from which to choose. Look for valid subject headings, and search more deeply than the first three or four records listed.

Results of the key-word search lead you to many possibilities, including "anabolic steroids." You find a website that addresses topics such as what they are, how they work, who uses them, how prevalent they are, the different types, drugs banned by the NCAA, and medical uses. Now you have other areas to pursue. Decide what aspects you want to cover that are relevant to the audience and can be discussed effectively within the given time constraints. Perhaps you are interested in who uses them, so you enter "Who uses anabolic steroids?" This leads you to a website on uses and abuses of steroids. You know you need to define what anabolic steroids are and to find out how they are used and abused. You can continue your research by examining both print and online resources for these specific aspects of performance enhancement drugs. Now you can develop a specific purpose statement and search for information to support it.

Librarians are experts in finding information efficiently to help save research time.

As you search for information, keep three aspects of research in mind: First, recognize the distinction between primary and secondary sources. **Primary sources** include firsthand accounts such as diaries, journals, and letters, as well as statistics, speeches, and interviews. They are records of events as they are first described. **Secondary sources** generally provide an analysis, an explanation, or a restatement of a primary source. If the U.S. Surgeon General issues a report on the dangers of smoking, the report itself (available from the U.S. Surgeon General's Office) is the primary source; newspaper and magazine articles about the report are secondary source material.

Second, there is a relationship between the length of your speech and the amount of time you must spend in research. Many students learn the hard way that five minutes of research will not suffice for a five-minute speech. Conventional wisdom suggests that for every one minute of speaking time, there is an hour of preparation needed. Whatever the length of the speech, you have to spend time uncovering facts and building a strong foundation of support.

Third, finding information is not enough; you must also be able to evaluate it (relevance, reliability, and so on), and utilize it in the most appropriate way in order to achieve your specific purpose. For example, your audience analysis may suggest that specific statistics are necessary to convince your audience. On the other hand, perhaps personal or expert testimony will be most persuasive. Overall, developing a research strategy is one of the most useful things you will learn in college.

Evaluating and using information appropriately is as important as finding it.

Specific library resources In addition to providing access to computers for online searches, each library houses a variety of research materials, including books, reference materials, newspaers, magazines, journals, and government documents. Microfilm, specifically for archived newspapers may still be available, but the government has stopped producing microfiche. If information is not housed in your library, you can electronically extend your search far beyond your campus or community library through interlibrary loan. It may take two weeks or longer to process requests, so planning is especially important when relying on interlibrary loan.

Each library is different. One may not have the same databases or reference materials as another. Some libraries are depositories for your state, and it may be one of a few that receives state documents automatically.

Books. Historically, libraries have been most noted for their collection of books. Many universities have several libraries so students may access the large volume of books in general collections, archived collections, and specific collections. Using the library catalog is essential. Most libraries today have online computer catalogs, which contain records of all materials the library owns. In addition to identifying what books are available and where to find them, an online catalog will also indicate whether a particular book is checked out and when it is due back. Keep in mind that the library groups books by subject, so as you look in the stacks for a particular book, it makes sense to peruse surrounding books for additional resources.

General reference materials. At the beginning of your search, it may be helpful to start with one or more general reference resources, including encyclopedias, dictionaries, biographical sources, and statistical sources. Most likely, your time spent with these materials will be short, but these resources can provide you with basic facts and definitions.

Unlike some of our experiences in primary school, seldom does a student's research start and end with the encyclopedia. The *World Book Encyclopedia* is helpful if you are unfamiliar with a topic or concept. It can provide facts that are concise as well as easy to read and understand. Encyclopedias are either general or specialized. **General encyclopedias** (e.g., *The Encyclopedia Americana* and *Encyclopedia Britannica*) cover a wide range of topics in a broad manner. In con-

General reference resources may be helpful as you begin your search for material.

trast, **specialized encyclopedias,** such as the *Encyclopedia of Religion*, and the *International Encyclopedia of the Social Sciences*, focus on particular areas of knowledge in more detail. Over the last decade, there has been an explosion of discipline-specific encyclopedias. Articles in both general and specialized encyclopedias often contain bibliographies that lead you to additional sources.

Although encyclopedias are helpful as a basic resource, they generally are not accepted as main sources for class speeches. Use them to lead to other information. CAUTION: Do not fall into Wikipedia's web of easy access and understanding. Its legitimacy is questionable. Stephen Colbert, host of the TV show *The Colbert Report*, asked his viewers to log on to the entry "elephants" on Wikipedia.com to report that the elephant population in Africa "has tripled in the last six months." This online encyclopedia noted a spike in inaccurate entries shortly after the show aired. Most instructors discourage use of this online resource.

During your research, you may consult a dictionary when you encounter an unfamiliar word or term. They also provide information on pronunciation, spelling, word division, usage, and etymology (the origins and development of words). As with encyclopedias, dictionaries are classified as either general or specialized. It is likely you have used some general dictionaries such as the *American Heritage Dictionary* or the *Random House College Dictionary*. The dictionary is also just a click away. You might try Merriam-Webster Online (www.m-w.com). Specialized dictionaries cover words associated with a specific subject or discipline, as in the following: *The American Political Dictionary, Black's Law Dictionary,*

Harvard Dictionary of Scientific and Technical Terms, and *Webster's Sports Dictionary*. Many disciplines use their own specialized terminology that is more extensive and focused, and those definitions are found in their journals and books. CAUTION: Check with your instructor before beginning your speech with, "According to Webster's dictionary, the word _____ means . . ." As Harris (2002) notes in his book, *Using Sources Effectively*, "Generally speaking, starting with a dictionary definition not only lacks creativity but it may not be helpful if the definition is too general or vague" (35).

Biographical sources. Biographical sources, which are international, national, or specialized, provide information on an individual's education, accomplishments, and professional activities. This information is useful when evaluating someone's credibility and reliability. A biographical index indicates sources of biographical information in books and journals whereas a biographical dictionary lists and describes the accomplishments of notable people. If you are looking for a brief background of a well-known person, consult the biographical dictionary first. If you need an in-depth profile of a lesser-known person, the biographical index is the better source. Some examples of these sources are Author Biographies Master Index, Biography Index, the New York Times Index, Dictionary of American Biography, European Authors, World Authors, and Dictionary of American Scholars.

Statistical sources. When used correctly, statistics can provide powerful support. Facts and statistics give authority and credibility to research. Many federal agencies produce and distribute information electronically. The *American Statistics Index* (ASI) includes both an index and abstracts of statistical information published by the federal government. Try also the *Index to International Statistics* (IIS) and the *Statistical Abstract of the United States*. The online source LexisNexis touts itself as providing "authoritative legal, news, public records and business information" (www.lexisnexis.com).

Magazines, newspapers, and journals. Magazines (also known as periodicals) and newspapers provide the most recent print information. Once you identify ideas that connect with the needs of your audience, you can look for specific information in magazines and newspapers. General indexes cover such popular magazines and newspapers such as *Time*, *Newsweek*, *U.S. News & World Report*, the *New York Times*, and the *Chicago Tribune*. The *Readers' Guide to Periodical Literature* is an index available online as well as in print form. Other popular indexes include: the *New York Times Index*, *Wall Street Journal*, *Christian Science Monitor*, *Los Angeles Times*, *The Education Index*, *Humanities Index*, *Public Affairs Information Service Bulletin*, *Social Sciences and Humanities Index*, and *Social Sciences Index*.

Newspapers and magazines can be distinquished from journals in many ways. First, the frequency of distribution is different. While newspapers can be accessed daily, and magazines are either weekly or monthly, journals are usually quarterly publications. Second, authors of articles in newspapers and magazines are generally paid by their publisher, whereas authors of journal articles (usually referred to as "researchers" rather than "authors") are generally experts in their particular fields, and have submitted their article(s) on a competitive, reviewed basis. In general, the more prestigious the journal, the more difficult it is to get an article printed in it. Journals may have editorials or book reviews, but they generally focus on qualitative and quantitative research conducted by professionals—doctors, professors, lawyers, and so on. Third, magazines and newspapers are written for general audiences, whereas journal articles are written for a specific audience; an example would be faculty or graduate students interested in communication apprehension. Many journals can be accessed online, but not all are available electronically.

Fourth, and very importantly, journals focus on original, qualitative, and quantitative research. Much of the content in a journal is considered to be a primary source because it reports findings from research conducted by the author.

Government documents. Government documents are prepared by agencies, bureaus, and departments that monitor the affairs and activities of the nation. Documents are issued by the Office of the President, the U.S. Congress, the departments of Commerce, Agriculture, Education, Navy and Army, Indian Affairs, the Veterans' Administration, the Food and Drug Administration, and the FBI.

Through the U.S. Government Printing Office (GPO) one can find unique, authoritative, and timely materials, including detailed census data, vital statistics, congressional papers and reports, presidential documents, military reports, and impact statements on energy, the environment, and pollution. Consult the Monthly Catalog of United States Government Publications, which is available online.

Online research As stated earlier, your librarian can lead you to a variety of material. An enormous amount of databases exist, and one can approach web research in many ways. Without help of some kind, looking for information on the web is like upending the library in a football field and being given a pen light to search for information. The librarian can at least provide you with stadium lights.

Consider using online databases such as InfoTrac and EBSCO. According to InfoTrac College Edition's website (infotrac. thomsonlearning.com), more than 20 million articles from nearly 6,000 sources are available to you. The advantage of using this resource is that you may access cross-disciplinary, reliable, full-length articles. It is free of advertising and available twenty-four hours a day. EBSCO (www.ebsco.com)

If you're unfamiliar with online databases, ask the librarian for assistance.

offers a similar service, and claims to be the most widely used online resource, with access to over 100 databases, and thousands of e-journals. By the time this book is printed, it is a sure bet that even more databases will be available.

Web evaluation criteria Many students will start their research online. Computers are in dorm rooms, dorm halls, academic buildings, and the library. It may take only a few steps to access one. While there is nothing inherently wrong with this, we urge you to proceed with caution. Evaluating the credibility of your online resources is critical. The quantity of information available via the Internet is colossal, and includes highly respected research as well as pure fiction presented as fact. Seek information from competent, qualified sources and avoid information from uninformed individuals with little or no credentials. Ultimately, you are held accountable for the quality and credibility of the sources you use.

As you access each website, it is important to evaluate its legitimacy as a source for your speech. Radford and his colleagues (2006) identify five web evaluation criteria that serve as useful standards for evaluating online information.

1. **Authority.** Authority relates to the concept of credibility. As we know, virtually anyone can become a web publisher. A website that passes this first test contains information provided by an individual, group, or organization known to have expertise in the area.

Questions to guide evaluation include the following:

- What type of group put up the site? (Educational institution? Government agency? Individual? Commercial business? Organization)
- Can you identify the author(s)? (What is the organization or who is the person responsible for the information?)
- What are the credentials of those responsible?

2. **Accuracy.** A website that is accurate is reliable and error-free. One aspect of accuracy is timeliness. If the last time the site was updated was two years ago and the site is discussing a bill before the legislature, then it is no longer accurate. One assumes more accuracy when it is clear that information is scrutinized in some way before being placed on the web. Accuracy is clearly related to authority, since the sites with greater authority are most likely to have mechanisms for determining how something becomes "site-worthy."

Questions to guide evaluation include the following:

- Is the information accurate?
- Does the information confirm or contradict what is found in printed sources?
- Are references given to the sources of information?

3. **Objectivity.** The extent to which website material is presented without bias or distortion relates to objectivity. As you examine the material, you want to determine if it is presented as opinion or fact.

Questions to guide evaluation include the following:

- What is the age level of the intended audience? (Adults? Teenagers? Children?)
- Is the information on the site factual or an expression of opinion?
- Is the author controversial? A known conservative? A known liberal?
- What are the author's credentials?

4. **Coverage.** Coverage refers to the depth and breadth of the material. It may be difficult to determine who the site is targeting. As a result, material may be too general or too specific. Determine if it meets your needs or if critical information is missing.

Questions to guide evaluation include the following:

- What is the intended purpose of the site? (Educational? Informational? Commercial? Recreational?)
- Who is the intended audience (General public? Scholars? Students? Professionals?)
- Is information common knowledge? Too basic? Too technical?
- Does information include multiple aspects of the issue or concern?

5. **Currency.** Currency refers to the timeliness of the material. Some websites exist that have never been updated. Information may be no longer valid or useful. If you look for "Most popular books of the year," and find a site from 2003, that information is no longer current or relevant. Looking at birth rates or literacy rates from the past would not produce relevant information if you are looking for the most recent information.

Photo courtesy of Charles Long

Questions to guide evaluation include the following:

- When was the site created?
- Is the material recent?
- Is the website updated?

It's easy to access computer resources, but make sure you carefully evaluate the material you find.

When using these five criteria to evaluate your online information, remember that *all* criteria should be met, not just one or two of the above. Accurate and current information must also be objective. If critical information is missing (coverage), no matter how accurate and current the information is, it should be eliminated as a source.

4. Interview, If Appropriate

Interviews are useful if you want information too new to be found in published sources or if you want to give your listeners the views of an expert. By talking to an expert, you can clarify questions and fill in knowledge gaps, and you may learn more about a subject than you expected. In the process, you also gather opinions based on years of experience.

Look around your campus and community. You will find experts who can tell you as much as you need to know about thousands of subjects. You can get opinions about the stock market, the effect of different types of running shoes on the development of shin splints, race relations, No Child Left Behind legislation, ethanol, water or air pollution, or curbside recycling.

If you decide to interview one or more people, we offer the following four suggestions:

Contact the person well in advance. Remember, *you* are the one who needs the information. Do not think that leaving one voice message is the extent of your responsibility. You may have to make several attempts to contact the person. Schedule a date and time to interview that leaves you with ample time to prepare your speech.

Prepare questions in advance. Make sure you know what topics need to be covered and what information needs to be clarified.

Photo courtesy of Charles Long

Develop questions in a logical order. One question should lead naturally to another. Place the most important questions at the top to guarantee that they will be answered before your time is up.

Stay within the agreed time frame. If you promise the interview will take no longer than a half hour, keep your word, if at all possible. Do not say, "It'll just take a minute," when you need at least fifteen minutes. Build in a little time to ask unplanned questions, questions based on the interviewee's answers or for clarification.

When you conduct an interview, make sure you schedule a date and time to interview that leaves you with ample time to prepare your speech.

After reading this section on research, hopefully you are aware that it involves a significant time commitment. It is never too early to start thinking about your next speech topic and where you might find sources. Explore a variety of resources. Ask for help from your instructor or the librarian. Make sure you know the constraints of the assignment.

Citing Sources in Your Speech

Any research included in your speech needs to be cited appropriately in order to give due credit. If you interviewed someone, your audience should know the person's name, credentials, and when and where you spoke with him or her. If you use information from a website, the audience should know the name of the website and when you accessed it. For print information, the audience generally needs to know the author, date, and type of publication. Your credibility is connected to your source citation. Expert sources and timely information add to your credibility. Essentially, all research used in your speech needs to be cited. Otherwise, you have committed an act of plagiarism. Following are ways to cite sources in your speech. *Consult with your instructor,* however, as he or she may have specific concerns.

Example 1

Correct source citation. In their 1995 book on family communication, researchers Yerby, Buerkel-Rothfuss and Bochner argue that it is difficult to understand family behavior "without an adequate description of the historical, physical, emotional, and relational context in which it occurs."

Incorrect source citation. Researchers on family communication argue that it is difficult to understand family behavior without an adequate description of the historical, physical, emotional, and relational context in which it occurs.

Explanation. We need the date to evaluate the timeliness of the material. We need to know that this information was found in a book, as opposed to a television show, a newspaper, magazine, or other source. We need the authors' names so we know who wrote the information, and so we can find the book.

Example 2

Correct source citation. According to a personal interview last week with Diane Ruyle, principal of Danube High School, fewer students are choosing vocational classes than they were ten years ago.

Incorrect source citation. According to Diane Ruyle, fewer students are choosing vocational classes.

Explanation. We need to know why the person cited Diane Ruyle. As a principal, she ought to be able to provide accurate information regarding course selection. Adding "than they were ten years ago" gives the listener a comparison basis.

Example 3

Correct source citation. According to an Associated Press article published in the *New York Times* on August 9, 2007, "unlike in South Carolina, state laws in Iowa and New Hampshire require officials there to hold the first caucus and primary in the nation, respectively."

Incorrect source citation. "Unlike in South Carolina, state laws in Iowa and New Hampshire require officials there to hold the first caucus and primary in the nation, respectively."

Explanation. First, if this is published information, it should be cited. Second, most of us do not know these facts, a citation is necessary. Otherwise, the speaker could be making this up. The date provided allows us to look up the source and shows us that the information is timely. No author was identified, and since Associated Press articles can be found in many newspapers, it is important to note this was found in the *New York Times*.

Example 4

Correct source citation. According to the current American Diabetes Association website, "Cholesterol is carried through the body in two kinds of bundles called lipoproteins—low-density lipoproteins and high-density lipoproteins. It's important to have healthy levels of both."

Incorrect source citation. Cholesterol is carried through the body in two kinds of bundles called lipoproteins—low-density lipoproteins and high-density lipoproteins. It's important to have healthy levels of both.

Explanation. This information is not common knowledge, so it should be cited. Many different organizations might include such information on their website, so it is important to note that it came from the American Diabetes Association (ADA). An audience would infer that the ADA is a credible organization regarding this topic. Using the word "current" suggests that one could find that information today on the ADA website, which reinforces the timeliness of the material.

In summary, remember that you *do not* need to cite sources when you are reporting your own original ideas or discussing ideas that are commonly held. You *must* cite sources when you are quoting directly or paraphrasing (restating or summarizing a source's ideas in your own words). You must also cite the source of an illustration, diagram, or graph. Providing the date of publication, date of website access, credentials of the source, and/or type of publication where applicable will allow the listener to evaluate the credibility of the information.

Supporting Your Speech

Imagine a chef with a piece of steak, some cauliflower, and rice, the main ingredients for a dinner special. What the chef does with these raw materials will influence the response of the consumers. The chef decides whether to grill, broil, bake, steam, or fry. Different spices can be used for different results. Numerous possibilities exist.

The research you have gathered for your speech can be viewed as the raw material. Now you need to figure out how to organize and present the material in the most effective way for your audience. This is where the concept of supporting material applies.

Supporting material gives substance to your assertions. If you say that *Casablanca* is the best movie ever produced in Hollywood, you are stating your opinion. If you cite a film critic's essay that notes it is the best movie ever, then your statement has more weight. You may also be able to find data that indicates how well the movie did, and a public opinion poll that had it ranked as the top movie. These different resources provide support. Just about anything that supports a speaker's idea can be considered supporting material.

When developing your speech, you also have many decisions to make. Consider the following example:

Your public speaking professor has just given your class an assignment to deliver an informative speech on the problem of shoplifting. These two versions are among those presented:

Version 1:
Shoplifting is an enormous problem for American retailers, who lose billions of dollars each year to customer theft. Not unexpectedly, retailers pass the cost of shoplifting onto consumers, which means that people like you and me pay dearly for the crimes of others.

Shoplifting is increasingly becoming a middle-class crime. Experts tell us that many people shoplift just for kicks—for the thrill of defying authority and for the excitement of getting away with something that is against the law. Whatever the reason, one in fifteen Americans is guilty of this crime.

Version 2:
Imagine walking up to a store owner once a year and giving that person $300 without getting anything in return. Could you afford that? Would you want to do that? Yet that's what happens. Every year, the average American family of four forks over $300 to make amends for the crimes of shoplifters.

Shoplifting is a big cost to big business. According to recent statistics from the National Association for the Prevention of Shoplifting, people who walk out of stores without first stopping at the cash register take with them more than $13 billion annually. That's more than $25 million per day. Their website claims that one out of eleven of us is guilty of this crime. To bring this figure uncomfortably close to home, that's at least two students in each of your classes.

Interestingly, shoplifting is no longer a poor person's crime. Hard as it is to imagine, many shoplifters can well afford to buy what they steal. Wynona Ryder received a great deal of unwanted press when she shoplifted $5,000 worth of merchandise at a Beverly Hills store in 2001.

Why do middle- and upper-income people steal? According to psychiatrist James Spikes, quoted in a recent *Ms.* magazine, shoplifters are "defying authority. They're saying, 'The hell with them. I'll do it anyway . . . . I can get away with it . . . .'" Psychologist Stanton Samenow, quoted in the July issue of *Life* magazine, agrees:

"Shoplifters will not accept life as it is; they want to take shortcuts. They do it for kicks" (Sawyer, Glenn Dowling 1988).

Although both versions say essentially the same thing, they are not equally effective. The difference is in the supporting materials.

Five Functions of Support

Support should strengthen your speech in five ways. Comparing Version 1 with Version 2 will help illustrate the value of supporting material.

1. *Support is specific.*
   Version 2 gives listeners more details than Version 1. We learn, for example, how much shoplifting costs each of us as well as the financial burden retailers must carry.

2. *Support helps to clarify ideas.*
   We learn much more about the reasons for shoplifting from Version 2. This clarification—from the mouths of experts—reduces the risk of misunderstanding.

3. *Support adds weight.*
   The use of credible statistics and expert opinion adds support to the second version's main points. This type of support convinces listeners by building a body of evidence that may be difficult to deny. The testimonies of Drs. Spikes and Samenow are convincing because they are authoritative. We believe what they say far more than we do unattributed facts.

4. *Support is appropriate to your audience.*

   Perhaps the most important difference between these two versions is Verssion 2's attempt to gear the supporting material to the audience. It is a rare college student who would not care about a $300 overcharge or who cannot relate to the presence of two possible shoplifters in each class. Also, movie star Wynona Ryder's shoplifting is noted in Version 2. Students are familiar with her name, but college students would not be as familiar with an older famous person who has shoplifted, such as Bess Myerson, winner of Miss America in 1945 and actress on several television shows in the 1960s.

Effective support is used to develop the message you send.

5. *Support creates interest.*

   Although Version 1 provides information, it arouses little or no interest. Listeners have a hard time caring about the problem or becoming emotionally or intellectually involved. Version 2, on the other hand, creates interest through the use of meaningful statistics, quotations, and an example. When used properly, supporting materials can transform ordinary details into a memorable presentation.

Effective support is used to develop the message you send to your listeners. It is through this message that communication takes place between speaker and audience. In public speaking, you cannot separate the act of speaking from the message the speaker delivers. Supporting your message is one of your most important tasks as you develop your speech.

Forms of Support

Effective speeches generally rely on multiple forms of support. To give your speech greater weight and authority, at least five forms of support can be used. These include facts, statistics, examples, testimony, and analogies. Each of these forms of support will be discussed, and guidelines for using them will be presented.

Facts Nothing undermines a presentation faster than too few facts. **Facts** are pieces of information that are verifiable and irrefutable. **Opinions** are points of view that may or may not be supported in fact. Too often, speakers confuse fact and opinion when adding supporting material to a speech. For example, while it is a fact that Forest Whitaker won the 2007 Academy Award for Best Actor, it is opinion to state that he is the best actor in Hollywood.

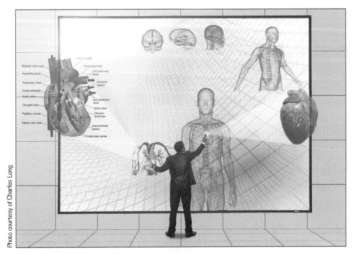

Include facts that will clarify the concepts you are describing in your speech.

Facts serve at least three different purposes:

1. *Facts clarify your main point.*
   They remove ambiguity, making it more likely that the message you send is the message your audience will receive.
2. *Facts indicate your knowledge of the subject.*
   Rather than say, "The League of Women Voters has been around for a long time," report, "The League of Women Voters was founded in 1919." Your audience wants to know that you have researched the topic and can discuss specifics about your topic.
3. *Facts define.*
   Facts provide needed definitions that may explain new concepts. If you are delivering a speech on "functional illiteracy," you may define the term in the following way:

   While an illiterate adult has no ability to read, write, or compute, relatively few Americans fall into this category. However, some 27 million Americans can't read, write, compute, speak, or listen effectively enough to function in society. They cannot read street signs, write out a check, apply for a job or ask a government bureaucrat about a Social Security check they never received. Although they may have minimal communications skills, for all intents and purposes, they are isolated from the rest of society. These people are considered functionally illiterate.

In the above example, you anticipated the potential confusion between the terms "illiteracy" and "functional illiteracy," and you differentiated between these terms. While you defined this term for your public speaking class, if your audience was comprised of literacy coaches, this would not be necessary.

Guidelines for using facts **Carefully determine the number of facts to use.** Too few facts will reveal that you spent little time researching, while too many may overwhelm your listeners. Sometimes, students want to impress their audience, or at least their instructor, with the amount of research completed for a particular speech. The desire to include all information may result in a "data dump," where facts are given in a steady stream with little or no connection to the speech or to each other. This results in an overload of information that is difficult to process.

To be effective, the number and complexity of your facts must be closely tied to the needs of your listeners. A speech to a group of hikers on poison ivy prevention may include practical issues such as identifying the plant and recognizing, treating, and avoiding the rash. However, if you are delivering a speech on the same subject to a group of medical students, a detailed explanation of the body's biochemical response to the plant is probably more relevant.

Make sure your meanings are clear. If you use words or phrases that have different meanings to you than they do to members of your audience, the impact of your speech is lessened. Misunderstandings occur when your audience attributes meanings to terms you did not intend. Think about the following words: success, liberal, conservative, patriot, happiness, good, bad, and smart. Collectively, we do not agree on the meanings of these words. One person may define success in terms of material wealth, while another may think of it in terms of family relationships, job satisfaction, and good health. When it is essential that your audience understand the meaning you intend, take the time to define it carefully as you speak.

Define terms when they are first introduced. The first time you use a term that requires an explanation, define it so that your meaning is clear. If you are talking about the advantages of belonging to a health maintenance organization, define the term the first time it is used.

Statistics The second form of supporting material is **statistics**: the collection, analysis, interpretation, and presentation of information in numerical form. Statistics give us the information necessary to understand the magnitude of issues and to compare and contrast different points. Basic measures include the mean, median, and mode, which are generally referred to as descriptive statistics, because they allow us to discuss a set of numbers easily. The **mean** is calculated by adding all the numbers in a group and dividing by the number of items. It is the most widely used statistical measure. The **median** measures the middle score in the group. That is, half the values fall above it and half fall below. The **mode** is the value that occurs most frequently.

But statistics can be misleading. For example, if one were to examine the National League Baseball (NLB) salaries for 2005, one would find the average, or mean, salary for those players was $2,585,804 (http://asp.usatoday.com/sports/baseball/salaries). However, the highest salary went to San Francisco Giant's Barry Bonds who earned $22 million.

Meanwhile, the median salary for all NLB players was $800,000. This means that half of the 439 players received more than $800,000 and half received less than that. In addition, the mode was $316,000. Twenty-six players received this amount. In this case, simply discussing these three statistical measures is not helpful, unless you want to make the point that salaries are not consistent. It might make more sense to discuss the range of salaries or look at a particular group of players' salaries. When using statistics in your speech, it is important to understand what they mean.

Guidelines for using statistics **Be precise.** Make sure you understand the statistics before including them in your speech. Consider the difference between the following statements.

> A 2-percent decrease was shown in the rate of economic growth, as measured by the gross national product, compared to the same period last year.
> The gross national product dropped by 2 percent compared to the same period last year.

In the first case, the statistic refers to a drop in the rate of growth—it tells us that the economy is growing at a slower pace but that it is still ahead of last year—while in the second, it refers to an actual drop in the gross national product in comparison to the previous year. These statements say two very different things.

It is critical that you not misinterpret statistics when analyzing the data. If you have questions, refer to a basic statistics text or another source that further explains the data.

Avoid using too many statistics. Too many statistics will confuse and bore your audience and blunt the impact of your most important statistical points. Save your statistics for the places in your speech where they will make the most impact.

Round off your numbers. Is it important for your audience to know that, according to the Census Bureau's daily population projection on March 3, 2006, the U.S. population reached 298,228,575? The figure will have greater impact—and your audience will be more likely to remember it—if you round it off to "more than 298,000,000."

Cite your sources. Because statistics are rarely remembered for very long, it is easy for speakers to misquote and misuse them—often in a calculated way for their own ends. As an ethical speaker, you need to make sure your statistics are correct and you need to quote your sources. For example, if you were talking about the history of Girl Scout cookies, you could mention that during peak production of Girl Scout cookies, according to the Little Brownie Bakery website (www.littlebrowniebakers.com), one of two bakers for the Girl Scouts, 1,050,000 pounds of flour a week are used in production.

Use visual aids to express statistics. Statistics become especially meaningful to listeners when they are presented in visual form. Visual presentations of statistics free you from the need to repeat a litany of numbers that listeners will probably never remember. Instead, by transforming these numbers into visual presentations, you can highlight only the most important points, allowing your listeners to refer to the remaining statistics at any time. For example, in a speech extolling the virtues of graduate school, a graph displaying average salaries by degrees earned would be helpful.(See Figure 7.1).

Examples Examples enliven speeches in a way that no other form of supporting material can. Grounding material in the specifics of everyday life has the power to create an empathic bond between speaker and audience, a bond strong enough to tie listeners to a speech and the speaker even after the example is complete.

Examples can be brief or extended, real or hypothetical, and narrative. Although examples differ in length, factual base, and source, their effectiveness lies in the extent to which they support the speaker's core idea.

Examples are brief or extended. Brief examples are short illustrations that clarify a general statement. If you made the following assertion: "Americans are more modest than Europeans," you could support it by using brief examples, such as, "If you take a walk on the beach in Italy or France, you should not be surprised to find women sunbathing topless. Also, many European countries, such as Sweden and Germany, have public saunas that are enjoyed by men and women—who are in the same sauna, sitting naked on their towels." Brief examples can be used effectively throughout a speech. Your decision to use them will depend on many factors, including the needs of your audience, the nature of your material, and your approach.

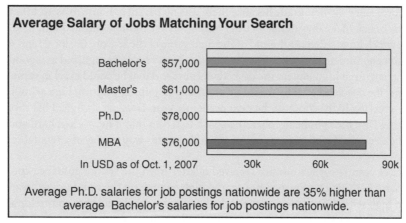

Figure 7.1 A bar graph can be used to clearly illustrate differences in values.

Extended examples are longer and richer in detail than brief examples. They are used most effectively to build images and to create a lasting impression on the audience, as can been seen in the following excerpt from a speech in 2006 given by Steven Darimont, candidate for sheriff in Coles County, Illinois. When making the point that money is spent unnecessarily on jail food, he stated:

> "Our food budget alone is at $140,000 and we will go over that by $12–15,000 this year. The sheriff has requested that (amount) be raised (an additional) $20,000, to $160,000 next year. The inmates currently get three hot meals a day. An example of this is breakfast: scrambled eggs, toast with butter and jelly, cold cereal with milk, hash browns, fruit, and juice. The Department of Corrections mandates only one hot meal per day, yet we feed three hot meals."

Providing more detail about the budget and the ample food choices creates a greater impact on the listener rather than saying, "We provide three hot meals a day, and we're going over budget."

Because of their impact, extended examples should not be overused or used at inappropriate points. As with other forms of support, they should be reserved for the points at which they will have the greatest effect: in clarifying the message, persuading listeners to your point of view, or establishing a speaker-audience relationship.

Examples are real or hypothetical. Sometimes the best examples are real, and come from your personal experience. By revealing parts of your life that relate to your speech topic, you provide convincing evidence and, at the same time, potentially create a powerful bond between you and your audience. Consider the student who has watched her mother die from lung cancer. The experience of hearing about the diagnosis, discussing treatment possibilities, and making final arrangements while her mother was alive can have a powerful effect on the audience. The words and emotion have great impact because the situation is real, not hypothetical, and the speaker provides a sense of reality to the topic.

At times, it suits the speaker's purpose to create a fictional example, rather than a real example, to make a point. Although these examples are not based on facts, the circumstances they describe are often realistic and thus effective.

As an educator and school administrator for more than twenty years, I have witnessed many transitions in the evolution of public education. I have also witnessed the effect that misguided politicians can have on the state of our educational process. I welcome the opportunity to share with you, using the case study method, how one such initiative *No Child Left Behind Act of 2001* affected the life of one disadvantaged student. The *No Child Left Behind Act of 2001* was based on the belief that by setting high standards and measurable goals, we can improve an individual's performance. As I share with you the case of Dwayne Jefferson, you can draw your own conclusion as to the success of this controversial initiative.

Dwayne Jefferson was a fourteen year old who attended school in a rural area in a southern town. He came from a single family home in which the mother worked two jobs to support him and his five brothers and sisters. Dwayne had below level reading scores since the first grade because there was no parent at home to assist him with homework and to encourage him to read. In lieu of a babysitter at an early age, Dwayne's mother enrolled him in an afternoon intramural basketball program in which he excelled. At the end of the final game of the season, the local high school basketball coach approached Dwayne to congratulate him on an excellent game. Never being recognized as a good student, Dwayne was excited that the coach recognized his talent on the basketball court and that he could excel in some aspect of his life. After congratulating Dwayne, the coach asked if he would be interested in joining the local high school basketball team in the fall since he would be entering high school in the next academic year. Dwayne shrugged his shoulders and said, "Sure, I'd like that." After taking Dwayne's phone number, the coach told him that if he worked hard and stayed out of trouble, he would have a great career, and by his senior year he would be on his way to play at a reputable college.

At the end of that school year, Dwayne's mother received a letter from the school guidance counselor stating that the school regretted to inform her that Dwayne had not scored high enough on the standardized reading test to matriculate from middle school to high school. Dwayne's mother asked the high school guidance counselor about her son's options. Her questions included: What programs have been put in place so that my son can continue his education with other students of his age? What assistance can I request to ensure that Dwayne receives the required score next year? Finally and most importantly, his mother asked, why haven't measures been taken prior to a test of this magnitude to ensure Dwayne was successful?

Needless to say, the case of Dwayne Jefferson is not uncommon. Early that fall Dwayne received a call from the basketball coach at the local high school. Unfortunately, Dwayne had only bad news to give the coach about his anticipated participation on the team. As you can imagine, the case of Dwayne Jefferson brings to the forefront many of the criticisms of the *No Child Left Behind Act of 2001,* from the allegation of "gaming" the system to illuminating the "problems" with standardized tests, the program has faced an uphill battle.

Hypothetical examples are useful when you want to exaggerate a point as the educator did. They are also useful when you cannot find a factual illustration for your speech. To be effective, they must be tied in some way to the point you are trying to illustrate.

It is important that your listeners know when you are using a hypothetical example and when you are not. Avoid confusion by introducing these examples in a direct way. You might start out by saying, "Imagine that you live next door to a college professor we'll call Dr. Supple," or "Let's talk about a hypothetical mother on welfare named Alice."

Examples can be in narrative form. Narratives are stories within a speech, anecdotes that create visual images in listeners' minds. In many ways, they take extended examples a step further by involving listeners in a tale that captures attention and makes a point—a story connected to the speaker's core idea. Many listeners love a good story, and when the speech is over, the narrative is what they remember.

Imagine Laura, a person who has traveled significantly, giving an informative speech on "The art of shopping outside the United States: Bartering made simple." She might include the following:

> My husband and I were in Morocco shopping with my mother and my aunt. They stopped to speak with a shop owner about carpets and my husband and I went on. About forty-five minutes later, we walked by to see them STILL speaking with the shop owner. Now, though, all three were seated, and they were drinking hot, mint tea. We approached the shopkeeper and introduced ourselves. He proceeded to tell us how different my mother and aunt were from most American women. He said that American women will ask the price of something, and he'll throw out some high price. Then the women will offer a significantly lower price. He rejects that but comes down on his original high price. The American women, usually, will accept his second price, no matter how high! Not these women! My mom and aunt bartered back and forth with the shopkeeper about the price, never giving in! The shopkeeper said he really enjoyed negotiating with them; that they were both friendly **and** insistent. They didn't back down easily, and, according to the shopkeeper, they ended up paying a reasonable price for their carpet.

By their nature, narratives demand that listeners take an active part in linking the story to the speaker's main point. The story moves from beginning to middle, to end. Even if the speaker supplies the link after the narrative, audience members still make the connections themselves as they listen.

A narrative can be used anywhere in a speech. No matter where it is placed, it assumes great importance to listeners as they become involved with the details. Through the narrative, speakers can establish a closeness with the audience that may continue even after the story is over.

Guidelines for using examples Examples add interest and impact. They should be representative because examples support your core idea only when they accurately represent the situation. No matter the type of example you use as supporting material, the following three guidelines will help you choose examples for your speeches:

Use examples frequently. Examples are often the lifeblood of a speech. Use them to make your points—but only in appropriate places. When using examples to prove a point, more than one example generally is needed.

Use only the amount of detail necessary. To make your examples work, you want to use only the amount of detail necessary for your audience and no more. The detail you provide in examples should be based on the needs of your audience. If your listeners are familiar with a topic, you can simply mention what the audience already knows. Interspersing long examples with short ones varies the pace and detail of your discussion.

Use examples to explain new concepts. Difficult concepts become easier to handle when you clarify them with examples. Keep in mind that although you may be comfortable with the complexities of a topic, your listeners might be hearing these complexities for the first time. Appropriate examples can mean the difference between communicating with or losing your audience.

Testimony The word testimony may conjure a vision of witnesses in a court of law giving sworn statements to a judge and jury, adding credibility to a case. In public speaking, testimony has nothing to do with the law, but it has everything to do with credibility. When you cite the words of others, either directly or through paraphrasing, you are attempting, in effect, to strengthen your position by telling your audience that people with special knowledge support your position or take your side. Testimony can cite either experience or opinion. Also, short quotations may be an effective way to provide testimony.

In order to be effective, however, testimony needs to be used in its proper context. Purposefully distorting the testimony of an expert to suit the needs of your speech is misleading and unethical. Be honest to your source as well as your audience.

Experience as testimony. Experience may be the most credible choice in some cases because someone was "on the scene." For example, hundreds of thousands of individuals were directly affected by hurricane Katrina. A student writer for the University of Texas at Austin newspaper interviewed Lorraine Brown about her personal experience during hurricane Katrina. The following account was printed in the September 6, 2005 issue of *The Daily Texan*.

> At 5 a.m. on Monday, after floodwaters breached the New Orleans levees, Brown awoke to find water seeping into her house. 'I saw the water on my kitchen floor, and I picked up a mop and started mopping. But then I looked out the window and saw that the water was already up to here,' she said, holding her hand at her waist.
>
> *September 6, 2005* by Delaney Hall. Copyright © 2005 by Daily Texan.

Lorraine Brown's experience as one of the survivors of the hurricane provides vivid imagery that helps the listener recognize the terror that many experienced.

It is possible to use your own testimony when you are an expert. If you are writing a speech on what it is like to recover from a spinal cord injury, use your own expert testimony if you have suffered this injury. Similarly, if you are talking about the advantages and problems of being a female lifeguard, cite your own testimony if you are female and have spent summers saving lives at the beach. When you do not have the background necessary to convince your audience, use the testimony of those who do.

Opinion as testimony. In some circumstances, the opinion of a recognized authority may provide the credibility needed to strengthen your argument or prove a point. Jimmy Carter, former president and winner of the Nobel Peace Prize in 2002, is an outspoken critic of the Iraqi War. At a news conference in July 2005, CBS News quoted him as saying,

"I thought then, and I think now, that the invasion of Iraq was unnecessary and unjust. And I think the premises on which it was launched were false" (www. cbsnews.com). While he is clearly stating an opinion, Carter carries a certain amount of credibility because of his previous position as president of the United States and as a Nobel Peace Prize winner.

Short quotations. A short quotation is a form of testimony, but its purpose is often different. Frequently, short quotations are used to set the tone for a speech, to provide humor, or to make important points more memorable. If you were receiving the MVP award for football at your high school or college, you might start out with something like this:

> "Wow. I'm reminded of John Madden's words when he was inducted into the Pro Football Hall of Fame in 2006, 'And right now, I don't have, I got like numb, you know, a tingle from the bottom of my toes to the top of my head.' Yep. That's exactly how I feel."

Madden's quote is not the most articulate or insightful comment, but it certainly expressed the emotion the football player was feeling, and this quote would set an engaging tone for an acceptance speech.

Shown here making a statement after receiving the Nobel Peace Prize, Jimmy Carter's opinions carry credibility because of his past accomplishments.

Sometimes quotations are too long or too complicated to present verbatim. You can choose to cite the source but paraphrase the message. Instead of quoting the following description of the effect crack cocaine has on the body, it might be more effective to paraphrase.

Quote:

> According to Dr. Mark S. Gold, nationally known expert on cocaine abuse, founder of the 800-COCAINE helpline, and author of *The Facts About Drugs and Alcohol*, "as an anesthetic, cocaine blocks the conduction of electrical impulses within the nerve cells involved in sensory transmissions, primarily pain. The body's motor impulses, those that control muscle function, for example, are not affected by low-dose use of cocaine. In this way cocaine creates a deadening blockage (known as a differential block) of pain, without interfering with body movement" (Gold 1986, 36).

Paraphrase: According to Dr. Mark S. Gold, nationally known expert on cocaine abuse,

> founder of the 800-COCAINE helpline and author of *The Facts About Drugs and Alcohol*, cocaine blocks pain without interfering with body movement.

The second version is more effective when speaking to a lay audience who knows little about medicine, while the former is appropriate for an audience of science students or physicians.

Guidelines for using testimony **Use only recognizable or credible testimony and quotations.** At a time when media exposure is so pervasive, it is easy to find someone who will support your point of view. Before citing a person as an authoritative source, be sure that he or she is an expert. If you are giving a speech on the greatest movies ever produced, it would make sense to quote Roger Ebert, film critic and author of numerous books on the subject of film. However, he would not be the proper choice for a speech on the joys of collecting and trading baseball cards.

As you review expert testimony, keep in mind that the more research you do, the more opinions you will find. Ultimately, your choice should be guided by relevance and credibility of the source. The fact that you quote Supreme Court Justice Sandra Day O'Connor in a speech on affirmative action is as important as the quote itself.

Choose unbiased experts. How effective is the following testimony if its source is the *owner* of the Oakland Athletics?

There is no team in baseball as complete as the Athletics. The team has better pitching, fielding, hitting, and base running than any of its competitors in the National or American League.

If the same quote came from a baseball writer for *Sports Illustrated* you would probably believe it more. Thus, when choosing expert testimony, bear in mind that opinions shaped by self-interest are less valuable, from the point of view of your audience, than those motivated by the merits of the issues.

Identify the source. Not all names of your experts will be recognizable, so it is important to tell your audience why they are qualified to give testimony. If you are cautioning overseas travelers to avoid tourist scams, the following expert testimony provides support:

At a time when media exposure is so pervasive, it is easy to find someone who will support your point of view.

> According to Rick Steves, travelers should be wary of "The 'helpful' local: Thieves posing as concerned locals will warn you to store your wallet safely—and then steal it after they see where you stash it. Some thieves put out tacks and ambush drivers with their "assistance" in changing the tire. Others hang out at subway ticket machines eager to "help" the bewildered tourist buy tickets with a pile of quickly disappearing foreign cash" (www.ricksteves.com).

Without knowing anything about Rick Steves, your readers will have no reason to trust this advice. However, if you state his credentials first, you can establish the credibility of your expert. So instead, the speaker could start begin with, "According to Rick Steves, host and producer of the popular public television series *Rick Steves' Europe* and best-selling author of thirty European travel books, travelers should be wary of . . ."

Develop techniques to signal the beginning and ending of each quotation. Your audience may not know when a quote begins or ends. Some speakers prefer to preface quotations with the words, "And I quote" and to end quotations with the phrase, "end quote." Other speakers indicate the presence of quotations through pauses immediately before and immediately after the quotation or through a slight change of pace or inflection. It may be a good idea to use both techniques in your speech to satisfy your listeners' need for variety. Just do not make quotation signs with your fingers!

Analogies At times, the most effective form of supporting material is the analogy, which points out similarities between what we know and understand and what we do not know or cannot accept. Analogies fall into two separate categories: figurative and literal. **Figurative analogies** draw comparisons between things that are distinctly different in an attempt to clarify a concept or persuade. Biology professor and world-renowned environmentalist Paul Erlich uses an analogy of a globe holding and draining water to explain the problem of the world population explosion. The following is an excerpt from a speech delivered to the First National Congress on Optimum Population and Environment, June 9, 1970:

> As a model of the world demographic situation, think of the world as a globe, and think of a faucet being turned on into that globe as being the equivalent of the birth rate, the input into the population. Think of that drain at the base of that globe—water pouring out—as being the equivalent to the output, the death rate of the population. At the time of the Agricultural Revolution, the faucet was turned on full blast; there was a very high birth rate. The drain was wide open; there was a high death rate. There was very little water in the globe, very few people in the population—only above five million. When the Agricultural Revolution took place, we began to plug the drain, cut down the death rate, and the globe began to fill up.

This analogy is effective because it helps the audience understand the population explosion. It explains the nature of the problem in a clear, graphic way. Listener understanding comes not from the presentation of new facts (these facts were presented elsewhere in the speech) but from a simple comparison. When dealing with difficult or emotionally charged concepts, listeners benefit from this type of comparative supporting material.

Keep in mind that although figurative analogies may be helpful, they usually do not serve as sufficient proof in a persuasive argument. Erlich, for example, must back his analogy with facts, statistics, examples, and quotations to persuade his listeners that his analogy is accurate—that we are indeed in the midst of a population crisis.

A **literal analogy** compares like things from similar classes, such as a game of professional football with a game of college football. If, for example, you are delivering a speech to inform your classmates about Russia's involvement in the war in Afghanistan, the following literal analogy might be helpful:

> The war in Afghanistan was the former Soviet Union's Vietnam. Both wars were unwinnable from the start. Neither the Vietnamese nor the Afghans would tolerate foreign domination. Acting with the determination of the Biblical David, they waged a struggle against the Goliaths of Russia and the United States. In large part, the winning weapon in both wars was the collective might of village peasants who were determined to rid their countries of the Superpowers—no matter the odds.

Literal analogies serve as proof when the aspects or concepts compared are similar. When similarities are weak, the proof fails. The analogy, "As Rome fell because of moral decay, so will the United States," is valid only if the United States and Rome have similar economic and social systems, types of governments, and so on. The fewer the similarities between the United States and Rome, the weaker the proof.

Guidelines for using analogies **Use analogies to build the power of your argument.** Analogies convince through comparison to something the audience already knows. It is psychologically comforting to your listeners to hear new ideas expressed in a familiar context. The result is greater understanding and possible acceptance of your point of view.

Be certain the analogy is clear. Even when the concept of your analogy is solid, if the points of comparison are not effectively carried through from beginning to end, the analogy will fail. Your analogy must be as consistent and complete as in the following example:

In political campaigns, opponents square off against one another in an attempt to land the winning blow. Although after a close and grueling campaign that resembles a ten-round bout, one candidate may succeed by finding a soft spot in his opponent's record, the fight is hardly over. Even while the downed opponent is flat against the mat, the victor turns to the public and tells yet another distortion of the truth. "My opponent," he says, "never had a chance." Clearly, politicians and prize fighters share one goal in common: to knock their opponents senseless and to make the public believe that they did it with ease.

Avoid using too many analogies. A single effective analogy can communicate your point. Do not diminish its force by including several in a short presentation.

Summary

Research gives you the tools you need to support your thesis statement. A solid research base increases your credibility. To begin your research strategy, assess your personal knowledge and skills. Then look for print and online resources. The librarian can lead you to valuable sources within the physical library as well as online. You may need to look up information in encyclopedias, dictionaries, books, newspapers, magazines, journal articles, and government documents. When using online resources, it is important to use website evaluation criteria and to question accuracy, authority, objectivity, coverage, and currency.

Supporting materials buttress the main points of your speech and make you a more credible speaker. Among the most important forms of support are facts—verifiable information. Facts clarify your main points, indicate knowledge of your subject, and serve as definitions. Opinions differ from facts in that they cannot be verified. Statistical support involves the presentation of information in numerical form. Because statistics are easily manipulated, it is important to analyze carefully the data you present.

Five different types of examples are commonly used as forms of support. Brief examples are short illustrations that clarify a general statement. Extended examples are used to create lasting images. Narratives are stories within a speech that are linked to the speaker's main idea. Hypothetical examples are fictional examples used to make a point. Personal examples are anecdotes related to your topic that come from your own life.

When you use testimony quotations, you cite the words of others to increase the credibility of your message. Your sources gain expertise through experience and authority. Analogies focus on the similarities between the familiar and unfamiliar. Figurative analogies compare things that are different, while liberal analogies compare things from similar classes. Literal analogies can often be used as proof.

Communication for Today's Student

Chapter 7 – Researching Your Topic

Exercise 7.1 – Support and Verbal Footnotes

Effective support is used to develop the message you send to your listeners. Support should strengthen your speech in five ways:

- Support is specific.
- Support helps to clarify ideas.
- Support adds weight.
- Support is appropriate to your audience.
- Support creates interest.

Using a topic of your choice, fictionalize an example of support that demonstrates your ability to develop support that is *specific, clear, weighty, appropriate* and *interesting*.

For example:
Topic: Pit Bulls

Support: According to Peter Daniels' book, *Dogs and Their Owners*, the pit bull was brought to America by English immigrants and were originally used as "gripping" dogs when hunting large game.

Does this support meet our five criteria? Is this verbal footnote specific, clear, weighty, appropriate, and interesting?

Now develop your own fictitious examples. Use the type of support indicated on the topic Pit Bulls. Remember, you can make up your sources and information, if you like. Be prepared to share.

Topic: Pit Bulls

Verbal footnote: Magazine

Topic: Pit Bulls

Verbal footnote: Newspaper

Topic: Pit Bulls

Verbal footnote: Website

*Try to vary your verbal footnote language.

Communication for Today's Student

Chapter 7 – Researching Your Topic

Exercise 7.2 – Formatting Sources for the Bibliography

Below are the components of resources that may be used as entries for a bibliography when using the MLA style. Using the MLA Style Manual, place the components in the correct order for each source. Do not forget to include punctuation as well.

Topic: *High Heels*

p. LZ06
British Woman's Revolt Against High Heels Becomes a Cause in Parliament
Dan Bilefsky
March 6
New York Times
2017

Topic: *Pit Bulls*

Peter Daniels
Kendall Publishers
New York, New York
2008
Pit Bulls and their Owners

Topic: *Interpersonal Relationships*

Interpersonal Relationships—The Good, the Bad and the Ugly
Karen Turner Ward
Tamara Williams
April 22
Relationships Matters Magazine
pages 211-212
2017

Topic: *Fitbit*

How Fit Is Your Heart?
Susie Jogger
eMD
July 8
www.eMD.com/how_ fit-heart.html
2017

Chapter 7 – Researching Your Topic

Exercise 7.2 Continued

Topic: *High Heels*

Topic: *Pit Bulls*

Topic: *Interpersonal Relationships*

Topic: *Fitbit*

ORGANIZING YOUR IDEAS
AND STRUCTURING YOUR OUTLINE

After reading this chapter, you should be able to:

- ☑ Explain the steps in the process of preparing an outline.
- ☑ Demonstrate an understanding of the correct use of attention getting devices.
- ☑ Determine the best pattern to use when organizing the main points of a speech.
- ☑ Demonstrate the correct use of transitions, signposts, internal previews, and internal summaries.
- ☑ Demonstrate the correct process for preparing the full sentence and keyword outlines.

Key Terms

Anecdote	Keyword outline	Sentence outline
Attention getters	Main points	Signposts
Brainstorming	Mapping	Specific purpose
Cause and effect pattern	Monroe motivated	Subordination
Chronological pattern	sequence pattern	Sub point
Coordination	Oral footnotes	Sub-sub point
General purpose	Problem-solution pattern	Topical pattern
Internal previews	Proximity pattern	Transitions
Internal summaries	Rhetorical questions	

8 Scenario

"Y ou hate my speech!" Nathalie groaned loudly.

"I don't hate it," Chris said. "I never said that."

"Well, you didn't say it was good either!" Nathalie fired at him.

"All I said is that it could use some work," Chris defended. "That's all."

"My speech is tomorrow!" Nathalie yelled. "Tomorrow! In front of the whole student body."

Nathalie was running for sophomore class president, and she was determined to win. She had run a pretty successful campaign. She had professional posters designed and buttons made. She even appointed Chris as her campaign manager. The only thing left was her speech, and according to her campaign manager, it was nowhere near perfect.

"I'm going to fall flat on my face." Nathalie buried her head in her hands.

"No, you're not," Chris said.

"Yes, I am because my speech sucks."

"It doesn't suck," Chris said. "It needs a little work."

"Work?"

"Yes, work."

"Like?"

Chris grabbed her speech and looked down at it. "It lacks organization," he said.

"Says the guy who loses his backpack every day!" Nathalie exclaimed.

"Hey now," Chris smirked. "Be nice."

"I know," said Nathalie as she shook her head.

"Let's go over this." Chris pulled Nathalie down on the bed next to him.

"Let's organize this. Now, we need to narrow down your main points and make sure you keep all of the relevant points. And, I think we can come up with a better attention grabber than this."

Nathalie arched her brow. Several of Chris's points made sense. Maybe making him her campaign manager wasn't a bad idea after all.

Why is organization so important when preparing an outline for a speech?

Respond Here

My daughter Jaden and I decided that for her 16th birthday we would take a cross country trip together. Needless to say, we were extremely excited about our adventure. In anticipation of our trip, we had taken care of what we assumed were the critical preparations. We had purchased numerous essential items for our excursion. We bought two sets of designer luggage and a complete wardrobe, including purses, jewelry and shoes. We stocked up on all of our hard to find toiletries. We purchased several types of cameras, including video and digital cameras with professional lenses. Lastly, we bought and packed numerous boxes of our favorite snacks. We loaded my daughter's IPod with all of our favorite playlists.   Unfortunately, we forgot to acquire a map to lead us to our destination. We had omitted the most important aspect of reaching our location successfully. Many speakers follow the same approach when they prepare a speech for an audience. As they begin to formulate their speeches, they neglect to prepare a blueprint, or outline for the speech. If your destination is a successful speech, it is important, just as with our cross country trip, that you have a map. Outlining is an instrumental process that serves as the structure of a speech to lead to an effective outcome. In this chapter, we will learn how to organize your ideas so that you may prepare a clear outline. Let's get started!

Organizing Your Ideas

Now that we have developed your research strategy, analyzed your audience, located sources, and identified forms of support, it is time to develop the framework for your speech. Every good speech begins with a well structured outline. The three major components of an outline are the introduction, body and conclusion. Outlines may be labeled differently depending upon the communication theorist, however, they serve the same function. Outlines must be clear, repetitive, and useful.

Principles for Preparing the Outline

When preparing an outline, the following structure should be used:
I. Main Point
   A. Subpoint
      1. Sub–Subpoint
      2. Sub–Subpoint
         a. Support Point
         b. Support Point

Main points are represented by Roman Numerals. For example, I., II., III., IV., V. Note that sub points are indicated with capital letters and sub-subpoints with standard numbers. Lowercase letters are used to indicate support points. Outlines should follow the principles of coordination and subordination. The principle of coordination requires that all information at a given level be of similar importance. The principle of **subordination** requires that the main points descend in weight from general main points to the concrete and specific subpoints (Osborn and Osborn 2003). The indentation of five spaces is used for the symbol above it when outlining. This is key for maintaining clarity and neatness in your outline.

Example:

II. The first thing Dr. King has inspired me to do is to work hard. **Main Point**

A. Dr. King was a diligent student. **Subpoint**

1. He worked hard to graduate from high school and enter Morehouse College at 15 years old. **Sub-Subpoint**

2. He continued his schooling at Crozer Theological Seminary and Boston University and earned multiple degrees. **Sub-Subpoint**

Based on your research, spend some time brainstorming to generate ideas for your speech.

Outline components

Speech outlines should cite the title, general purpose, specific purpose, thesis statement, attention getter, and pattern of organization. The general purpose gives the overall objective of the speech. It serves as the umbrella under which the other outline components fall. The ***general purpose*** is the overall goal of a speech and serves one of three overlapping functions: to *inform, to persuade, or to entertain* (Seiler and Beall 2005). If the function of the general purpose is to inform your audience, your information should serve to emphasize that function. This does not mean that the information in your speech cannot be entertaining. However, in keeping true to the purpose of informing, the general purpose should primarily enhance an audience's knowledge and understanding by explaining what something means, how something works, or how something is done. You may ask, "Why is the general purpose so important in the preparation of a speech?" The answer is simple. The general purpose helps the speaker remain on target.

The ***specific purpose*** is a single phrase that defines precisely what is to be accomplished in a speech. It is typically worded by including the general purpose followed identifying the audience and presenting the exact topic to be covered. When developing an effective specific purpose, remember the following:

In an informative speech on civil rights, you would likely include information about Rosa Parks' contributions to the cause.

1. Specific purpose should be carefully worded.
2. Specific purpose should never be posed as a question.
3. Specific purpose should always express a single thought or idea.
4. Most importantly, the specific purpose should include the verb that supports the general purpose.

Example

General Purpose: **To inform**

Specific Purpose: To inform my audience about the life and legacy of Martin Luther King, Jr.

The Body of your Speech

The body of your speech contains the main content of what you intend to say. It articulates your thesis statement. As you prepare the body of the speech, it is important to first develop the main points. ***Main points*** are the principal sub-divisions of a speech and are often expressed within the specific purpose. One strategy used to generate main points is brainstorming. ***Brainstorming*** is a technique used to generate as many unedited ideas as possible in a limited amount of time. A good technique to use when brainstorming is ***mapping*** or clustering. Once you have generated your ideas using brainstorming, use the mapping technique to ready the content for the outline. This is done by using geometric shapes and arrows to indicate the relationships among them. Mapping enables you to reach your goal of not just planning what should be included in the outline but also creating coherence and unity in your speech. When developing your main points, keep the following suggestions in mind:

1. ***Limit the number of main points.*** Since most classroom speeches are never more than ten-to-fifteen minutes, the need to use more than five main points is rare. The use of too many main points will result in a speech that is difficult to follow and, even more importantly, difficult to remember.

2. ***Check main points for relevance and importance.*** Main points should stress the major considerations of your thesis statement. Each mainpoint should be distinct and should not overlap. They should relate directly to the topic and be major factors of significance.

3. ***State your main points in a parallel format.*** Parallelism increases comprehension and assists with delivery.

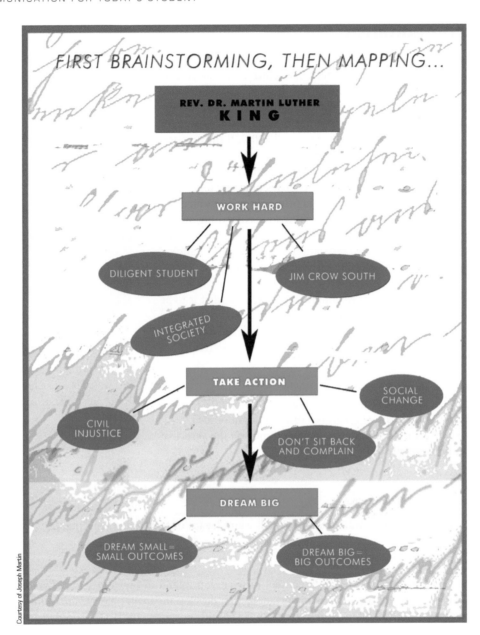

Courtesy of Joseph Martin

Thesis Statement

While the specific purpose states what you wish to accomplish with your speech, the thesis statement specifically states what is going to be discussed in the speech. The thesis statement will concisely state the contents of the speech. The thesis statement is a crucial step in narrowing a broad topic.

Example 1

Specific purpose: To inform my audience about the life and legacy of Rev. Dr. Martin Luther King, Jr.

Thesis Statement: Rev. Dr. Martin Luther King, Jr. was a dedicated husband, father, theologian, and civil rights activist.

Example 2

Specific Purpose: To inform my audience about the three major tourist attractions in the United States.

Thesis Purpose: Today, I would like to take you on a tour of the three major tourist attractions in the United States, including Niagara Falls, Disney World, and Washington National Zoo.

Attention Getters

One of the functions of the introduction in a speech is to capture the attention of the audience. There are numerous ways to gain an audience's attention through what public speakers refer to as attention getting devices.

1. **Ask Rhetorical Questions.** *Rhetorical questions* are useful attention devices because they offer the audience an opportunity to engage in reflection and apply the circumstances to their lives. While some speechmakers endorse the use of questions, it is not generally advised because you can not totally predict an audience's response.

2. **Tell Anecdotes.** An *anecdote* is a personal story that peeks an audience's interest because it presents a lighter and sometimes humorous element to the subject matter.

3. *Use Quotations.* When quotations are directly relevant to your topic they arouse the audience's attention. Quotations are effective if they are precise and use memorable syntax. In addition, quotations, when borrowed from a reputable source, can increase a speaker's credibility.

4. *Cite a Startling Statement or Fact.* A statement that is interesting and surprising to an audience will often make them pay closer attention to a speaker. The true test of this type of attention getter cannot be measured until it is actually presented to an audience. This sometimes proves to be a disadvantage of using this device.

5. **Employ Riddles.** Riddles are one of the oldest types of attention getters. They require the speaker to demonstrate the ability to be clever while exercising poise. Riddles are most effective when they are introduced at the beginning of the speech and answered in the conclusion.

Organizing Your Main Points

Once you have identified your main points, the next step is to determine a logical order for them. There are several patterns of arrangement that can be used. The pattern should be selected based upon the main points that you have determined should be included in a speech. Let's examine a few of the most frequently used patterns.

1. **Topical Pattern.** The *topical pattern* of arrangement is based upon categories or subject matter. It is the most popular arrangement pattern used among speech makers because it can be adapted to a variety of speech subjects. Placing main points in a parallel structure is easy to accomplish when using the topical pattern. When using the topical pattern of arrangement, you must first identify commonalities. In the topical pattern, the main topic is divided into a series of related subtopics.

Example

Topic: The Rev. Dr. Martin Luther King, Jr.

Main points

    I.   Rev. Dr. Martin Luther King, Jr. inspired me to work hard.

    II.   Rev Dr. Martin Luther King, Jr. inspired me to take action.

    III.   Rev. Dr. Martin Luther King, Jr. inspired me to dream big.

2. **Chronological Pattern.** When using the chronological pattern, information is arranged according to periods of time. Information may begin at some point in time and either continues forward or backwards. Additionally, topics which deal with steps in a process or the development of a series of events or ideas are best utilized with the chronological pattern. It is important to keep in mind when using the chronological pattern that it is effective only when applied uniformly and consistently.

Example

Topic: Making Chocolate Chip Cookies

Main points

    I.   The first step in making chocolate chip cookies is to gather the ingredients.

    II.   The second step in making chocolate chip cookies is to mix the ingredients.

    III.   The third step in making chocolate chip cookies is to place the batter in the oven.

3. **Proximity Pattern.** When organizing main points according to the proximity pattern, the content of the speech is organized according to relationships in space. Main points are arranged in accordance to distances, directions or physical surroundings. Keep in mind, the proximity pattern is sometimes referred to as the spatial or space pattern of organization.

Example

Topic: Rap Music: Does Geography Influence Rap Music Sales?

    I.   East Coast rappers accounted for 30% of rap music sales in 2010.

    II.   "Dirty South" rappers accounted for 24% of rap music sales in 2010.

    III.   West Coast rappers accounted for 44% rap music sales in 2010.

4. **Problem-Solution Pattern.** The problem-solution pattern utilizes two main points: the problem and the solution. The problem establishes the need and describes what is wrong. The solution proposes remedies or eliminates the problem without creating an additional difficulty or issue.

Example

Topic: Texting While Driving

Problem: In 2010, 2,200 people in the United Stated died as a result of texting while driving.

Solution: Congress should pass strict legislation to deter texting while driving with a penalty of life imprisonment.

5. **Cause and Effect Pattern.** The cause and effect pattern is very similar to the problem-solution pattern in that it consists of two basic parts: the cause and the effect. The cause describes something that has happened or is happening. The effect predicts the outcome possibilities. Frequently, public speakers reverse the order of this pattern. This is an acceptable practice; however, at least three of the following items should be present when following this pattern.

- A definition and description of the problem
- An analysis of the problem
- Suggestions of possible solutions
- Recommendation for the best possible solutions
- Discussion of the best solution to put into operation(Seiler and Beall 2005)

6. **Monroe Motivated Sequence Pattern.** The Monroe Motivate Sequence, named after its originator, Alan H. Monroe, is a variation of the problem - solution pattern. This pattern, which is used primarily in persuasive speeches, combines logic and practical psychology. The sequence, consisting of five steps, is effective in persuasive speaking because it follows the human thinking process and motivates listeners to take some type of action. The sequence, as detailed in Chapter 11, includes: *Attention, Need, Satisfaction, Visualization, and Action.*

Developing Subpoints

Subpoints are used to further explain and support the main points of your speech. As supporting material is added to the outline, the body of the speech should expand. Supporting materials should be relevant to the main point, as well as related to the topic, specific purpose, and thesis. Typically, the main point is supported by two or more subpoints. In addition, it is critical that the support is logically organized. The subpoints that follow the mainpoint should make that point understandable, believable and compelling (Oliver, Zelko, and Holtsman, 1968). While establishing good form in an outline, its' important to remember to limit the number of support points. In order to keep your speech from becoming convoluted and difficult to follow, when you find you have too many subpoints, it may be necessary to reevaluate to determine if they are in fact, sub-subpoints. Subpoints sometimes require further clarity and specificity.

Making Connections

When you begin to compose an essay for an English composition class, you include major ideas which may be expressed in paragraphs ranging from three to five sentences each. You have been instructed that in order to make your essay "read well" and effectively communicate your ideas, you must smoothly guide the reader as your topic is being presented. The same approach must be taken when preparing an oral presentation. As the speaker, you must communicate effectively with an audience and, in doing so, it is important to effectively incorporate connecting devices. Speeches that lack such devices will make your speech seem disjointed and be difficult for your listeners to follow. The most common connections in public speaking are transitions, internal previews and summaries, and signposts.

1. **Transitions.** Transitions are words or phrases that link the introduction and body of the speech, the main ideas and supporting material, and the body and conclusion. Transitions serve to assist listeners in connecting one idea to another. Transitions are usually simple short phrases or stock words that can be directly linked to a specific function within a speech.

Transitions can be classified in the following ways:

- *Time Changes*—until, now, since, previously, later, earlier, in the past, in the future, meanwhile, five years ago, just last week, tomorrow, following, before, presently, eventually, sooner or later.
- *Numerical Order*—first, second, third, last, to begin with, initially, next, finally.
- *Spatial Relations*—to the north, alongside, to the left, above, moving eastward, in front of, behind, nearby, below.
- *Importance*—most importantly, above all, remember, take note of, keep this in mind.
- *Comparisons*—compared with, both are, likewise, in comparison, similarly, like, just as, another type of.
- *Cause/Effect*—therefore, thus, consequently, accordingly, so, as a result, hence, since, because of.
- *Contrast*—but, yet, however, on the other hand, still, otherwise, in contrast, unfortunately, on the contrary.
- *Explanation*—to illustrate, for example, for instance, case in point, in other words, to simplify, to clarify.
- *Additions*—moreover, in addition, furthermore, besides.
- Conclusions—finally, in short, in conclusion, to summarize. (Osborn and Osborn 2003)

2. **Signposts**. Signposts are words, phrases or short statements that indicate to an audience the direction a speaker will take next. Just as traffic signs let us know when take a turn or warn us about upcoming conditions when traveling, signposts operate in much the same manner. Signposts can include questions as well as in many cases, they are used to indicate to the audience that the upcoming information is very important.

Examples of signposts include: *my next point is . . . next. . . . lastly . . . what happened next?. . . . what is our next plan of action?. . . . the most critical point I'd like to make is. . . .*

3. **Internal Previews.** Internal Previews consist of short statements that give advance warning to the audience of what is going to be discussed in the speech.

Examples of internal previews: *Next, we'll take a close look at the early career of Michael Jordan. . . . Now, lets examine additional causes of teenage drug use. . . . Lastly, we will consider the most important reason for giving to the victims of Hurricane Katrina.*

Photo courtesy of Charles Long

Persuasive speeches often present an audience with a problem and examine potential solutions.

4. ***Internal Summaries.*** Internal summaries are unique transitions in that they remind listeners of what has been previously been said in order to move on to a new point. Internal summaries should be brief and to the point. An internal summary should be used at the end of each main point. Internal summaries are especially important when using the cause-effect and problem–solution patterns of arrangement because they condense lengthy material into abbreviated material which can serve as support for a persuasive argument.

An example of an internal summary is *"Now that we have looked at the commitment of Rev. Dr. Martin Luther King, Jr. to his family and his leadership in the Civil Rights Movement, let's examine closely the impact of his tragic end on the world."*

Jesse Jackson's key role as a leader in the Democratic party could be a main point in a topical organizational pattern speech on civil rights.

The Conclusion

Most speech writers assert that the only part of a speech that is more important than the introduction is the conclusion. Given that, perhaps we should prepare the conclusion as we prepare the introduction. Some writers find that doing so eliminates fatigue and "speaker's block." Have you ever sat in an audience and witnessed an ill prepared speaker reach the conclusion saying phrases like, "That's all," "That ends my speech," "That's all I have to say," or even "Well, I'm finished." Prior to the conclusion you had higher expectations of the speaker's ability. If you have witnessed this as an audience member, it should be enough to persuade you to construct your speech conclusion carefully. Whether you are a believer of the primacy effect or the recency effect, you should concur that concluding remarks leave a lasting impression on your audience. This should not be taken lightly. The conclusion should bring the most important points together in a condensed and uniform way. It is always helpful when the speaker can connect the conclusion in some way to the introduction of the speech. Additionally, ensure the audience that you are finishing your speech. This may be done by using a simple transition such as, "In conclusion," "Finally," or," "As I conclude." The conclusion is an excellent opportunity for the speaker to reiterate or, perhaps in some cases, make the thesis clearer. If the speaker decides to repeat the main points, this is always helpful. In repeating the main points, it advisable to reword or restate to prevent boredom. Lastly, the conclusion should always include a memorable thought and may even utilize the attention getting device that was presented in the introduction.

Preparing the Outline

There are two types of outlines: the sentence and the keyword outline. The keyword outline, while serving as the blueprint or skeleton of the speech, serves as a preliminary sketch of the main points and subpoints. The keyword outline helps the speaker remember the information that they would like to include in the presentation. The keyword outline should include verbal footnotes. This is the only case in which full sentences are permissible in the outline. Since the speaker will use this outline when delivering the speech, it is beneficial to highlight the verbal footnotes in the outline. Once the keyword outline has been completed, the full sentence outline can be prepared. All items in the full sentence outline should be written in complete sentences. This includes the sub-points and sub-subpoints. A good sentence outline is detailed, but should not present more than one sentence per Roman numeral, letter or number. Additionally, the full sentence outline should include all verbal footnotes.

Verbal footnotes are citations within the speech which give credit to the source of the support information. Verbal footnotes increase the credibility of the speaker.

The main objective in preparing a full sentence outline is to provide the speaker with the syntax that will be used as the speech is delivered. It becomes easier to speak using the key word outline, once you have practiced with the sentence outline.

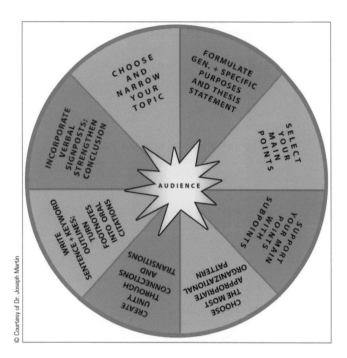

© Courtesy of Dr. Joseph Martin

Summary

The outline serves as the blueprint for your speech. It provides an overview of what you plan to say and the manner in which you plan to say it. Overall it is the tool that will help you achieve your purpose. When preparing the outline, it is important to remember that the two types of outlines, sentence outlines and keyword outlines, should be closely coordinated. As you prepare the outlines, keep in mind that audiences will be able to follow your speech if the main points are presented using a standard pattern of organization. We discussed several in this chapter. In choosing a pattern of organization, first consider the topic and the type of information that you have found in your research. The outline consists of three key components: introduction, body and conclusion. However, do not dismiss the importance of transitions, signposts, previews, and internal summaries. Without transitions, your speech will appear disjointed and often times less coherent. The introduction of a speech should fulfill the objectives of gaining attention, connecting with the audience, and previewing your topic. The body of the outline presents the major ideas, and the conclusion should summarize and leave your audience with a memorable message.

When Jaden and I planned our cross country trip, we made a major mistake because we did not consider the primary thing that would ensure our safe and successful arrival to our destination. Something as simple as a map could have prevented us from having a memorable vacation. After reading this chapter, you should see the significance of having a map or blueprint to ensure the success of your speeches. Your destination in public speaking is a speech that is informative, logical, and memorable. A well constructed outline will help you reach your goals. After completing your outline, ask yourself:

- Have I gained my audience's attention?
- Did I establish a connection between my audience, my topic and me?
- Did I provide a preview of my speech?
- Did I select no more than five main points?
- Did I present them in parallel format?
- Did I use an acceptable and applicable pattern of organization?
- Did I incorporate transitions?
- Were there opportunities to include signposts?
- Is my speech lengthy enough to necessitate internal summaries?
- Did I include an indication that I was completing my speech?
- Did I summarize and restate my main points?
- Did I leave my audience with a memorable thought?

Communication for Today's Student

Chapter 8 – Organizing Your Ideas and Structuring Your Outline

Exercise 8.1 – Structure of Outlining

Instructions: Indicate the parts of the outline in the blanks provided. Follow the example given.

Example (<u>General Purpose</u>): To inform

Specific Purpose: To inform my audience about how Rev. Dr. Martin Luther King, Jr. inspired me to work hard, take action, and dream big.

Attention-Getter: Startling Statement

Pattern of Organization: Topical

I. (_____) April 4, 1968. None of us were around to remember what happened this day, but our parents could probably tell us exactly what they were doing when they heard that one of the most influential men that has ever lived had been murdered.

   A. The death of Dr. King will always be a painful memory, but his life should be greatly celebrated for the inspiration he gave.
   B. Good morning, my name is Brittany Jackson and my purpose today (_____) is to tell you how the life of one man has inspired me to work hard, take action, and dream big.

II. The first thing Dr. King has inspired me to do is to work hard. (_____)

   A. (_____) Dr. King was a diligent student.
      1. He worked hard to graduate from high school and enter Morehouse College at 15 years old.
      2. He continued his schooling at Crozer Theological Seminary and Boston University and earned multiple degrees.
   B. It was not common that a young black man growing up in the Jim Crow South had the opportunity or the drive to go this far in education.
   C. Today, in an integrated society, I realize that I have more opportunities and an even greater chance to succeed.

III. The next thing (_____) that Dr. King has inspired me to do is to take action.

   A. During a time when civil injustice was at its peak, many people complained but were afraid to do anything about it.
   B. Dr. King saw the need for a social change.
      1. In December 1965, he organized a bus boycott, which led to the Supreme Court ruling bus segregation unconstitutional.
      2. (_____) Dr. King was arrested, his home was bombed, and he received personal abuse.
   C. Whatever you see that you feel needs to be changed, don't sit back and complain about it. TAKE ACTION!

IV. Lastly, Dr. King has inspired me to dream big. (_____)

Chapter 8 – Organizing and Outlining Your Ideas

Exercise 8.1 Continued

    A. Mostly, everyone is familiar with Dr. King's famous "I Have a Dream" speech.
       1. In that speech, he stated that one of his dreams was that his children would be judged by the content of their character and not the color of their skin.
       2. Dr. King never saw his dream come true, but he never gave up on believing in it.
    B. The most valuable lesson I have learned from Dr. King is to dream big, even though it seems impossible.

V. (_____) In conclusion, we all have dreams, and even though they may not be dreams that will change humanity, they are still important to us.

    A. If you dream small, the outcome is likely to be small.
    B. If you dream big, then the possibilities are endless.

Communication for Today's Student

Chapter 8 – Organizing and Outlining Your Ideas

Exercise 8.2 – Outlining

Instructions: Transform the sentence outline on Dr. Martin Luther King into a key word(s) outline.

General Purpose:
Specific Purpose:
Attention-Getter:
Pattern of Organization:

I.

    A.

    B.

II.

    A.

        1.

        2.

    B.

    C.

III.

    A.

    B.

        1.

        2.

    C.

IV.

    A.

        1.

        2.

    B.

V.

    A.

    B.

DELIVERING THE SPEECH

After reading this chapter, you should be able to:

- ☑ Indentify the four methods of the delivery of a speech.
- ☑ Explain the aspects of vocal delivery when giving a speech.
- ☑ Explain the aspects of physical delivery when giving a speech.
- ☑ Describe the aspects of the effective delivery of a speech.

Key Terms

Additions	Gestures	Pronunciation
Articulation	Habitual pitch	Public-speaking anxiety
Bel	Impromptu speaking	Rate
Decibel	Inflection	Slurring
Deletion	Loudness	Stress
Enunciation	Manuscript delivery	Substitution
Ethos	Memorization delivery	Transposition
Extemporaneous speaking	Pathos	Vocal fillers
Eye contact	Pauses	Volume
Facial expression	Pitch	

Facing image Photo courtesy of Charles Long.

9 Scenario

Nathalie stood behind the curtain of the school auditorium with her note cards in her hand. She could hear her opponent giving his speech. It was not going horribly. He was a comedian and a class clown, so he had the audience under his comedic charm. She began to warm up, waking up her articulators with a few exercises she had learned from her oral communication class. She was stretching her tongue when Chris walked back stage.

"Why are you here?" Chris asked walking over to Nathalie. "I told you I'd get you from the dressing room when it was your turn."

"I wanted . . ." Nathalie sighed. "Staying in that dressing room would have made me more nervous to be honest."

"Cameron's a clown," Chris muttered. "He's not talking about anything important. It's like he's having his own comedy hour up there."

"He's sticking to his strengths," Nathalie said as she arranged her cards in order. "Can't fault him for that."

Chris shook his head, "I gave the guy on the teleprompter your speech. I had him check the order twice."

"Thanks, but I won't need it," Nathalie said confidently, handing him the notecards. "I know this speech backwards and forwards. I've done the work."

The crowd clapped as Cameron left the stage. The host was now introducing Nathalie. Nathalie grabbed her water bottle from a nearby table and took a quick sip before placing it back.

"Wish me luck," Nathalie winked as she walked on stage.

Chris smiled and watched her take the podium. "You don't need it."

Nathalie feels confident that she doesn't need to utilize note cards or the teleprompter to deliver her speech. What are some pitfalls of delivering a speech from memory?

Respond Here

Demonthenes, believed to be the greatest orator in the ancient world, mastered his delivery by taking extreme measures. Having suffered from a speech impediment, he was said to have practiced his speech with pebbles in his mouth while running up stairs and hills to strengthen his breathing capacity. To increase his ability to project, Demonthenes stood by the ocean when practicing in an attempt to speak over the roar of the waves. He was also known to practice in front of a large mirror to perfect his gestures and body language.

The ancient Greeks placed great emphasis on not only what was said but also how it was said. Delivery, the fifth canon of Aristotle's *Canons of Rhetoric*, was believed to be essential in creating both ethos (credibility) and pathos (emotion) in speaking.

In my numerous years of teaching, conducting workshops, and attending conferences, I have had the experience of witnessing thousands of speeches with various purposes, in diverse venues, by speakers with various levels of professionalism. Many of the speeches have been extraordinary.

Lecomte du Nouy, Jean Jules Antoine (1842–1923).

Oftentimes, I am asked if I can identify the best speech I have ever heard? This is not just a difficult question, but an impossible one for me to answer with integrity. I can say, however, that the most memorable speeches I have witnessed were memorable not because of the speaker's message or the speech's occasion, but because of the speaker's dynamic delivery.

The Greeks and Romans described delivery as "the appropriate management of voice, gestures, and appearance (Ridolfo). Surprisingly, our view of delivery is not very different from that held by the Greeks and Romans.

Communication theorists assert, and we have learned in previous chapters, that the public presentation of a speech involves conceptionalizing, researching, and organizing your topic. However, in order be effective as a public speaker, you must always be cognizant of the fifth canon of rhetoric, delivery. Delivery occurs when the visuals and verbal components of the topic merge in front of an audience. Let us face it, whether you are presenting a speech in front of hundreds of people, or a few, delivering an effective speech is a challenge.

The first advice for preparing to deliver a speech is to envision your success in front of the extended audience. Professional speakers suggest that you visualize your success, by imagining yourself standing in front of a warm smiling enthusiastic audience. If you view the audience in this manner then more than likely you will feel good about your presentation.

The second sage advice dispensed by seasoned speakers is to keep your speech audience centered. Remember, you are never giving the speech for yourself, but for the audience. Therefore, you must prepare your speech for the audience and from the audience's perspective. Much like the great Athenian orator Demonthenes, you must practice your delivery to ensure the audience receives the full benefit of your message.

In this chapter, we will examine the essential elements of a dynamic delivery. *Where should I look during my speech? Should I place my hands on the podium, in my pockets, or behind my back while I am speaking? Am I gesturing too much or not enough? Should I stand behind the podium or is it acceptable to move around? Am I using too many vocal filers? Is my voice monotonous? Do I sound conversational?* These are just some of the issues that will be addressed as we take a close look at the vocal and physical aspects of delivery.

Before we delve into the elements of delivery, let us examine the methods of delivering a speech. Keeping in mind that the delivery of your speech should be compatible with the topic, audience, and occasion, the speaker should decide which of the following methods of delivery is appropriate:

Each method has specific advantages and disadvantages which are greatly dependent upon the communication situation or context.

impromptu, manuscript, memorized, or extemporaneous. As each is discussed, see if you can determine which you will be utilizing in this class, and then speculate as to the reason why.

Methods of Delivery

Impromptu Delivery

Nathalie bites her nails and feels a sudden pain in the pit of her stomach when professor Young asks her to stand and describe the War of 1812. She thinks to herself for a moment about the reading she did last night in preparation for today's history class. As she begins to recall her reading, she quickly jots down a few terms in the margin of her spiral notebook. She then takes a deep breath, stands, and begins to respond to Professor Young's request. Before she realizes it, she is fully engaging her audience. Her delivery is energetic and her enthusiasm for history has consumed her anxiety. When Professor Young tells Nathalie thank you, she feels as if she could continue to speak for much longer. Nathalie has just delivered an impromptu speech.

Photo courtesy of Charles Long

Be sure to develop an outline that contains main points and sub points before moving on to key-words only.

An impromptu speech is a speech that is delivered without prior notice, and it is typically presented by a speaker who has a great deal of knowledge on the topic or subject matter. Speaking without the benefit of a prior notice or planning can be nerve-wracking and cause speech anxiety regardless of how much knowledge the speaker may possess on the topic. Becoming proficient at impromptu speaking requires practice.

Below are some suggestions to help you become a stronger impromptu speaker:

Keep it formal. Always consider the speaking engagement as formal. Be reserved even if the setting does not appear to call for it. Use appropriate language. Never engage in slang. Do not get too comfortable.

Organize your thoughts. Prepare a brief "mini" outline of your ideas. This will keep you on track and assist with your audience's comprehension in some cases. The napkin outline, as it is sometimes called, is basically four or five words written on any type of paper within the speaker's reach, for example, a napkin at the banquet table, that helps the speaker stick to the point.

Be brief. Resist the tendency that some speakers have to ramble as an extension of their nervousness. When you finish your mini outline, say thank you and take your seat. As simple as this may seem, sometimes taking a seat is a great challenge for speakers. It is a challenge either because they think they are performing well and want to make the experience last or because they do not realize they have accomplished their objective. In either case, failing to sit down when finished can diminish the speaker's sense of accomplishment.

Use the speech context. Consider what has just occurred before you speak or what is supposed to occur after you finish as a means of connecting with the audience. If appropriate, you may even mention the occasion. Sometimes, this puts you and your audience at ease.

The more opportunities you have to give impromptu speeches, the better you will become at delivering them. You will begin to develop a sense of spontaneity and the ability to organize your thoughts quickly. Also, you will stockpile a reservoir of attention getters to gain your audience's attention and keep it.

Improvised speaking is a learned technique. Those speakers who master it and demonstrate an undeniable ability to do it well are quite impressive.

Manuscript Delivery

When President Obama stands at the podium to present the State of Union Address to Congress, it may appear as if he is looking directly at the audience. However, he is actually looking at two teleprompters and reading the entire text of his speech. This method of delivery is referred to as manuscript delivery. The teleprompters are designed so that the speaker can view the script though it is invisible to the audience.

In manuscript speeches, each word is written out and then spoken verbatim. This method is used when it is important that the exact wording is used or when the timing of the speech must be exact. The speaker can minimize errors in word choice and grammar when using the manuscript method. The speaker has an opportunity to read the speech prior to delivery to ensure the wording is correct and that the intended message is indeed the one being conveyed. Most speakers believe that manuscript delivery is easy. It appears simple because it only involves writing out the speech and reading it to the audience.

Can you think of any reason why "public reading" is frowned upon in most speech contexts? Most speakers who use the manuscript method of delivery become dependent upon the script. This insecurity can lead to a lack of eye contact and vocal variety.

Memorized Delivery

As children we were often put in a speech context, such as a church program, in which we were required to present a poem or short speech. In these contexts, we were required to memorize the poem or short speech. Memorized delivery entails the speaker committing the entire speech to memory and then presenting it to an audience. The memorized speech is beneficial when the speaker seeks to minimize the risk of presenting information that is inaccurate or sounding unprepared. A memorized delivery can be advantageous when used in small doses.

It is beneficial to memorize specific sections of your speech. Speech instructors encourage young speakers to memorize the introduction and conclusion when preparing to deliver a speech. Also, it is always advisable to memorize transactional phrases. If the context calls for memorized delivery, it is important to appear spontaneous. Work on the vocal variation and inflection to prevent the speech from sounding stilted or dronish.

Extemporaneous Delivery

The preferred method of delivery in most speech contexts, hands down, is extemporaneous. When preparing to speak using an extemporaneous delivery, the speaker performs thorough research, organizes ideas and findings, prepares an outline, rehearses the speech using the outline, and then delivers the speech with the aid of the outline. This is the desired method because it enables the speaker to "appear" spontaneous, adapt to the audience and environment, and engage the listeners. In simplistic terms, the extemporaneous method of delivery allows for spontaneity while utilizing an effective structure.

Expressing yourself naturally helps you connect with your audience.

	Characteristics	Benefits	Challenges	Contexts
Impromptu	Speech is delivered with little or no preparation and the speaker has knowledge of the topic.	✒ Speak informally ✒ Maintain eye contact	✒ May lack research ✒ May lack clear organization	✒ Meetings at work ✒ Classroom
Memorized	Speech is written out word for word and recited with the use of notes	✒ Maximizes eye contact ✒ Allows for careful wording ✒ Allows for exact timing	✒ May sound over-rehearsed and stilted ✒ May limit ability to adapt to audience ✒ May forget information or get lost	✒ Introductions ✒ Acceptance ✒ Announcements ✒ Brief remarks ✒ Commentary
Manuscript	Speech is written out word for word and read from the script	✒ Reduces risk of misspeaking	✒ May reduce eye contact	✒ Introductions ✒ Acceptance ✒ Announcements ✒ Remarks ✒ Commentary ✒ Political Speeches
Extemporaneous	Speech is prepared and delivered from notes	✒ Allows for research, planning, and practice ✒ Allows for spontaneity	✒ May call for preparation that is time consuming	✒ Professional presentations in various contexts

How Do I Deliver an Effective Speech?

According to research on public speaking anxiety conducted by Walechinsky et al., the fear of speaking in public is only second to the fear of dying. While most of us may believe speech anxiety is fairly common, we may not realize just how prevalent it is among speakers. Speech anxiety is so prevalent that one study found that eighty-five percent of the general population report experiencing some level of fear or anxiety about public speaking (Burnley et.al., 1993). There is no wonder that each time students are presented with an opportunity to speak in

Photo courtesy of Charles Long

Extemporaneous speaking allows you to move freely and emphasize points with gestures.

James McCroskey's
Personal Report of Public Speaking Anxiety **(PRPSA)**

Directions: Below are thirty-four statements that people sometimes make about themselves. Please indicate whether or not you believe each statement applies to you by marking whether you:

Strongly Disagree = 1; Disagree = 2; Neutral = 3; Agree = 4; Strongly Agree = 5.

1. While preparing for giving a speech, I feel tense and nervous.
2. I feel tense when I see the words "speech" and "public speech" on a course outline when studying.
3. My thoughts become confused and jumbled when I am giving a speech.
4. Right after giving a speech I feel that I have had a pleasant experience.
5. I get anxious when I think about a speech coming up.
6. I have no fear of giving a speech.
7. Although I am nervous just before starting a speech, I soon settle down after starting and feel calm and comfortable.
8. I look forward to giving a speech.
9. When the instructor announces a speaking assignment in class, I can feel myself getting tense.
10. My hands tremble when I am giving a speech.
11. I feel relaxed while giving a speech.
12. I enjoy preparing for a speech.
13. I am in constant fear of forgetting what I prepared to say.
14. I get anxious if someone asks me something about my topic that I don't know.
15. I face the prospect of giving a speech with confidence.
16. I feel that I am in complete possession of myself while giving a speech.
17. My mind is clear when giving a speech.
18. I do not dread giving a speech.
19. I perspire just before starting a speech.
20. My heart beats very fast just as I start a speech.
21. I experience considerable anxiety while sitting in the room just before my speech starts.
22. Certain parts of my body feel very tense and rigid while giving a speech.
23. Realizing that only a little time remains in a speech makes me very tense and anxious.
24. While giving a speech, I know I can control my feelings of tension and stress.
25. I breathe faster just before starting a speech.
26. I feel comfortable and relaxed in the hour or so just before giving a speech.
27. I do poorer on speeches because I am anxious.
28. I feel anxious when the teacher announces the date of a speaking assignment.
29. When I make a mistake while giving a speech, I find it hard to concentrate on the parts that follow.
30. During an important speech I experience a feeling of helplessness building up inside me.
31. I have trouble falling asleep the night before a speech.
32. My heart beats very fast while I present a speech.
33. I feel anxious while waiting to give my speech.
34. While giving a speech, I get so nervous I forget facts I really know.

Continued

Scoring: To determine your score on the PRPSA, complete the following steps:

Step 1. Add scores for items 1, 2, 3, 5, 9, 10, 13, 14, 19, 20, 21, 22, 23, 25, 27, 28, 29, 30, 31, 32, 33, and 34.

Step 2. Add the scores for items 4, 6, 7, 8, 11, 12, 15, 16, 17, 18, 24, and 26.

Step 3. Complete the following formula:

PRPSA = 72 – Total from Step 2 + Total from Step 1

Total: _____

Your score should be between 34 and 170. If your score is below 34 or above 170, you have made a mistake in computing the score.

High = > 131
Low = < 98
Moderate = 98–131

Courtesy of Dr. James C. McCroskey, Department of Communications Studies, University of Alabama-Birmingham

public they experience not just nervousness, but speech anxiety. Speech anxiety manifests itself through various physiological symptoms. Speakers have been known to suffer with severe perspiration, trembling, excessive use of vocal fillers, dry mouth, digestive issues, and even fainting.

A surprising example of speech anxiety gained national attention when Florida Republican Senator Mark Rubio gave the Republican response to President Barack Obama's 2013 State of the Union Address. Rubio's apparent nervousness manifested itself by him continuously reaching for a bottle of water during the live broadcast.

Rubio's response to the President Obama's 2013 State of the Union Address marked the first time the GOP selected a Cuban immigrant to deliver the response. Some political analysts speculated that this speech should have positioned Rubio on the platform for the GOP nomination in the 2016 presidential election. While in some political circles the Senator's speech was hailed as the best response to the State of the Union Address ever seen, it was overshadowed by headlines such as "Marco Rubio Pauses Speech for Water Break." Senator Rubio's reach for that bottle of water became the obsession of the media and comedians the next day, airing 184 times and leading to questions of his readiness for the national platform.

President Obama is known for his effective delivery.

Given what we know about public speaking anxiety, Senator Rubio's thirst was mostly likely the result of one of the most common symptoms of speech anxiety, dry mouth.

Would you say that audience members believe what they see more than what they hear? Even though Senator Rubio's speech was viewed as a well-written speech, his effectiveness was called into question because of his nonverbal cues. As we look at the aspects of an effective delivery, we need to remember that speech anxiety may affect the vocal and physical aspects of the delivery.

One of the most prolific and respected scholars in the area of speech anxiety, James McCroskey, developed an evaluative instrument known as the Personal Report of Public Speaking Anxiety (PRPSA). The PRPSA is an excellent measure for researchers in the area of speech anxiety. Let us test your speech anxiety by answering a few sample questions.

Now that you have completed the PRPSA to determine the level of your public speaking anxiety, consider how your level of anxiety may impact your delivery. Numerous studies have found that affective strategies can minimize public speaking anxiety. It has been proven that students experienced significantly less anxiety after they had been taught how to manage their distress by using means of affective strategies (M. K. and M. Bobanović 5).

As we address the aspects of verbal and physical delivery, bear in mind how your anxiety may have a direct impact on both aspects of your delivery.

Aspects of Vocal Delivery

A speaker's credibility and ultimate success greatly depends on the ability to create an image for the audience by using vocal cues. While there is no magic formula to achieve this goal, a speaker must always be cognizant of the fact that, first, he or she must be understood so that the message is conveyed. Second, the speaker must deliver the message with a conversational quality so that the audience will take a genuine interest in the message. To achieve these two objectives, the speaker should give significant consideration to the vocal aspects of delivery, including volume, pitch, articulation, rate, and pauses.

Volume

The greatest disservice a speaker can commit when presenting a speech to an audience is to not be heard. It is, to say the least, a minimal expectation. *Loudness* or intensity of sound is measured in units of *bels*. A *decibel* is one-tenth of a bel. You may recognize the word decibel as it is derived from the inventor of the telephone, Alexander Graham Bell. *Volume* is the degree of loudness. It is important that the speaker determine the degree at which he or she can he heard by all of the participants in the speech setting or context. Since there will be no decibel reader in the room, it is important that the speaker has a good sense of what is considered the necessary level of loudness by listening to others who may speak in the room prior to him or her taking the stage.

Try these on for size:

A whisper	20 decibels
Natural conversation	40–60 decibels
Symphony orchestra playing Wagner at full blast	100 decibels
Pain and danger level	120 decibels
Rock group playing	141 decibels (Mayer 51)

When determining the volume to use when delivering your message, keep in mind that you should speak loud enough so that the audience member who is furthest away from you can hear you without having to strain. Additionally, try varying the volume to create a dramatic effect that will intensify the message. This technique is referred to as emphasis or stress. Emphasis is the degree of prominence given to a phrase or thought group while stress is the degree of emphasis given to a syllable within a word or a word within a phrase or a sentence. Lyle Mayer states that the "stressed syllable is made louder and is often higher in pitch than its neighbors (304, 305)."

Do not stress about stressing. This technique will require practice, but typically it becomes more natural with practice. Lastly, learn to use a microphone. Contrary to popular thought, there is a technique to using microphones. Never think that you can simply speak into the microphone and all will be well. Simply put, sound reinforcement is exactly what it indicates, reinforcement. Do not rely on a microphone to do your work for you. You should never rely on the microphone for projection. Microphones are devices designed for amplification, not projection. Therefore, when using a microphone, a speaker must support the sound by placing it forward toward the audience.

Articulation

Another important variable in effective delivery is articulation. Articulation is the production of clear and distinct speech sounds. It is a process by which individual sounds are produced by using the tongue, lips, teeth, and velum (soft palate) to modify the outgoing stream of air from the air passage.

Surprisingly, few people place much emphasis on articulation unless speaking intelligibility is a necessity or requirement of job performance.

> Can you name five occupations that require good articulation?
> 1.
> 2.
> 3.
> 4.
> 5.

Oftentimes, when we refer to clarity and distinctness in speech, we use the terms diction or enunciation, as well as articulation. But do not be surprised if you hear the terms articulation, diction, and enunciation used interchangeably, as all three terms refer to the accuracy and clarity of speech. The preferred reference is articulation because we engage in this process of speech clarity by manipulation of the articulators.

Pronunciation, on the other hand, is quite different from these terms. As described by Lee and Gura, *pronunciation* is acceptable when all the sounds of a word are uttered correctly in their proper order and with accent (stress) on the proper syllable (86).

Articulation is more concerned with the production of sounds to ensure clarity and intelligibility, whereas the emphasis in pronunciation is upon the structure of the sounds that form the English language. In either case, meaning can be lost if the speaker is not articulate and does not pronounce each word correctly.

What does it matter? Which of the following concern articulation (A) and which concern pronunciation (P)?

A or P?

Aks	ask
Warsh	wash
Getting	getting
Gitcha	get you
Pacific	specific

> Unfortunately, often times we are unaware we pronounced a word incorrectly until a listener points it out to us.

The most common articulation problems can be minimized or even eliminated with awareness and practice.

Common articulation problems are presented below.

Deletion is when sounds are omitted from a word. *Addition* occurs when a speaker adds extra sounds to a word. *Substitution* occurs when a speaker replaces an acceptable sound with an incorrect replacement (e.g., <u>dis</u> for <u>this</u>).

Slurring is when a speaker combines two or more words into one word as in the case of *I'm going* to *I'magoing*.

Transposition is defined as reversing two sounds in a word. An example is *prespective* instead *perspective*.

Remember, mispronouncing words will detract from a speaker's credibility, and possibly from the listeners' comprehension.

Oftentimes, a speaker's dialect can interfere with a listener's comprehension. A *dialect* is the pronunciation of words that is consistent with an ethnic group or geographic region. Mayer explains further that a dialect is a variety of a language that is distinguished from other varieties of the same language. The variation of the language is typically spoken by groups that have been separated by ethnicity or location (7).

There are four major terms that are used to identify dialects in the United States. They are Southern, Eastern, New England, and Standard American. Standard American is spoken by the majority of the people in the United States, largely in the Midwest and as far south as the Mason-Dixon Line. People who reside in the West, Southwest, Alaska, and Hawaii are known to speak Standard American. Since this dialect is considered the standard, the other dialects are compared to it. Standard American is the dialect that is used by professional actors, television personalities, newscasters, commentators, and the list continues.

New England and Eastern dialects have the smallest numbers of users. The New England dialect is spoken in Massachusetts, Rhode Island, Connecticut, Vermont, New Hampshire, and Maine. The Eastern dialect is used in the Middle Atlantic States like New York and New Jersey. It is important to remember that these dialects vary from city to city within each state. No dialect is absolute. This is most evident in the Southern dialect or the states of the Old Confederacy. A single state can have numerous subdialects, yet each dialect will always be recognized as Southern (Mayer 7–8).

Pitch

One of the quickest ways to lose an audience's attention is for the speaker to lack vocal variation or speak in a monotone. Speakers with vocal monotony are often referred to as drones. It is, therefore, important that the speaker delivers the speech in a vocal quality that is interesting and engaging. A drone delivery is commonly attributed to personality traits or the type of material being addressed. Regardless of the cause of this problem, it is fatal to the overall successful delivery of the speech. It is a plague that can strike speakers of all ages and from any profession. A speaker can avoid this plague through variation in inflection.

The informal, careless speech you use when talking with friends is not polished enough for a presentation.

According to Lee and Gura, "most people have in their daily speech a characteristic pattern of inflections, which is a part of their own personalities" (83). *Inflection* is when the speaker raises or lowers the pitch when pronouncing words. *Pitch* refers to how low or high your voice sounds. Mayer tells us that the slower the vibration cycles of the vocal folds, the lower the pitch. The faster the vibration cycles, the higher the pitch (215). Pitch is determined

Pausing during a presentation can help listeners process the information you are conveying.

Pause for two or three seconds when displaying a visual to let your audience read it without missing your next comment.

by several factors that include age, sex, and one's emotional state. Additionally, the length, thickness and mass, and tension of the vocal folds can impact pitch.

Everyone speaks at a habitual pitch. A speaker's habitual pitch is not to be confused with speaking in monotone. A *habitual pitch* is the range of voice a speaker uses during normal conversation. Your habitual pitch can be typically low or high, but to make your voice more interesting to listen to during delivery, always vary your pitch from high to low. The lack of variation in pitch can be one of the most distracting traits in a speaker.

Rate

Rate is another very important aspect of delivery that should be given careful consideration. Rate is defined as the number of words spoken per minute. The fastness or slowness of speaking includes the quantity or duration of sounds and the length and number of pauses (305). As you practice your speech, remember there is no best speaking rate. Speakers should determine the best speaking rate by assessing their personal delivery style and the message context.

The novice speaker will often choose a rate which is too fast. This is attributed to speaker anxiety which will sometimes cause the speaker to rush through the delivery of the speech. Even more detrimental than a speaker rushing the delivery is one who speaks too slowly. Speaking too slowly will cause your audience to lose interest. Unless the subject matter is extremely complex the audience will grasp the information much faster than you can say it. An experienced speaker will vary the rate by including pauses to add emphasis and vocal variety.

Pause

Speakers must exercise caution when using pauses. Pauses must always remain pauses. Avoid the temptation of inserting sounds within the pause. These vocalized pauses are referred to as fillers. Examples of frequently used fillers are *uhm*, *you know*, and *like*. The excessive use of vocal fillers will become annoying to an audience and prevent them from focusing on your very important message. Unfortunately, the habit of using vocalized pauses is extremely difficult to break. If used correctly, however, the pause can establish and sustain the emotional intent of the moment as well as build suspense.

Aspects of Physical Delivery

When you enter the room or auditorium, your delivery begins and it does not end until you are out of the view of the audience. The audience members begin to assess your ability to inform, persuade, or entertain them before a word is ever uttered. The audience members will predict whether you will be an effective speaker by the nonverbal cues that you send them. Further, communication research purports that audience members are more likely to trust the nonverbal cues when listening to a speaker than they are the words that are spoken. To ensure you establish a credibility with your audience, speakers must give consideration to all of the aspects of the physical delivery including eye contact, body language, gesture, movement, posture, facial expression, and personal appearance.

Eye Contact

Eye contact is the most significant factor in establishing a speaker's credibility. Research states that "eye contact with your audience opens the lines of communication, makes you more believable, and keeps your audience interested" (Beebe & Beebe, 2006).

Your audience will believe you are interested in the process of communicating with them if you establish and maintain eye contact with them during your speech from start to finish. Most students are familiar with the old adage, when you give a speech you can avoid looking directly at the audience by staring at the back wall directly over the audience members' heads. Nothing could be farther the truth. Not only will the audience know that you are looking at the back wall, but you will not be able to adjust to the audience's feedback if you are not looking at them. The audience wants speakers to engage them. When eye contact is made, the audience members are drawn into the experience of exchanging information.

It is also important for you as the speaker to include the entire audience. In public speaking this is often referred to as three-way scanning. Three-way scanning requires the speaker to include the entire audience and not direct his or her attention to only one area. When a speaker uses three-way scanning, the speaker divides the audience into the three sections: A, B, and C. During the speech, the speaker delivers several lines of the speech to the area labeled section A, then directs several lines to section B, and lastly, section C. The speaker should select individuals within these areas to look at directly. When three-way scanning is practiced effectively, the speaker and audience are free to engage in the context and the expectation of inclusiveness is met.

Expressing yourself naturally helps you connect with your audience.

Body Language

Body language is a key element of nonverbal behavior that is directly linked to the delivery of an effective speech. Communication theorists assert that audience members pay more attention to nonverbal language in public speaking. The controversial research conducted by Dr. Albert Mehrabian claimed body language and voice intonation together are very important, accounting for perhaps seventy-five to eighty percent of the meaning a listener gets from a speaker, including how the speaker feels about his topic, his audience, and himself.

The role body language plays in establishing a speaker's ethos or credibility cannot be disputed. In many ways, audience members *listen* to body language for nonverbal messages that reinforce competence and believability.

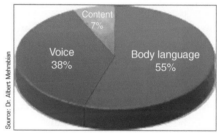

How do we *listen* to body movement? Try this exercise to find out how this occurs. Watch and record a TV show with which you are not familiar, but turn the volume completely down. Observe the characters for three or four minutes. Then, write out what you believe each character said. Next, play the segment that you recorded and listen to the actual dialogue. How accurate was the dialogue you wrote from the actual dialogue in the show? What clues did you get from the body movement? What could you determine about the relationship between the characters by their gestures, movement, facial expressions, or posture? In order for a public speaker to be effective, the speaker must consider all the aspects of body language so that it can reinforce the verbal message. Let us take a closer look at each.

Gestures

Many beginning speakers are hesitant to use gestures. Gestures serve valuable purposes in public speaking. In fact, we find that gestures used when giving a speech serve a similar function and relay a similar meaning as those that we use in our day-to-day communication. Gesture serves to emphasize or reinforce the verbal message. We do this naturally when speaking face-to-face with another person. Yet, when we are in a public speaking environment, needless to say, it becomes a challenge for us to incorporate them. Most times, we appear awkward and seldom do we know what to do with our hands once we stand behind the lectern. Some speakers engage in behavior that truly relays the wrong message to the audience. One common mistake is grasping the podium so tightly that a crowbar could not pry your hands away. Another common mistake is clasping your hands behind your back. Neither of these options will help speaker convey their message more effectively. Here are a few tips that will help you incorporate gestures when preparing for your next speaking engagement.

1. *Gesture should serve a purpose.* Plan the use of gestures by determining their purpose. Never use frivolous gestures. It will appear as if you are signing.
2. *Gesture should be natural.* Even if the act of using gestures makes you feel awkward, practice them to the point where they seem an effortless and natural aspect of your presentation of self.
3. *Gestures should vary.* Do not continue to use the same gestures repetitively unless there is a strong reason for doing so.
4. *Gestures should always be appropriate for the audience.* Keep in mind the demographic composition of your audience. Also, be certain to consider the size of the space. In an intimate space, a speaker can use smaller and fewer gestures, whereas in a large venue, these gestures would lose impact.

When speaking to a large audience, gestures play a key part in reinforcing the ideas in your message.

Movement

As in the case of gestures, movement during your delivery should be given major consideration. When preparing an effective presentation, being aware that the communication context will help you make good decisions regarding movement.

Should I stand behind the lectern? Is it appropriate to walk among the audience members? Will the audience be distracted if I move from left to right and then return to the lectern? These questions can be answered by placing the audience's experience first and foremost in your speech. All movement should be purposeful. Your decision to incorporate movement should contribute to your goal of engaging the audience. Avoid any movement that is distracting and incorporate movement that complements the verbal message. If the audience members recognize movement when you are speaking, the movement was not a good choice.

Another factor to keep in mind when deciding to include movement is physical barriers that may be inherent to the physical environment. The physical barrier can be a raised stage that separates the speaker from the audience, a podium or lectern, rows of chairs or tables, or even audiovisual equipment setups. All these can affect the speaker's ability to incorporate movement. Your movement choices may need to be adjusted to accommodate these types of barriers and oftentimes cannot be determined until you are able to see the physical space.

When making a decision to incorporate movement, the speaker should consider using movement as a device to signal a change in the focus of the speech. Oftentimes, movement is used to signal the beginning of a presentation, a transition in subject, or even a shift in mood. However, even in these instances, the speaker should exercise caution in making choices that shift the focus away from the intended message. Always keep in mind that it may be better to avoid movement altogether than to make a bad choice.

Posture

Stand up straight! Do not lean on the podium! Do you realize you lean your head to the left when you speak?

These are comments that may sound familiar to speakers who are unaware of their physicality when delivering a public speech. Posture or stance is major aspect of establishing an effective presence when presenting a speech. Issues with a speaker's posture are difficult to address because the speaker is seldom cognizant of bad posture until it is offered as a criticism or the speaker views a recording of himself delivering the speech. The good news is that posture is an easy idiosyncrasy to recognize. The bad news is that since the speaker is unaware when he is demonstrating bad posture, it becomes difficult to correct with any consistency. It is important that you remember that posture is an indication of how the speaker feels about himself or herself, how he feels about the occasion, and in many cases, how he feels about the topic.

Given this, a speaker should place great importance on posture. The advice regarding gestures and movement also apply to posture.

Facial Expression

Most have used or heard the saying, "it's written all over your face." This is an important expression to remember when preparing to speak before an audience. Before a single word is uttered at the podium our facial expression serves to establish the tone or emotional climate of the speech. Even though in studying nonverbal communication we learn that the human face is capable of demonstrating more than 200,000 expressions, we can categorize the emotions we express to an audience using six primary emotions to include happiness, anger, disgust, fear, sadness, and surprise.

When taking that first step toward the lectern, the speaker must be cognizant that audience members observe their faces and do not determine one single emotional state but a general mood that is being conveyed. When we begin the speech, we must make certain that regardless of the way we feel at that particular moment, the audience is convinced that we are experiencing the emotional state that is indicated by the occasion and topic.

Understanding and realizing the expectations of the audience and committing to fulfill those expectations are key to a successful delivery. If the occasion is a solemn one, the facial expression of the speaker will convey that to the audience. If the speech is being given at a celebratory occasion, the facial expression of the speaker will convey this mood to the audience. It is important to remember that it is more challenging to control nonverbal behavior than it is verbal behavior. Therefore, when preparing to take the podium it is important to stay focused or, as it is sometimes referred to, "stay in the moment."

Additionally, it is important that your facial expressions reinforce your enthusiasm to present your speech while not appearing fake or phony. Sometimes it helps to rehearse your speech in front of a mirror, realizing that when you are standing in front of the mirror you are standing in front of your biggest critic.

Lastly, keep in mind that facial expressions reveal our innermost thoughts. Always remember one of the principles of the transactional theory of communication discussed earlier in chapter 1, "communication is continuous and simultaneous," or "we cannot not communicate." So, oftentimes what we are thinking will be written all over our faces.

Personal Appearance

When preparing to present a speech, a great deal of consideration should be given to personal appearance which includes grooming, clothing, and accessories. Research conducted by author, columnist, and consultant John T. Malloy claims that dressing for success conveys a person's professional potential and serves as an indicator of future performance. Further, it has been proven that people who dress well and have impeccable grooming are treated with more dignity and respect. While Malloy's best-known works, *New Dress For Success* and *New Woman's Dress For Success*, focus primarily on dressing for the workplace, much of his advice extends to all professional contexts, including speaking in public. We know that being well-groomed and well-dressed increases the credibility of the speaker. Audience members' response to the message is directly impacted by the speaker's dress and overall appearance. If the speaker violates the audience's expectations by the manner in which he or she is dressed, the speaker may not be successful in reaching the objective. It is important that the speaker understands that prior to the speaking occasion, the audience has certain expectations with regard to a speaker's appearance. Therefore, you must always meet or exceed those expectations if you want to be successful.

Here are some tips that will help you prepare for your appearance:

1. Dress conservatively. Regardless of the speaking occasion, always select the most conservative, yet appealing attire possible. Use your audience as a gauge and dress more conservatively than you believe your audience will be dressed. Make certain your attire sets the bar for the best dressed at the engagement. Black or navy dresses and suits are always the acceptable and preferred attire in formal settings. Ties are recommended for men. Bow ties, though fashionable, are not recommended.
2. Regardless of your personal style, you should get a haircut, remove facial hair, manicure your nails, and be mindful of oral hygiene.
3. Minimize jewelry. Jewelry and all accessories should complement your wardrobe and never detract from it. Avoid wearing large earrings and multiple bracelets that jingle or make noise when you move. Men should avoid wearing jewelry altogether. It is advisable to limit jewelry to a watch and ring.
4. Remember, when giving a speech, all eyes are on you! The audience will critique you and your appearance from head to toe before you say one word.
5. Lastly, if you are not certain about your dress and appearance, seek assistance. Some consultants advise speakers to seek the services of a personal stylist or choose a role "model" who is a recognized professional to use as a guide when making decisions about your attire and personal appearance.

Suggestions for an Effective and Successful Delivery

When former President Bill Clinton stepped on the stage at the 2012 Democratic Convention in Charlotte, North Carolina, the crowd roared and the commentators buzzed in anticipation of once again being dazzled by the natural ease and unmatched theatricality of what has come to be known as the Clinton brand. The forty-second President did not disappoint. CNN Wolf Blitzer called it, "the best speech I've heard Bill Clinton deliver" (Lattimer). When former President Clinton left the stage that night, his success was measured by the audience's thunderous applause, numerous accolades from spin doctors, and most importantly, a big hug of appreciation from President Obama. President Clinton, along with so many other celebrated orators, including

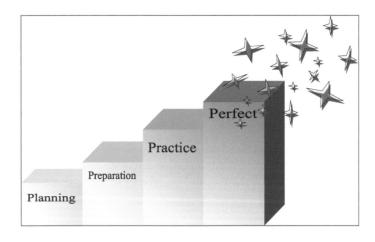

Demonthenes, President John F. Kennedy, Dr. Martin Luther King, Maya Angelou, Governor Ann Richards, and President Barack Obama, would concur that the key to an effective delivery of a speech is no secret. Having listened to thousands of speeches and coached hundreds of speakers, I can attest that the keys to a successful delivery of a speech are planning, preparation, and practice.

Prior to giving any speech or presentation, remember to do the following:

- Know your audience, occasion, and setting.
- Dress for the occasion.
- Prepare using your sentence outline first; then practice with your keyword(s) or phrase outline.
- Practice your speech as parts of a whole.

- Articulate!
- Vary your rate, pitch, volume, and avoid vocal fillers.
- Maintain eye contact with your entire audience and use facial animation.
- Maintain good posture and include purposeful gestures.
- Remain within the established speaking space and avoid extraneous movement and pacing.
- Visualize your success.

Summary

In this chapter, we addressed the key elements of the effective delivery of a speech. Using the discipline of the ancient Greek orator Demonthenes as an example, we concluded that delivery is essential in establishing both credibility and emotion as a speaker.

An effective speaker should always assess the topic, occasion, audience, and his or her own speaking style to determine the best method of delivering the speech. There are four possible methods of delivering a speech. They include impromptu, manuscript, memorized, and extemporaneous. Impromptu speeches are delivered without the use of notes and with little or no preparation. When using the manuscript method of delivery, the speaker writes the speech out word for word and uses it to read the speech to the audience. The memorized method of delivery is typically used for short speeches because the speaker must memorize the speech and deliver it errorless to the audience without the assistance of notes or a script. The final method of delivery, extemporaneous, is the preferred method. When delivering a speech using the extemporaneous method, the speaker uses an outline. This enables the speaker to talk to the audience using a conversational quality while still having the benefit of referring to their notes.

When preparing to deliver a speech, regardless of the method of delivery, the speaker must be concerned with the vocal and the physical aspects of delivery. The main two objectives of the vocal delivery are to be understood and to maintain interest. As a speaker, you can accomplish these two objectives through the effective use of articulation, volume, pitch, rate, and pauses. The physical aspects of delivery play an equally important role in a successful speech. You should be aware that the audience members are influenced just as much, if not more, by what they see as what they hear. As a speaker, you should be aware of the message you send the audience through the physical aspects so that your nonverbal messages reinforce your verbal messages. To strengthen the physical aspects of delivery, a speaker should be cognizant of eye contact, body language, movement, gestures, posture, and facial expressions. Additionally, remember your physical appearance, including grooming, dress, and hygiene, is a significant factor in establishing speaker credibility.

Lastly, it is a known fact that with all the satisfaction that comes with the delivery of a successful speech, there is always just as much, if not more anxiety. Public speaking anxiety affects people in different ways and to various degrees. Whether you break out in a sweat, begin trembling uncontrollably, or pass out on the floor, public speaking anxiety is to be expected to some degree. There is good news. Communication research shows that the more speeches you deliver and the more practice you obtain, the easier it will be to overcome public speaking anxiety and . . . Deliver!

Communication for Today's Student

Chapter 9 – Delivering the Speech

Exercise 9.1 – Methods of Delivery

	Characteristics	Benefits	Challenges	Contexts
Impromptu				
Memorized				
Manuscript				
Extemporaneous				

Communication for Today's Student

Speech Evaluation Form

Name_____   Time_____   Grade_____   Date_____

Thesis Statement _____

Type (purpose) of Speech _____

| **1 = Excellent** | **2 = Good** | **3 = Average** | **4 = Fair** | **5 = Poor** |

Adaptation
___ Awareness of listeners

___ Adaptation to conditions

___ Appropriate topic

___ Friendliness

Language
___ Appropriateness

___ Economy

___ Vividness ___ Clarity

___ Sentence Structure

Content
___ Accuracy of material

___ Familiarity of material

___ Specific evidence

Sources Cited & Qualified
___ Source 1   ___ Source 4

___ Source 2   ___ Source 5

___ Source 3   ___ Source 6

___ Source 7

Physical Delivery
___ Posture and movement

___ Facial expression

___ Gestures

___ Eye contact

Vocal Delivery
___ Pitch ___ Quality

___ Rate ___ Loudness

___ Sound production

___ Conversational quality

Organization
___ Introduction ___ Thesis

___ Body   ___ Transitions

___ Previews   ___ Conclusion

___ Internal summaries

Paperwork Submitted
___ Sentence outline

___ Keyword(s) outline

___ Bibliography

Overall Rating of Speech with General Comments: _____

_____

_____

_____

_____ Examiner: _____

SPEAKING TO INFORM

After reading this chapter, you should be able to:

- ✅ Distinguish between informative and persuasive intent.
- ✅ Describe the different types of informative speeches.
- ✅ Indentify the goals and strategies for informative speaking.

Key Terms

Definition through example
Operational definitions

Speeches of demonstration
Speeches of description

Speeches of explanation
Repetition

Facing image Photo courtesy of Charles Long

Makay et al: From *Public Speaking: Choices for Effective Results* by John Makay, Mark Butland, and Gail Mason.
Copyright © 2008 by Kendall Hunt Publishing Company. Reprinted by permission.

10 Scenario

Cassandra rubbed her temples as she looked at her ball gown hanging in her closet. Her mother sent her the gown for the AIDS Awareness Gala. Cassandra was given the honor of giving a speech about the AIDS research her university was conducting on campus. It was thought that if the alums and other esteemed members of the city heard how beneficial the research was to her education that it would encourage more donations.

The words of Dr. Watkins, Cassandra's mentor and professor, swam around in her head. Dr. Watkins stressed that if they garnered more financial support, Cassandra would be a part of the research for the next three years of her undergraduate career and beyond. Aside from this amazing opportunity to advance her education, she wanted to honor everyone on the project and those fighting on the front lines of the war on AIDS.

That all created pressure for Cassandra. As a result, her document was empty and the cursor was blinking annoyingly at her. The first two drafts of her script were scattered all over the room in the form of crumpled up balls of paper. Her first draft read like a scientific journal, overloaded with facts that most people without a science background wouldn't understand. Her second draft was too heavy for a gala; it was a party after all.

Cassandra glanced down at the paper balls, wondering if somehow she could combine the drafts in some way.

"It may work," Cassandra mumbled, picking up several sheets of paper. "It just may work."

Are Cassandra's concerns about the first and second drafts of her speech on AIDS legitimate ones?
Is her solution a viable one?

Respond
Here

Informative Speaking

When you deliver an **informative speech,** your goal is *to communicate information and ideas in a way that your audience will understand and remember.* Whether you are a nurse conducting CPR training for new parents at the local community center, a museum curator delivering a speech on impressionist art, or an auto repair shop manager lecturing to workers about the implications of a recent manufacturer's recall notice, you want your audience to gain understanding of your topic. An important caveat for students of public speaking to remember is that the audience should hear *new* knowledge, not facts they already know. For example, the nurse conducting CPR training for new parents would approach the topic differently than if the audience was comprised of individuals from various fields working on their yearly recertification. New parents may have never had CPR training, whereas the others receive training at least once a year.

In this chapter, we first distinguish an informative speech from a persuasive one. The different types of informative speeches are identified, and goals and strategies for informative speaking are presented.

Informative versus Persuasive Intent

When you deliver an informative speech, your intent is to enlighten your audience—to increase understanding or awareness and, perhaps, to create a new perspective. In contrast, when you deliver a persuasive speech, your intent is to influence your audience to agree with your point of view—to change attitudes or beliefs or to bring about a specific, desired action. In theory, these two forms are distinctly different. In practice, as we noted earlier, this may not be the case.

For example, if during an informative speech on the ramifications of calling off a marriage you suggest to the engaged couples in your audience that safeguards may have to be taken to prevent emotional or financial damage, you are being persuasive implicitly. If you suggest to the men in your audience that they obtain a written statement from their fiancées pledging the return of the engagement ring if the relationship ends, you are asking for explicit action, and you have blurred the line between information and persuasion.

The key to informative speaking is intent. If your goal is to expand understanding, your speech is informational. If, in the process, you also want your audience to share or agree with your point of view, you may also be persuasive. In describing the different kinds of assault rifles available to criminals, you may persuade your audience to support measures for stricter gun control. Some of your listeners may write to Congress while others may send contributions to lobbying organizations that promote the passage of stricter gun control legislation. Although your speech brought about these actions, it is still informational because your intent was educational.

To make sure your speech is informational rather than persuasive, start with a clear specific purpose signifying your intent. Compare the following two specific purpose statements:

Specific purpose statement #1 (SPS#1) To inform my listeners about the significance of the bankruptcy of the leading American energy company, Enron Corporation

Is your goal to expand the audience's understanding of a topic? If this doctor is outlining the latest advances in neurosurgery, he is giving an informational speech.

Specific purpose statement #2 (SPS#2) To inform my listeners why the investment firm Drexel Burnham Lambert was a symbol of Wall Street greed, power, and the corruption that marked the decade of the 1980s

While the intent of the first statement is informational, the intent of the second is persuasive. The speaker in SPS#1 is likely to discuss the fallout of Enron's bankruptcy, such as decrease in consumer confidence, changes in federal securities laws, and how employees were affected. The speaker in SPS#2 uses subjective words such as "greed, power, and corruption." Most likely this speech would focus more on the unethical practices that resulted in employees and investors losing their life savings, children's college funds, and pensions when Enron collapsed.

Types of Informative Speaking

Although all informative speeches seek to help audiences understand, there are three distinct types of informative speeches. A speech of **description** helps an audience understand *what* something is. When the speaker wants to help us understand *why* something is so, they are offering a speech of **explanation.** Finally, when the focus is on *how* something is done, it is a speech of **demonstration.** Each of these will be discussed in more detail.

Speeches of Description

Describing the circus to a group of youngsters, describing the effects of an earthquake, and describing the buying habits of teenagers are all examples of informative speeches of description. These speeches paint a clear picture of an event, person, object, place, situation, or concept. The goal is to create images in the minds of listeners about your topic or to describe a concept in concrete detail. Here, for example, is a section of a speech describing a reenactment of the 1965 civil rights march in Selma, Alabama. We begin with the specific purpose and thesis statement:

> **Specific purpose.** To have my audience learn of the important connections between the civil rights marches in Selma, Alabama in 1965 and 2005.

> **Thesis statement.** Civil rights marchers returned to Selma, Alabama, in 2005 to commemorate the violence-marred march forty years earlier.

> Thousands of civil rights marchers came together in Selma, Alabama, to walk slowly across the Edmund Pettus Bridge. The year was 2005 and the reason for the march was to commemorate the brutal and violent march that took place in Selma forty years earlier. The first march awakened the country to the need to protect the civil liberties of African Americans, but this one was a time of celebration and rededication to the cause of civil rights.

> The 2005 march was peaceful. Only sound effects reminded participants of the billy club-wielding state troopers, of the screams and clomping horse hoofs, of the beatings and the inhumanity (Smothers, 1990).

In this excerpt, the speaker is making a contrast between two similar events that occurred forty years apart. Audience members are provided with images of what was named "Bloody Sunday," in 1965, and they can picture the peaceful, even celebratory, mood of the similar event forty years later. Specific, concrete language conveys the information through vivid word pictures.

Speeches of Explanation

Speeches of explanation deal with more **abstract** topics (ideas, theories, principles, and beliefs) than speeches of description or demonstration. They also involve attempts to simplify complex topics. The goal of these speeches is audience understanding.

Speeches of explanation may come from a corporate officer outlining business policy to people in the company.

A psychologist addressing parents about the moral development of children or a cabinet official explaining U.S. farm policy are examples of speeches of explanation.

To be effective, speeches of explanation must be designed specifically to achieve audience understanding of the theory or principle. Avoid abstractions, too much jargon, or technical terms by using verbal pictures that define and explain. Here, for example, a speaker explains the concept of depression by telling listeners how patients describe it.

> Serious depression, a patient once said, is "like being in quicksand surrounded by a sense of doom, of sadness." Author William Styron described his own depression as "a veritable howling tempest in the brain" that took him down a hole so deep that he nearly committed suicide.
>
> Veteran and senior CBS correspondent Mike Wallace reached a point in his life where he found himself unable to sleep, losing weight, and experiencing phantom pains in his arms and legs. "Depression is palpable," explained Wallace. "You begin to feel like a fake and a fraud. You second guess yourself about everything" (1990, 48–55).

Compare this vivid description with the following, more abstract version:

> Severe depression involves dramatic psychological changes that can be triggered by heredity or environmental stress. Depression is intense and long lasting and may result in hospitalization. The disease may manifest itself in agitation or lethargy.

If the second is presented alone, listeners are limited in their ability to anchor the concept to something they understand. The second explanation is much more effective when combined with the first.

Speeches of explanation may involve policies: statements of intent or purpose that guide or drive future decisions. The president may announce a new arms control policy. A school superintendent may implement a new inclusion policy. The director of human resources of a major corporation may discuss the firm's new flextime policy.

A speech that explains a policy should focus on the questions that are likely to arise from an audience. For example, prior to a speech to teachers and parents before school starts, the superintendent of a school district implementing a new inclusion policy needs to anticipate what the listeners will probably want to know—when the policy change will be implemented, to what extent it will be implemented, when it will be evaluated, and how problems will be monitored, among other issues. When organized logically, these and other questions form the basis of the presentation. As in all informative speeches, your purpose is not to persuade your listeners to support the policy, but to inform them about the policy.

Speeches of Demonstration

Speeches of demonstration focus on a process by describing the gradual changes that lead to a particular result. These speeches often involve two different approaches, one is "how," and the other is a "how to" approach. Here are four examples of specific purposes for speeches of demonstration:

- To inform my audience *how* college admissions committees choose the most qualified applicants
- To inform my audience *how* diabetes threatens health
- To inform my audience *how to* sell an item on Ebay
- To inform my audience *how to* play the Internet game Bespelled

Speeches that take a "how" approach have audience understanding as their goal. They create understanding by explaining how a process functions without teaching the specific skills needed to complete a task. After listening to a speech on college admissions, for example, you may understand the process but may not be prepared to take a seat on an admissions committee.

Let us look more closely at a small section of a "how" speech.

> How are shows selected by the networks to be placed in prime time for an upcoming television season? The answer to this question describes a complex process involving a host of people ranging from developers with an idea to advertising executives responsible for deciding whether or not to sponsor a program. When the proposed television programs are presented to

advertisers, the process engaged is one which can allow advertisers to have some influence over the content of programs they choose to sponsor. Before this sort of influence takes effect, the network officials and advertising executives go through what is called "speculation season." In early spring those involved in the decision-making process may consider about 100 hours' worth of programs. Usually no more than 23 to 25 hours of airtime eventually make it. The networks may develop 30 to 40 projects, while many more do not get past a one-page plot outline (Carter 1992).

Although this sample begins to explain how television programs are selected for the fall season, its primary goal is understanding, not application.

In contrast, *"how to"* speeches try to communicate specific skills, such as selling an item on Ebay, changing a tire, or making a lemon shake-up. Compare the previous "how" example discussing network television show selection with the following "how to" presentation on "how to" make a lemon shake-up.

In front of me are all the ingredients for a lemon shake-up: lemons, water, sugar, a knife, and two cups. First, cut the lemons into quarters. If you love the tart taste of lemons . . .

The main object of Bespelled is to win points by connecting letters or "tiles" on a board to spell words that are at least three letters long. After downloading the game from msn.com and pressing "play," look at the board. Seven rows of seven letters are arranged randomly, and to the left of the board, you'll see a wizard and a score box. Look for words arranged in any fashion. One letter of a word must be connected to the next letter. You use the mouse to highlight each letter, and then click when you have finished the word.

Points are based on two things: the length of the word, and value of the letters. A second object is to keep letters or "tiles" that catch on fire from reaching the bottom of the board. The game is over when a burning tile ignites the whole board. So, you need to put out the fire by creating a word that incorporates the burning letter. If you avoid one burning tile, more will appear. Each burns the tile beneath them, and at some point, the board goes up in flames . . .

At the end of this speech of demonstration, the listener should know the ingredients and how to make a lemon shake-up.

One clear difference between the speech of demonstration and the speeches of presentation and explanation is that the *speech of demonstration benefits from presentational aids.* When your goal is to demonstrate a process, you may choose to complete the entire process—or a part of it—in front of your audience. The nature of your demonstration and the constraints of time determine your choice. If you are giving CPR training, a partial demonstration will not give your listeners the information they need to save a life. If you are demonstrating how to cook a stew, however, your audience does not need to watch you chop onions; prepare in advance to maintain audience interest and save time.

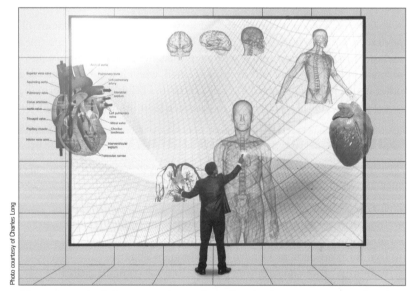

After a speech of demonstration on how the circulatory system works, the listener should be able to identify the major organs in the system.

Goals and Strategies of Informative Speaking

Although the overarching goal of an informative speech is to communicate information and ideas in a way that the audience will understand, there are other goals that will help you create the most effective informative speech.

Whether you are giving a speech to explain, describe, or demonstrate, the following five goals are relevant: be accurate, objective, clear, meaningful, and memorable. After each goal, two specific strategies for achieving that goal are presented.

1. Be Accurate

Facts must be correct and current. Research is crucial to attaining this goal. Do not rely solely on your own opinion; find support from other sources. Information that is not current may be inaccurate or misleading. Informative speakers strive to present the truth. They understand the importance of careful research for verifying information they present. Offering an incorrect fact or taking a faulty position may hurt speaker credibility and cause people to stop listening. The following two strategies will help speakers present accurate information.

Question the source of information. Is the source a nationally recognized magazine or reputable newspaper, or is it from someone's post on a random blog? Source verification is important. Virtually anyone can post to the Internet. Check to see if your source has appropriate credentials, which may include education, work experience, or verifiable personal experience.

Photo courtesy of Charles Long

Research is crucial to attain correct information to present in your speech.

Consider the timeliness of the information. Information can become dated. There is no hard and fast rule about when something violates timeliness, but you can apply some common sense to avoid problems. Your instructor may take this decision-making out of your hands by requiring sources from the last several years or so. If not, the issue of timeliness relates directly to the topic. If you wanted to inform the class about the heart transplant process, relying on sources more than a few years old would be misleading because scientific developments occur continuously.

2. Be Objective

Present information that is fair and is unbiased. Purposely leaving out critical information or "stacking the facts" to create a misleading picture violates the rule of objectivity. The following two strategies should help you maintain objectivity.

Take into account all perspectives. Combining perspectives creates a more complete picture. Avoiding other perspectives creates bias, and may turn an informative speech into a persuasive one. The chief negotiator for a union may have a completely different perspective than the administration's chief negotiator on how current contract negotiations are proceeding. They may be using the same facts and statistics, but interpreting them differently. An impartial third party trying to determine how the process is progressing needs to listen to both sides and attempt to remove obvious bias.

Show trends. Trends put individual facts in perspective as they clarify ideas within a larger context. The whole—the connection among ideas—gives each detail greater meaning. If a speaker tries to explain how the stock market works, it makes sense to talk about the stock market in relation to what it was a year ago, five years ago, ten years ago, or even longer, rather than focus on today or last week. Trends also suggest what the future will look like.

3. Be Clear

To be successful, your informative speech must communicate your ideas without confusion. When a message is not organized clearly, audiences can become frustrated and confused and, ultimately, they will miss your ideas. Conducting careful audience analysis helps you understand what your audience already knows about your topic and allows you to offer a clear, targeted message at their level of understanding. The following five strategies are designed to increase the clarity of your speech.

Carefully organize your message. Find an organizational pattern that makes the most sense for your specific purpose. Descriptive speeches, speeches of demonstration, and speeches of explanation have different goals. Therefore, you must consider the most effective way to organize your message. *Descriptive speeches* are often arranged in spatial, topical, and chronological patterns. *Speeches of demonstration* often use spatial, chronological, and cause-and-effect or problem-solution patterns. *Speeches of explanation* are frequently arranged chronologically, or topically, or according to cause-and-effect or problem-solution.

Define unfamiliar words and concepts. Unfamiliar words, especially technical jargon, can defeat your purpose of informing your audience. When introducing a new word, define it in a way your listeners can understand. Because you are so close to your material, knowing what to define can be your hardest task. The best advice is to put yourself in the position of a listener who knows less about your topic than you do or ask a friend or colleague's opinion. In addition to explaining the dictionary definition of a concept or term, a speaker may rely on two common forms of definitions: operational and through example.

Operational definitions specify procedures for observing and measuring concepts. We use operational definitions to tell us who is "smart," based on a person's score on IQ test. The government tells us who is "poor" based on a specified income level, and communication researchers can determine if a person has high communication apprehension based on his or her score on McCroskey's Personal Report of Communication Apprehension.

Definition through example helps the audience understand a complex concept by giving the audience a "for instance." In an effort to explain what is meant by the term, "white-collar criminal," a speaker could provide several examples, such as Jeff Skilling, (former Enron executive convicted on federal felony charges relating to the company's financial collapse), George Ryan (former Illinois governor indicted on federal racketeering, fraud, and conspiracy charges), and Duke Cunningham (former congressional representative from California, convicted of various bribery and fraud charges).

4. Be Meaningful

A meaningful, informative message focuses on what matters to the audience as well as to the speaker. Relate your material to the interests, needs, and concerns of your audience. A speech explaining the differences between public and private schools delivered to the parents of students in elementary and secondary school would not be as meaningful in a small town where no choice exists as it would be in a large city where numerous options are available. Here are two strategies to help you develop a meaningful speech:

Consider the setting. The setting may tell you about audience goals. Informative speeches are given in many places, including classrooms, community seminars, and business forums. Audiences may attend these speeches because of an interest in the topic or because attendance is required. Settings tell you the specific reasons your audience has gathered. A group of middle-aged women attending a lifesaving lecture at a local YMCA may be concerned about saving their husbands' lives in the event of a heart attack, while a group of nursing students listening to the same lecture in a college classroom may be doing so to fulfill a graduation requirement.

The setting makes a difference as to what information is important to people, and you should plan your focus accordingly.

Avoid information overload. When you are excited about your subject and you want your audience to know about it, you can find yourself trying to say too much in too short a time. You throw fact after fact at your listeners until you literally force them to stop listening. Saying too much is like touring London in a day—it cannot be done if you expect to remember anything.

Information overload can be frustrating and annoying because the listener experiences difficulty in processing so much information. Your job as an informative speaker is to know how much to say and, just as importantly, what to say. Long lists of statistics are mind-numbing. Be conscious of the relationship among time, purpose, and your audience's ability to absorb information. Tie key points to anecdotes and humor. Your goal is not to "get it all in" but to communicate your message as effectively as possible.

5. Be Memorable

Speakers who are enthusiastic, genuine, and creative and who can communicate their excitement to their listeners deliver memorable speeches. Engaging examples, dramatic stories, and tasteful humor applied to your key ideas in a genuine manner will make a long-lasting impact.

Speakers who are enthusiastic, genuine, and creative make a long-lasting and favorable impression upon their audience.

Use examples and humor. Nothing elicits interest more than a good example, and humorous stories are effective in helping the audience remember the material. When Sarah Weddington (1990), winning attorney in the Roe v. Wade Supreme Court case, talks about the history of discriminatory practices in this country, she provides a personal example of how a bank required her husband's signature on a loan even though she was working and he was in school. She also mentions playing "girls" basketball in school and being limited to three dribbles (boys could dribble the ball as many times as they wanted). While these stories stimulate interest and make the audience laugh, they also communicate the message that sex discrimination was pervasive when Weddington was younger.

Physically involve your audience. Ask for audience response to a question: "Raise your hand if you have . . . " Seek help with your demonstration. Ask some audience members to take part in an experiment that you conduct to prove a point. For example, hand out several headsets to volunteers and ask them to set the volume level where they usually listen to music. Then show how volume can affect hearing.

Guidelines for Effective Informative Speeches

Regardless of the type of informative speech you plan to give, there are characteristics of effective informative speeches that cross all categories. As you research, develop, and present your speech, keep the following nine characteristics in mind.

Consider Your Audience's Needs and Goals

Considering your audience is the theme of the book, but it is always worth repeating. The best informative speakers know what their listeners want to learn from their speech. A group of Weight Watchers members may be motivated to attend a lecture on dieting to learn how to lose weight, while nutritionists drawn to the same speech may need the information to help clients. Audience goals are also linked to knowledge. Those who lack knowledge about a topic may be more motivated to listen and learn than those who feel they already know the topic. However, it is possible that technology has changed, new information has surfaced, or new ways to think about or do something have emerged. The speaker needs to find a way to engage those who are less motivated.

Make connections between your subject and your audience's daily needs, desires, and interests. For example, some audience members might have no interest in a speech on the effectiveness of half-way houses until you tell them how much money is being spent on prisons locally, or better yet, how much each listener is spending per year. Now the topic is more relevant. People care about money, safety, prestige, family and friends, community, and their own growth and progress, among other things. Show how your topic influences one or more of these and you will have an audience motivated to listen.

Photo courtesy of Charles Long

The best informative speakers know what their audiences want to learn from their message.

Consider Your Audience's Knowledge Level

If you wanted to describe how to use eSnipe when participating in Ebay auctions, you may be speaking to students who have never heard of it. To be safe, however, you might develop a brief pre-speech questionnaire to pass out to your class. Or you can select several individuals at random and ask what they know. You do not want to bore the class with mundane minutia, but you do not want to confuse them with information that is too advanced for their knowledge level. Consider this example:

> As the golf champion of your district, you decide to give your informative speech on the game. You begin by holding up a golf club and saying, "This is a golf club. They come in many sizes and styles." Then you hold up a golf ball. "This is a golf ball. Golf balls are all the same size, but they come in many colors. Most golf balls are white. When you first start playing golf, you need a lot of golf balls. So, you need a golf club and a golf ball to play golf."

Expect your listeners to yawn in this situation. They do not want to hear what they already know. Although your presentation may be effective for an audience of children who have never seen a golf club or ball, your presentation has started out too simplistic even for people who have some knowledge of the game.

Capture Attention and Interest Immediately

As an informative speaker, your goal is to communicate information about a specific topic in a way that is understandable to your listeners. In your introduction, you must first convince your audience that your topic is interesting and relevant. For example, if you are delivering a speech on white-collar crime, you might begin like this:

> Imagine taking part of your paycheck and handing it to a criminal. In an indirect way, that's what we all do to pay for white-collar crime. Part of the tax dollars you give the federal government goes into the hands of unscrupulous business executives who pad their expenses and over-charge the government by millions of dollars. For example, General Dynamics, the third-largest military supplier, tacked on at least $75 million to the government's bill for such "overhead" expenses as country-club fees and personal travel for corporate executives . . .

This approach is more likely to capture audience attention than a list of white-collar crimes or criminals.

Sustain Audience Attention and Interest by Being Creative, Vivid, and Enthusiastic

Try something different. Change your pace to bring attention or emphasis to a point. Say the following phrase at a regular rate, and then slow down and emphasize each word: "We must work together!" Slowing down to emphasize each word gives the sentence much greater impact. Varying rate of speech can be an effective way to sustain audience attention.

Also, show some excitement! Talking about accounting principles, water filters, or changes in planet designations with spirit and energy will keep people listening. Delivery can make a difference. Enthusiasm is infectious, even to those who have no particular interest in your subject. It is no accident that advertising campaigns are built around slogans, jingles, and other memorable language that people are likely to remember after a commercial is over. We are more likely to remember vivid language than dull language.

Show some excitement regardless of your topic!

Cite Your Oral Sources Accurately

Anytime you offer facts, statistics, opinions, and ideas that you found in research, you should provide your audience with the source. In doing this, you enhance your own credibility. Your audience appreciates your depth of research on the topic, and you avoid accusations of plagiarism. However, your audience needs enough information in order to judge the credibility of your sources. If you are describing how the HBO show *Deadwood* became an acclaimed yet controversial drama, it is not sufficient to say, "Ashley Smith states . . ." because Ashley Smith's qualification to comment on this show may be based on the fact that she watches television regularly. If the speaker said, "Ashley Smith, television critic for the Chicago Tribune, states . . ." then we know she has some expertise in the area.

Signpost Main Ideas

Your audience may need help keeping track of the information in your speech. Separating one idea from another may be difficult for listeners when trying to learn all the information at once. You can help your audience understand the structure of your speech by creating oral lists. Simple "First, second, third, fourth . . ." or "one, two, three, four . . ." help the audience focus on your sequence of points. Here is an example of signposting:

> Having a motorized scooter in college instead of a car is preferred for two reasons. The first reason is a financial one. A scooter gets at least 80 miles per gallon. Over a period of four years, significant savings could occur. The second reason a scooter is preferred in college is convenience. Parking problems are virtually eliminated. No longer do you have to worry about being late to class, because you can park in the motorcycle parking area. They're all around us . . .

Signposting at the beginning of a speech tells the audience how many points you have or how many ideas you intend to support. Signposting during the speech keeps the audience informed as to where you are in the speech.

Relate the New with the Familiar

Informative speeches should introduce new information in terms of what the audience already knows. Analogies can be useful. Here is an example:

A cooling-off period in labor management negotiations is like a parentally-imposed time-out. When we were children, our parents would send us to our rooms to think over what we had done. We were forbidden to come out for at least an hour in the hope that by the time we were released our tempers had cooled. Similarly, by law, the President can impose an 80-day cooling-off period if a strike threatens to imperil the nation's health or safety.

Most of us can relate to the "time out" concept referred to in this example, so providing the analogy helps us understand the cooling-off period if a strike is possible. References to the familiar help listeners assimilate new information.

Use Repetition

Repetition is important when presenting new facts and ideas. You help your listeners by reinforcing your main points through summaries and paraphrasing. For example, if you were trying to persuade your classmates to purchase a scooter instead of a car, you might have three points: (1) A scooter is cheaper than a car; (2) A scooter gets better gas mileage than a car; and (3) You can always find a nearby parking spot for your scooter. For your first point, you mention purchase price, insurance, and maintenance cost. As you finish your first point, you could say, "So a scooter is cheaper than a car in at least three ways, purchase price, insurance, and maintenance." You have already mentioned these three sub-points, but noting them as an internal summary before your second main point will help reinforce the idea that scooters are cheaper than cars.

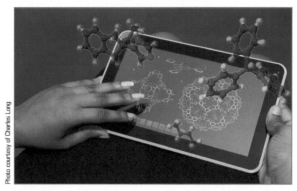

Use effective presentational aids in your informative speech to hold your audience's attention.

Offer Interesting Visuals

Using pictures, charts, models, PowerPoint slides, and other presentational aids helps maintain audience interest. Jo Sprague and Douglas Stuart, (1988) explain:

> "Your message will be clearer if you send it through several channels. As you describe a process with words, also use your hands, a visual aid, a chart, a recording. Appeal to as many senses as possible to reinforce the message . . . If a point is very important or very difficult, always use one other channel besides the spoken word to get it across" (299).

Use humorous visuals to display statistics, if appropriate. Demonstrate the physics of air travel by throwing paper airplanes across the room. With ever-increasing computer accessibility and WiFi in the classroom, using computer-generated graphics to enhance and underscore your main points and illustrations is a convenient and valuable way to help you inform your audience effectively.

Ethics of Informative Speaking

Think about the advertising you see on television and the warning labels on certain products you purchase. Listening to a commercial about a new weight-loss tablet, you think you have just found a solution to get rid of those extra twenty pounds you carry with you. Several happy people testify about how wonderful the drug is, and how it worked miracles for them. At the end of the commercial, you hear a speaker say, "This drug is not for children under 16. It may cause diarrhea, restlessness, sleeplessness, nausea, and stomach cramps. It can lead to heat strokes and heart attacks. Those with high blood pressure, epilepsy, diabetes, or heart disease should not take this medicine . . . " After listening to the warnings, the drug may not sound so miraculous. We have government regulations to make sure consumers make informed choices.

As an individual speaker, *you need to regulate yourself*. A speaker has ethical responsibilities, no matter what type of speech he or she prepares and delivers. The informative speeches you deliver in class and those you listen to on campus are not nearly as likely to affect the course of history as those delivered by high-ranking public officials in a time of war or national political campaigns. *Even so, the principles of ethical responsibility are similar for every speaker.*

The President of the United States, the president of your school, and the president of any organization to which you belong all have an obligation to inform their constituencies (audiences) in non-manipulative ways and to provide them with information they need and have a right to know. Professors, doctors, police officers, and others engaged in informative speaking ought to tell the truth as they know it, and not withhold information to serve personal gain. You, like others, should always rely on credible sources and avoid what political scientists label as "calculated ambiguity." **Calculated ambiguity** is a speaker's planned effort to be vague, sketchy, and considerably abstract.

You have many choices to make as you prepare for an informative speech. Applying reasonable ethical standards will help with your decision-making. An informative speech requires you to assemble accurate, sound, and pertinent information that will enable you to tell your audience what you believe to be the truth. Relying on outdated information, not giving the audience enough information about your sources, omitting relevant information, being vague intentionally, and taking information out of context are all violations of ethical principles.

Summary

Informative speeches fall into three categories. Speeches of description paint a picture of an event, person, object, place, situation, or concept; speeches of explanation deal with such abstractions as ideas, theories, principles, and beliefs; and speeches of demonstration focus on a process, describing the gradual changes that lead to a particular result.

A somewhat blurry line exists between informative and persuasive speaking. Remember that in an informative speech your goal is to communicate information and ideas in a way that your audience will understand and remember. The key determinant in whether a speech is informative is speaker intent.

As an informative speaker, you should strive to be accurate, objective, clear, meaningful, and memorable. Preparing and delivering an effective informative speech involves applying the strategies identified in this chapter. In order to increase accuracy, make sure you question the source of information, consider the timeliness, and accurately cite your sources orally. Being objective includes taking into account all perspectives and showing trends. Crucial to any speech is clarity. To aid your audience, carefully organize your message, define unfamiliar words and concepts, signpost main ideas, relate the new with the familiar, and use repetition.

Audience members have gathered for different reasons. No matter what the reason, you want your speech to be meaningful to all listeners. In doing so, consider the setting, your audience's needs and goals and knowledge level, and try to avoid information overload. An informative speaker also wants people to remember his or her speech. In order to meet that goal, try to capture attention and interest immediately, sustain audience attention and interest by being creative, vivid, and enthusiastic, use examples and humor, offer interesting visuals, and physically involve your audience.

As you prepare your informative speech, make sure the choices you make are based on a reasonable ethical standard. You have an obligation to be truthful, and we presented many ways to accomplish this as you prepare your speech as well as when you deliver it.

TTYL (Talk to Your Listener)

In an informative speech, you are likely to encounter questions, comments, and interruptions while you speak. Here are some tips to cope with these unpredictable events.

Decide whether you want questions during your presentation or at the end. If you prefer they wait, tell your audience early in your speech or at the first hand raised something like, "I ask that you hold all questions to the end of this presentation, where I have built in some time for them."

When fielding questions, develop the habit of doing four things in this order: thank the questioner, paraphrase the question in your own words (for the people who may not have heard the question), answer the question briefly, and then ask the questioner if you answered their question.

Note that the second step in answering questions is to paraphrase the question in your own words. This provides you with the opportunity to point questions in desirable directions or away from areas you are not willing to go. Paraphrasing allows the speaker to stay in control of the situation.

For any question, you have five options: (1) answer it, and remember "I do not know" is an answer; (2) bounce it back to the questioner, "Well, that is very interesting. How might you answer that question?"; (3) Bounce it to the audience, "I see, does anyone have any helpful thoughts about this?"; (4) Defer the question until later, "Now you and I would find this interesting, but it is outside the scope of my message today. I'd love to chat with you individually about this in a moment"; (5) Promise more answer later, "I would really like to look further into that. May I get back to you later?" Effective speakers know and use all five as strategies to keep their question-and-answer period productive and on track.

When random interruptions occur, do not ignore them. Call attention to the distraction. This allows your audience to get it out and then return their attention to you. One speaker was interrupted when a window washer suspended outside the building dropped into view, ropes and all. The speaker paused, looked at the dangling distraction and announced, "Spiderman!" Everyone laughed, and he then returned to his speech. At a banquet, a speaker was interrupted by the crash of shattering dishes from the direction of the kitchen. She quipped, "Sounds like someone lost a contact lens." Whether humorous or not, calling attention to distractions is key to maintaining control.

The heckler is a special kind of distraction that requires prompt attention. If you notice a man in the audience making comments for others to hear that undercut your message, first, assume he is trying to be helpful. Ask him to share his comments for all to hear. This will usually stop the heckler. If it does not, ask him his name, and use it as often as you can in your message. This usually works because oftentimes the heckler simply wants more attention. When all else fails, enlist the assistance of your audience. Ask if anyone wants to hear what you have to say more than what the heckler is saying. (Your audience will indicate they do.) Then ask if there is a volunteer, preferably a big one, who can help us all out. The combination of humiliation and the implied threat should do the trick.

Communication for Today's Student

Chapter 10 – Speaking to Inform

Exercise 10.1 – Types of Informative Speeches

Part One

Communication for Today's Student states that there are three types of informative speeches: Speeches of Description, Speeches of Explanation and Speeches of Demonstration. Select an informative speech topic. Write a key word outline for your topic first as a *speech of description*, then as a *speech of explanation* and lastly as a *speech of demonstration*.

General Purpose:
Specific Purpose:
Attention-Getter:
Pattern of Organization:

Speech of Description	Speech of Explanation	Speech of Demonstration
I.	I.	I.
A.	A.	A.
B.	B.	B.
II.	II.	II.
A.	A.	A.
B.	B.	B.
C.	C.	C.
III.	III.	III.
A.	A.	A.
B.	B.	B.
C.	C.	C.
IV.	IV.	IV.
A.	A.	A.
B.	B.	B.
C.	C.	C.
V.	V.	V.
A.	A.	A.
B.	B.	B.

Chapter 10 – Speaking to Inform

Exercise 10.1 Continued

After making your topic selection, explain how the three types of speeches differ and how are they similar.

Explain: _____

_____

_____

Part Two

Regardless of whether you are giving a speech to *explain*, *describe,* or *demonstrate,* your speech should meet the five goals of informative speaking. Does it?

Five goals of informative speaking	Explain how the goal is met
Be accurate	
Be objective	
Be clear	
Be meaningful	
Be memorable	

Communication for Today's Student

Chapter 10 – Informative Speech

Exercise 10.2 – Informative Speech Topic Approval

Name: _____

Date: _____

Remember:
Numbers are not
used when preparing
the Bibliography for
submission

Sources **(in MLA format)**
1.

2.

3.

Circle One: (Person, Place, Object, or Process)

Topic One: _____

General Purpose: _____

Specific Purpose: _____

Pattern of Organization: _____

Chapter 10 – Speaking to Inform

Exercise 10.2 Continued

> **Remember:**
> *Numbers are not used when preparing the Bibliography for submission*

Circle One: (Person, Place, Object, or Process)

Topic Two: _____

General Purpose: _____

Specific Purpose: _____

Pattern of Organization: _____

Sources (in MLA format)

1.

2.

3.

Remember:
Numbers are not used when preparing the Bibliography for submission

Circle One: (Person, Place, Object, or Process)

Topic Three: _____

General Purpose: _____

Specific Purpose: _____

Pattern of Organization: _____

Sources **(in MLA format)**

1.

2.

3.

Write sources in MLA format. Remember only one (www) website may be used for this speech.

How many minutes is your informative speech? _____

How many oral footnotes must you include? _____

Approved Topic: _____

Instructor Comments:

_____

_____

_____

_____

SPEAKING TO PERSUADE

After reading this chapter, you should be able to:

- ✓ Describe the elements of persuasion.
- ✓ Describe the dimensions of speaker credibility.
- ✓ Discuss pathos and the power of emotion.
- ✓ Discuss logos and the power of logical appeals and arguments.
- ✓ Explain the three types of inductive reasoning.
- ✓ Demonstrate an understanding of deductive reasoning.
- ✓ Discuss the goals of persuasion.
- ✓ Identify persuasive aims.
- ✓ Explain the types of persuasive claims.
- ✓ Discuss the use of Monroe's Motivation Sequence as a method of organizing persuasive argument.
- ✓ Demonstrate an understanding of the role that ethics play in persuasive speaking.

Key Terms

Adoption	Discontinuance	Logos	Reasoning
Analogies	Dynamism	Monroe's Motivation Sequence	Reasoning from sign
Belonginess and love needs	Ethics	Pathos	Safety needs
Causal reasoning	Esteem needs	Physiological needs	Self actualization
Continuance	Ethos	Proposition of fact	
Deductive reasoning	Inductive reasoning	Proposition of policy	
Deterrence	Inference	Proposition of value	

11 Scenario

"I want to do my speech on how McDonald's fries are better than Burger King's fries," Kevin announced in class. The whole class erupted with laughter. Kevin looked around genuinely confused as to why everyone was laughing, including his friend Damien.

Mr. Nahuel contained his laughter as he waved his hands. "Class settle, settle. I'm sure Kevin has a good explanation for his speech topic."

"I do have a good explanation," Kevin said. "It's the truth! McDonald's fries are indeed the best fries."

"Do you think this is the best way for you to go, Kevin?" Mr. Nahuel asked. "How can you prove this?"

"I can conduct a taste test," Kevin said quickly. "Or even a survey."

"That's a dumb topic," Maria teased. "You make laughing at you too easy, Kevin."

"Harsh, Maria," Mr. Nahuel said. "I wouldn't call Kevin's idea dumb; it's just a little underdeveloped."

"Underdeveloped?"

"Yes," Mr. Nahuel said. "I think you can go further."

"Mr. Nahuel, I'm passionate about this," Kevin said.

"You're passionate about french fries!" Maria giggled.

"Are you a french fry expert?" Mr. Nahuel asked.

"No, I'm not," Kevin sighed.

"But you are getting your degree in nutrition," Mr. Nahuel said. "That makes you an expert in that field. In a persuasive speech, you have to convince the audience you are educated enough in your topic to make this speech. Think about how you can use your background in nutrition and your passion for fast food to create a speech. Think about it."

Kevin sighed and nodded. "I'll give it some thought, I guess."

What role does passion play when attempting to persuade?
Which is more effective in persuasion: passion or logic? Why?

Individuals engage in persuasive speaking at all levels of communication. Interpersonally, we try to convince people to share our opinions or attitudes about very small things ("Burger King fries are better than McDonald's fries") and very significant things ("We shouldn't have children until we've been married for ten years"). We also engage in persuasive discourse at a societal level ("Homosexuals should be allowed to marry"). The ability to express one's self is a cornerstone of our democracy. The power of free speech is most clearly realized in speeches to persuade. Here is one example.

After the defeat of the "Clinton health care program" in the fall of 1994, Hillary Clinton stepped up the efforts to bring a more universalized system of healthcare to the American public. Her steadfast belief in this cause resulted in extensive worldwide campaigning, which led to her giving a speech before the World Health Organization (WHO) on September 5, 1995.

Photo courtesy of Charles Long.

Sharing your opinion on something even as simple as where you will go to eat lunch involves persuasion skills.

> At long last, people and their governments everywhere are beginning to understand that investing in the health of women and girls is as important to the prosperity of nations as investing in the development of open markets and trade . . . (Remarks to the World Health Organization Forum on Women and Health Security. Delivered in Beijing, China.)

Clinton's speech stressed the need to come together as a worldwide community with the goal of bettering the health and well-being of all women and families so the new century would open with marked improvement in the lives of women.

Clinton continued by outlining the basic needs that women have not had access to in the past. Women have lived without the necessities that help anyone look forward to a full life of health and productivity. These necessities include medical care, education, legal protection, the chance to better their economic position, and human rights. There are many places in the world where womens' health is in jeopardy because health care is not available or does not do enough to adequately meet needs. Often health care is simply too expensive for those who need it. Even the most basic needs, such as good, clean drinking water and good nutrition are not readily available. Moreover, many women are the victims of sexual abuse and ignorance of health concerns.

Too many women have been suffering for too long, Clinton proclaimed. She said the state of their health is one of continuous pain. The women who are suffering could be any woman in the world or any girl in the world. You could be looking in the mirror at that woman. Or it could be another person very close to you . . . your friend, your sister, your child, your neighbor.

In her speech, Clinton quoted compelling statistics about how many women in the world die or nearly die because of serious difficulties during childbirth. She expanded the information about reproductive issues, citing statistics about women who do not use any family planning methods due to a lack of education, no access to such services, or just because of their poverty. Because of this, Clinton stated that millions of women end up having abortions that are unsafe and ultimately result in lifelong medical problems or even death. More women are facing unplanned, unwanted pregnancies when they themselves can scarcely be called women, as young as they are. Good opportunities available for those babies born to very young mothers are few and far between. Mother and child both suffer in so many ways.

Another topic Clinton spoke out against was violence, saying that women not only suffer because of violence, but they also die. Violence takes many forms against women, whether it takes place within the home or outside the home. She said that violence, too, is an issue of health.

Breast cancer statistics also served as startling reminders to show the numbers of women throughout the world who suffer from this disease and who ultimately die because of it. Clinton even mentioned how many women would have died in the amount of time it took for her to deliver her speech that day.

Clinton remarked that using tobacco products kills as well and it is a killer that can be prevented. Even though it is not one of those things that people immediately think of as being deadly, it is one that causes horrible suffering to those who are affected by it. Along with such diseases as AIDS, there needs to be a focus on this killer as well. There is much that can be done to prevent those deaths that are caused by tobacco use.

Clinton closed her speech with a plea for all the nations who had representatives present that day to make every effort to ensure that the childbearing years of womens' lives should be a healthy and safe time. She implored every nation to do everything possible to make health care accessible and affordable for all women. She made a call for action on the issue.

Although retrospectives of Clinton's stay as First Lady often point to the failure of the "Clinton health care plan," her remarks before the WHO led to a substantial change in the healthcare of both women and their children.

Elements of Persuasion

Hillary Clinton's speech embodies the critical elements of persuasion that have been defined by generations of rhetorical scholars, starting with Aristotle. Persuasion is intended to influence choice through appeals to the audience's sense of ethics, reasoning, and emotion. Aristotle's views on the use of what he termed ethos, pathos, and logos provide the underpinnings of our modern study of persuasion.

Ethos and the Power of the Speaker's Credibility

Aristotle believed that **ethos,** which refers to speaker credibility, makes speakers worthy of belief. Audiences trust speakers they perceive as honest, especially "on points outside the realm of exact knowledge, where opinion is divided." In this regard, he believed, "we trust [credible speakers] absolutely. . . ."(Cooper 1960, 8). Hillary Clinton appealed to her audience through her own credibility as First Lady of the United States and as Chairwoman of the Task Force on National Health Care Reform. Due to her experiences with health and healthcare, Clinton was viewed as a credible source on several dimensions.

Dimensions of Speaker Credibility

What your audience knows about you before you speak and what they learn about your position during your speech may influence your ability to persuade them. Credibility can be measured according to four dimensions: perceived competence, concern for the audience, dynamism, and ethics.

Perceived competence. In many cases, your audience will decide your message's value based on perceived speaker competence. Your listeners will first ask themselves whether you have the background to speak. If the topic is crime, an audience is more likely to be persuaded by the Atlanta chief of police than by a postal worker delivering his personal opinions. Second, your audience will consider whether the content of your speech has firm support. When it is clear

Photo courtesy of Charles Long

Persuasive speakers have the ability to convey to listeners that you are on their side.

that speakers have not researched their topic, their ability to persuade diminishes. Finally, audiences will determine whether you communicate confidence and control of your subject matter through your delivery.

Concern for audience. Persuasion is also influenced by concern for your audience. Communication Professor Richard L. Johannesen (1974) differentiates between speakers who engage in "dialogue" and those who engage in "monologue." A **dialogue** takes into account the welfare of the audience; a **monologue** focuses only on the speaker's self-interest (95). Audiences sense a speaker's concern by first analyzing the actions a speaker has taken before the speech. If the group has formed to protest the location of a highway through a residential community, the audience will consider what the speaker has already done to convince highway officials to change their minds. Second, audiences listen carefully to the strength and conviction of the speaker's message. For instance, does the speaker promise to fly to Washington, D.C., if necessary, to convince federal officials to withhold funds until a new site is chosen? Persuasive speakers are able to convince their audiences that they are on their side.

Dynamism. Your credibility and, therefore, your ability to persuade are also influenced by the audience's perception of you as a dynamic spokesperson. A person who is dynamic is lively, active, vigorous, and vibrant. Your listeners will ask themselves whether you have the reputation for being someone who gets the job done. They will listen for an energetic style that communicates commitment to your point of view, and for ideas that build upon one another in a convincing, logical way.

Ethics. Finally, your ability to persuade is influenced by the audience's perception of your ethical standards. If you come to the lectern with a reputation for dishonesty, few people will be persuaded to trust what you say. If your message is biased and you make little attempt to be fair or to concede the strength of your opponent's point of view, your listeners may question your integrity. They may have the same questions if you appear manipulative (Sprague and Stuart 1988, 208–10).

If you analyze Hillary Clinton's speech to the WHO, all four dimensions of speaker credibility can be seen. *Perceived competence* is illustrated by her official positions (First Lady and Chair of the Task Force on National Health Care Reform) and her research. She cites several statistics related to childbirth complications, violence against women, breast cancer, and tobacco usage. *Concern for audience* is found in her topic selection and approach. Her target audience is members of the World Heath Organization, so the variety of health-related topics addressed by Hillary Clinton is appropriate. Also, she shares information rather than lectures, and approaches the topics as issues "we" need to address rather than what "you" need to be concerned about. *Dynamism* is shown through her articulate and energetic presentation, and the straight-forward approach. Known concern for women's health issues and use of statistics suggest a solid set of *ethics*.

Does credibility make a difference in your ability to persuade? Researchers have found that, in many cases, the most credible speakers are also the most persuasive (Aronson, Turner, and Carlsmith 1963). One powerful way speakers enhance their credibility is by creating a strong sense of identification in their audiences.

The Strategy of Identification: Seeking Common Ground

Your credibility and your ability to persuade may increase if you convince your audience that you share "common ground." In his classic work, *Public Speaking*, published in 1915, James A. Winans introduced the concept of "common ground." "To convince or persuade a man," he writes, "is largely a matter of identifying the opinion or course of action which you wish him to adopt with one or more of his fixed opinions or customary courses of action. When his mind is satisfied of the identity, then doubts vanish" (Day 1959).

Labor leader Cesar Chavez forged a common bond with his audience after a twenty-day fast in 1968 to call attention to the plight of California farm workers by proclaiming that the end of his fast was not the true reason for the gathering. Rather, people had come to observe that, "we are a family bound together in a common struggle for justice. We are a

Union family celebrating our unity and the nonviolent nature of our movement." Chavez explained why he had fasted: "My heart was filled with grief and pain for the suffering of farm workers. The Fast was first for me and then for all of us in this Union. It was a Fast for nonviolence and a call to sacrifice." Chavez concluded with, "We have something the rich do not own. We have our own bodies and spirits and the justice of our cause as our weapons. It is how we use our lives that determines what kind of men we are. . . . I am convinced that the truest act of courage, the strongest act of manliness is to sacrifice ourselves for others in a totally nonviolent struggle for justice. To be a man is to suffer for others. God help us to be men" (Hammerback and Jensen 1987, 57).

In this instance, Chavez establishes a common ground through identifying with his audience and provoking them to identify with him. Moreover, Chavez also makes effective use of emotional arguments, which Aristotle referred to as *pathos*.

Cesar Chavez established a common ground with his audience and effectively used emotional arguments.

Pathos and the Power of Emotion

Aristotle believed in the power of speakers to persuade through emotional appeals. He explained, "Persuasion is effected through the audience, when they are brought by the speech into a state of emotion; for we give very different decisions under the sway of pain or joy, and liking or hatred. . . ."(Cooper 1960, 9). Hillary Clinton appealed to the emotions of her listeners with the words, "In too many places, the status of women's health is a picture of human suffering and pain. The faces in that picture are of girls and women who, but for the grace of God or the accident of birth, could be us or one of our sisters, mothers, or daughters." This call to visualize harm to one's own family members served as a powerful example of utilizing emotion to appeal to the sensibilities of her audience members.

Appeal to Audience Emotion

Emotional appeals have the power to elicit happiness, joy, pride, patriotism, fear, hate, anger, guilt, despair, hope, hopelessness, bitterness, and other feelings. George Kennedy (1991), a scholar of classical rhetoric, tells us, "Emotions in Aristotle's sense are moods, temporary states of mind (123–4). But according to persuasion theorists Martha Cooper and William Nothstine (1992), "modern research into motivation and the passions moved beyond Aristotle's emphasis on the emotions themselves and moved extensively into broader theories of human psychology" (74). The persuader, they advise us, can influence his or her audience by using appeals to create an emotional, as well as a cognitive, state of imbalance in listeners, which arouses feelings that something is wrong and something must be done. By taking the essential needs of an audience into consideration, the persuader can develop lines of reasoning that respond to pertinent needs. Yes, human needs can be described in terms of logic or what makes sense to a listener, but needs are immersed in emotions of the individual as well.

Psychologist Abraham Maslow classified human needs according to the hierarchy pictured in figure 11.1. An analysis of these needs will help you understand audience motivation as you attempt to persuade. Maslow believed that our most basic needs—those at the bottom of the hierarchy—must be satisfied before we can consider those on the next levels. In effect, these higher level needs are put on "hold" and have little effect on our actions until the lower level needs are met.

Physiological needs. At the bottom of the hierarchy are our biological needs for food, water, oxygen, rest, and release from stress. If you were delivering a speech in favor of a proposed new reservoir to a community experiencing problems with its water supply, it would be appropriate to appeal to the need for safe and abundant water.

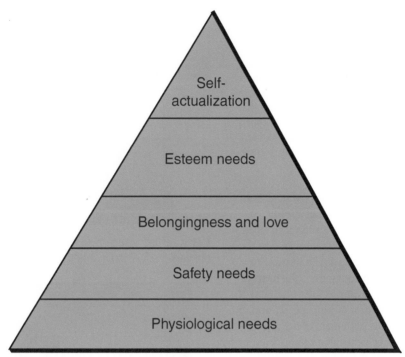

Figure 11.1 Maslow's Hierarchy of Needs

Safety needs. Safety needs in-clude the need for security, freedom from fear and attack, a home that offers tranquility and comfort, and a means of earning a living. If you are delivering the same speech to a group of unemployed construction workers, you might link the reservoir project to jobs and a steady family income.

Belongingness and love needs. These needs refer to our needs for affiliation, friendship, and love. When appealing to the need for social belonging, you may choose to emphasize the camaraderie that will emerge from the community effort to bring the reservoir from the planning stage to completion.

Esteem needs. Esteem needs include the need to be seen as worthy and competent and to have the respect of others. In this case, an effective approach would be to praise community members for their initiative in helping to make the reservoir project a reality.

Self-actualization needs. People who reach the top of the hierarchy seek to fulfill their highest potential through personal growth, creativity, self-awareness and knowledge, social responsibility, and responsiveness to challenge. Addressing this audience, you might emphasize the long-range environmental and ecological implications of the reservoir. Your appeal may include the need to safeguard the water supply for future generations.

Maslow's Hierarchy of Needs can guide you in preparing a persuasive speech when you think about the feelings of your audience and how you can reach them in combination with the factors of credibility and sound argument. Understanding the basis for Maslow's hierarchy is critical to your success as a persuasive speaker, for if you approach your listeners at an inappropriate level of need, you will find them unable or unwilling to respond.

Our emotions are powerful ingredients in our human composition. You accept an ethical responsibility when you use emotional appeals. *The ethically responsible speaker does not distort, delete, or exaggerate information for the sole purpose of emotionally charging an audience in order to manipulate their feelings for self-centered ends.*

Yet, emotional appeals are often the most persuasive type of appeal because they provide the motivation listeners need to change their minds or take action. Instead of simply listing the reasons high fat foods are unhealthy, a more effective approach is to tie these foods to frightening consequences:

> Jim thought nothing could ever happen to him. He was healthy as an ox—or so he thought. His world fell apart one sunny May morning when he suffered a massive heart attack. He survived, but his doctors told him that his coronary arteries were blocked and that he needed bypass surgery. "Why me?" he asked. "I'm only 42 years old." The answer, he was told, had a lot to do with the high fat diet he had eaten since childhood.

Some subjects are more emotionally powerful than others and lend themselves to emotional appeals. Stories such as personal health crises, children in need, or experiences with crime and deprivation engage the emotions of listeners. Delivery also has an impact. Your audience can tell if you are speaking from the heart or just mouthing words. They respond to the loudness of your voice, the pace and rhythm of your speech, and to your verbal cues. Finally, the placement of the appeal is important. Corporate speech consultant James Humes suggests using an emotional ending to motivate an audience to action. In his view, the same emotions that stir people in their private lives motivate audiences. He explains, "CEOs tell me, 'Listen, Jim, I'm not trying to save England, I'm just trying to get a message across to the company.' Well, you still want to ask the employees to join you in something. End on an emotional pitch. Work that audience up" (Kleinfeld 1990).

Because of their power, emotional appeals can be tools of manipulation in the hands of unscrupulous speakers who attempt to arouse audiences through emotion rather than logic. These speakers realize that fear and other negative emotions can be more powerful persuaders than reason when the audience is receptive to their emotional message.

Everyone has attachment needs and can identify with appeals for friendship and camaraderie.

Your audience can tell if your expressions, tone, and gestures are genuine.

Logos and the Power of Logical Appeals and Arguments

In addition to ethical (ethos) and emotional (pathos) appeals and arguments, logos or logical appeals and arguments are critical to the persuasive process. A logical appeal is rational and reasonable based on evidence provided. For example, if a friend tried to convince you *not* to buy a new car by pointing out that you are in college, have no savings account, and are currently unemployed, that friend would be making a logical argument. Aristotle saw the power of persuasion relying on logical arguments and sound reasoning. Clinton appealed to her audience's reasoning by constructing an inequality of healthcare as evidenced by the positions of doctors, scientists, and nurses.

Reasoning refers to the sequence of interlinking claims and arguments that, together, establish the content and force of your position. Although we believe the treatment of public speaking throughout this book promotes being reasonable, *no aspect of our book is more instrumental in guiding you to improve your critical thinking than reasoning as logical appeal.* Logical thought as critical thinking is intended to increase your ability to *assess, analyze*, and *advocate* ideas. As a persuasive speaker you will reason logically either through induction or deduction. Your responsibility is to reason by offering your audience factual or judgmental statements based on sound inferences drawn from unambiguous statements of knowledge or belief (Freeley 1993, 2).

To construct a sound, reasonable statement as a logical appeal for your audience you need to distill the essential parts of an argument:

1. The evidence in support of an idea you advocate;
2. A statement or contention the audience is urged to accept; and,
3. The inference linking the evidence with the statement.

Of the three parts to an argument, the most difficult part to understand is often the inference. It may be an assumption that justifies using evidence as a basis for making a claim or drawing a conclusion. For example, suppose you take a big bite out of food you have taken for dinner in your cafeteria or apartment and claim, "This is the worst piece of meat I have ever put in my mouth." With this claim you are making a statement that you *infer* from tasting the meat.

What is the evidence? The meat before you. The statement or contention is, "The meat is awful." The relation of the evidence to the claim is made by an inference, which may be an *unstated belief* that spoiled, old, or poorly prepared meat will taste bad. Stephen Toulmin, the British philosopher acknowledged as an expert on argument, speaks of the inferential link between evidence and claim as the *warrant.* Toulmin points out that a warrant is the part of the argument that states or *implies* an inference (Vancil 1993, 120–24).

When you reason with your audience by trying to persuade the listeners with an argument you want them to accept and act upon, you must use evidence, inferences, and statements as contentions the audience can understand and accept. Sound reasoning is especially important when your audience is skeptical. Faced with the task of trying to convince people to change their minds or do something they might not otherwise be inclined to do, your arguments must be impressive.

Supporters in an audience may require arguments in the form of reinforcement. You may have to remind a sympathetic crowd of the reasons your shared point of view is correct. This reminder is especially important if your goal is audience action. If you want a group of sympathetic parents to attend a board of trustees meeting to protest tuition increases, you must persuade them that a large turnout is necessary. It is up to you, through the presentation of an effective argument, to make action the most attractive course.

In persuasion, ethical and emotional appeals may be powerful factors, but reasoning or logical appeal can be your most effective tool. Well-developed reasons stated without exaggeration tell your listeners that you trust them to evaluate the facts on their merit rather than emotional appeal. Through the framework of a logical appeal, we piece together important elements to persuade listeners to accept our position and respond to a call to action. The framework for logical appeal is based on inductive and deductive modes of reasoning, in particular reasoning by analogy, reasoning from cause, and reasoning from sign.

To persuade your audience that a claim or conclusion is highly probable, you must have strong evidence and show that you have carefully reasoned the support of your points. Only when strong probability is established can you ask your listeners to

Photo courtesy of Charles Long

You must have strong evidence and show that you've carefully supported your points to convince your audience that your claim has merit.

make the inductive leap from specific cases to a general conclusion, or to take the deductive move from statements as premises to a conclusion you want them to accept. We will look more closely now at inductive and deductive reasoning.

Inductive Reasoning

Aristotle spoke of inductive reasoning in his *Rhetoric* (Cooper 1960, 10). Through inductive reasoning, we generalize from specific examples and draw conclusions from what we observe. Inductive reasoning moves us from the specific to the general in an orderly, logical fashion.

When you argue on the basis of example, the inference step in the argument holds that what is true of specific cases can be generalized to other cases of the same class, or of the class as a whole. Suppose you are trying to persuade your audience that the disappearance of downtown merchants in your town is a problem that can be solved with an effective plan you are about to present. You may infer that what has worked to solve a similar problem in a number of highly similar towns is likely to work in the town that is the subject of your speech.

One problem associated with inductive reasoning is that individual cases do not *always* add up to a correct conclusion. Sometimes a speaker's list of examples is too small, leading his/her audience to an incorrect conclusion based on limited information. Here, as in all other cases of inductive reasoning, you can never be sure that your conclusions are absolutely accurate. Because you are only looking at a sample, you must persuade your audience to accept a conclusion that is probable, or maybe even just possible.

Reasoning by Analogy

Analogies establish common links between similar and not-so-similar concepts. They are effective tools of persuasion when you can convince your audience that the characteristics of one case are similar enough to the characteristics of the second case that your argument about the first also applies to the second.

A **figurative analogy** draws a comparison between things that are distinctly different, such as "Eating fresh marshmallows is like floating on a cloud." Figurative analogies can be used to persuade, but they must be supported with relevant facts, statistics, and testimony that link the dissimilar concepts you are comparing.

Although figurative analogies can provide valuable illustrations, they will not prove your point. For example, before the United States entered World War II, President Franklin D. Roosevelt used the analogy of a "garden hose" to support his position that the United States should help England, France, and other European countries already involved in the war. In urging the passage of the Lend-Lease Bill, he compared U.S. aid to the act of lending a garden hose to a neighbor whose house was on fire. Although this analogy supplied ethical and emotional proof, it did not prove the point on logical grounds. It is vastly different to lend a garden hose to a neighbor than it is to lend billions of dollars in foreign aid to nations at war (Freeley 1993, 119).

Whereas a figurative analogy compares things that are distinctly different and supply useful illustrations, a literal analogy compares things with similar characteristics and, therefore, requires less explanatory support. One speaker in our class compared the addictive power of tobacco products, especially cigarettes, with the power of alcoholic beverages consumed on a regular basis. His line of reasoning was that both are consumed for pleasure, relaxation, and often as relief for stress. While his use of logical argument was obvious, the listener ultimately assesses whether or not these two things—alcohol and tobacco are sufficiently similar. It may be that their differences diminish the strength of the speaker's argument. The distinction between literal and figurative analogies is important because only literal analogies are sufficient to establish a logical proof. The degree to which an analogy works depends on the answers to the following questions:

1. Are the cases being compared similar?
   Only if you convince your listeners of significant points of similarity will the analogy be persuasive.
2. Are the similarities critical to the success of the comparison?

The fact that similarities exist may not be enough to prove your point. Persuasion occurs when the similarities are tied to critical points of the comparison.

3. Are the differences relatively small?
   In an analogy, you compare similar, not identical, cases. Differences can always be found between the items you are comparing. It is up to you as an advocate for your position to decide how critical the differences are.
4. Can you point to other similar cases?
   You have a better chance of convincing people if you can point to other successful cases. If you can show that the similarities between your position and these additional cases are legitimate, you will help sway audience opinion (Freely 1993, 119–20).

Reasoning from Cause

When you are reasoning from cause the inference step is that an event of one kind contributes to or brings about an event of another kind. The presence of a cat in a room when you are allergic to cats is likely to bring about a series of sneezes until the cat is removed. As the preceding example demonstrated, causal reasoning focuses on the cause-and-effect relationship between ideas.

> **Cause:** inaccurate count of the homeless for the 2000 census
>
> **Effect:** less money will be spent aiding the homeless

An advocate for the homeless delivered the following message to a group of supporters:

> We all know that money is allocated by the federal government, in part, according to the numbers of people in need. The census, conducted every ten years, is supposed to tell us how many farmers we have, how many blacks and Hispanics, how many homeless.
>
> Unfortunately, in the 2000 census, many of the homeless were not counted. The government told us census takers would go into the streets, into bus and train station waiting rooms, and into the shelters to count every homeless person. As advocates for the homeless, people in my organization know this was not done. Shelters were never visited. Hundreds and maybe thousands of homeless were ignored in this city alone. A serious undercount is inevitable. This undercount will cause fewer federal dollars to be spent aiding those who need our help the most.

When used correctly, causal reasoning can be an effective persuasive tool. You must be sure that the cause-and-effect relationship is sound enough to stand up to scrutiny and criticism. To test the validity of your reasoning, ask yourself the following questions:

1. Do the cause and effect you describe have anything to do with one another?
   Some statements establish a cause-and-effect relationship between ideas when the relationship is, at best, questionable. Ask yourself whether other factors contributed to the change. You may be attributing cause and effect where there is only coincidence.
2. Is the cause acting alone or is it one of many producing the effect?
   Even if the connection you draw is valid, it may be only one of several contributing factors that bring about an effect. To isolate it as solely responsible for an effect is to leave listeners with the wrong impression.
3. Is the effect really the effect of another cause?
   To use a medical example, although fatigue and depression often occur simultaneously, it may be

Photo courtesy of Charles Long

Causal reasoning is effective if your argument can withstand scrutiny.

a mistake to conclude that depression causes fatigue when other factors may also be involved. Both conditions may be symptoms of other illnesses such as mononucleosis, or the result of stress.

4. **Are you describing a continuum of causes and effects?**
When you are dealing with an interrelated chain of causes and effects, it is wise to point out that you are looking at only one part of a broader picture.
5. **Are the cause and effect related but inconsequential?**
Ask yourself whether the cause you are presenting is sufficient to bring about the effect you claim.
6. **Is your claim and evidence accurate?**
To be an effective persuasive tool, causal reasoning must convince listeners that the link you claim is accurate. Your listeners should be able to judge probability based on your supporting evidence. They will ask themselves if your examples prove the point and if you explain or minimize conflicting claims (Sprague and Stuart 1988, 165–66).

To be effective, causal reasoning should never overstate. By using phrases like, "This is one of several causes," or "The evidence suggests there is a cause-and-effect link," you are giving your audience a reasonable picture of a complex situation. Public speakers could learn from medical researchers who are reluctant to say flatly that one thing causes another. More often than not, researchers indicate that cause-and-effect relationships are not always clear and that links may not be as simple as they seem.

Reasoning from Sign

In the argument from sign, the inference step is that the presence of an attribute can be taken as the presence of some larger condition or situation of which the attribute is a part. As you step outside in the early morning to begin jogging, the gray clouds and moist air can be interpreted as signs that the weather conditions are likely to result in a rainy day. Argumentation Professor David Vancil (1993) tells us that, "arguments from sign are based on our understanding of the way things are associated or related to each other in the world with them, [so] we conclude that the thing is present if its signs are present. The claim of a sign argument is invariably a statement that something is or is not the case" (149).

The public speaker who reasons from sign must do so with caution. Certainly, there are signs all around us to interpret in making sense of the world, but signs are easy to misinterpret. Therefore, the responsible speaker must carefully test any argument before using it to persuade an audience.

Deductive Reasoning

Aristotle also spoke of deduction as a form of reasoning in persuasive argument. Through deductive reasoning, we draw conclusions based on the connections between statements that serve as premises. Rather than introducing new facts, deductions enable us to rearrange the facts we already know, putting them in a form that will make our point. Deductive reasoning is the basis of police work and scientific research, enabling investigators to draw relationships between seemingly unrelated pieces of information.

At the heart of deductive reasoning is the syllogism, a pattern of reasoning involving a major and a minor premise and a conclusion. Syllogisms take this form:

a = b
b = c
c = a

Here is an example:

1. All basketball players can dribble the ball.
2. Anthony is a basketball player.
3. Anthony can dribble the ball.

Using this pattern of logic, the conclusion that Anthony can dribble the ball is inescapable. If your listeners accept your premise, they are likely to accept your conclusion. The major premise in this case is statement (1) "All basketball players can dribble the ball," while the minor premise is statement (2) "Anthony is a basketball player." Whether the deductive reasoning is stated in part or not, it leads us down an inescapable logical path. By knowing how two concepts relate to a third concept, we can say how they relate to each other.

Recognizing that people do not usually state every aspect of a syllogism as they reason deductively, Aristotle identified the **enthymeme** as the deductive reasoning used in persuasion. Because speakers and listeners often share similar assumptions, the entire argument may not be explicitly stated, even when the elements of a syllogism are all present. This truncated, or shortened, form of deductive reasoning is the enthymeme. The inference step in reasoning with an enthymeme is that the audience, out of its judgment and values, must supply and accept the missing premises or conclusions. If a classmate in a persuasive speech makes the claim that a newly elected congressional representative will probably take unnecessary trips costly to the taxpayers, your classmate's claim is drawn from the major premise (unspoken) that most, if not all, congressional representatives engage in unnecessary and costly travel.

The interrelationships in a syllogism can be established in a series of deductive steps:

1. **Step One:** Define the relationship between two terms.
   Major premise: Plagiarism is a form of ethical abuse.
2. **Step Two:** Define a condition or special characteristic of one of the terms.
   Minor premise: Plagiarism involves using the words of another author without quotations or footnotes as well as improper footnoting.
3. **Step Three:** Show how a conclusion about the other term necessarily follows (Sprague and Stuart 1988, 160).
   Conclusion: Students who use the words of another, but fail to use quotations or footnotes to indicate this, or who intentionally use incorrect footnotes, are guilty of an ethical abuse.

Your ability to convince your listeners depends on their acceptance of your original premise and the conclusion you draw from it. The burden of proof rests with your evidence. Your goal is to convince your listeners through the strength of your supporting material to grant your premises and, by extension, your conclusion. Considering persuasion from the vantage point of such outcomes will be considered next.

Outcomes and the Power of Goals, Aims, and Claims

Since Aristotle, scholars have focused on the elements of ethos, pathos, and logos as the primary aspects of persuasion. Some researchers have added to these principles an emphasis on outcomes. Gary Woodward and Robert Denton, Jr. (1992), explain: "Persuasion is the process of preparing and delivering messages through verbal and nonverbal symbols to individuals or groups in order to alter, strengthen, or maintain attitudes, beliefs, values, or behaviors" (18–19). Careful consideration of the goals of persuasion, the aims of your speech, and the type of claim you are making will help your message achieve the influence that will allow you to advance your agenda.

Goals of Persuasion

Critical to the success of any persuasive effort is a clear sense of what you are trying to accomplish. As a speaker, you must define for yourself your overall persuasive goals and the narrower persuasive aims. The two overall goals of persuasion are **to address attitudes** and **to move an audience to action.**

Speeches that focus on attitudes. In this type of speech, your goal is to convince an audience to share your views on a topic (e.g., "The tuition at this college is too high" or "too few Americans bother to vote"). The way you approach your goal depends on the nature of your audience.

When dealing with a negative audience, you face the challenge of trying to change your listeners' opinions. The more change you hope to achieve the harder your persuasive task. In other words, asking listeners to agree that U.S. automakers need the support of U.S. consumers to survive in the world market is easier than asking the same audience to agree that every American who buys a foreign car should be penalized through a special tax.

By contrast, when you address an audience that shares your point of view, your job is to reinforce existing attitudes (e.g., "U.S. automakers deserve our support"). When your audience has not yet formed an opinion, your message must be geared to presenting persuasive evidence. You may want to explain to your audience, for example, the economic necessity of buying U.S. products.

Speeches that require action. Here your goal is to bring about actual change. You ask your listeners to make a purchase, sign a petition, attend a rally, write to Congress, attend a lecture, and so on. The effectiveness of your message is defined by the actions your audience takes.

Motivating your listeners to act is perhaps the hardest goal you face as a speaker, since it requires attention to the connection between attitudes and behavior. Studies have shown that what people feel is not necessarily what they do. That is, little consistency exists between attitudes and actions (Wicker 1969, 41–70). Even if you convince your audience that you are the best candidate for student body president, they may not bother to vote. Similarly, even if you persuade them of the dangers of smoking, confirmed smokers will probably continue to smoke. Researchers have found several explanations for this behavior.

First, people say one thing and do another because of situational forces. If support for your position is strong immediately after your speech, it may dissipate or even disappear in the context in which the behavior takes place. For example, even if you convince listeners to work for your political campaign, if their friends ridicule that choice, they are unlikely to show up at campaign headquarters.

Researchers have found that an attitude is likely to predict behavior when the attitude involves a specific intention to change behavior, when specific attitudes and behaviors are involved, and when the listener's attitude is influenced by firsthand experience (Zimbardo 1988, 618–19). Firsthand experience is a powerful motivator. If you know a sun worshipper dying from melanoma, you are more likely to heed the speaker's advice to wear sun block than if you have no such acquaintance. An experiment by D. T. Regan and R. Fazio (1977) proves the point:

> A field study on the Cornell University campus was conducted after a housing shortage had forced some of the incoming freshmen to sleep on cots in the dorm lounges. All freshmen were asked about their attitudes toward the housing crisis and were then given an opportunity to take some related actions (such as signing a petition or joining a committee of dorm residents). While all of the respondents expressed the same attitude about the crisis, those who had had more direct experience with it (were actually sleeping in a lounge) showed a greater consistency between their expressed attitudes and their subsequent behavioral attempts to alleviate the problem (28–45).

Therefore, if you were a leader on this campus trying to persuade freshmen to sign a petition or join a protest march, you would have had greater persuasive success with listeners who had been forced to sleep in the dorm lounges. Once you establish your overall persuasive goals, you must then decide on your persuasive aims.

Persuasive Aims

The aims of persuasion, or the type and direction of the change you seek, is the important next consideration. You must define the narrower aims of your speech. Four persuasive aims define the nature of your overall persuasive goal.

Adoption. When you want your audience to start doing something, your persuasive goal is to urge the audience to adopt a particular idea or plan. As a spokesperson for the American Cancer Society, you may deliver the following message: "I urge every woman over the age of forty to get a regular mammogram."

Continuance. Sometimes your listeners are already doing the thing you want them to do. In this case, your goal is to urge continuance. For example, the same spokesperson might say:

I am delighted to be speaking to this organization because of the commitment of every member to stop smoking. I urge all of you to maintain your commitment to be smoke free for the rest of your life.

Speeches which urge continuance are necessary when the group is under pressure to change. In this case, the spokesperson realized that many reformed smokers constantly fight the urge to begin smoking again.

Discontinuance. You attempt to persuade your listeners to stop doing something:

I can tell by looking around that many people in this room spend hours sitting in the sun. I want to share with you a grim fact. The evidence is unmistakable that there is a direct connection between exposure to the sun and the deadliest of all skin cancers—malignant melanoma.

Deterrence. In this case, your goal is avoidance. You want to convince your listeners not to start something, as in the following example:

We have found that exposure to asbestos can cause cancer twenty or thirty years later. If you have flaking asbestos insulation in your home, don't remove it yourself. Call in experts who have the knowledge and equipment to remove the insulation, protecting themselves as well as you and your family. Be sure you are not going to deal with an unscrupulous contractor who is likely to send in unqualified and unprotected workers likely to do a shoddy job.

Speeches that focus on deterrence are responses to problems that can be avoided. These messages are delivered when a persuasive speaker determines that an audience possesses something which the speaker sees as highly threatening or likely to result in disaster. The speaker may try to bring about some sort of effective block or barrier to minimize, if not eliminate, the threat or danger. New homeowners, for example, may find themselves listening to persuasive presentations about the purchase of a home security system. The thrust of such a persuasive speech is the need to prevent burglary through use of an effective and economical security system.

Types of Persuasive Claims

Within the context of these persuasive goals and aims, you must decide the type of persuasive message you want to deliver. Are you dealing with a question of fact, value, or policy? To decide, look at your thesis statement which expresses your judgment or point of view. In persuasive speeches, the thesis statement is phrased as a proposition that must be proved.

For example, if your thesis statement was, "All college students should be required to take a one-credit Physical Education course each year," you would be working with a proposition of policy. If instead, your thesis statement was, "Taking a Physical Education course each year will benefit all college students," this would be a proposition of value.

Propositions are necessary because persuasion always involves more than one point of view. If yours were the only way of thinking, persuasion would be unnecessary. Because your audience is faced with differing opinions, your goal is to present your opinion in the most effective way. The three major types of propositions are those of *fact*, *value*, and *policy*.

Proposition of fact. Because facts, like beauty, are often in the eye of the beholder, you may have to persuade your listeners that your interpretation of a situation, event, or concept is accurate. Like a lawyer in a courtroom, you have to convince people to accept your version of the truth. Here are two examples of facts which would require proof:

1. Water fluoridation can lead to health problems.
2. American corporations are losing their hold on many world markets.

When dealing with propositions of fact, you must convince your audience that your evaluation is based on widely accepted standards. For example, if you are trying to prove that water fluoridation can lead to health problems, you might point to a research article that cites the Environmental Protection Agency (EPA) warning that long-term exposure to excessive fluoridation can lead to joint stiffness and pain and weak bones. You may also support your proposition by citing another research study that reports that children who are exposed to too much fluoridation may end up having teeth that are pitted and/or permanently stained.

Informative speakers become persuasive speakers when they cross the line from presenting facts to presenting facts within the context of a point of view. The informative speaker lets listeners decide on a position based on their own analysis of the facts. By contrast, the persuasive speaker draws the conclusion for them.

Proposition of value. Values are deep-seated beliefs that determine what we consider good or bad, moral or immoral, satisfying or unsatisfying, proper or improper, wise or foolish, valuable or invaluable, and so on. Persuasive speeches that deal with propositions of value are assertions based on these beliefs. The speaker's goal is to prove the worth of an evaluative statement, as in the following examples:

1. It is *wrong* for men to leave all the housework and childcare to their working wives.
2. Plagiarism is terribly *dishonest* for anyone who engages in it to complete an assignment.

   When you use words that can be considered judgments or evaluations, such as those italicized above, you are making a proposition of value.

Proposition of policy. Propositions of policy are easily recognizable by their use of the word "should":

1. Campus safety should be the number one priority of the college.
2. Student-athletes should adhere to the same academic standards as other students.

   In a policy speech, speakers convince listeners of both the need for change and what that change should be. They also give people reasons to continue listening and, in the end, to agree with their position and to take action.

A speaker's persuasive appeal, in summary, derives from the audience's sense of the speaker's credibility as well as from appeals to an audience's emotion and logic. At times, one persuasive element may be more important than others may. Many speakers try to convince audiences based primarily on logical appeal, some use mainly emotional appeals, and others rely on their image and credibility as a speaker. The most effective speakers consider their intended outcomes and appropriately combine all persuasive elements to meet a variety of audience needs and achieve their ultimate persuasive ends. Now we will turn our attention to a powerfully influential sequence of steps often used to organize persuasive messages.

Monroe's Motivated Sequence

As emphasized throughout this text, communication is a process connecting both speaker and audience. This awareness is particularly important in speeches to persuade, for without taking into account the mental stages your audience passes through, your persuasion may not succeed. The *motivated sequence*, a widely used method for organizing persuasive speeches developed by the late communication professor Alan H. Monroe (1965), is rooted in traditional rhetoric and shaped by modern psychology.

The method focuses on five steps to motivate your audience to act, and as Monroe would tell his students, they follow the normal pattern of human thought from attention to action. The motivated sequence clearly serves the goal of action if all five steps are followed. When the goal is to move your audience to act, each of the following five steps would be needed.

If someone wants only to persuade the audience there is a problem, then only the first two steps are necessary. If the audience is keenly aware of a problem, then a speaker may focus only on a solution.

Attention. Persuasion is impossible without attention. Your first step is to capture your listeners' attention in your introduction and convince them that you have something to say that is of genuine importance to them. You have several possibilities, including making a startling statement, using an anecdote, and asking a rhetorical question.

Need. In the *need step*, you describe the problem you will address in your speech. You hint or suggest at a need in your introduction, then state it in a way that accurately reflects your specific purpose. Your aim in the need step is to motivate your listeners to care about the problem by making it clear the problem affects them. You can illustrate the need by using examples, intensifying it through the use of carefully selected additional supporting material, and *linking* it directly to the audience. Too often the inexperienced speaker who uses the motivated sequence will pass through the need step too quickly in haste to get to the third step, the satisfaction step.

Satisfaction. The *satisfaction step* presents a solution to the problem you have just described. You offer a proposal in the form of an attitude, belief, or action you want your audience to adopt and act upon. Explanations in the form of statistics, testimony, examples, and other types of support ensure that your audience understands exactly what you mean. You clearly state what you want your audience to adopt and then explain your proposal. You have to show your audience how your proposal meets the need you presented. To be sure everyone understands what you mean, you may wish to use several different forms of support accompanied by visuals or audiovisual aids. An audience is usually impressed if you can show where and how a similar proposal has worked elsewhere. Before you move to the fourth step, you need to meet objections that you predict some listeners may hold. We are all familiar with the persuader who attempts to sell us a product or service and wants us to believe it is well worth the price and within our budget. In fact, a considerable amount of sales appeal today aims at selling us a payment we can afford as a means to purchasing the product, whether it is an automobile, a vacation, or some other attractive item. If we can afford the monthly payment, a major objection has been met.

How can you capture an audience's attention in your introduction to keep them listening?

Visualization. The *visualization step* encourages listeners to picture themselves benefiting from the adoption of your proposal. It focuses on a vision of the future if your proposal is adopted and, just as important, if it is rejected. It may also contrast these two visions, strengthening the attractiveness of your proposal by showing what will happen if no action is taken.

Positive visualization is specific and concrete. Your goal is to help listeners see themselves under the conditions you describe. You want them to experience enjoyment and satisfaction. In contrast, negative visualization focuses on what will happen without your plan. Here you encourage discomfort with conditions that would exist. Whichever method you choose, make your listeners feel part of the future.

Action. The *action step* acts as the conclusion of your speech. Here you tell your listeners what you want them to do or, if action is not necessary, the point of view you want them to share. You may have to explain the specific actions you want and the timing for these actions. This step is most effective when immediate action is sought.

How far would any politician get if he/she failed to directly ask people to vote for him?

Many students find the call to action a difficult part of the persuasive speech. They are reluctant to make an explicit request for action. Can you imagine a politician failing to ask people for their vote? Such a candidate would surely lose an election. When sales representatives have difficulty in closing a deal because they are unable to ask consumers to buy their products, they do not last long in sales. Persuasion is more likely to result when direction is clear and action is the goal.

In review, remember the five-step pattern if you want to lead your audience from attention to action. The motivated sequence is effective, and like all tools of persuasion, can be misused. The line between use and abuse of persuasive tools warrants further examination.

Ethics and Persuasive Speaking

Do you want to be lied to—by anyone? Even when the truth hurts, we prefer it to deception. Telling the truth is the paramount ethical standard for the persuasive speaker. The importance of ethics in public speaking is stressed both implicitly and explicitly throughout this book. Ethics provide standards for conduct that guides us. Persuasive speaking requires asking others to accept and act on ideas we believe to be accurate and true. The ethics of persuasion merit particular consideration in our plans for persuasion.

Think for a few moments about rhetoric as persuasive speaking. Rhetoric is framed and expressed in language and presents ideas within a range of choice. As a speaker, when you make choices, some degree of value is involved in your choosing, whether you speak about the quality of the environment or television programs to select. When choice is involved, ethics are involved. Rhetoric and ethics are bound together.

As a speaker, you must decide not only what to tell your audience, but also what you should avoid saying. In a persuasive speech, you are asking listeners to think or act in ways needed to achieve your specific purpose, a desired response. Emotional appeals entail ethical responsibility, and this responsibility extends to other appeals as well. Consider the four habits as applied to ethical persuasion:

1. **The habit of search**, in which we look for information to confirm or contradict a point of view, demands that we express genuine knowledge of our subject and an awareness of its issues and implications. As a persuasive speaker, you know that controversy exists in matters requiring persuasion. Your task, within the time constraints you face and resources you utilize, is to develop sound and good reasons for the response you desire from an audience. This task is centered in a careful search for the truth.
2. **The habit of justice** asks that you be fair in your search, selection, and presentation of facts for the audience to consider and accept. You should not distort ideas or hide information that an audience needs to properly evaluate your speech, neither should you use loaded language or guilt-by-association tactics.
3. **The habit of preferring public to private motivation** stems from the fact that when you are involved in public speaking, you act as public persons. As such, you have a responsibility to disclose any special bias, prejudice, and private motivations in your sources and in your own motives. There are times in our society when political, religious, or economic spokespersons will articulate a public position that clearly indicates motives in the public interest when, in fact, their persuasive message is actually rooted in a private agenda that is self-serving.
4. **The habit of respect for dissent** requires that, as a persuasive speaker, you must recognize the legitimate diversity of positions that differ from yours. As a persuader, you are not compelled to sacrifice principle but, as Karl Wallace (1955) puts it, you should "prefer facing conflict to accepting appeasement" (9). Leaders who serve as spokespersons, from local community centers to the centers of power in Washington, DC, are constantly being challenged about their opinions, policies, and actions. As a persuasive speaker, you can ask with respect for dissent: "Can I freely admit the force of opposing evidence and argument and still advocate a position that represents my convictions?"

The ethics of persuasion call for honesty, care, thoroughness, openness, and a concern for the audience without manipulative intent. The end does *not* justify the means at all costs. In a society as complex as ours, one marked in part by unethical as well as ethical persuaders, the moral imperative is to speak ethically.

Summary

Your credibility as a speaker is determined by the way the audience perceives you. Credibility is measured in terms of perceived competence, concern for the audience, dynamism, and ethics. According to rhetorical theorist Kenneth Burke, you can increase your credibility and ability to persuade if you convince your audience that you share "common ground" by identifying with your listeners.

Emotional appeals (pathos) can be powerful because they provide the motivation for action and attitude change. Through emotional appeals you can elicit the full range of human feelings in your listeners. To strengthen your appeal, use concrete detail and emotional language, and concentrate on delivering your speech effectively. Persuasive speaking also invites ethical responsibility (ethos). As a persuasive speaker, you should be conscious of ethical standards and what the implications are of the choice you are asking your audience to make. The audience needs to be treated to the truth, without manipulative intent.

Understanding Abraham Maslow's hierarchy of human needs is helpful to persuasive speakers. The five levels of Maslow's hierarchy form a pyramid, with the basic levels forming the base. From bottom to top, these needs are physiological, safety, belongingness and love, esteem, and self-actualization. If you approach your listeners at an appropriate level of need, you will find them more able or willing to respond.

When making logical arguments (logos), one can take an inductive or deductive approach. Inductive reasoning enables you to generalize from specific instances and draw a conclusion from your observations. Deductive reasoning draws a conclusion based on the connections between statements. Depending on your purpose for persuasion, you may choose to reason from examples, analogies, causal relations, or with enthymemes. Choosing the right amount of support, the most persuasive kind of evidence, and then reasoning carefully are essential for successful persuasion.

The two overall persuasive goals are to address audience attitudes and to move an audience to action. Four specific persuasive aims define the focus of your speech. These aims include adoption, continuance, discontinuance, and deterrence. Your point of view, or thesis statement, is expressed in the form of a proposition that must be proved. Propositions take three basic forms: fact, value, and policy.

An effective method for organizing a persuasive speech is Monroe's Motivated Sequence that includes five steps designed to motivate the audience to action: attention, need, satisfaction, visualization, and action. The motivated sequence is a widely used method for organizing persuasive speeches which follows the normal pattern of human thought from attention to action.

Communication for Today's Student

Chapter 11 – Speaking to Persuade

Exercise 11.1 – Strategies of Persuasion

Today's student is bombarded by thousands of persuasive messages each day. *Oral Communication for Today's Student* traces persuasion from Aristotle's elements of ethos, pathos, and logos to persuasive claims to Monroe's Motivated Sequence, etc. The list of the methods of persuasion is lengthy.

Part One: **Monroe Motivated Sequence**

Describe what information might be included to persuade an audience to "stop smoking."

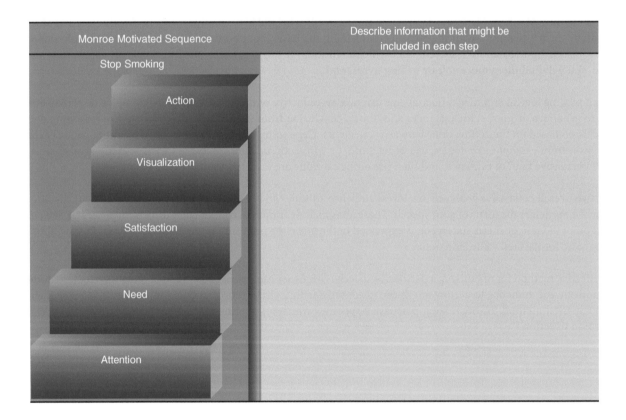

Chapter 11 – Speaking to Persuade

Exercise 11.1 Continued

Part Two: **Maslow's Hierarchy of Human Needs**

Use *Maslow's Hierarchy of Human Needs* to persuade an audience to "Get a Graduate Degree."

Describe the information that may be used in each level to persuade us.

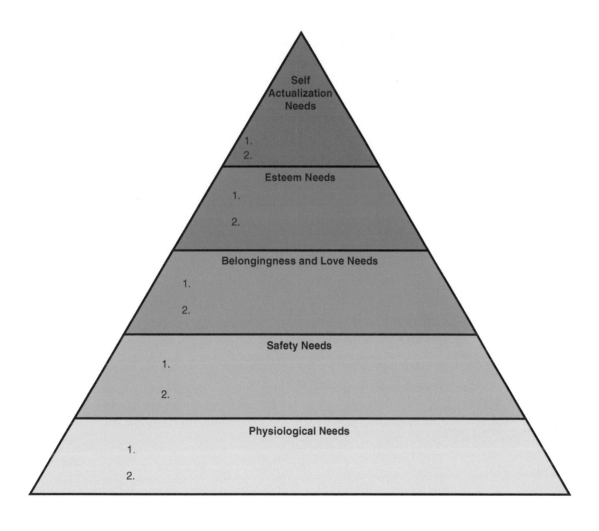

Communication for Today's Student

Chapter 11 – Speaking to Persuade

Exercise 11.2 – Persuasive Speech Topic Approval

Name: _____

Date: _____

> **Remember:**
> *Numbers are not used when preparing the Bibliography for submission*

Circle One: (Person, Place, Object, or Process)

Topic One: _____

General Purpose: _____

Specific Purpose: _____

Sources (in MLA format)

1.

2.

3.

4.

5.

Chapter 11 – Speaking to Persuade

Exercise 11.2 Continued

> *Remember:*
> *Numbers are not*
> *used when preparing*
> *the Bibliography for*
> *submission*

Circle One: (Person, Place, Object, or Process)

Topic Two: _____

General Purpose: _____

Specific Purpose: _____

Sources (in MLA format)

1.

2.

3.

4.

5.

Remember:
Numbers are not
used when preparing
the Bibliography for
submission

Circle One: (Person, Place, Object, or Process)

Topic Three: _____

General Purpose: _____

Specific Purpose: _____

Sources **(in MLA format)**

1.

2.

3.

4.

5.

Chapter 11 – Speaking to Persuade

Exercise 11.2 Continued

Write sources in MLA format. Remember only one (www) website may be used for this speech.

How many minutes is your persuasive speech? _____

How many oral footnotes must you include? _____

What persuasive strategy are you considering? (e.g., Monroe's Motivated Sequence)

Approved Topic: _____

Instructor Comments:

_____

_____

_____

_____

WHAT ARE THE ROLES OF LEADERSHIP AND POWER IN GROUP DYNAMICS?

After reading this chapter, you should be able to:

- ⊘ Define and distinguish between leadership and power.
- ⊘ Discuss the different types of leadership syles.
- ⊘ Discuss the six basic bases of power in small groups.
- ⊘ Describe the types of conflict that can occur in small groups.
- ⊘ Discuss the role of culture and conflict management strategies in small groups.

Key Terms

Autocratic leader	Influence	Power distance	Superiority quality
Certainty	Interpersonal linkage	Problem orientation	Task leaders
Coercive power	Intrinsic conflict	Provisionalism	Task Roles
Collectivistic cultures	Laissez-Faire leader	Reciprocal	Theory X
Democratic leader	Leadership	Referent power	Theory Y
Empathy	Legitimate power	Reward power	Transformational
Expert power	Low context culture	Situational leadership	Transformational leader
Extrinsic conflict	Maintenance leaders	Spontaneity	Uncertainty avoidness
High context culture	Neutrality	Strategy	
Individualistic cultures	Power	Substantive conflict	

12 Scenario

Mario inhaled deeply before directing his attention back to his test. He was taking a test for the student ambassadors program for the university.

Student ambassadors were the official representatives for the university. They were able to travel internationally, attend alumni functions, and work alongside the university's esteemed president. After sitting in on the informational meeting, he realized that he was perfect for the program.

Mario had a long background in leadership.He had been class president in school since the fifth grade. He held several seats in student government organizations. Mario hoped to one day be President of the United States, and he believed that the student ambassadors program could help cultivate his ability to be a leader.

The test had been fairly easy until he reached the part which addressed the different types of leaders. Each blank required the definition of each leader. Mario never knew there were that many different types of leaders. He was completely over-whelmed. Unable to answer the questions, he left the section blank and turned in his test.

As he walked out, he knew he wouldn't make the student ambassadors program this year. He had a lot to learn about the different types of leaders before he could ever be one.

What type of leader are you?
What are the traits of a good leader?

 Respond Here

Introduction

How can my group manage itself to be productive and make quality decisions? That's a very hard question! One way to get some insight is to learn the chapter objectives. Even if you have the best group staffed with very bright and highly motivated members, most groups still need some help. You will have to find ways to help the group coordinate all its efforts, as well as help the members remain civil with each other. After all, the groups we are talking about are challenged with complex problems requiring information gathering, analysis, debate, and commitment. All that activity needs to be coordinated to keep the group on track. The members will require occasional motivation and, perhaps, even some discipline. In addition, because this process is rarely completed overnight, the potential for conflict is very high. It's natural for people to become

Groups are challenged with complex problems requiring a coordinated work approach.

irritated with each other and argue, especially when they spend a lot of time together. We're people; it's what we do! We have to find ways to keep that conflict under control and to use it to help our groups make the best decisions.

To help answer all these questions, this chapter addresses three separate but related topics: leadership, power, and conflict.

Are Power and Leadership the Same Thing?

Leadership is the ability to influence the behavior of others. A leader is someone who can use interpersonal *influence* to move people to action. A person exercising leadership uses persuasion to motivate people to action. **Power,** by contrast, is the ability to *control* the behavior of others. Power can be based on legitimate authority or position, access to information, or access and control of desired resources.

The use of power and the use of influence are not the same thing. It is possible to use one without using the other. For example, a group member in a leadership role could be very successful at motivating other members to complete tasks in the effort to accomplish the

How does a leader motivate others in the group?

group goal, but that leader could have no source of power. Conversely, a group member with some form of power (control over desired resources, for example), might be able to control the behavior of other group members, but he or she might not be personally persuasive or motivating.

In reality, many leaders likely use a combination of influence and power to accomplish tasks with groups of people. Good leaders try not to rely on power to motivate people, because a reliance on power damages the motivation and creativity of group members, and it results in flawed decisions and inferior products.

Leadership and power will be treated separately because they are different, but the discussion will emphasize the relationship between the two concepts.

What Is the Role of Leadership?

Forsyth says that leadership is a specialized form of social interaction. It is a "reciprocal, transactional, and sometimes transformational process in which cooperative individuals are permitted to influence and motivate others to promote the attainment of group and individual goals." Let's look at the parts.

Reciprocal suggests that leadership is an ongoing process and is defined by the leader, the group members, and the particular situation that the group happens to be experiencing. There is a give-and-take relationship between the leader and the members in which the followers allow themselves to be influenced by the leader. There is no leadership without followers.

Leaders and group members work together in a *transactional* process "exchanging their time, energies, and skills to increase their joint rewards." The leader specifies what follower behaviors are needed to solve the problem and how the group's or followers' needs would be satisfied as a result.

In a give-and-take relationship, followers allow themselves to be influenced by the leader.

Transformational means that leaders can communicate a group vision that members find appealing. This vision motivates and empowers followers to become leaders themselves and influence the outcomes of group tasks. The leader's task is to make the vision clear to the followers. It asks them to make the group goals perhaps more important than their own individual goals.

As we mentioned earlier, leadership is really a *cooperative* process that uses persuasion instead of power and control. Members with the most influence usually emerge as leaders over time, and they are followed by the other members of the group. Remember that we are talking about the member with the most influence, and not *necessarily* the person who was appointed or elected leader of the group. Finally, leadership should function to help the group to adapt to changing circumstances and remain focused on *accomplishing goals*. Leadership helps to provide the direction that moves the group toward its objectives.

Influence of a Leader

Leadership is not "built in" to particular people who possess certain personality characteristics. That is, people are not born or destined to be leaders or followers. Instead of leadership being determined by a set of personality traits, we suggest that it depends more on experience and skills that can be learned and developed. Leadership is given or attributed to a person by others in the group. Even though we have suggested that personality characteristics or traits do not determine who has the ability to lead others, personal qualities do seem to affect *perceptions* of leadership.

If your group does have an appointed leader, it doesn't necessarily mean that he or she will be the most influential

How can you emerge as a leader within your group?

Take a Closer Look

A study by Geier reports that a process of elimination of contenders for leadership takes place in the initial meetings of any group. If you want to contribute to the goals of the group and become a leader, take these steps:8

1. *Be informed:* Being uninformed is seen as a negative characteristic that eliminates most contenders.
2. *Participate:* Groups typically judge quiet members as nonparticipative and unsuitable for leadership.
3. *Be flexible:* Try to remain open to new ideas or methods, especially when your ideas or methods are in conflict with group norms or goals, and be willing to compromise.
4. *Encourage:* Encourage other members to participate; don't try to make all the decisions yourself or dominate the discussion.

---

person in the group. Leadership is not the sole possession of *the* leader. Many members of the group could provide leadership in different areas or at different times as the group progresses through a task. For example, if your group is working on a project related to the responsible use of energy resources, and even though you might not be *the* leader, you could be influential in decision making because you know a lot about the issue, because you are interested in energy policies, or because you belong to an active energy conservation organization. Whenever you influence the course the group takes, or when you help move the group toward the accomplishment of its goals, you have provided *leadership*.

Task and Maintenance Leadership

Task roles are oriented toward helping the group accomplish it's goals, while maintenance roles are focused on the social and relational issues that arise whenever people work together.

Consistent with this model, **task leaders** are those group members who help the group with organization and advancement toward making a decision of completing a job. They are sometimes perceived as the leader of the group, but they can also be group members who are influential in a particular situation. Task leaders often *emerge* from the interaction of the group over time, but they could also be appointed or elected by the members. The presence of effective task leadership results in the group spending more time on task and staying focused on specific topics. Groups with leaders have longer attention spans than groups without leaders.

Photo courtesy of Charles Long

What role does a task leader play in a group?

Maintenance leaders focus on relational issues, the development of an open and supportive climate, motivation of members, and conflict management. This type of leader also emerges from the interaction of the group. This function is far more than a cruise director sort of position. Maintenance leaders are critical to quality decision making because they mediate differences of opinion and interpersonal conflicts, maintain a high set of standards for group behavior and contributions, and encourage the participation of all the group members.

Both task and maintenance functions are essential to groups interested in making important decisions or completing complex tasks. Keep in mind these important functions of leaders as you consider the three perspectives on leadership presented in the next section.

Leadership Styles

The **styles approach** to leadership is focused on the behaviors of the leader. McGregor tells us that the behavior of a leader is based on assumptions that he or she makes about the members of the group. These assumptions are divided into two groups, Theory X and Theory Y, which were designed to show leaders two ends of a continuum of leadership possibilities.

Theory X Assumptions
- People don't like to work and require the control of a leader.
- People do not like responsibility and they will resist it.
- People are not creative problem solvers.
- People are motivated by lower level needs such as security, food, and money.

Theory Y Assumptions
- People like to work; it comes as naturally as play to them.
- People are capable of self-direction.
- People are attracted to self-control and responsibility.
- People are creative and imaginative in problem solving and like to make decisions.
- People are motivated by higher-level needs such as recognition and self-actualization.

Theory Y assumes that people are creative and imaginative in problem solving.

The practical application of these assumptions can be seen in the leadership styles: autocratic, laissez-faire, and democratic. Autocratic and democratic leadership capture the ends of the continuum, and those will be the primary focus of our illustration.

The autocratic leader. The **autocratic leader** follows the Theory X assumptions most closely and creates an authoritative atmosphere that is based on direction and control. This type of leader does not solicit follower feedback. Instead, he or she makes the decisions and supervises followers to make sure the task is being accomplished. Members do not communicate much with each other. Instead, they communicate mostly with the leader, and communication is mostly task-related questions. There is very little discussion. An example of autocratic leadership can often be found in military organizations and on the shop floor in factories geared for high-volume production.

What does the autocratic style of leadership accomplish?

The autocratic style normally results in high efficiency and a high quantity of work, but it is low on cohesiveness, creativity, and member satisfaction. Lewin found that groups with autocratic leaders had the highest incidents of aggressive activity and exhibited the most productivity, but only when closely supervised. Additionally, employees who had low needs for independence and were authoritarian performed best under autocratic supervision.

The laissez-faire leader. The **laissez-faire leader** is one who takes a hands-off approach to leadership and provides very little direction to those being led. This leader seems to be a nonleader, because he or she does so little to guide the group. He or she abdicates responsibility, delays decisions, gives no feedback, and makes little effort to help followers satisfy their needs. There is no exchange with followers or any attempt to help them grow. This is rarely an effective style.

The democratic leader. The **democratic leader** adopts the Theory Y assumptions and creates an atmosphere of member integration, self-control, and participatory decision making; the input of subordinates is encouraged and is used to make decisions. This type of leadership is most effective with groups who have some knowledge about how to complete the task at hand and are fairly motivated to do so. Followers tend to be motivated by higher-level needs such as self-esteem and job satisfaction. In this case, a leader who is too authoritative will only serve to inhibit the group's creative processes.

Why are democratic conditions better when searching for a creative solution?

The democratic leader facilitates group discussion and participation in the decision-making process. In Lewin's study, groups with democratic leaders had the highest levels of individual satisfaction and functioned in the most positive and orderly fashion. Likewise, employees with a high need for independence and who are not authoritarian performed best under a democratic supervisor.

The strength of the styles approach is its focus on leader behaviors and assumptions made by leaders about followers. Some styles would only be effective in particular situations. For example, the autocratic style should be useful in a factory type setting where work is repetitive and high quantity is expected. By contrast, a group trying to find a creative solution to a complex problem would probably perform better in a democratic condition. The situation, the task, and the composition of the group members will determine what style will produce the best outcomes.

Situational Leadership

Situational leadership assumes that a leader's effectiveness is contingent, or dependent, upon how well the leader's style fits the context. The situational leadership model by Hersey, Blanchard and Johnson argues that leadership effectiveness is built on a combination of task-based and relationship-based behaviors of the leader. The composition of the group will determine what leadership approach will work best. People in leadership positions should first analyze the group, and then implement one of a variety of leadership styles designed to address the situation.

How does a leader effectively analyze the group?

The primary factors that leaders look for are the ability of members to complete a particular task and their motivation to do so. As we discussed earlier, groups function on two levels: a task level (which is focused on goal achievement) and a relationship level (which is focused on maintaining the group as a unit and motivating members). As such, after situational leaders examine the abilities and motivation levels of followers, they must determine what combination of task and relationship leadership behaviors will work for the group in this situation. Hersey, Blanchard, and Johnson have outlined four leadership styles that consider these issues: telling, selling, participating, and delegating.

1. *Telling.* A high-task and low-relationship approach is used when group members have low levels of ability and low motivation. Groups that are not motivated to perform a task need and expect the leader to be direct in telling them what they should do. Communication is one-way and the leader decides what should be done and how. This leader typically uses a clear, confident, and directive communication style.

2. *Selling.* A high-task and high-relationship approach is used when the members have low levels of ability but high motivation to complete the task. The leader is comparable to a salesperson and works to gain acceptance of a particular course of action by explaining why it is the right or best one to take. The communication used by this leader offers emotional support, and it is motivational, encouraging, and, at times, stern.

3. *Participating.* A low-task and high-relationship approach is used when the members have high levels of ability but low motivation to complete the task. The leader and the group work together to determine what should be done, how, and when. It is similar to the democratic style mentioned earlier. It requires the leader to be less directive, more supportive, and to include the members in decision making. The leader utilizes an open communication style conducive to facilitating discussion, sharing ideas, and encouraging input.

4. *Delegating.* A low-task and low-relationship approach is used when the members have high levels of ability, as well as high levels of motivation to complete the task. This group needs very little guidance or motivation. The leader outlines what needs to be accomplished and the group gets the job done its own way and at its own pace. This requires the leader to use feedback as well as clear communication that fosters a supportive climate, while still maintaining a sense of his or her role as a facilitator. The leader demonstrates confidence in the group by delegating more responsibilities.

The strength of the situational approach to leadership is its focus on member assessment and thinking through what and why a particular leadership approach should be used. For example, we may be more authoritative when a quick response is due and more facilitative when we are working with a mature group and have the time for facilitation. In addition, individuals from high context and collectivistic cultures may not ever use an authoritative (i.e., telling) style, as this approach would cause both leaders and followers to lose face. Please see the cultural discussion later in this chapter.

Transformational Leadership

A **transformational leader** is someone who possesses the charisma necessary to motivate followers and evoke change. Transformational leaders have charisma and vision, provide intellectual stimulation, and inspire their followers:

- They stimulate interest among colleagues and followers to view their work from new perspectives.
- They generate an awareness or a vision of the mission for the group.
- They develop colleagues and followers to higher levels of ability and potential.
- They motivate colleagues and followers to look beyond their own interests toward those that will benefit the group.

Transformational leaders are visionary and inspire followers to achieve higher goals. Lee Iacocca, a transformational leader, joined the Chrysler Corporation in 1978 when the company was on the verge of bankruptcy. From 1979 to 1986, Iacocca was able to turn the company around and make it profitable. Stephen Sharf, who was the head of manufacturing for Chrysler when Lee Iacocca took over, attributed the Chrysler transformation to Iacocca's leadership style. Iacocca is described as someone who knew what he was doing, someone who was well liked, and a person who took charge. Sharf states: "His tremendous self-confidence radiated to whomever he talked to—workers, suppliers, banks, and the government. He was articulate and a motivator. There was no doubt in his mind that he could turn Chrysler around and people began to believe he really could." Iacocca was a transformational leader and a visionary who was able to share that vision with others and transform Chrysler's way of doing business. Lee Iacocca is still regarded as a folk hero because of his leadership and achievements at Chrysler.

Other examples of transformational leaders include John Kennedy, Sam Walton, Steve Jobs, Abraham Lincoln, and Franklin D. Roosevelt.

As with the other leadership approaches mentioned in this chapter, there are some weaknesses of transformational leadership. One is the possibility that passion and confidence may be mistaken for truth and reality. Additionally, the energy these leaders exert can become unrelenting and exhausting because the followers and leaders of this type tend to see the big picture at the expense of the details. However, this approach helps us to understand why some leaders are more successful than other leaders. They can empower individual members to perform beyond their own expectations. This kind of motivation can create strong group identity and often changes the culture of entire organizations.

How to Destroy a Group: Understanding What Not to Do

In order to improve our communication skills, understanding what not to do is important. Communication scholar D. M. Hall jokingly suggests eight ways in which a group member should not behave in groups:

1. Never prepare in advance; speak spontaneously. It keeps things on a superficial level.
2. Always take your responsibility lightly. This reduces your anxiety level and increases the frustration levels of others.
3. Never try to understand the group's purposes. This guarantees you'll accomplish nothing.
4. Always do the lion's share of the talking. None of the others have good ideas anyway.
5. Never give credit; hog it all for yourself. The rest love a braggart.
6. Always speak of your many years of experience. This compensates for your lack of ability.
7. Never tell anyone how to do it, else you may lose your prestige and position.
8. Always encourage the formation of cliques. The group can't last long when they begin to fight among themselves.

   Have you engaged in any one of these communication behaviors?

   If so, what can you do to avoid doing so in the future?

Source: Written by D. M. Hall, summarized by Murk (1994).

You don't need to be born with certain personality traits to be a good leader. You can rise to leadership if you take the time to develop the skills and gain experience. Hackman and Johnson tell us that skill development is a continuous, life-long process. The moment you think you have "arrived" as a leader, the progress stops.

From the discussion of leadership styles and types in this chapter, you should learn that a single leadership type will not always be successful. There is no absolute or formula that will be perfect in every situation. To be a successful leader, you should be able to analyze the task, the context of the task, and the group of people who will be making the decision or working on the task. When you have completed that analysis, you should gain some insight into what kind of leadership approach will be most useful in that situation.

Good leaders always adapt their approach as the group changes.

However, you should not get comfortable! Groups mature, motivation levels change, and the nature of the task could vary as you move toward completion. You should always pay attention to these changes and be ready to adapt and to alter your leadership approach as needed to best achieve your group's goals.

What Is the Role of Power?

At the beginning of this chapter, we defined power as the ability to control the behavior of others. As you read before, power can be based on legitimate authority or a person's position in an organization, access to information, and access to or control of desired resources. It is possible to use power without being influential (i.e., exhibiting leadership), and it is possible to be influential without using power. The best situation exists when leadership and power are combined: the influential leader who uses power at the appropriate times and in moderation can be very successful at helping groups accomplish goals.

French and Raven identified five foundations of power that are typically used in small groups:

1. Legitimate power
2. Coercive power
3. Reward power

4. Expert power
5. Referent power

This section looks more closely at these five power sources, plus one more—interpersonal linkage.

Legitimate Power

Legitimate power exists as a function of someone's position in an organization. Followers defer to the *authority* carried by the position regardless of who occupies the position. Respect for the individual in the position of legitimate power is not required for control. The higher the position in the organization, the more legitimate power a person typically has. An example of the amount of influence and psychological effects legitimate power can have over an individual can be found in the studies of Stanley Milgram. This series of

Is using coercive power an effective way to lead?

studies found that people would obey legitimate power even when it conflicted with what they believed to be the right thing to do. The best condition exists when the person holding the legitimate power in the organization is also respected by the subordinates. In this condition, the power can be used to direct activities rather than to control group members.

Coercive Power

Coercive power could also be called power to punish. Members follow leaders with coercive power because they want to avoid reprimand or punishment. Followers allow themselves to be controlled in order to avoid the punishments or sanction that could be associated with the failure to comply. Such punishments could include criticism, social ostracism, poor performance appraisals, reprimands, undesirable work assignments, or dismissal.

Coercive power ends when the power holder is no longer able to inflict punishment. Unless it is necessary, it is a good idea to avoid the use of this type of power because it is uncomfortable for most people and it can have a negative effect on the motivation and creativity of group members.

Reward Power

Reward power is just the opposite of coercive power. Where coercive power threatens to punish (or remove access to some desired resource) for noncompliance, reward power offers access to some desired resource as payment for compliance. The primary motivation of the follower is to comply with the leader to get the reward. Your teacher could reward you with bonus points for coming to class on a very cold day, or your boss could give you a bonus for completing a project on time or under the budget. Other rewards at your workplace could include pay increases, recognition, interesting job assignments, or promotions.

Like coercive power, this individual's power ends when he or she is no longer able to provide rewards. Individuals with only reward and not coercive power promise fewer rewards than someone who has both coercive and reward power. Likewise, those who possessed coercive power without reward power were more likely to invoke coercive power more frequently.

These first three power bases can be considered as what Porter and his colleagues termed *position power,* which includes power that is granted as a result of a person's position in an organization rather than by the unique characteristics of the individual. Position-based power is an impersonal source of power. It is also granted to those who have supervisory positions.

The last two bases of power identified by French and Raven and one identified by Hocker and Wilmot are forms of personal power. Unlike position power, these are granted based on individual knowledge, skills, or personality. These power bases often transfer from role to role and are used by either supervisors or subordinates.

Expert Power

A person with **expert power** is able to assist the group in reaching its goals because of his or her expertise on a given topic. Group members comply because they don't have the knowledge to complete the task without help. Followers perceive that the expert has the knowledge to achieve the group's goals. This person can easily lose power if his or her knowledge base is needed for just one subject and if the knowledge is no longer needed or desired.

Referent Power

Referent power is based on the personal liking or respect that one person has for another. The person with referent power is influential because others respect or admire the way he or she does a job or if the power holder possesses personal qualities that others would like to emulate. When people admire you and want to be liked or admired by you, they are often willing to be influenced. You could say that people who have referent power have charisma. As long as followers feel connected with this leader, he or she will exert referent power. If, for some reason, followers' perceptions are altered, then this leader's power is diminished.

Interpersonal Linkages

In addition to the five bases of power identified by French and Raven, Hocker and Wilmot identified a power base that comes from the power holder's access to people who control desired resources. The **interpersonal linkage** is power based on who you know and what resources those people control. If your group needs information from a government agency, for example, and you happen to know somebody at that government agency who can get the information for you, then that can be a source of influence. You don't have access to the information, but you know somebody who does!

A person with referent power is influential because others respect or admire the way he/she works.

Power bases give us insight into the reasons that some leaders are effective. Power can be based on one's position in a company, as we see with legitimate, coercive, and reward power. Power such as expert, personal linkage, and referent can be based on one's individual qualities. Any group member can have this kind of power, and it is dependent on the context and task facing the group. When you possess this kind of power, it is essential that you are ethical with its use. You should be aware of the unethical use of power and question it when it comes in direct conflict with your moral and ethical standards.

Does My Group Have to Have Conflict?

Just as you can count on the sun coming up in the morning, you can count on the presence of conflict in small groups. Whenever you get two or more people together who are trying to do something, there will be conflict! Even though many of us are quite similar, we still have individual differences that make us unique. We see the world around us in our own unique ways. When we come together as a small group, those individual differences are going to clash to create misunderstandings and disagreements. Conflict!

How is group conflict a good thing?

Conflict involves disagreement over task and procedural issues, over personality and affective issues, and over competitive tensions among group members. It can arise from differences of opinion, incompatible personalities, and even from geographical and cultural differences.

Conflict is inevitable in small groups. It is not something that you can avoid. But don't walk away from this discussion with the idea that conflict is always a bad thing. Conflict is a central and essential element for groups trying to solve complex problems. One of the primary reasons that groups make better decisions than individuals working alone is the multiple perspectives that group members bring to the table. It is when these perspectives conflict that new ideas, points of view, and solutions are created. This is group synergy in action!

Conflict related to the problem challenging a small group is central to the group's success, but it has a darker side. Conflicts based on personality clashes or competitive group members can be a distraction to groups, prevent the group from thoroughly completing the decision-making plan, and even threaten the existence of the group. However, personality-related conflicts can serve a maintenance function. Members of even friendly and cohesive groups get upset with each other now and then. Conflict provides those members with an outlet for hostile feelings, and it can facilitate a close examination of relationships. The bottom line is that if conflict is properly managed, it can be productive on both the task and relationship levels.

As you might have guessed by now, we will be discussing two kinds of conflict: conflict *intrinsic* to the task and conflict *extrinsic* to the task.

Intrinsic Conflict

Intrinsic conflict usually centers on disagreements related to the task facing the group. Intrinsic conflict can take two forms. It can be *substantive conflict,* which involves issues directly related to the content of the decision being made. It is unrelated to personal tensions that might exist between group members. Substantive conflict helps groups achieve their goals. Intrinsic conflict can also be *procedural,* which involves group policies and methods of solving problems. Members could disagree, for example, on what is the best way for reaching agreement. Some members might favor voting, for example, while other members believe that all decisions made by the group should have the complete agreement of all members. To prevent procedural issues from taking too much time, some groups adopt explicit policies that specify member responsibilities and decision making processes. Some groups even adopt standard policies such as *Robert's Rules of Order.*

Young, et al. provide us with a comparison of three standard procedures for reaching decisions: voting, compromise, and consensus. If your group gets stuck deciding how to decide, consider adopting of these procedures as your standard policy. Before you choose one, however, carefully look at the strengths and weaknesses of each procedure. We have ranked them good, better, and best, but all decision making experts might not agree with our assessment.

Standard Procedures for Reaching Decisions

- *Good: Voting.* Voting is quick and it solves the problem efficiently, but it creates a majority and a minority. The majority gets everything it wants, so its members are satisfied and committed to carrying out the decision. The minority gets nothing that it wants, so the commitment level of its members is often low, which results in a lack of motivation to follow through with implementation.
- *Better: Compromise.* In this situation, the members made trade-offs to make the decision. All of the members get some of what they want, and all of the members have to give up something to gain the agreement of the group. The resulting level of commitment is only moderate from all members, so follow through on decision implementation could be weakened. Compromise is not as quickly accomplished as voting.
- *Best: Consensus.* Consensus implies unanimous agreement of all members. Because all the members are satisfied and take ownership of the outcome, commitment to the decision is high and all are motivated to follow through on implementation. Consensus could take a very long time with complex issues. You should also beware that a consensus decision, because it has to please all the members to gain agreement, might not always be the most creative or best decision.

If your group gets stuck on substantive or procedural differences, then you should consider adopting a policy that will help you resolve or manage them. If intrinsic conflict is not managed well, it distracts from the group working on the task. In addition, it could get out of control and lead to extrinsic conflict. The decision-making plan (DMP) is a comprehensive procedure designed to help you understand and solve complex decisions. The three strategies just described will be very useful as your group navigates its way through the DMP procedure.

Extrinsic Conflict

When most people think of conflict, they are probably thinking of **extrinsic conflict**. This kind of conflict is related to the personalities and relationships between members. It can arise when you *just don't like* another group member, or when some basic incompatibility exists between members that cause tension.

There are multiple causes of extrinsic conflict:

- Recall that group communication implies interdependence among the people. When the communication becomes less interdependent and more competitive, the potential for conflict is high. Group members who are committed to the group's goals (creative solution to the problem facing the group) are at odds with members who are more committed to their own individual goals (promotion, money, job recognition).
- The use of power such as threats and punishments and the poor application of legitimate power by leaders or other members can lead to extrinsic conflict.
- Extrinsic conflict can arise when individuals do not understand the reasons for the behaviors of others. If the reasons are not understood, then the behaviors can easily be misinterpreted and lead to resentment. For example, geographic diversity and cultural differences are often a source of conflict. These will be described in the next section.
- Extrinsic conflict often arises from the ways the members communicate with each other. Sometimes it is not *what* you say but *how* you say it that creates the problem. If communication makes another member defensive, then extrinsic conflict becomes more likely. The final section of this chapter looks at communication that can create defensive climates and strategies that can help you avoid conflict.
- Extrinsic conflict can arise because you just don't like another group member. Maybe he or she reminds you of the kid who broke your pencil in kindergarten or the bully who beat you up. If it's all inside your head, then here's some friendly advice: *It's time to be an adult and let go of it!* If, however, the other person feels the same way about you, you should handle the problem in private. If you and the other member can't resolve these differences, try to agree on a strategy for at least managing your relationship while you are working with the group. If you can both commit to the goals of the group, petty differences can be put aside and maybe you can share a friendly, professional relationship.

As stated before, extrinsic conflict can serve a useful maintenance function. However, unmanaged extrinsic conflict often causes harm to a group. If unmanaged, even minor extrinsic conflicts can turn into major problems. Conflicts that go unresolved or unmanaged generally do not go away. They can "explode," and the group cannot go about the business of making decisions because it is caught up in destructive conflict.

Whatever the kind of conflict that arises in your group, the key to making it work for you is **conflict management.** Some strategies you can use for managing extrinsic conflict include the following.

1. *Do everything you can to encourage cooperation among group members.* Look for opportunities to agree whenever possible. Small agreements can eventually lead to larger agreements and cooperation.
2. *Try to encourage participation of all members.* Approach reticent or shy members in a nonthreatening way and ask for their opinions. Listen to their answers. When they realize that other members listen to them, participation will increase.
3. *Be honest about your intentions.* Don't play games or try to manipulate other members.
4. *Maintain a supportive climate.* Look at the final section of this chapter and be able to recognize the difference between defensive and supportive climates. If the climate in your groups becomes defensive, use some of the strategies suggested to move toward a more supportive, cooperative atmosphere.
5. *Keep the group goals as a priority.* They should take precedence over the individual goals of members.

Example: Countering Extrinsic Conflict

A group member complains, "Steve is always late for our meetings. He says we meet too far from his house. That really burns me up. Let's throw him out of the group!"

Problem: Extrinsic conflict leads to low member satisfaction, a lack of agreement, the loss of the cooperative climate, low productivity, and even the disintegration of the group. What do you do when you see escalating extrinsic conflict?

Strategy: Individual group members can successfully counteract extrinsic conflict by turning disruptive acts (that would normally escalate the conflict) into constructive contributions. This helps defuse the situation and refocus the attention of each member to the task at hand. You could turn that expression of anger into a constructive suggestion by saying, "Let's meet at Steve's house. That way, he can't be late! Besides, we can watch the game on his HDTV and his refrigerator is always full of food!"

How Can Cultral Differences Lead to Extrinsic Conflict?

Cultural influences have a profound effect on decision quality and the overall decision-making process. Chances are, you have already worked in a group made up of people from a variety of cultural and ethnic backgrounds. If not, get ready! The world is becoming increasingly *flat*. This means that collaboration and competition for jobs is open to people from all over the world, not just those who live near you or even in your country! Instantaneous communication technology in the "digital age" is shaping the way we manage our lives and do business, and that business is increasingly conducted with others around the globe. Because diverse groups are more likely to experience extrinsic conflict than homogeneous groups, we will briefly examine some of the cultural dimensions that affect groups.

How has the "digital age" changed the way we do business?

If you are aware of the cultural influences on others, and if you are aware of your own cultural influences and biases, you will be better able to adapt to new situations when they present themselves. Instead of moving directly to an extrinsic conflict situation, you should be willing to understand (and possibly explain to others in the group) that the source of your differences is culture related and perhaps not a fundamental interpersonal disagreement.

Geert Hofstede used the term *cultural dimensions* to refer to the common elements or the key issues of a culture that can be studied and analyzed in meaningful ways. Hofstede's value orientations are used to test and understand culture's influence in today's digital world. Some of these dimensions can be directly applied to the small-group context.

Individualism/Collectivism

In **individualistic cultures,** people are taught personal autonomy, privacy, self-realization, individual initiative, independence, individual decision making, and an understanding of personal identity as the sum of an individual's personal and unique attributes. People from individualistic cultures are taught that their needs and interests are just as important, if not more important, than the needs and interests of others. Some examples of individualistic societies are Australia, Great Britain, Canada, and the United States.

Group members from individualistic cultures are most comfortable working on projects alone and have a tendency to do all the work or none at all. This is not because they are uncooperative or difficult. Rather, it is because they are not socialized to collaborate like those from collectivistic cultures. For individualists, the group experience can be exceedingly frustrating. When an individualist approaches group projects and collaboration with a collectivistic mindset, he or she may find that to put group goals before personal goals is not necessarily a losing position.

Collectivism characterizes a culture in which people, from birth, are integrated into strong, cohesive in-groups. Collectivistic cultures emphasize emotional dependence on groups and organizations, less personal privacy, and the belief that group decisions are superior to individual decisions. They believe in interdependence, an understanding of personal identity as knowing one's place within the group, and concern about the needs and interests of others.

Group members from individualistic cultures are most comfortable working on projects alone.

Collectivistic cultures include China, Hong Kong, India, Japan, Pakistan, and Taiwan. Group members from collectivistic cultures experience less frustration when working with group members who also have collectivistic tendencies. This is largely due to the practice they have had collaborating with their own families, friends, and colleagues. Their frustration with groups is more likely experienced when they are collaborating with people who approach group work as individualists.

High Power Distance/Low Power Distance

Power distance is the extent to which the less powerful members of organizations and institutions accept and expect that power is distributed unequally. Individuals from low power-distance cultures believe that inequality in society should be minimized, that all individuals should have equal rights, that power should be used legitimately, and that powerful people should try to look less powerful than they are. Individuals from high power-distance cultures stress coercive and referent power and believe that power holders are entitled to privileges, and that powerful people should try to look as powerful as possible.

Participating effectively in small groups may be more challenging for group members from high power-distance cultures. Likewise, decision-making processes and approaches to conflict resolution are likely to be influenced by the group's power distance level. For instance, conflict management in teams with a low power-distance factor is based on principles of negotiation and cooperation, while in high power-distance teams, conflict is resolved primarily by the power holder. On the one hand, those who come from low power-distance cultures think that group decisions should be made by consensus, should have shared leadership, and that role responsibilities should be based on expertise. On the other hand, people from high power-distance cultures use voting, expect leaders to lead, and are uncomfortable in teams where they are asked to take on more autonomy and responsibility.

Uncertainty Avoidance

Uncertainty avoidance refers to the extent to which risk and ambiguity are acceptable conditions. Hofstede suggests that it is the extent to which the members of a culture feel threatened by uncertain or unknown situations. This is one of the cultural dimensions most problematic for groups. Group members from high uncertainty avoidance cultures interact based on a need for rules, suppression of deviant ideas and behavior, and resistance to innovation. They are motivated by security, esteem, and belongingness. Some countries with high uncertainty-avoidance cultures are Greece, Portugal,

Guatemala, Uruguay, and Japan. Low uncertainty-avoidance cultures include the United States, Sweden, Jamaica, Singapore, and Hong Kong.

Group members from low uncertainty-avoidance cultures are more tolerant of different opinions, prefer as few rules as possible, are more calm and contemplative, and they are not expected to express emotions. They are better able to function within a group that is less structured. Such groups are characterized by loose deadlines, undefined roles, few rules, and a high tolerance for innovation and "outside-of-the-box" thinking. Understanding the uncertainty avoidance tendencies of members can help groups structure a productive decision-making environment. Such an environment would provide a balance of structure for those high in uncertainty avoidance. They would still maintain a spirit of innovation and encourage unique approaches to decision making for those who are low in uncertainty avoidance.

High Context/Low Context

Hall divided cultures into high and low context according to their ways of communicating. A **high-context culture** uses communication in which most of the information is either in the physical context or internalized in the person. To understand high-context communication, one should consider the content of the messages and the context together. Context is the situation, background, or environment connected to an event, a location, or an individual. Very little is explicitly stated. High-context communication is typically indirect, ambiguous, harmonious, reserved, and understated. A **low-context culture** is just the opposite. The majority of information is stated explicitly. Low-context communication is direct, precise, dramatic, open, and based on feelings or true intentions.

High Context Cultures

Japan
Arab Countries
Greece
Spain
Italy
England
France
North America
Scandinavian Countries
German-speaking
    Countries

Low Context Cultures

Source: Hall & Hall (1990) Understanding Cultural Differences

When interacting with people who are from a high-context culture, using communication that is too direct can result in embarrassment or even anger. Likewise, when interacting with someone from a low-context culture, using communication that is indirect or implied can result in confusion and frustration because it is perceived that the communicator does not say what he or she means. For instance, if a North American supervisor is unsatisfied with a subordinate's sales proposal, the response will probably be explicit and direct: "I can't accept this proposal as submitted, so come up with some better ideas." A Korean supervisor, in the same situation, might say, "While I have the highest regard for your abilities, I regret to inform you that I am not completely satisfied with this proposal. I must ask that you reflect further and submit additional ideas on how to develop this sales program." The message is essentially the same, but as you can see, the approach is different.

In addition to personal and ideational differences that normally exist between people, multicultural groups have a high potential for intrinsic conflict based on their different points of view. The potential for extrinsic conflict is even higher, considering the number of potential misunderstandings and interpersonal transgressions resulting from the clash of cultural expectations. An awareness of different cultural expectations will help keep nonproductive conflict to a minimum and promote the level of communication, understanding, and cooperation necessary for making creative decisions.

How Is Communication a Source of Extrinsic Conflict?

A frequent source of extrinsic conflict is communication itself. Sometimes it's not what people say that creates the problem but the way they say it.

Control/Problem Orientation

Most of us need to feel we have some control over our lives. So we respond to control with *psychological reactance*. In response to feeling controlled, we do the opposite of what we are told to do. Communication typical of **control strategies** includes statements such as, "You need to be more considerate," "You must stop procrastinating," and "You have to listen to me." Statements like these create psychological reactance and lead to defensiveness, which leads to extrinsic conflict. Gibb says that hidden in attempts to control is the assumption by the controlling person that the other is somehow inadequate. Wouldn't that make you feel defensive?

Using a **problem orientation** allows others an equal contribution to the discussion and decision making. It sends the relational message that the other's position, opinions, and concerns are important. When you take a problem orientation approach to interacting with others, they are likely to be more committed to the resolution of the problem. Just as individuals may respond with psychological reactance when feeling controlled, individuals who feel they have a voice in decision making are more likely to commit to the decision's implementation. Statements that illustrate a problem orientation include, "We are in this together," "What can we do to solve this problem?" and "What do you think?"

> ## Defensive versus Supportive Behaviors
> Defensive and supportive climates can be created and maintained with communication behaviors
>
> **Defensive Behaviors**
> 1. Control strategies
> 2. Superiority
> 3. Evaluation
> 4. Neutrality
> 5. Strategy
> 6. Certainty
>
> **Supportive Behaviors**
> 1. Problem orientation
> 2. Equality
> 3. Description
> 4. Empathy
> 5. Spontaneity
> 6. Provisionalism

Take a Closer Look

Sometimes when your group has a competitive environment or spirit, it means that there is a lack of compatibility between group goals and the goals of individual members. What should you do?

Try this: Create a cooperative climate!

Instead of allowing the competitive attitudes of group members to become more intense and inhibit cooperation in the group, try to find something on which all members can agree. Even if the members don't go along with you, discovering these opportunities to agree should push the group climate toward the more cooperative end of the continuum. Agreement tends to be reinforcing in that, before too long, others in the group will begin to "pay back" your agreement with their cooperation. Over time, the environment of your group should become more cooperative.

Superiority/Equality

Communicating **superiority** creates defensiveness by demonstrating that we perceive ourselves to be better than others, and that quickly leads to extrinsic conflict. Superiority is characterized by comments such as, "You do not know what you are doing," and, "I have had more experience with this type of situation; I will handle it." This sends the relational message that the other's opinion is not worthy, his expertise is not valued, or that he is not important.

Equality, by contrast, involves treating others with respect and valuing their thoughts and opinions, regardless of their knowledge about the topic, their status, age, or position. People who *appear* to be of lower status or position are capable of having profound insights. Communication illustrating equality would be, "What do you think?" and, "I never thought of it that way; let's explore this idea together further."

Evaluation/Description

If a communicator appears to be evaluating you, either through tone of voice, expression, or message content, you will likely go into a protection mode. This kind of communication is often perceived as an attack on a person's self-esteem. The person feeling attacked then focuses energy on defense, which draws his or her focus from the problem to be solved.

When communicating with others, you should first *describe* before forming evaluations. This is not to say that you cannot evaluate behavior, but before jumping to conclusions, you should demonstrate that you are attempting to understand. Through description, you may create a more supportive climate. To be descriptive is to be factual without offering an opinion.

If you look at the descriptions provided in the box, can you say with certainty that the behaviors indicate rudeness, pushiness, or unfairness? Based on the behaviors described, there *may* be other possible interpretations. Could Kate have not realized she bumped into someone? Or did she softly say she was sorry but was not heard? Could Tom have had an urgent message? Could Stacey have valid reasons for her decision that were, indeed, fair? The answers to these questions are, *maybe*. We cannot be entirely sure without more information. The point is we need to be descriptive if we want to avoid extrinsic conflict by creating a defensive climate.

Neutrality/Empathy

One of the best ways to devalue someone is to respond in a way that communicates a lack of caring. **Neutrality** communicates that you simply do not care about the person or what he or she is saying. Using the supportive strategy of **empathy** means approaching a discussion with the intent to understand the other person's position from his or her point of view. This is not to be confused with sympathy, or responding with how we would feel in a particular situation. To be empathic is to express genuine interest in hearing what others have to say; it is one of the most confirming communication forms. Some examples of empathic responses are, "Kate, you must feel very upset by your layoff," and, "Stacey, I can only imagine how you must feel right now." To respond with neutrality, you might use responses like, "It doesn't matter to me," and, "Whatever you want."

If you want to create and maintain a supportive climate in your group, practice responding in ways that demonstrate that you care and understand.

Take a Closer Look

Kate is rude.	**Tom is pushy.**	**Stacey is unfair.**

Each of these statements is an evaluation. Now, if we were to take the time to describe the behavior that made us conclude that Kate is rude, Tom is pushy, and Stacey is unfair, we might come up with the following descriptive statements:

- Kate bumped into me without acknowledging it. She didn't say she was sorry or excuse herself.
- Tom kept phoning me after I told him I was too busy to talk.
- Stacey didn't give me the opportunity to work on the marketing project.

Strategy versus Spontaneity

To use **strategy** is to communicate that you have a hidden agenda. There is something motivating your communication that is not initially revealed to others. You try to manipulate others in the effort to gain some advantage. Have you ever had someone ask you, "What are your plans Friday night?" And you respond with, "I am free. Do you want to do something?" only to hear, "Oh good, can you babysit?" Somehow, this approach asking us to babysit feels like a trick. Another stereotypical example is the feeling when you walk into a sales presentation. You suspect that everything from the first handshake to the free dinner is carefully scripted to get you to buy something. Your defenses are activated and you begin to interpret everything that is said to you as part of a sneaky plot to buy that time-share in an exotic resort area. Strategic communication is revealed when you feel that people are flattering you for their own personal gain, or using self-disclosure to get you to reciprocate.

Spontaneity is characterized by honesty, directness, and good faith. It is saying: "I really need a babysitter Friday night; if you are free I would greatly appreciate your help." In a spontaneity condition, you probably won't be as suspicious of others and you will take things they say at face value. If they attempt to shake your hand, you can be sure it's an invitation to friendship and nothing else. When you get into the defensive mode, it is easy to misinterpret and start looking for hidden meanings in things that people say.

Certainty versus Provisionalism

People who communicate **certainty** seem to know all the answers. There is nothing they don't know, and they are quite sure about it. We tend to see this dogmatic individual as needing to be right and "wanting to win an argument rather than solve a problem." This behavior communicates to others a lack of interest in their position on an issue. The defensiveness that is created by certainty can be countered by provisionalism. **Provisionalism** means trying to explore issues, look for solutions, and consider the points of view of other group members.

Research tells us that supportive climates not only produce happier and more satisfied group members, but that groups with predominately supportive climates are more productive. When the climate becomes defensive, group members become distracted by the suspicion that they are being manipulated or attacked, the potential for destructive extrinsic conflict is high, messages are consistently misinterpreted, and the group loses sight of the problem to be solved. All the assumptions that we make about groups making better decisions are based on the broad assumption that the members are fully engaged in the solution of the problem. When the attention of the group is distracted from that problem-solving goal, defective decisions will be the result.

Summary

There was a lot of territory covered in this chapter, so we'll try to boil down the answer to the question, "What should I take from this chapter?" First, you should understand that every group member has the potential for leadership. You don't have to be *the* leader to exhibit leadership; you just have to use influence to help the group somehow mover closer to its goals. You should also understand that every group is unique, and that there is no single leadership style or approach that is going to be successful in every group. You will have to understand the functions of leadership, and then you will have to adapt what you know to each particular situation. There are many suggestions in this chapter to help you accomplish this. Look at the leadership styles approach, the situational leadership approach, and the information on transformational leadership to get some insight about how to adapt to your group.

You should also try to understand the bases of interpersonal power and how they can be used as a tool of leadership. Remember that those power bases can be easily abused, especially legitimate and coercive power, and that abuse can prevent your group from accomplishing its goals.

Finally, you should take with you an appreciation for conflict. If you are a member of a small decision making group, conflict can be your best friend and your worst enemy. Conflict related to the task, intrinsic conflict, unleashes the real power of small groups by allowing the clash of divergent points of view. This clash leads to a synthesis of ideas which the group members could not have created if they were working alone. This clash exploits the synergy of the group and makes the solution of complex problems possible.

However, conflict can also be your worst enemy. Extrinsic conflict, related to personalities, can distract your group from its task and even destroy the group itself. Although there are a lot of sources of extrinsic conflict, this chapter explored two common causes: differences in culture (very important in the age of the global economy), and the defensive climates that are created when interpersonal sensitivity is overlooked in conversations. Being aware of the roots of conflict and understanding management strategies can help your group stay together, make complex decisions, and provide all the members with a satisfying experience!

Communication for Today's Student

Chapter 12 – What are the Roles of Leadership and Power in Group Dynamics?

Exercise 12.1 – Leadership Strengths and Weaknesses

Answer the survey below to determine your strengths and weaknesses as a transformational leader. Would you make an excellent, fair, or poor candidate for the student ambassador program?

5 Strongly Agree   4 Agree   3 Somewhat Agree   2 Disagree   1 Strongly Disagree

I handle difficult people well in difficult situations.

I listen to conflicting opinions without criticism.

When I critique others, I focus on their actions and not their personality.

I encourage others to give input when working in a group.

I contribute valuable information when working in a group.

I encourage suggestions that are divergent from groupthink.

I am adaptable in stressful situations.

I do not participate in sidebar conversations.

I am punctual and encourage others to be.

I use humor when dealing with stressful tasks.

TOTAL

SMALL GROUP PRESENTATIONS

After reading this chapter, you should be able to:

- Discuss the aspects of participating in a small group.
- Describe the characteristics of small groups.
- Explain the role responsibilities of small group members.
- Identify ways to create effective small group experiences.
- Explain the application of the reflective thinking process in small group problem solving.
- Describe the small group presentation formats.

Key Terms

Brainstorming	Primary audience	Self-oriented goals
Forum	Process	Small group
Group-oriented goals	Reflective thinking process	Symposium
Panel discussion	Secondary audience	

Facing image Photo courtesy of Charles Long.

Makay et al: From *Public Speaking: Choices for Effective Results* by John Makay, Mark Butland, and Gail Mason.
Copyright © 2008 by Kendall Hunt Publishing Company. Reprinted by permission.

13 Scenario

Ariel threw her phone across the room.

"Calm down, Ariel," Cassandra said.

"I can't stand working in groups," Ariel yelled.

"What happened now?" Cassandra asked as she readied herself for her date.

"Mya is ignoring my calls," Ariel said. "She's not even giving me the respect of letting it ring and then go to voice mail. She's sending me straight to voicemail. Then Ryan is using the whole 'I'm a student athlete' excuse as his reason for not showing up. Kevin is a fool. There's no need to explain that."

"You have Kevin in your group?" Cassandra sighed. "Good luck."

"I have no luck," Ariel groaned. "Not with this group."

"Sorry, Ariel," Cassandra said, grabbing her coat. "I'm heading out. Don't stress too much. We all get horrible groups."

"I guess," Ariel muttered as she pressed "send" to call Mya, only to be greeted with her voice mail again.

What suggestions would you give Ariel to help her corral her group members into a cohesive, productive, task-oriented group?

Respond Here

Small Groups in Life

Small groups are a part of life. If you are on the editorial board of your school newspaper or are an organizer of the community blood drive, you are a member of a small group. If you are a member of a church, a musical, athletic, or academic group, you are a member of a small group. Think about how many groups you have participated in, and realize your membership in small groups may increase after you leave college. In business, academic life, government, and civic affairs, tasks are defined and completed through small-group communication. Many of the major decisions affecting your life are made by small groups. College admissions departments, school boards, and zoning boards are a few groups whose policies directly influence behavior.

As a homeowner, you may have an opportunity to present before a governing board. Perhaps you are a budding environmentalist who has noticed that the city has been pruning trees excessively or is making plans to eliminate landmark trees in order to widen streets. You take an opportunity to encourage the city council to approach city growth in a more "green" fashion. As a parent, you speak before the school board to convince them to eliminate vending machine drinks that contain sugar and/or caffeine. You argue that these are not healthy choices for young school children. In these situations, you have asked to speak before some group. As a professional, however, you receive requests to speak before a group because of your expertise. A state senator might talk to the local League of Women Voters about proposed state legislation. An

Small groups are a part of life and you may have opportunities to speak before your city council, school board, or other community groups.

insurance agent presents a bid before the city council or school board. As the chair of a university-funded organization, you present a budget request before the school's Apportionment Board, the group that allocates funds to college organizations.

Participating in a Small Group

The most common way to be involved in groups is to participate in a small group. Groups meet for a variety of purposes. Sometimes the purpose of a small group meeting is to discuss a current problem. For example, if your organization is low on funds. You must find a way to raise money. A group of individuals wanting to become a recognized group on campus, needs to think of a strategy for presenting your case to the appropriate governing body. Everyone contributes to the discussion, and usually a designated leader facilitates the discussion. In college, study groups, sororities and fraternities, residence halls, honorary societies, academic groups, athletic groups, and church groups are just some of the possible ways you connect with others through small group communication.

Speaking as an Individual Before a Group

A second way to be involved with a small group is by speaking before one. This is considered public speaking and is the focus of this text book. Unlike regular

Chances are you've been involved in various small groups, such as a study group, during college.

public speaking, however, you may have two audiences, not one. The *primary audience* is the small group, such as a seven-member school board, a five-member city council, or a ten-member Apportionment Board. Your purpose is to provide information, to express a concern, or attempt to persuade. Also in attendance, however, may be a *secondary audience*. This is a collection of individuals who attend the open meeting for any number of reasons, including simply observing its proceedings. It's possible these individuals may have no knowledge or interest in your specific topic, and did not know you were planning to speak.

In a situation involving both primary and secondary audiences, do you construct a message for the primary audience, accepting the fact that the secondary audience may not understand the context, concern or content? Or do you construct a message that takes into account both audiences, knowing that for members of the primary audience, some of the information will be unnecessary or redundant? Complexity of the issue, size of the secondary audience, and time constraint are a few of the factors to consider before developing your message.

Speaking as a Member of a Group Before a Group

Alternatively, you may find yourself in a third speaking situation where you are a member of a small group presenting before another group. This may occur in your business class when you are part of a group presenting a case study, in a psychology class when your group presents results of its research project, or in a public relations class when you are asked, as a group, to present your public relations campaign. There are many instances in college when you work as a group to accomplish a task and report the results to your classmates. In your community, as a health care professional, you may be asked to join a panel with several other health care professionals to discuss the health care crisis before a group of senior citizens. The focus is not just on you, but on your group.

Many contexts are possible with the small group presentation, including being the only person who speaks before a small group or being one of many individuals who speak before a group. In some instances you will find yourself on a panel with individuals you have never met and in others you will participate in significant small group interaction before your group presents. Given our interest in helping you become the most effective speaker possible regardless of context, this chapter will focus on (1) working in small groups, and (2) presenting in small groups. In order to work in a small group, it is helpful to know the characteristics of small groups, including purpose, goals, and size. When presenting in small groups, each person should understand his or her role responsibilities, and the members should consider which group format is most appropriate for the purpose and audience. Included in this chapter are suggestions for working in a small group and small group performance guidelines.

Photo courtesy of Charles Long

When presenting in small groups, members need to consider which format is most appropriate for the occasion.

Working in a Small Group

In a college classroom, whether or not you were able to choose your "groupmates," the members of your group, these are the individuals with whom you must interact and cooperate. Each person brings to the group his or her own predispositions, attitudes, work ethic, personality, knowledge, and ability. You may find your groupmates friendly, fascinating, frustrating, or infuriating. Likewise, they will have their own perceptions of you and of each other. Regardless, in all but the most dire circumstances, you will traverse the hills and valleys of group work with these people.

Characteristics of Small Groups

We should acknowledge that many academic institutions have semester-long courses devoted to the topic of small group communication, and we could discuss small group characteristics indefinitely. However, for our purposes, three characteristics seem to be most relevant to the public speaking classroom.

Shared purpose. One characteristic of a small group is that group members share a purpose for communication, unlike a collection of individuals who share the same physical space. Seven people waiting in line for tickets to see the Los Angeles Lakers are not considered members of a small group. Neither are five people sharing a taxi from the Dallas-Fort Worth airport or eight people sitting in a dentist's waiting room. They lack a communication purpose. But if the individuals waiting in line for tickets interact with each other to form a cooperative so that only one of the seven individuals will wait in line for tickets at subsequent games, they would then have a shared purpose that would guide communication in all future meetings.

Group-oriented and self-oriented goals. A second characteristic of small groups is that members usually have both group-oriented and self-oriented goals. **Group-oriented goals** center around specific tasks to be performed, whereas **self-oriented goals** relate to the individual's personal needs and ambitions. Say you are a member of a small group charged with the responsibility of determining policies of a new campus radio station. Some of the tasks you face are developing station operating policies, purchasing equipment, and attracting advertisers. As an individual, however, a self-oriented goal may be to emerge as leader of the group in order to demonstrate leadership potential. Self-oriented goals may complement group-oriented goals, or they may provide distracting roadblocks.

A group with an even number needs to determine what to do in the event of a tie vote on an issue.

Size. A third characteristic of small groups is group size. Scholars agree that a group must have a minimum of three members to be considered a small group. Communication professor Vincent DiSalvo notes that the ideal group size is from five to seven members (DiSalvo 1973, 111–112). According to Philip E. Slater, "These groups are large enough for individuals to express their feelings freely and small enough for members to care about the feelings and needs of other group members" (Slater 1958). However, a three-person group may lose effectiveness if one member is left out or if one member withdraws or chooses not to contribute. Also, groups with even numbers need to have some mechanism in place for solving the problem of a potential tie. As groups grow in numbers, the need for coordination and structure increases.

Role Responsibilities

When you become a group member, how you communicate is shaped, in large part, by your role in the group. If you have been appointed leader or have a special expertise that sets you apart from the other members, you may be given more responsibility than the other members.

Group roles evolve quickly and if you are the appointed leader, you will likely have more responsibility than other members.

Roles quickly emerge in small groups. While one group member emerges as the leader, taking the initiative in setting the group's agenda, another is uncommunicative and plays a minor role in group discussions. Still other members of the group may try to dominate the discussion, oppose almost every point raised, and close their minds before the discussion begins (Bales 1953, 111–61).

The role you assume determines how you will communicate in the group and how effective the group will be. Although there are many types of roles, we focus on two broad categories: your role as a group leader and your role as a group member.

Leader Responsibilities

You may be elected or appointed as leader of a group, or you may emerge as leader over time. As leader, you need to be aware of the group's *process and the relationships* among group members. Behaviors that relate to *process* are designed to help the group complete the task. These include *providing direction and purpose, keeping the group on track, and providing clarifying summaries.*

Provide direction and purpose. As part of your responsibility to provide direction and purpose, you may choose to open the meeting with action-directed comments ("We are here to establish whether or not it is feasible to add another organization to our college") or to examine items on an agenda. Once the discussion begins, others will contribute, but it is the leader's role to focus the meeting at the start.

Keeping the group on track. Keeping the group on track simply means making sure the group does not drift too far from the task at hand. If you are talking about offering healthy alternatives in the cafeteria line, it is easy to start talking about favorite foods or incidents that occurred in the cafeteria or people who work or who eat in the cafeteria. While *some* extraneous conversation help build relationships among group members, the leader is responsible for making sure time is not wasted and the group does not get side-tracked on irrelevant issues.

Provide a clarifying summary. Groups, like the individuals who comprise them, can be confused by the information they hear. Warning signs include questions for clarification, puzzled looks, and drifting attention. When you sense confusion, one of the best ways to move forward is to provide a clarifying summary, which recaps what has just occurred. For example, after hearing evidence and testimony at a student disciplinary hearing, the board voted that a student (Martin) was guilty of vandalism. After some time, the group was getting nowhere in terms of determining a punishment. As a leader, you say,

> We've agreed that Martin is guilty of vandalism, and that his actions are worthy of punishment, but we seem to be stuck on the concept of expulsion. We agree that suspension is too lenient, and expulsion is more warranted. The confusion seems to rest on how we are interpreting 'expulsion,' with some thinking the student may never return to our school and others thinking the student may return after a specified period of time, provided certain conditions are met.

With this type of clarifying summary, you have eliminated suspension from further discussion and identified the source of confusion. Clarifying summaries help bring focus back to the meeting.

In addition to facilitating the group's *process*, an effective group leader is concerned with *relationship* aspects, which facilitate communication. An effective leader will draw information from participants, keep group communication from being one-sided, and try to maintain the cohesiveness of the group. Ultimately, the relationship aspects allow the group to accomplish its task.

Draw information from participants. Each person has something to contribute to the group, whether it is in the form of offering specific information, analyzing the issue, or being creative. However, some people are hesitant to speak even when they have something valuable to contribute. Their reasons may range from communication anxiety to uncertainty about their role in the group. As a leader, draw information from participants by directing questions to those who remain silent, asking each group member to speak, and being supportive when a normally quiet member makes a comment in the hope of encouraging additional responses at a later time. Getting everyone to contribute is particularly important when one or more members of the group seem to dominate the discussion. It is up to the group leader to make sure the group benefits from the combined wisdom of all its members.

Try to keep group communication from being one-sided. A leader should try to keep group communication from being one-sided. We often have preconceived ideas of how something should be done. While dissent is healthy, these ideas may be obstacles to group communication if the leader allows the discussion to become one-sided. The leader needs to recognize when one point of view is dominating the discussion. Inviting others into the discussion or providing a varying opinion yourself may open up the discussion for multiple perspectives.

Photo courtesy of Charles Long.

How can a group leader encourage everyone to contribute to the discussion?

Try to maintain the cohesiveness of the group. As a leader, you should try to maintain the cohesiveness of the group. You want the group to see themselves as a group and function as a group, not as a collection of individuals. Everyone needs to work toward the group goal, while not ignoring his or her personal goals. Nothing is inherently wrong with a heated discussion, especially when the issue is controversial. But when the discussion turns into a shouting match, it is no longer productive. In a conflict situation, the leader should acknowledge the person's point of view but suggest that the problem be analyzed from other perspectives as well. Conflict is healthy, but unproductive conflict is a major obstacle to task completion. Keeping communication flowing effectively and making sure members feel their contributions are valued are important to the overall cohesiveness of the group.

Member Responsibilities

Being an active participant is the most important responsibility of each group member. An active participant contributes to the discussion, shares responsibility for task completion, and works effectively with other group members. Some group members believe that their participation is unnecessary because others will pick up their slack. Others view the experience as less important than other college work or activities. Complaining about group members is nothing new. Here are common complaints about other group members:

- Doesn't work or prepare enough
- Others have to nag group members to get work done
- Procrastinates
- Doesn't keep group members informed of content of presentation
- Information in presentation overlaps too much
- Information is excessive or too brief
- Too controlling
- Too apathetic
- Doesn't return calls or email
- Difficult to contact
- Doesn't stay after class to check with group
- Doesn't come to class on group work days
- Doesn't proofread PowerPoint

The previous is only a partial list of complaints we hear about group members. We understand that students take several academic courses. They have a social and/or work life, and priorities differ among students. But once you are part of a group, your actions have an impact on the other people in that group. In a classroom setting, you may not be thrilled with the topic, the assignment, or the other group members. But you do need to work with your group in order to complete the required assignment. Actively working to complete your individual tasks and being available and cooperative will make the situation better for all involved. Fulfill a commitment to the group.

Suggestions for Group Members

The following seven suggestions are designed to create the most effective small group experience within the context of your classroom. Many of these translate easily to experiences outside the college classroom. The suggestions are derived partially from *Speak from Success* by Eugene Ehrlich and Gene R. Hawes (1984, 133).

Know the constraints of the assignment. Read the syllabus or any other material given to you related to the assignment. Make sure everyone agrees as to the constraints of the assignment. The following are some questions that may guide your group:

- When does the group present?
- How much time does the group have to present?
- Does each speaker have the same amount of time?
- What information needs to be included in the presentation?
- Are presentational aids required?
- Does each speaker use a set of note cards? Is there a restriction?
- Is there audience involvement at some point during the group presentation?
- Can group members interrupt each other to comment or add insight?
- Is there a paper required? Or an outline?
- How many and what type of sources are required, and should they be cited during the presentation?
- Does the group choose its format, or is there a particular format that is required?
- Are students being graded individually, as a group, or both?
- Will there be any peer evaluations?

Photo courtesy of Charles Long

Most of your group work occurs before you present, as you spend time defining your purpose, researching, and organizing your message.

Work to achieve group goals. Instructors understand that each individual is concerned about his or her own grade. However, the purpose of a group assignment is to work collectively and collaboratively. Make group goals your top priority. Making a commitment to the group means making a commitment to achieve group goals at each meeting. When you feel strongly about your position, it is legitimate to try to convince the group you are correct. But if others disagree, it is important that you listen to their objections and try to find merit in them. You need an objective detachment from your own proposals to enable you to place the group's goals above your own. A group needs a shared image of the group, in which individual aspirations are subsumed under the group umbrella that strives for the common good.

Be responsible for completing your part of the assignment. Group membership brings with it a set of roles and responsibilities. It may not have been your choice to work in a group or to work with that specific group of individuals. The fact is, the assignment is mandatory. Everyone has a life. Everyone has distractions in their lives. You may be very busy, or you may be uninterested, but your group needs your help. If a group member volunteers to make the PowerPoint presentation consistent from speaker to speaker, you need to make sure that person has your slides when they are requested. If you are supposed to make contact with city officials or individuals who may help with a fundraising idea, you need to come to the group with that information. Do not be responsible for the group's progress being delayed, or the task not completed. If you cannot attend a meeting, make sure someone knows. Send your work with someone else. If you do get behind, make sure group members know so they have an opportunity to respond in some way.

Research sufficiently. Most group work involves research of some type. When you are finished researching, you should feel confident that you have ample support or that the topic or issue has been covered in enough depth. Depending on the group's purpose or goal, research may involve surfing the Internet, conducting a library search, looking through the local Yellow Pages, calling different social service agencies in town, or interviewing members of the local city council. If your group sought to determine what Americans consider the most important political issues for the 2008 presidential campaign, locating *one* website or *one* magazine article is not sufficient. If your group wanted to determine which pizza place in town served the best pizza, selecting two from the Yellow Pages is not sufficient, particularly in a city that has ten or more places that sell pizza. If you have been assigned to interview city council members, talking to one person for five minutes is not sufficient.

Communicate effectively and efficiently. Different people bring to a group a wide range of knowledge and views that help complete the task. Group discussion often produces creative approaches that no one would have thought of alone. Group involvement through communication increases the likelihood that the group's decision will be accepted and supported by all group members and by the broader community. Do not waste time and do not monopolize the group discussions or the presentation.

Most group work involves some research so you feel confident that the topic has been covered in enough depth.

Avoid personal attacks. Comments like, "You have to be an idiot to believe that will work," or "My six-year-old cousin has better ideas than that," accomplish nothing. On the contrary, these comments are so antagonistic that they make it virtually impossible for people to work together. If you do not like an idea, say so directly by focusing on the idea, not the person, such as "It may be difficult to get funds for that project," or "I don't think parents will want to volunteer their time for that." Try not to make your disagreement too negative. Find areas of agreement, where possible.

Leave personal problems at home. Group conflicts are often the result of personal problems brought to the group meeting. A fight with a family member, a poor test grade, an alarm clock that failed to ring, a near-accident on the highway, or school or work pressure can put you in a bad mood for the meeting and lessen your tolerance for other group members. Although an outburst of anger may make you feel better for the moment, it can destroy the relationships you have with other members of the group.

Antagonistic comments can be permanently damaging and make it impossible for the group to function.

Reflective Thinking Process

You may be called upon in a college course or in an organization to work with others on a problem-solving task. On campus for example, the Student Senate needs to find ways to get more students involved in campus events, while off campus the local Chamber of Commerce is trying to find ways to entice new businesses to join their organization. Groups are faced with small and large problems on a regular basis. Almost 100 years ago, John Dewey developed a theory of reflective thinking that is now applied to group communication (1910). If you are working on a problem-solving task, consider following the following seven steps:

1. Identify and Define the Problem

The first step of this process is to make sure group members understand and agree on what the problem is. Otherwise, the discussion may scatter into many different directions and time will be misused, for example, a newly elected Student Senate member wants to work with a group to deal with student complaints about residence hall assignments. One problem is that students are not given enough options about where they may live or with whom. A second problem is that the administration does not process complaints effectively. Third, students are unhappy about meal plan options and residence hall rules and contracts. Does the group want to take on all of these problems, or to focus on the complaint process? The first thing the group needs to do is identify the problem.

2. Analyze the Problem

In the process of analyzing the problem, group members need to identify what they know about the problem, what they do not know, and what resources are available to help them acquire more information. In this step, group members should find out what caused the problem, how long the problem has been an issue, and the extent of the problem. If only one student has complained about her residence hall assignment, there is not much of a problem. But if significant staff time is devoted to addressing students' complaints, then the problem is significant. Perhaps the problem started when a new administrator took office. Perhaps the problem is ongoing. This is the information-gathering, sorting, and evaluation stage of the reflective thinking process.

3. Determine Criteria for an Acceptable Solution

Many groups skip this step, whether they are newly formed groups in a college classroom or well-established policy groups in a community. However, it is a mistake to come into the problem-solving process with a firm idea of what you think is the best solution. Whatever solution your group suggests must meet agreed-upon criteria or standards. Criteria will differ vastly from situation to situation. For example, if four students turned in a group paper that was clearly plagiarized, before determining the punishment, an instructor might consider the following criteria:

In order to present a solution, there needs to be sufficient information-gathering, sorting, and evaluation of the problem.

- Is (the punishment) it fair (to the four students and the rest of the class)?
- Is it appropriate (given the nature of the misconduct)?
- Will it deter future misconduct (on the part of the students who cheated as well as other students who might be contemplating misconduct)?

Criteria related to the residence hall complaints issue might include the following:

- Does the solution consider both the needs of students and college administrators?
- Does the solution apply to all students living in residence halls, not just incoming freshmen?
- Does the solution allow students to change residence halls?
- Does the solution recognize that freshmen do not have cars?

Establishing criteria keeps group members from simply proposing their solution. Any solution presented needs to meet the criteria established by group members.

4. Generate Possible Solutions

According to Dewey, suspended judgment is critical at this point in the decision-making process (Ross and Ross 1989, 77). Group members need to identify available options without stifling the process by providing immediate evaluation. **Brainstorming,** which involves generating as many solutions as possible without critical evaluation, may be useful during this step of the reflective thinking process. Be creative. Encourage group members to think "outside the box." Avoid the temptation to say, "that won't work," "that's not possible," or worse, "that's a dumb idea." Instead, generate ideas until you agree you have exhausted the possibilities. If possible, give yourselves time to think about these solutions before evaluating or moving on to the next step. For the teacher who caught the group of students plagiarizing, some of the punishment options include ignoring it, talking to the students, requiring them to give a group presentation on the evils of plagiarism, requiring them to write another paper, lowering their grade on the paper, failing them for the assignment, failing them for the semester, and reporting the students to the Office of Judicial Affairs.

Regarding the problem of residence hall complaints, the group may develop several options, including changing the forms students fill out, suggesting a policy change, providing clearer, more specific information to students, and establishing a committee to hear complaints not resolved between students and administration. The important thing is to *have* alternatives, and not be single-minded in your approach.

5. Choose the Solution That Best Fits the Criteria

Each solution identified in Step Four needs to be evaluated based on the criteria established in Step Three. Ideally, the best solution is one that meets all the established criteria. If that does not happen, the group may need to revisit the possible solutions, and determine if amending one of the solutions might result in it meeting all of the established criteria. The instructor who caught students plagiarizing needs to evaluate her possible options by the criteria she has set. For example, if she ignores the misconduct, is that fair to those in the class who did not plagiarize? Is failing the students for the course an appropriate punishment for the students' misconduct?

In terms of the residence hall complaints, does changing the form students fill out meet both the needs of students and administrators? Will the form address the issue of changing residence hall assignments? Will a committee be formed to hear complaints from all students in residence halls? An option might not meet each of the criteria perfectly, but the point of this step is to choose the solution that best meets the criteria. If multiple options are acceptable, the group needs to determine how it will decide on which solution to implement.

6. Implement the Solution

Implementing the solution means putting it into effect. It is one thing to decide that a car wash will raise the most money; it is another thing to advertise, staff, supply, and conduct the fundraiser. The work involved in implementing the solution will vary according to the problem. For example, an instructor dealing with plagiarism can determine the best solution and then communicate that decision to the students and/or administration. If the group dealing with residence hall complaints decides to form a committee to hear complaints, then implementing the solution entails setting up committee structure, policies and procedures, soliciting membership, and informing students about the committee.

In a public speaking class, your group may be involved in determining a solution and suggesting how it could be implemented, but it is possible the group will not be involved with the actual implementation. For example, your group may be given the task of determining how to get students more involved in their department's activities. Your group could work through Step Five and decide that the best solution is to advertise activities earlier so that students can work them into their schedules. As a group, you may present Steps One through Five to a faculty committee, but Step Six might ultimately be the committee's responsibility.

7. Reassess

Reassessing at some point prevents the group from saying "we're done" after implementing the solution. It is an important part of the process because you evaluate your group's success or lack thereof. Fundraisers are carefully planned and executed, but still may fail. New policies are developed with the best intentions, but may still be ineffective. Do you try the same fundraiser again? Do you keep the new policy? Before you answer "yes" or "no" to these questions, the group needs to answer some other questions. Did the fundraiser fail because it was held at a bad time? Was it advertised sufficiently? Did it ask too much of the people working it or attending the fundraiser? In other words, the group needs to decide what contributed to the lack of success. Similarly, with the ineffective policy, did administration evaluate its effectiveness too soon? Were students inadequately informed? Was administration insufficiently trained? Those engaged in reassessment need to discuss what factors influenced the lack of success. In a sense, this final step can be the beginning step of a new process, if the solution has not been effective.

The seven-step reflective thinking process is one way to help groups move through the problem-solving process. It is certainly not the only way. However, regardless of the approach groups take, it is important that a clear process be established that allows for rational, deliberative discussion of all relevant aspects of the problem. A leader should help the group through this process, and group members should contribute productively throughout the process.

Presenting in Small Groups

Just because you are part of a small group discussion does not mean that you will report your results through some type of oral presentation. Some groups prepare written reports that some administrator, council, or committee will evaluate. Sometimes the results of your deliberation are presented before a group, and in many instances a group presents before another group for other reasons. For example, a group of teachers who attended a workshop on working with gifted students present their observations of the workshop to the group of teachers who were unable to attend. Members of the League of Women Voters who attended the national convention present a summary of their experiences to the rest of the membership. Also, many careers have national conferences where people with similar interests have the opportunity to attend or present seminars and panel presentations.

Photo courtesy of Charles Long

When speaking in a small group format, you need to be aware of how your message fits in with those of the other group members.

Whether presenting as a group or as an individual to a group successful public speaking strategies are necessary. So all information presented in this textbook is relevant to this context. Audience analysis is essential. Any presentation you prepare should have a clear introduction, body, and conclusion. Your presentation should be well-research, sufficiently supported, and organized effectively. Your delivery should be engaging and extemporaneous. Be sure you are not too dependent on notes.

Speaking as a member of a group, however, involves additional reflection. First, it is important to find a small group format that best suits your purpose. Second, it is important that the speeches all group members give flow as though they were one coherent speech. The last section of this chapter describes a variety of small group formats concerns that need to be addressed before the group speaks, and makes suggestions for the presentation.

Small Group Formats

Most of your group work in class occurs before the day you present. You spend time defining your purpose, setting goals, distributing the work load, researching your topic/issues, and organizing your research into something meaningful. If in business or civic life, you are already an expert on the topic, your task is to determine what you need to bring to this particular presentation. It is possible that you never meet the other group members until moments before the presentation.

In a public speaking class, your instructor may suggest a particular small group format. In business or civic life, a moderator or facilitator decides how the group should present. It is also possible that you determine your format. Regardless, there are three main small group formats: panel discussion, symposium, and forum.

Panel Discussion

In a panel discussion, group members have an informal interchange on the issues in front of an audience. The positive and negative features of issues are debated, just as they were in the closed group meeting, but this time in front of an audience. When you are part of a panel discussion, it is important to keep in mind that you are talking for the benefit of the audience rather than for other group members. Although your responses are spontaneous, they should be thought out in advance, just as in any other public speaking presentation.

Panel discussions are directed by a moderator who attempts to elicit a balanced view of the issues and to involve all group members. The role of the moderator is to encourage the discussion—he or she does not take part in the debate. Moderators coordinate and organize the discussion, ask pertinent questions, summarize conclusions, and keep the discussion moving. Once the discussion is over, the moderator often opens the discussion to audience questions.

When you feel strongly about your position, you can try to convince others that you're correct. Ultimately, though, you need to put the group's goals above your own.

As you can tell from the previous description, the critical elements of a panel discussion are: (1) it is an informal discussion moderated or facilitated by someone who is not an active participant, (2) interaction should be distributed equitably among group members with no pre-determined time limit for each group member, and (3) generally, there are no prepared remarks.

Symposium

A symposium is more formal and predictable than a panel discussion. Instead of focusing on the interaction among group members, it centers on prepared speeches on a specified subject given by group members who have expertise on the subject. The topic and speakers are introduced by a moderator. A symposium is structured, and speakers are generally given a time frame for their comments. After the formal presentation, a panel discussion or forum may follow. This allows for interaction among group members, and for the audience to ask questions of individual speakers.

Forum

In a forum, group members respond to audience questions. Someone may provide a prepared statement, but it is also possible to introduce group members and their credentials, and then ask for audience questions. Unlike a panel discussion or the second half of a symposium, a forum does not include interactions among group members. The forum is very audience-centered.

The success of the forum depends on how carefully the audience has thought about the topic (the topic is announced in advance) and the nature of their questions. For example, school boards hold public hearings about their annual budget. In addition to the school board, the superintendent and district financial officer will be present. Generally, there is a presentation by the financial officer, and then anyone present at the meeting may ask questions. Questions could be asked about transportation, food service, athletics, computer equipment, and so on. If several concerned citizens show up with questions in mind, the meeting could last for hours. If no one in the community attends the meeting, then it will be very short.

A forum also needs a moderator. When the League of Women Voters holds a candidates' forum, selected League members collect questions from the audience and give them to the moderator who then addresses questions to the appropriate panelists. A forum is not just a collection of individuals, but a group of people who have been chosen for their interest in the topic/issue or because of their expertise.

Preparing to Present as a Group

When you prepare a speech for class, you are responsible for all aspects of the speech. As an individual, you need to prepare, practice, and present. Once you join a group, however, you need to be prepared, but you also need to be aware of how your speech fits into the other speeches, and the group needs to make sure everyone is viewing the presentation from a similar perspective. With this interest in mind, we present the following aspects of the presentation to consider *before* the group speaks. All group members should know and be in agreement with the following:

1. Speaker order
2. Formality of the presentation
   Can group members interrupt each other?
   Can group members wander from their prepared remarks?
3. Determine where will the group sit/stand?
   Group members need to realize that if they are all in front of the class, whether standing or speaking, audience members will be aware of them, even when they are not speaking.
   Will all sit and then stand up to speak or will all stand throughout the entire presentation?
   Should the group sit to the side and have the speaker stand in the middle of the front of the class?
4. Delivery
   Use note cards? Legal pad? PowerPoint slides?
   Prepare individually—think about eye contact (speak to the group, not the instructor), gestures, and vocal aspects
5. Time constraints for each speech
6. Determine how to signal if someone is speaking too long or if the group is going too long
7. Introduction, body, conclusion
   Who will deliver the group's introduction and conclusion?
   How will each person's introduction and conclusion relate to the group?
   How do you make transitions between speeches so all presentations are connected?
8. Presentational aids
   What is available in the classroom?
   Will they benefit the presentation?
   Who will be responsible for making them and setting them up?

If group members wait until they approach the front of the room to address these concerns, they will appear unprepared. Deciding where to stand, how to signal each other, and what the speaking order is will reduce awkwardness and uncertainty, and should give a more professional, polished look to the presentation.

General Suggestions for Presenting in a Small Group

The following guidelines will help you be a successful participant in a panel discussion, symposium, or forum. Many of the guidelines apply to all three group formats, but others apply just to one.

Limit the number of points you make. Since you will be given some time constraints, limit the number of points you make. Remember that each person has information to present. Your audience cannot process an overload of material. Be brief. Make your point as briefly and clearly as possible and do not confuse your listeners with too many details.

Avoid repetition. Avoid repetition by learning in advance what the other panelists will cover in their speeches. The job of assigning topics should be the responsibility of the presentation organizer. If the organizer is negligent, you may want to get in touch with the other panelists yourself. Keep communication channels open with your group members so you do not find yourself giving the same presentation as the person who spoke before you.

Try to meet in advance. Try to meet your fellow panelists in advance. When group members meet for the first time on stage, there is often an awkwardness in their interchange that comes from not knowing one another. This discomfort may be communicated to the audience.

Restrict your speech to the allotted time. If speakers exceed the time limit, the audience will find it difficult to sit through the entire program, and little opportunity will remain for a panel interchange or a question-and-answer period. In addition, by violating the time constraints, you may cause another speaker to modify his or her speech significantly. Staying within the allotted time frame is a necessary courtesy to the other group members.

Prepare for audience questions. Because the question-and-answer period is often the most important part of the program, spend as much time preparing for the questions as you did for your formal remarks. Anticipate the questions you are likely to be asked and frame your answers. During the question-and-answer period, be willing to speak up and add to someone else's response if none of the questions are being directed to you. When a fellow panel member finishes a response, simply say, "I'd like to make one more point that . . ." If, on the other hand, a question is directed to you that you think would be better handled by another panel member, say, "I think that considering her background, Therese is better able to answer that question."

Consider enhancing your presentation with visual aids. Simple visual aids are as appropriate in group presentations as they are in single-person public speaking. Coordinate the use of visual aids so information is not repeated by multiple speakers. Be consistent and professional. It is inconsistent to allow one group member to use the blackboard when the rest of the group has PowerPoint slides.

Photo courtesy of Charles Long

Simple visual aids are appropriate for group presentations, as long as you coordinate with other members.

Summary

We are all involved in small group activities whether they occur within or outside of the classroom. Opportunities exist for interacting within a group or speaking before a group. As a speaker, consider both primary and secondary audiences. As group members, we share a purpose for communication. Also, group members usually have both group-oriented and self-oriented goals, and group size influences the need for structure and how we communicate.

Each individual has responsibilities within the group setting regardless of the person's role. As leader, you can contribute to the group's process by providing direction and purpose, especially at the beginning of the meeting, keeping the group on track throughout the meeting, and providing a clarifying summary when appropriate. In terms of helping the group communicate effectively, the leader should draw information from participants, try to keep group communication from being one-sided, and try to maintain the cohesiveness of the group.

As a group member, you have several responsibilities, including knowing the constraints of the assignment, working to achieve group goals, being responsible for completing your part of the assignment, researching sufficiently, communicating effectively and efficiently, avoiding personal attacks, and leaving your personal problems at home. Following the seven-step reflective process helps to keep the group organized and focused and helps to make sure that members do not jump to quick solutions without sufficient analysis and deliberation.

When the occasion arises for you to present as a group member before an audience, it is important to determine whether a panel discussion, symposium, or forum best suits your needs and the needs of your audience. Your knowledge of public speaking and your individual skills come into play as you present before the group. However, it is important to meet as a group beforehand to determine such things as speaker order, amount of speaking time allotted for each individual, whether or not presentational aids will be useful, and who will be responsible for preparing such aids. Each person's presentation should cover only a few points. The presentations should not overlap, and group members should be prepared for audience questions. An effective presentation involves preparation on the part of all group members as well as attention to detail regarding content connection, transitions from speaker to speaker, and overall professional performance.

Communication for Today's Student

Chapter 13 – Small Group Presentations

Exercise 13.1 – Group Presentation

Groups are organized for a wide variety of reasons. Most often groups meet to discuss and solve a current problem. In this exercise, after agreeing on a leader and a set of operating rules, your group will follow the Reflective Thinking Process to solve a problem.

After completing the process, the group leader should prepare the group survey to submit to the instructor. The group reporter should be prepared to share the group experience with the class.

Part One:

Group membership:

_____

_____

_____

_____

_____

_____

Group Rules:

1.

2.

3.

4.

5.

6.

7.

8.

9.

10.

*Leader _____

Topic: _____

Step One: **Identify and Define the Problem**
Application:

Step Two: **Analyze the Problem**
Application:

Step Three: **Determine Criteria for an Acceptable Solution**
Application:

Step Four: **Generate Possible Solutions**
Application:

Step Five: **Choose the Solution that Best Fits the Criteria**
Application:

Step Six: **Implement the Solution**
Application:

Step Seven: **Reassess**
Application:

Part Two:

Group Membership:

_____

_____

_____

_____

_____

_____

Chapter 13 – Small Group Presentations

Exercise 13.1 Continued

Submit a copy of the survey below. All group numbers must have input in the final responses of the survey. PLEASE USE THE TERMINOLOGY FROM THE CHAPTER WHEN RESPONDING TO EACH QUESTION.

A. Identify the type of group in which you have just participated.

B. Who is the leader of the group?

C. What type of leader is he/she? Why?

D. Did you use the <u>seven</u> suggestions to create the most effective small group experience? Give us an example of how some of the suggestions were used.

E. What conflict did the group experience? What was the reason?

F. How was the conflict solved?

If your group were to be convened to address another problem, what recommendations would you make to ensure the group operates effectively?

*Leader_____

ENDNOTES

Avtgis, T., West, D., and Anderson, T. "Relationship Stages: An Inductive Analysis Indentifying Cognitive, Affective, and Behavioral Dimensions of Knapp's Relational Stages Model." *Eastern Communication Association: Communication Research Reports 15 (3)*.

Beebe, S. and Beebe, S. *Public speaking: An audience-centered approach*. 6th ed. Upper Saddle River, New Jersey: Pearson Education, 2006. Print.

Bobananovic, M.K. and Bobananovic, M. *Coping with Public Speaking Anxiety*. np. 2004.

Burnley, M., Cross, P. A., and Spanos, N. P. "The effects of stress inoculation training and skills training on the treatment of speech anxiety." *Imagination, Cognition and Personality* 12 (1992):355–366.

Cochran, Sylvia. List of Ivy League Colleges Online. 7 December 2011. web 26 May 2012 <http://www.brighthub.com/education/online-learning/articles/29201.aspx>.

Conner, Michael. Internet Addiction and Internet Sex. 2004. web 26 May 2012 <http://www.crisiscounseling.com/Articles/InternetAddiction.htm>.

Conner, Michael. Internet Addiction and Internet Sex. 2004. web 26 May 2012 <http://www.crisiscounseling.com/Articles/InternetAddiction.htm>.

Contributors of CBS. Tyler Clementi: Rutgers Suicide. 2010. web 24 May 2012 <http://www.cbsnews.com/2300-504083_162-10005019.html>.

Contributors of Divorce.com. "Worldwide Divorce Statistics." 2011. divorce.com. web 23 May 2012.

Contributors of Linguistics (2003, 5 May). Language and Power. web May 23, 2012, from Linguistics 50: http://www.linguistics.ucsb.edu/faculty/cumming/ling50/emcdefinitions.htm

Contributors of Teacher Today. Teach Today: What are the effects of Cyber Bullying. 2011. web 26 May 2012 <http://www.teachtoday.eu/en/Teacher-advice/Cyberbullying/What-are-the-effects-of-cyberbullying.aspx>.

Crannell, Kenneth. *Voice and Articulation: Developing Career Speech*. 2nd ed. Belmont, CA: Wadsworth, 1991.Print.

Knapp, M. Social Discourse. Boston: Allyn and Bacon, 1978. Print.

Knapp, M., and Vangelisti, A. Interpersonal Communication and Human Relationships, 3rd ed. Boston: Allyn and Bacon, 1995. Print.

Latimer, Matt. "Ex-Bush Aide on How Bill Clinton's Speech Bested Mitt Romney's." thedailybeast.com. *The Daily Beast*, 6 September 2012. Web. 16 June 2014.

Lee, Charlotte and Gura, Timothy. *Oral Interpretation*. Boston, MA: Houghton Mifflin, 1997. Print.

Malloy, John T. *New Men's Dress for Success*. New York, NY: Warner Books, 1988. Print.

Malloy, John T. *New Women's Dress for Success*. New York, NY: Grand Central Publishing, 1996. Print.

Mayer, Lyle. *Fundamentals of Voice and Diction*. New York, NY: McGraw-Hill, 2013. Print.

McCroskey, J. C. "Measures of Communication-Bound Anxiety." *Speech Monographs* 37 (1970): 269–277. Print.

National Center for Victims of Crime. National Center for Victims of Crime: Cyberstalking. 2003. web 25 May 2012 <http://www.ncvc.org/ncvc/main.aspx?dbName=DocumentViewer&DocumentID=32458>.

NHTSA contributors. Distracted Driving | National Highway Traffic Safety Administration | Texting and Driving. web 26 May 2012.

Oliver, R., Zelko., H and Holtzman, P. Communicative Speaking and Listening. New York: Holt, Rinehart and Winston, 1968. Print.

Osborn, M., and Osborn, S. Public Speaking 6th ed. Boston: Houghton Mifflin, 2003. Print.

Palika, Liz. "How Pets Help You Live Longer." 15 December 2008. petside.com. web 23 May 2012 <http://www.petside.com/article/how-pets-help-you-live-longer>.

Presley, Bill. CyberBullying.org. 2010. web 26 May 2012 <cyberbullying.org>.

Pring, Cara. The Social Skinny. 12 February 2012. web 18 May 2012 <http://thesocialskinny.com/100-more-social-media-statistics-for-2012/>.

Ridolfo, Jim. "Rhetorical Delivery as Strategy: Rebuilding the Fifth Canon from Practitioner Stories." *Rhetoric Review* 31.2 (2012): 117–129. Print.

Sameer Hinduja, Ph.D. and Justin W. Patchin, Ph.D. State Cyber Bullying Laws. April 2012. web 26 May 2012 <http://www.cyberbullying.us/Bullying_and_Cyberbullying_Laws.pdf>.

Savage, Dan. It Gets Better Project. 7 October 2010. web 26 May 2012 <http://www.itgetsbetter.org/blog/entry/welcome-to-the-it-gets-better-project/>.

Seiler, W., and Beal, M. Communication: Making Connections (6th ed.) New York: Harper Collins, 2005. Print.

Wallechinsky, D., Wallace, D., and Wallace, H. *The Book of Lists*. New York, NY: Bantam Books, 1977. Print.

GLOSSARY

A

Acceptance: Refers to our awareness of the feelings and emotions involved in diverse approaches to relationships and communication.

Acronym: A word abbreviated in such a way that it creates a new word or phrase so that something (a concept or process) is easy to remember.

Action-oriented listener: Listeners that prefer error-free and concise messages and they get easily frustrated with speakers who do not clearly articulate their message in a straightforward manner.

Active strategies: Require us to engage in interactions with others to learn additional information about others.

Adaptors: Behaviors that can indicate our internal conditions or feelings to other people.

Addition: This term refers to the extra sounds that a speaker adds to a word.

Adoption: When you want your audience to start doing something.

Affect display: A form of nonverbal behavior that expresses emotions.

Aggression: Occurs when one person voices concerns and frustration about a conflict without considering the other person's thoughts or feelings.

Aggressive talk: Talk that attacks a person's self concept with the intent of inflicting psychological pain.

Ambushing: Type of listener who will listen for information that they can use to attack the speaker.

Analogy: Establishes common links between similar and not-so-similar concepts.

Appreciative listening: This type of listening is for the pure enjoyment of listening to the stimuli.

Articulation: The verbalization of distinct sounds and how precisely words are formed.

Assertiveness: Taking the responsibility of expressing needs, thoughts, and feelings in a direct, clear manner.

Attitudes: Deeply felt beliefs that govern how one behaves. Also, a group of beliefs that cause us to respond in some way to a particular object or situation.

Attitudes: Learned predispositions to respond in favorable or unfavorable ways toward people or objects.

Attribution theory: The dominant theory that explains how people explain their own and others' behavior.

Autocratic leader: Leadership method based on direction and control of the leader. There is little discussion among followers.

Avoidance: A refusal to deal with conflict or painful issues.

Avoidance: Occurs when one or both individuals in a relationship do not address issues of conflict.

B

Bel: The unit to measure the intensity of a sound.

Beliefs: One's own convictions; what one thinks is right and wrong, true and false. Also, they are classified as statements of knowledge, opinion and faith.

Beliefs: Our personal convictions regarding the truth or existence of things.

Belonginess and love needs: Human need that refers to affiliation friendship and love.

Biased information search: Our propensity to seek out certain types of information and avoid others.

Bid: A question. Gesture, look, touch, or other single expression that says, "I want to feel connected to you."

Blind area: The part of the self known to others but not known to oneself.

Blind pane: That area in the Johari Window as an accidental disclosure area.

Body: Includes your main points and supporting material that reinforces your specific purpose and thesis statement.

Brainstorming: Generating as many solutions as possible without critical evaluation.

Brainstorming: Generating a list of ideas consistent with the goals of your speech.

Brainstorming: Is a technique used to generate as many unedited ideas as possible in a limited amount of time.

Breadth: The range of topics about which an individual discloses.

C

Causal reasoning: A persuasive and logic appeal which expresses a cause and therefore uses the word because which is either implicitly or explicitly.

Cause and Effect: Focus on way something happens and what the consequences of the event or action were.

Certainty: Behavior that communicates to others a lack of interest in their position on an issue; the person seems to know all the answers.

Channel: The route traveled by a message; the means it uses to reach the sender-receivers.

Chronemics: Communication through the way we conceptualize and adhere to time.

Chronological: Arrangement pattern in accordance to time.

Close relationship: Is strong, frequent and that lasts over a considerable period of time.

Clothing and Artifacts: The manner in which we communicate through our clothing choices and preferences as well as the adornment of our bodies with accessories; serves the purpose of beautification or identification.

Coercive power: Power to punish; members follow coercive leaders to avoid reprimand or punishment.

Collectivistic cultures: Cultures in which people practice collaboration with family, friends, and colleagues.

Commitment: A strong desire by both parties for the relationship to continue. In groups, is it the willingness of members to work together complete the group's task.

Communication: Any process in which people share information, ideas, and feelings.

Compatibility: Similar attitudes, personality, and a liking for the same activities.

Complaint: Expression of dissatisfaction with the behavior, attitude, belief, or characteristics of a partner of or someone else.

Comprehensive listening: This type of listening involves mindfully receiving and remembering new information.

Computer-mediated communication (CMC): A wide range of technologies that facilitate both human communication and the interactive sharing of information through computer networks, including e-mail, discussion groups, newsgroups, chat rooms, instant messages, and web pages.

Concrete: Refers to messages that are well-defined.

Conclusion: Supports the body of your speech, reinforces your message and brings your speech to a close.

Conflict resolution: Negotiation to find a solution to the conflict.

Connotative meanings: Reflect your personal, subjective definitions.

Consensus: Considers whether the behavior is unique to the individual or if they are behaving in the way that would be typically expected of others.

Consistency: Refers to whether an individual behaves the same way across contexts and at various times.

Constitutive rules: Tell us how to "count" different kinds of communication, revealing what we feel is appropriate.

Constructivism: Refers to the process we use to organize and interpret experiences by applying cognitive structures labeled schemata.

Content-oriented listener: Listeners that focus on the details of the message, and they pick up on the facts of the story and analyze it from a critical perspective.

Context: The place that the communication occurs.

Continuance: When your listeners are already doing the thing you want them to do.

Coordination: Requires that all information at a given level be of similar importance.

Costs: The problems associated with relationships.

Covariation theory: The idea that we decide whether peoples' behavior is based on either internal or external factors by using three different and important types of information: distinctiveness, consensus, and consistency.

Criticism: A negative evaluation of a person for something he or she has done or the way he or she is.

Cultural information: Information used in making predictions based on person's most generally shared cultural attributes such a language, shared values, beliefs, and ideologies.

Culture: Shared perceptions which shape the communication patterns and expectations of a group of people.

Culture: The ever-changing values, traditions, social and political relationships, and worldview created and shared by a group of people bound together by a combination of factors (which can include a common history, geographic location, language, social class, and/or religion.

Culture: Community of meaning; we all belong to multiple cultures and we come into contact with other cultures on a professional and social basis every day; people belong to a variety of nations, traditions, groups and organizations, each .of which has its own point of view, values and norms

D

Decibel: A decibel is one-tenth of 1 bel. It is named after Alexander Graham Bell, inventor of the telephone.

Decoding: Once the message is perceived and understood by the receiver, the decoding process occurs and that process is reversed.

Deductive reasoning: Drawing conclusions based on the connections between statements that serve as premises.

Deductive reasoning: Drawing conclusions based on the connections between statements that serve as premises.

Defensive Communication: When one partner tries to defend himself or herself against the remarks or behavior of the other.

Defensive listening: This type of listener perceives a threatening environment.

Definition through example: Helps the audience understand a complex concept by giving the audience a "for instance."

Definition through example: Assistance in understanding a complex concept by using "for instance".

Deletion: It is the omission of a sound(s) from a word.

Democratic leader: Adopts the Theory Y assumptions and creates an atmosphere of member integration, self-control, and participatory decision making; the input of subordinates is encouraged and is used to make decisions.

Denotative meanings: Literal, dictionary definitions that are precise and objective.

Depth: The level of personal information a person reveals on a particular topic.

Derogatory language: Consists of words that are degrading or tasteless.

Deterrence: Your goal is to convince your listeners not to start something.

Disconfirming: Listeners that deny the feelings of the speaker.

Discontinuance: An attempt to persuade your listeners to stop doing something.

Discriminate listening: This type of listening helps us understand the meaning of the message.

Distinctiveness: Refers to whether or not a person typically behaves the same way with the target, or receiver, of the behavior.

Diversity: Refers to the unique qualities or characteristics that distinguish individuals and groups from one another.

Dual perspective: Recognize another person's point of view and take that into account as you communicate.

Dynamism: A lively, active, vigorous, and vibrant quality.

E

Emblem: A nonverbal behavior that has a distinct verbal referent or even a denotative definition, and it is often used to send a specific message to others.

Emotional intelligence: The ability to understand and get along with others.

Emotional intelligence Is described as the ability to understand and get along with others.

Empathetic listening: This type of listening is used to help others.

Empathy: Approaching a discussion with the intent to understand the other person's position from his or her point of view.

Empathy: The process of mentally indentifying with the character and experiences of another person. The ability to recognize and identify with someone's feelings.

Emphasis: To draw attention to a specific word or phrase.

Empty words: Overworked exaggerations.

Encoding: The process of transforming mental images into words and placing these words into logical messages with meaning.

Enunciation: Refers to the clarity, accuracy, and distinctness in speech.

Equality pattern: Giving equal time to each point.

Equivocal words: Have more than one correct denotative meaning.

Esteem needs: Human need to be seen as worthy and competent and to have the respect of others.

Ethical Communication: Communication that is honest, fair, and considerate of others' rights.

Ethics: The rules we use to determine good and evil, right and wrong. These rules may be grounded in religious principles, democratic values, codes of conduct, and bases of values derived from a variety of sources.

Ethnicity: Refers to the common heritage, or background, shared by a group of people.

Ethnocentrism: Refers to the tendency to perceive our own ways of behaving and thinking as being correct, or acceptable, and judging other behaviors as being "strange," incorrect, or inferior.

Ethos: Ethical appeal, makes speakers worthy of belief.

Evaluative listening: This type of listening involves critically assessing messages.

Evaluative statements: Expressions that involve a judgment.

Examples: Support that helps illustrate a point or claim.

Expectancy violations theory: Suggests that we hold expectations about the nonverbal behavior of others, and when communicative norms are violated, the violation may be perceived either favorably or unfavorably, depending on the perception that the receiver has of the violator.

Expert power: A person who is able to assist the group in reaching its goals because of his or her expertise on a given topic.

Explicit learning: Learning that involves actual instructions regarding the preferred way of behaving.

Extemporaneous speaking: A method of delivery that involves using carefully prepared notes to guide the presentation.

External attribution: Situational factors.

External Noise: Includes any factors outside of the communicators that make it difficult or prevent the message from being understood.

Extrinsic conflict: Conflict related to the personalities and relationships between members.

Extrinsic Costs: The sacrifices, loses, or suffering as a result of things that occur outside the relationship (could not include having as much time for your friends or sharing your friends with your partner).

Extrinsic Rewards: The gifts, prizes, and recompenses that occur outside the relationship (could include liking the people your partner has introduced you to or the friends he or she hangs out with).

Eye contact: Direct visual contact made with another person; helps us to communicate in at least four ways: it can open a channel of communication, demonstrate concern, gather feedback, and moderate anxiety.

Eye contact: The connection you form with listeners through your gaze.

F

Facial expression: All of the aspects of the physical delivery including eye contact, body language, gesture, movement, posture, facial expression, and personal appearance.

Forum: Group members respond to audience questions.

Fundamental attribution error: When attempting to explain others' negative behaviors, we tend to overestimate the internal factors or causes and underestimate the external factors or causes.

G

Gestures: Using your arms and hands to illustrate, emphasize, or provide a visual experience that accompanies your thoughts.

Grammar: Syntax, a patterned set of rules that aid in meaning.

Group-oriented-goals: Centered around specific tasks to be performed.

H

Habitual pitch: Refers to the range of voice one uses during a normal conversation; it could be high or low.

Haptics: The way humans communicate by using or not using touch; closely linked to culture.

Hearing: Involves the physical process of sound waves traveling into the ear canal, vibrating the ear drum, and eventually sending signals to the brain.

Hearing: A passive physiological process where the ear receives sound.

Hidden area: The part of the self that contains information about the self known to oneself but that is hidden from others.

Hidden pane: That area of the Johari Window where self-knowledge is hidden from others- a deliberate non-disclosure area in which there are certain things you know about yourself that you do not want known and deliberately conceal them from others.

Homophily: The idea that we choose to be with people who are similar to us.

I

Illustrator: A gesture that is used with language to emphasize, stress, or repeat what is being said.

"I" messages: Non-evaluative responses that convey our feelings about the nature of a situation.

Implicit learning: Learning that occurs via observation.

Impromptu speaking: Involves little or no preparation time; using no notes or just a few.

Indirect aggression: (Also called passive aggression) People who use this form of communication often feel powerless and respond by doing something to thwart the person in power.

Individualistic cultures: Cultures in which people are taught personal autonomy, privacy, self-realization, individual initiative, independence, individual decision making, and an understanding that their needs and interests are just as important, if not more important, than the needs and interests of others.

Inductive reasoning: Generalizing from specific examples and drawing conclusions from what we observe.

Inference: Implies.

Inflection: Refers to different pitches that a speaker uses to pronounce certain words—either lowering or raising the pitch.

Instrumental costs: The problems associated with relationships.

Instrumental rewards: The pleasures that come as result of being in a relationship.

Intentionality: Described as being stable or persistent and often refers to behaviors that are likely to be exhibited repeatedly across a variety of contexts.

Interactive strategies: Typically involve a face-to-face encounter between two individuals to reduce uncertainty.

Intercultural Communication: When a message is created by a member of one culture, and this message needs to be processed by a member of another culture.

Internal attribution: Dispositional factors.

Internal previews: Extended transitions that tell the audience, in general terms, what you will say next.

Internal summaries: Follow a main point and act as reminders; useful to clarify or emphasize what you have just said.

Internal Noise: Interference with the message that occurs in the minds of the sender-receivers when their thoughts or feelings are focused on something other than the communication at hand.

Internal previews: Consist of short statements that give advance warning to the audience of what is going to be discussed in the speech.

Internal summaries: Are unique transitions in that they remind listeners of what has been previously been said in order to move on to a new point.

Interpersonal Communication: One person interacting with another on a one-to-one basis, often in an informal, unstructured setting.

Interpersonal communication: Communication that takes place between two persons who establish a communicative relationship, which includes conversations, interviews, and small group discussions.

Interpersonal linkage: Power based on who you know and what resources these people control.

Interpretation: The subjective process of making sense of our perceptions.

Interpretation: Assigning meaning to your perceptions.

Intersubjective: Meaning can exist only when people share common interpretations of the symbols they exchange.

Intrapersonal Communication: Communication that occurs within you; it involves thoughts, feelings, and the way you look at yourself.

Intrinsic conflict: Conflict that centers on disagreements related to the task facing the group.

Intrinsic costs: The obligation to return the attention, warmth, and affection you receive, and the time you will spend listening, communicating, and self-disclosing.

Introduction: Supports the body of your speech and should capture your audience's attention and indicate your intent.

Intrusion of territory: Violation, invasion, or contamination of your space.

J

Jargon: Specialized professional language.

Johari Window: A model of the process of disclosure in interpersonal relationships, developed by Joseph Luft and Harry Ingham.

Johari Window: A model containing four panes that is used to explain the roles that self-awareness and self-disclosure play in relationships.

K

Key word outline: An outline containing important words or phrases that assist in reminding the speaker of the ideas within the speech.

Kinesics: The study of our use of the body to communicate.

Knowledge: Refers to the theoretical principles and concepts that explain behaviors occurring within a specific communication context. Also refers to understanding what reaction or action is best suited for a particular situation.

L

Laissez-faire leader: One who takes a hands-off approach to leadership and provides very little direction to those being led.

Language: A shared system of symbols structured in organized patterns to express thoughts and feelings.

Leadership: The ability to influence the behavior of others to move people to action.

Legitimate power: Exists as a function of someone's position in an organization.

Limited capacity processors: We are described as this because we have innate limitations in our ability to process information.

Linear Communication: One-way communication that has no feedback.

Listening styles: A set of attitudes, beliefs, and predispositions about the how, where, when, who, and what of the information reception and encoding process.

Listening: Involves the physical process of hearing, but it also involves the psychological process of attending to the stimuli, creating meaning, and responding.

Listening: The active process of receiving, constructing meaning from, and responding to spoken and/or nonverbal messages.

Loaded words: Sound like they're describing, but they're actually revealing your attitude.

Logos: An appeal that is rational and reasonable based on evidence provided.

Loudness: The intensity of a sound, which is measured in units of bels.

M

Main Point: The information that consist of the broad or general ideas which support the central idea

Main Points: Are the principal sub-divisions of a speech and are often expressed within the specific purpose.

Maintenance leaders: Focus on relational issues, the development of an open and supportive climate, motivation of members, and conflict management.

Manuscript: Writing your speech out word from word then reading it.

Manuscript delivery: A pre-written speech that is delivered using a promptor or some medium.

Mapping: Clustering the content for the outline.

Meaning: Symbols must be shared in order to be understood.

Meaningfulness: Refers to the ways that we project comprehension or understanding onto perceptions.

Memorization delivery: Writing your speech out, committing it to memory, and delivering it word for word.

Message credibility: The extent to which the speech is considered to be factual and well-supported through documentation.

Message: The ideas and feelings that a sender-receiver wants to share.

Model of social penetration (Altman & Taylor): A way of looking at the process of disclosure as you work toward achieving intimacy in a relationship, social penetration.

Monopolizing: Involves taking the focus off the speaker and redirecting the conversation and attention to themselves.

Monroe's Motivation Sequence: A five step method of organizing a persuasive speech, which follows a pattern of human thought from attention to action.

N

Needs: Strong feelings of discomfort or desire which motivate to achieve satisfaction or comfort.

Negative criticism: Occurs when one person in the relationship evaluates the other person in the relationship in a negative manner.

Negative feedback: Refers to verbal and nonverbal behaviors that are often discouraging to a source to continue communicating.

Neutrality: Communicates that you simply do not care about the person or what he or she is saying.

Noise: Interference that keeps a message from being understood or accurately interpreted.

Noise: Refers to anything that interferes with the reception of a message.

Non-fluencies: Meaningless words that interrupt the flow of our speech; also known as filled pauses or vocal fillers.

Nonverbal Communication: Information we communicate without using words.

Novelty: Refers to the tendency to pay attention to stimuli that new or different.

O

Oculesics: The communication that takes place through eye behavior: the least controllable area of the face.

Olfactics: The communicative attributes of smell and scents; can be responsible for strong reactions both positive and negative.

Open pane: The area of the Johari Window that involves information about yourself that you are willing to communicate, as well as information you are unable to hide.

Operational definitions: Specify procedures for observing and measuring concepts.

Opinions: Points of view that may or may not be supported in fact.

Organization of ideas: The placement of lines of reasoning and supporting materials in a pattern that helps to achieve your specific purpose.

Organization: Refers to the process of placing stimuli or information into categories in order to make sense of it.

Organization: The arrangement of ideas in a speech.

Organization: Structuring perceptions in order to make sense of them.

Outline: Serves as the blueprint for your speech.

Owned message: (Also known as an I-message): An acknowledgement of subjectivity by a message-sender through the use of first-person singular terms.

P

Panel discussion: Group members have an informal interchange on the issues in front of an audience.

Paralanguage: Nonverbal behavior that focuses on how something is said and not what is said; includes vocal characteristics such as rate, pitch, volume, vocal quality, dialect, articulation and diction, fillers, dialect, etc.

Paraphrasing: Involves restating a message in your own words to see if the meaning you assigned was similar to that which was intended.

Passive strategies: Typically involve observation and social comparison to learn information about others.

Past-Present-Future: Chronological pattern used when developing a speech for a topic or a issue that has relevant history or future direction.

Pathos: Persuading through emotional appeals.

Pauses: Suspension or break in a speech pattern to create and effect.

People-oriented listener: Listeners that seek common interests with the speaker and are highly responsive; interested in the speaker's feelings and emotions.

Perception: How we interpret and assign meaning to others' behaviors and messages based on our background and past experiences. The process of selecting, organizing, and interpreting stimuli into something that makes sense or is meaningful.

Perception: Our set of beliefs concerning what is out there.

Personal constructs: Bipolar dimensions of meaning used to predict and evaluate how people behave.

Personal orientation system: Predispositions that are comprised of one's needs, beliefs, values, and attitudes.

Personal space: A small amount of portable space that you carry with you all the time; you control who is and who is not permitted inside that space.

Phonological rules: Regulate how words sound when you pronounce them.

Physiology: Physical sensory ability.

Pitch: Vocal range or key, the highness or lowness of your voice produced by the tightening and loosening of your vocal folds.

Planning outline: Full content outline that includes most of the information that would be presented in a speech.

Positive feedback: Refers to verbal and nonverbal behaviors that encourage the speaker to continue communicating.

Power distance: The extent to which the less powerful members of organizations and institutions accept and expect that power is distributed unequally.

Primary audience: Small group to whom you provide information, express concern, or attempt to persuade.

Primacy and recency: Refers to arguments delivered first and last.

Primacy effect: The belief that it is the first point in your speech that listeners will most likely remember.

Primary sources: Firsthand accounts such as diaries, journals, and letters, as well as statistics, speeches, and interviews. They are records of events as they are first described.

Primary territory: Space on those items you personally control.

Problem orientation: Allows others an equal contribution to discussion and decision making.

Problem Solution: Arrangement pattern according to two sections one dealing with the problem and the other dealing with the solution.

Process: Systemic approach to reaching a solution.

Progressive pattern: Using your least important point first and your most important point last.

Pronunciation: Knowing how to say a word and say it correctly.

Proposition of fact: Persuading your listeners that your interpretation of a situation, event, or concept is accurate.

Proposition of policy: Persuading your listeners to take a specific course of action and usually contains the words should, ought and must.

Proposition of policy: Easily recognizable by their use of the word "should."

Proposition of value: Persuading your listeners based on deep-seated beliefs.

Prototypes: Refers to knowledge structures which represent the most common attributes of a phenomenon.

Provisionalism: Behavior that tries to explore issues, look for solutions, and consider the points of view of other group members.

Proxemics: Communicative behavior through the use of space and distance; best explicated by using zones and territories.

Proximity: Refers to the physical distance between two people.

Proximity: The close contact that occurs when people share an experience such as work, play, or school.

Pseudo-listening: This type of listening is used when we are pretending to listen.

Psychological information: The kind of information that is the most specific and intimate because it allows you to know individual traits, feelings, attitudes, and important personal data.

Physiological needs: Human needs which deals with our basic biological needs including food, water, oxygen, rest and release from stress.

Psychological Noise: Idiosyncrasies that occur within the speaker that interfere with the speaker's ability to express or understand the intended message.

Public Communication: The sender-receiver (speaker) sends a message (the speech) to an audience.

Public-speaking anxiety: The fear of speaking in public that affects people in different ways such as breaking into a sweat, trembling, or dry mouth.

Public territory: Available to anyone; so any space you try to claim is only temporary.

R

Race: The term used to refer to genetically inherited biological characteristics such as hair texture and color, eye shape, skin color, and facial structure.

Rapport talk: Analogous to small talk or phatic communication.

Rate: The pace at which you speak.

Reasoning from sign: The inference step is that the presence of an attribute can be taken as the presence of some larger condition or situation of which the attribute is a part.

Reasoning: The process of using known and believed information to explain or prove other statements less well understood or accepted. Refers to the sequence of interlinking claims and arguments that, together, establish the content and force of your position.

Recency effect: The belief that it is the last point in your speech that listeners will most likely remember.

Reference(s): Consist of thoughts, experiences, and feelings about the referent.

Referent power: Based on the personal liking or respect that one person has for another.

Referent: The thing that we want to communicate about that exists in reality.

Reflective thinking Process: John Dewey's seven step approach to problem solving.

Regional differences: Speech patterns, attitudes, and values may differ significantly depending on the geographic location.

Regionalisms: Words or phrases that are specific to one part of the country.

Regrettable Talk: Saying something embarrassing, hurtful, or private to another person.

Regulative rules: Tell us when, how, where, and with whom we can talk about certain things.

Regulator: A turn-taking signal that helps control the flow, the pace, and turn-taking in conversations.

Reinforce: Refers to messages that are consistent with our views.

Repetition: Reinforcing main points through summaries and paraphrasing.

Report talk: Involves discussions about facts, events, and solutions. Refers to talking to accomplish goals.

Research: The raw material that forms the foundation of your speech.

Response to a bid: A positive or negative answer to somebody's request for emotional connection.

Reward power: Offers access to some desired resource as payment for compliance.

Rewards: The pleasures that come as a result of being in a relationship.

S

Safety needs: Human need for security, comfort and freedom from fear.

Schemata: Refers to mental filing cabinets with several drawers or organized clusters of knowledge and information about particular topics.

Script theory: The idea that we often interact with others in a way that could be described as "automatic" or even "mindless."

Scripts: Knowledge structures that guide and influence how we process information.

Secondary audience: Collection of individuals in attendance who may have no knowledge or interest in your topic and did not know you were planning to speak.

Secondary sources: Generally provide an analysis, an explanation, or a restatement of a primary source.

Secondary territory: Not your private property; not owned by you, but typically associated with you.

Selection: We are continually making choices about the amount and type of information that we choose to notice.

Selection: A method of focusing that narrows your attention to selected stimuli; determining your topic and purpose, meeting the audience's needs and expectations, and recognizing the kinds of supporting materials you will use to build the message.

Selective attention: Refers to the decision to pay attention to certain stimuli while simultaneously ignoring others.

Selective exposure: Refers to the choice to subject oneself to certain stimuli.

Selective listening: Type of listening that occurs when a listener focuses only on parts of the message.

Selective retention: Refers to the choice to save or delete information from one's long-term memory.

Self actualization: The need for fulfillment of one's highest potential.

Self-disclosure: Involves divulging personal information to another individual and is often delivered through face-to-face or computer mediated channels.

Self-disclosure: Process by which one person tells another something he or she would not tell just anyone.

Self-disclosure: The process of revealing to another person information about the self that he or she would not otherwise know.

Self-oriented goals: Relate to the individual's personal needs and ambitions.

Self-serving bias: States that we tend to manufacture, or construct, attributions which best serve our own self-interests.

Semantic rules: Govern the meaning of specific symbols.

Semantic triangle: A model that demonstrates how words come to have meaning.

Sender-receivers: In communication situations, those who simultaneously send and receive messages.

Setting: Where the communication occurs.

Signposts: Are words, phrases or short statements that indicate to an audience the direction a speaker will take next.

Situational leadership: Assumes that a leader's effectiveness is contingent, or dependent, upon how well the leader's style fits the context.

Size: Refers to the magnitude of the stimuli.

Skills: Specific communication behaviors which contribute to competent and effective interpersonal communication.

Slang: Consists of words that are short-lived, arbitrarily changed, and often vulgar ideas.

Slurring: Combining two or more words into one word when speaking.

Small group: Small number of people who meet to solve a problem or interact to maintain relationships.

Small Groups: Gatherings of 3 to 13 who meet to do a job, solve a problem, or maintain relationships.

Small talk: Social conversation about unimportant topics that allows a person to maintain contact with a lot of people without making a deep commitment.

Small talk: Discussions that focus on topics of general interest ad have little emotional or personal significance, such as the weather, sports, or other matters not requiring self disclosure.

Small-group Communication: It occurs when a small number of people meet to save a problem. The group must be small enough so that each member has a chance to interact with all the other members.

Social class: Stratification based on educational, occupational, or financial backgrounds, resulting in classifications and status differentials.

Social identity theory: An explanation for our tendency to evaluate in-groups more positively than out-groups.

Social penetration: The process of increasing both disclosure and intimacy in a relationship.

Social penetration model: Model describing how intimacy can be achieved via the breadth and depth of self disclosure.

Social penetration theory: The theory that states that our relationships begin with relatively narrow breadth and shallow depth and develop over time.

Socialization: Refers to the process of learning about one's cultural norms and expectations.

316 COMMUNICATION FOR TODAY'S STUDENT

Sociological information: Information that tells you something about others' social groups and roles.

Spatial Organization: The sequence of ideas moves from physical point to another.

Speaker credibility: The extent to which a speaker is perceived as a competent spokesperson.

Speakers notes: Abbreviated key-word outline.

Specific purpose: The precise response you want from your audience.

Speech of demonstration: When the focus is on how something is done.

Speech of description: Helps an audience understand what something is.

Speech of explanation: Helps an audience understand why something is so.

Spontaneity: Communication characterized by honesty, directness, and good faith.

Stability: Refers to the predictability that we need in life.

Statistics: The collection, analysis, interpretation, and presentation of information in numerical form.

Stereotypes: Impressions and expectations based on one's knowledge or beliefs about a specific group of people which are then applied to all individuals who are members of that group.

Step-by-step: A chronological pattern that is used when describing a process.

Strategy: 1. a plan; 2. a form of communication often making others defensive because they suspect a hidden agenda.

Stress: Refers to the degree of emphasis given to a syllable within a word or a word within a phrase or a sentence.

Strongest point pattern: You spend the most time in your speech on the first point; less time on the second point, and even less time on the last point of your speech.

Subordination: Requires that the main points descend in weight from general main points to the concrete and specific subpoints.

Subjectivity: Perceptions that are unique to your personal experience, views, or mental state.

Substitution: It is the replacement of an acceptable sound with an incorrect one.

Symbol: Something that sends for something else.

Symbols: Arbitrary labels that we give to some idea or phenomenon.

Symposium: Centers on prepared speeches on a specified subject given by group members who have expertise on the subject.

Syntactical rules: Present the arrangement of a language; how the symbols are organized.

T

Task leaders: Group members who help the group with organization and advancement toward making a decision or completing a job.

Task roles: Contribute to the group's productivity and are concerned with moving the group toward achieving its goals.

Testimony: Citing the experience or opinion of others; either directly or through paraphrasing.

Thesis statement: The core idea; identifies the main ideas of your speech.

Time-oriented listening: Listeners that are particularly interested in brief interactions with others.

Transactional Communication: Communication that involves three principles: (1) people sending messages continuously and simultaneously; (2) communication events that have a past, present, and future; and (3) participants playing certain roles.

Transformational leader: Someone who possesses the charisma necessary to motivate followers and evoke change.

Transitions: Are words or phrases that link the introduction and body of the speech, the main ideas and supporting material, and the body and conclusion.

Transitions: Verbal bridges between ideas; words; phrases, or sentences that tell your audience how ideas relate.

Transposition: It is the reversal of two sounds in a word.

Trite words: Words that have been overused and lose power or impact.

Topical Organization: Arrangement pattern according to subject matter.

Transitions: Verbal bridges between ideas; words; phrases, or sentences that tell your audience how ideas relate.

Transitional sentences: Linked various main points within the body and serves as internal previews and summaries.

U

Understanding: Applying knowledge to specific situations in an attempt to explain the behaviors that are occurring.

Unknown pane: Area of the Johari Window that is known as a nondisclosure area and provides no possibility of disclosure because it is unknown to self or to others.

Utility: The perception that particular messages are immediately useful.

V

Verbal footnotes: Are citations within the speech which give credit to the source of the support information.

Verbal Symbol: A word that stands for a particular thing or idea.

Vocal fillers: The insertion of sounds within a pause. These vocalized pauses are referred to as fillers. Examples of frequently used fillers are uhm, you know, and like.

Volume: The loudness of your voice, controlled by how forcefully air is expelled through the trachea onto the vocal folds.

Y

"You" Messages: Responses that place blame on another person.

INDEX

I

J